MARITIME SUFFOLK
A history of 1,500 years of seafaring

Further details of Poppyland Publishing titles can be found at
www.poppyland.co.uk
where clicking on the 'Support and Resources' button will lead to pages
specially compiled to support this title.

MARITIME SUFFOLK

A history of 1,500 years of seafaring

Robert Malster

Right: The frigate HMS *Lowestoft* on a visit to the town in 1976. One of nine ships of the Rothesay class, she was completed at Govan on the Clyde in 1961 and was modernised and equipped with a Wasp anti-submarine helicopter some twenty years later. Over the centuries many warships have carried the names of Suffolk towns and villages.

Opposite page: The Anglo-Saxon royal burial ground at Sutton Hoo seen from the air. In 1939 one of the mounds was found to contain a large ship and also a fabulous treasure that had originated from all parts of the then-known world. The mound on the right has been restored by the National Trust to its original height.

Below: A replica of the *Godspeed* in Jamestown, Virginia. The original *Godspeed*, captained by Bartholomew Gosnold of Otley Hall, was employed by the Virginia Company to carry settlers to Jamestown in 1607; Gosnold is credited by American sources as being 'the prime mover of the colonization of Virginia'.

Maritime Suffolk completes Robert Malster's pioneering study of the maritime history of the east of England and tells of Suffolk's many links with the sea over the centuries. Two companion volumes, *Maritime Norfolk* parts one and two, tell the story of Norfolk's seamen and fishermen while another, *North Sea War 1914-1919*, relates the significant contribution made by the East Anglian ports and by the east coast fishermen during the First World War. Another companion volume by Julian Foynes, *East Anglia against the Tricolor*, tells of the region's involvement in the Revolutionary and Napoleonic wars against France.

ISBN 978 1 909796 36 2
Published by Poppyland Publishing, Cromer NR27 9AN

Picture credits:

Clarges Gallery 91.
Creative Commons 13.
David Cleveland collection 146, 183.
John Cragie 186, 194, 246 (bottom).
Ted Frost 253 (margin), 248, 249, 250-251.
Lowestoft Maritime Museum 168, 181.
National Maritime Museum (© National Maritime Museum Greenwich, London) xii-xiii (top), 55, 67.
Robert Malster front cover, ix, xvi, 4, 14, 23 (bottom), 24 (top), 46, 68 (bottom), 113, 130, 134, 135, 149, 151, 153, 198, 204, 205, 218 (bottom), 225, 246 (top), 247 (bottom), 252 (bottom), 253 (top), 257 (top & bottom), 259, 264 (bottom), 265, 268 (top), 270,
Robert Malster collection ii-iii, x, xiv, xv, 24 (bottom), 25, 32, 33, 34, 35, 36, 38, 40, 57, 64, 65, 67, 68 (top), 70, 75, 82, 83, 84, 85 (top), 86, 87, 88, 89, 90, 91, 92, 93, 94, 96, 98, 99, 100, 101, 102, 103, 104, 105, 106 (top), 107, 108 (top), 109, 110, 111, 112, 114, 116, 117, 118, 120, 123, 124, 126, 129, 133, 138, 139, 141, 143, 144, 145, 150, 154, 156, 158, 161, 162, 163, 164, 166, 167, 169, 171, 174, 178, 182, 184, 188, 193, 195, 196, 197, 200, 201, 202, 206, 207, 208, 210, 211, 212, 213, 214, 215, 216, 218 (top), 219, 221, 222, 223, 224 (top), 226, 227, 232, 233, 234, 235, 237, 238, 242, 244, 245, 247 (top), 252 (top), 255, 262, 263 (top), 266, 267, 271 (margin), 275 (bottom), 276.
British Museum Trustees 3.
National Portait Gallery 71.
Norfolk Record Office 31.
Over Stoke History Group 240 (top).
Mike Page iv, 26, 260, 275 (top).
Peter Page 107 (bottom), 108.
Poppyland Publishing v, iix, 2, 5, 12, 23 (top), 29, 39, 48, 50, 51, 52, 191, 253 (bottom), 254, 257 (centre), 264 (top). 268 (bottom), 269, 271 (top).
Poppyland collection 72, 80, 170, 180, 185, 203, 220, 228.
R.G. Pratt/Hugh Moffat, Ipswich Transport Museum 22, 85 (bottom), 95, 106 (bottom), 132, 137, 239, 240, 263 (bottom).
Suffolk Record Office 6, 238 (margin).
Victoria and Albert Museum © 148.
John Wells 224.
Nicholas Wiggins 233.

In memory of Hugh Moffat, whose pioneering research into the maritime history of his native county has contributed so much to this book.

Cover picture: The spritsail barge *Xylonite*, built at Mistley in 1926 and thus one of the last trading barges to be launched, sailing hard while competing in a Pin Mill Barge Match.
Title Page: The barquentine *J.S.Sterry* is towed through the Lowestoft swing bridge at the turn of the twentieth century.

Contents

The 196-ton tug *Nafka* is launched from the Lowestoft shipyard of Richards Shipbuilders in 1978. One of many ships launched from Lowestoft yards over the years, the *Nafka* was built for the Ethiopian government and operated in the Red Sea port of Assab, now as a result of political tumult in the Horn of Africa in Eritrea.

Prince Philip with shipmate Commander Jenkins at the opening of the Lowestoft Maritime Museum on 12th June 1978.

Preface

The writing of this book, which completes a trilogy on the maritime history of East Anglia, has been made possible only by the help of many friends who have shared information and provided illustrations, answered questions and offered generous support in a variety of ways. There is so much to tell about more than 1,500 years of seafaring that it has been difficult to fit everything into a single volume, yet the economics of publishing decreed that the story must be told in just the one book.

So it is that one must begin with an apology to those friends who feel disappointment that there are so many subjects that have not found a place; it has proved necessary to make painful decisions as to what is to be left out. Jack Mitchley, were he still with us, would be severely critical of the absence of any account of the North of Europe Steam Navigation Company that operated from Lowestoft and other places in the mid-nineteenth century; David King would have been most upset that there is so little about the rise of the trawling industry; Hugh Moffat might well have asked why there is no mention of the introduction of the first lightship by his ancestor Robert Hamblin.

When I began my research sixty years ago I had a great deal of friendly help from the founder members of the Port of Lowestoft Research Society, and more recently I have enjoyed both the friendship and the assistance of current members of that organisation, of which I am proud to be a member. I have also been given a great deal of friendly help by those concerned with the splendid little Lowestoft Maritime Museum at Sparrows Nest. And over the years I have had both help and support from David Butcher, who has given me the benefit of his scholarly researches into the history of Lowestoft and the tape-recordings he made of men and women involved in the town's fishing industry.

Another friend, Suffolk historian Peter Northeast, provided me with many a photocopy of reports from his beloved 'Blue Books' and other sources as well as much excellent advice, and I also enjoyed the friendship and willing help of Hugh Moffat, whose book *Ipswich Ships and Shipyards 1700-1970* is a superb contribution to the maritime history of the east coast; his notes from the Ipswich Journal, now in the Ipswich Transport Museum, have proved invaluable.

Special thanks must go to another friend, Peter Stibbons, not only for publishing these books on East Anglia's maritime history but for help that has gone far beyond what one expects from one's publisher. I must also acknowledge with gratitude the help I always receive from the friendly and obliging staff of the Suffolk Record Office at both Ipswich and Lowestoft; how fortunate we are in Suffolk to have so outstanding an institution.

At an early stage in the preparation of these three books I received wonderful help and support from two good friends, Edward Paget-Tomlinson and Mike Stammers; sadly neither of them is still with us. Others who have helped in the work of gathering information and sorting out the facts over the years include Jonathan Abson, Captain John Cragie of Southwold, David Cleveland, John Fairclough, Linda Fitzpatrick of the Scottish Fisheries Museum at Anstruther, Julian Foynes, Jill Freestone, Dr Deirdre Heavens, John Mills, Adrian Osler, Linda Pargeter, Des Pawson, Philip Rumbelow and Richard Smith. Nicholas Amor, whose book *Late Medieval Ipswich: Trade and Industry* has made such a welcome contribution to the history of the town's trade, has kindly permitted me to make use of his research.

I thank them all. Seeing there are so many, it might be thought that the author has had but a minor role in the compilation of this book. If it be that my main contribution has been to introduce a number of mistakes and errors, I pray forgiveness.

R. & W. Paul maltings and Cranfield Brothers' flour mill beside Ipswich Dock in the 1970s. New brickwork on the top floor of the old malting indicates where repairs were made after bombing during the Second World War.

Introduction

Fishing punts on Southwold beach about 1890. What appears to be an old yawl is coming under inspection near the water's edge. The nearest shed bears on its end wall a name board from the *Alma*, wrecked on the Sizewell Bank in 1874 with a cargo of Norwegian ice; the lifeboat *Ipswich* from Thorpeness rescued the crew of twelve and the pilot.

Suffolk is, as John Kirby points out in the first sentence of *The Suffolk Traveller* (1784), a maritime county. It has a history of seafaring, fishing and trading that stretches over more than 1,500 years.

People have been coming and going to and from the Suffolk coast throughout history. It is highly likely that the Romans had a port at the mouth of the River Orwell during the four centuries that they occupied Britain and that supplies of grain and other agricultural produce went north to the Tyne for the garrisons on Hadrian's wall as well as to Roman towns in the Rhineland.

After the end of the Roman occupation settlers came from Scandinavia, people who buried their kings and chieftains in worn-out boats. We know from the gravegoods that they buried with their dead rulers that they traded not merely with the near Continent but with far-off countries in eastern Europe and beyond.

They were succeeded by other seafarers who came as marauders and remained as traders and later as residents. To them and to their descendants the North Sea was not a boundary but a link with their former homelands and with other distant lands.

In the fifteenth and sixteenth centuries Suffolk merchants were trading with Iceland for dried fish in one direction and with Gascony on the Bay of Biscay for wines in another. East Anglia was not then a region on the way to nowhere, as so many people choose to regard it today, but the most heavily populated area of England and a vibrant region that was in touch by sea with Europe, Scandinavia, the Mediterranean and many other parts of the world.

The Suffolk shore is composed largely of sand and shingle and lacks the rocky cliffs and promontories of some other parts of Britain's east coast. The nature of the material of which it is made up causes the coast of the county to be particularly liable to erosion and also in other places to accretion, while the sandbanks that lie offshore are constantly changing, making navigation of the channels between them hazardous, especially to those mariners who do not have a satisfactory knowledge of their situation at a particular time.

It is for this reason that charts of the area have to be kept constantly up to date, with amendments being announced from time to time by *Notices to Mariners*. From quite an early period fishermen and others with an intimate knowledge of the banks and the channels between them acted as pilots, either official or otherwise, to assist shipmasters in finding their way through these waters.

In the days of sail it was all too easy for vessels to be cast on to the sandbanks or on to the shore by wind and tide, even efficiently navigated ships sometimes being at the mercy of severe weather. It was natural that groups of longshoremen should be formed in the coastal settlements such as Lowestoft and Pakefield, Kessingland, Southwold and Aldeburgh to take supplies to shipping anchored close to the shore, sheltering from stormy weather or awaiting a favourable wind, and to assist vessels that got into trouble. The nineteenth-century beach companies were co-operative organisations that did much good work, while often being accused of benefiting from the misfortunes, or the mistakes, of others.

It is perhaps not surprising that the world's first sailing lifeboat was built and operated in Suffolk. Manned by the beachmen and pilots of Lowestoft, that boat, the *Frances Ann*, saved a great number of lives and was the forerunner of many later lifesaving craft.

There has been considerable change in the coastline over the centuries. It is impossible to know just what the coast was like when the Roman armies occupied Britain, but it is suggested that the coastline then was some distance to seaward of the present shore, and there might well have been settlements that are now a mile and more out to sea. The Roman Saxon Shore fort known in medieval times as Walton Castle – the Roman walls then gave shelter to a Norman castle – disappeared beneath the waves progressively in the eighteenth and nineteenth centuries, and the presence on the West Rocks in the Harwich approaches of Roman relics and building materials suggests that there might have been a town, perhaps a port, on that site in Roman times.[1]

The story of how the important medieval town and seaport of Dunwich was overwhelmed by the sea is well known; today it is possible only to stand on the western rampart of the town and look out to sea over the site of what was once a large and populous community and one of the kingdom's principal

Shipbuilding on the Orwell: a painting by the elder John Cleveley of the *Hampshire* ready for launching at John's Ness, the *Biddeford* being towed to Harwich for fitting out, and the bomb ketch *Granado* at anchor. All three warships were built by John Barnard, and it is thought the painting was probably commissioned by him. See chapter 19.

ports. At Aldeburgh the Moot Hall, which stood in the middle of the medieval 'Old Borough', is today just at the back of the beach.

In more recent times the building of a sea wall to protect that part of the town of Lowestoft known as the Beach – now more usually called the Beach Village – from the incursions of the sea led to erosion further south at Pakefield that carried away the lifeboat station and ate into the cliff to the extent that several houses collapsed on to the beach.

The Suffolk ports are most favourably placed for trade with the Continent and particularly with the Low Countries; the people of Lowestoft have been known to point out that the town is nearer to Amsterdam than it is to London. Indeed, the most easterly point of Britain is Lowestoft Ness, abreast of the town of Lowestoft and some 1,150 yards north of the entrance to Lowestoft's present-day harbour. The longitude of the Ness is approximately 1° 46'E.

South of the harbour the coast inclines slightly to the west of south until Benacre Ness is reached, and it then runs about SSW to Southwold; the longitude of Benacre Ness is roughly 1° 45'E.

The earliest available map showing the Suffolk coast is Christopher Saxton's of 1575,[2] which shows Easton Ness to extend to a longitude just to the east of that of Lowestoft. This has led to an assertion that in the Middle Ages the country's most easterly point was just north of Southwold, but how much reliance should be placed on this evidence?

Saxton's map does not appear to be based on an entirely satisfactory survey,

since the relative positions of some towns and villages would seem to be the result of guesswork. To give just one example, the settlements of Thorpe and Aldringham have been transposed, with Aldringham on the coast close to Thorpeness.

Interestingly, there is on Saxton's map a stretch of water between South Cove and Wangford running south-west to north-east, with no outlet to the sea; if extended to the north-east it would meet the sea at Covehithe. It probably did not flow towards that ancient port, however, for it appears to relate to the marshy valley that meanders southwards from Frostenden to Reydon and contains a minor river that runs under Potter's Bridge and into Easton Broad. There is a suggestion that at a very distant period this was a navigable stream giving access to a quay at Frostenden, and we need not doubt that in the sixteenth century this valley contained a quite extensive shallow lake.[3]

Less easily accepted is the bulbous shape of the Orford Ness shingle bank which Saxton depicts as swelling into a broad peninsula where he shows the Ore discharging into 'Orford Haven'. We know from other sources that the name Orford Haven relates not to the 'Mayne Sea' or to Hollesley Bay but to the channel of the river east of Havergate Island and also to that part of the river above Orford.

Saxton shows the Butley River, which he does not name, with a separate outlet to the sea to the west of the mouth of the Ore. This is clearly erroneous, for we know from Ananias Appleton's map of Orford Ness, 1588, and John Norden's painstaking survey of the same area made in 1600 and 1601 that

Orford Castle served during the eighteenth and nineteenth century wars with France as a naval signal station, as seen in this print of 1810.

'Buttley Crycke' or 'Chilsforde fleet' (now known as the Butley River) ran into the Ore some distance above its mouth at that period, much as it does today. It appears that Saxton drew this part of the Suffolk coast not from his own survey but from someone else's rather vague description, and the error does not encourage confidence in the accuracy of his work.

The same bulbous and demonstrably inaccurate shape of the Orford Ness area is depicted on John Speed's *Suffolke described* of 1610 and on almost every map produced in the following hundred years. Yet Norden's survey demonstrates that the shingle spit cutting off the River Ore from the sea was in 1601 remarkably similar in its basic form to its layout 400 years later.

John Speed, whose map appears to be a mere copy of Saxton's, shows Easton Ness in the same position as on Saxton's, though the name Easton is changed to Easton Baven [Easton Bavents]. Some have found the repetition of features such as the eminence of Easton Ness as confirmation of the accuracy of Saxton's map; it is nothing of the kind, being confirmation of nothing more than the fact that seventeenth-century county cartographers cheerfully copied one another's 'surveys' – and their mistakes.

An exception to this is Robert Morden, whose map of Suffolk, 1695, does appear to be the result of a fresh survey. 'Lestoff' reaches the extreme edge of the map and Easton Ness is a quarter-inch clear of the edge, while the Butley River flows into the Ore just above its mouth and the shape of the Orfordness bank is quite different from the standard earlier version repeated by successive mapmakers.

One might have expected later mapmakers to copy Morden's, yet as late as 1713 Henry Overton was clearly copying earlier maps so far as the coastline and Orford Haven are concerned. One is forced to the conclusion that Saxton was in error in showing that great carbuncle at Easton, and that the error was copied time and again over a period of more than a century.

Orfordness shingle spit gave shelter to the town and harbour of Orford, which at the time of the building by Henry II of the castle with its polygonal keep was already a fishing port with saltpans producing a commodity essential for the preservation of fish. Although when the Domesday Book was compiled it was merely a part of the manor of Sudbourne, in later days it became a borough in its own right and a prosperous port; John Norden in his map of 1601, now to be seen in the Suffolk Record Office at Ipswich, shows any number of ships moored in Orford Haven and elsewhere in the river.

Orford was fortunate in having a convenient harbour formed by the River Ore. Aldeburgh, whose shipping in the post-medieval period used the same river, in earlier times might have had a harbour to the north of the town; its entrance silted up and the one-time harbour became no more than an area of marsh and shallow freshwater.

Ipswich, founded as the royal trading centre of Gipeswic by those Saxon royalty who had their burial ground at Sutton Hoo on the bluff above the Deben, lies some miles up the Orwell from the commodious harbour of Harwich over which the town authorities once claimed control. And the smaller port of Woodbridge benefited from being near the head of navigation on the Deben, on the west bank facing Sutton Hoo.

In the lower part of the Deben there was once a wide expanse of water that formed the port of Goseford, the 'goose fjord' of the Norsemen. Edward III assembled his ships in Goseford and in the similar 'port' of Orwell in 1340

The ruin of All Saints' church, Dunwich, photographed about 1880. The one-time status of this town can be judged from the size of the medieval building which was taken by the sea bit by bit until the last remaining section of the tower fell down the cliff in 1919.

before sailing to victory over the French at the epic battle of Sluys.

Dunwich, which was reputed at one time to have been as great a trading centre as any in Suffolk until the sea that brought it prosperity began to devour its buildings, had its harbour in the mouth of the River Blyth, which had been diverted southwards by a spit in just the same way that the Alde/Ore was deflected by the shingle of Orfordness. As the sea ate away at the town and blocked up Dunwich harbour the men of Southwold laboured to direct the waters of the Blyth into the sea closer to their own town, at one time sending a drummer around the streets to muster workers to dig out a new channel.

Other places that could never boast a harbour nevertheless sent ships to sea from off their hospitable beaches. Lowestoft, which had no harbour until the nineteenth century, Kirkley, Pakefield, Covehithe, whose name indicates a haven and whose part-ruined church is evidence of its former prosperity, Easton Bavents, Thorpe, a maritime hamlet of the inland parish of Aldringham, and other places along the coast looked firmly towards the sea in the medieval period, sending their ships not only coastwise but to the near Continent and to Iceland.

As in Norfolk and elsewhere, some coastal communities such as Dunwich and Sizewell continued to receive their coal supplies in small ships that lay on the beach between the tides until the coming of the railways in the nineteenth century.

Although George Rope, who was involved with the operation of a small fleet of trading vessels sailing from Orford, blamed the arrival of the railways for the decline of the coasting trade, the nineteenth century was a period of development and expansion for two Suffolk ports. A scheme for making a Norwich and Lowestoft Navigation resulted in the building of a harbour at Lowestoft, and although it proved a failure so far as the inland navigation was concerned it led to the rise of Lowestoft as a major fishing and trading port. For many years Lowestoft was one of Britain's chief herring ports, and drifters from the town worked not only in the North Sea but all around the British Isles in search of herring and mackerel.

At Ipswich the making of a dock that was at the time of its construction far larger than any dock on the Thames or the Humber not only gave the Suffolk port a place in international trade that it had lacked in earlier days but boosted the town's industries, allowing them to take full advantage of the period of industrial expansion that proved so beneficial to the country as a whole. Today the old Wet Dock is a yacht marina, but commercial traffic still uses quays on both banks of the Orwell a little way downriver.

The opening of a much smaller dock at Felixstowe on the north side of Harwich harbour in 1886 did not prove an immediate success, largely due to the opposition of a railway company that had its own port on the Essex side of the harbour. In more recent years, however, that little dock has blossomed into the country's major container port handling enormous container ships from all over the world. Rows of towering container cranes loom over the site of the now-filled dock that had failed to realise the hopes of its creator, the rich and enigmatic George Tomline, in his lifetime.

The story of maritime Suffolk is by no means merely a matter of past history.

One of the smaller Lowestoft sailing trawlers or toshers, the *Glimpse*, LT413, built at Brixham in 1888, entering Lowestoft harbour on her return from a fishing trip. The bowsprit has been run in preparatory to entering the dock, the jib is hanging loosely and the topsail has been dropped.

Shipping at Ipswich in the early nineteenth century before the construction of the Wet Dock.

Saxon seamen   1

The rhythmical creaking of oars against tholes came across the water as the long double-ended boat crept slowly up the Deben. A hoarse cry echoed over the river as the lookout in the bows of the oncoming vessel called to the helmsman at the steering oar; the boat changed direction and headed towards the eastern shore, following the wandering river channel.

The voyage had begun in the Uppsala region of eastern Sweden some time earlier. The boat and its crew had headed south between the islands of Oland and Gotland, around the south of Sweden, through the Sound and the Kattegat, and by way of the Skagerrak to the North Sea. Turning south again, they had made their way by stages through the Frisian Islands and along the low-lying coast of Holland until they reached the mouth of the Maas, whence they had struck out westwards across the southern North Sea, travelling little more than a hundred miles to reach the Deben.[1] They had avoided the sandbanks that had trapped some of those who had sailed the same route before them, and here they were at last in the sheltered waters of the broad but shallow river.

Years afterwards that boat, or perhaps another similar craft, would be hauled from the Deben up a valley on to the heath above to provide an appropriate burial for one of the Wuffing kings who had their royal dwelling at Rendlesham, a few miles to the north of the burial site. It would be loaded with all the stores that the dead king would need on his voyage to the afterlife, and with a treasure drawn from all parts of the then known world, as far as Constantinople and even beyond, and would be covered over with a great mound that would hide it for more than a thousand years.

There were two such burial mounds on the heath overlooking the Deben, dating from the period when East Anglia was ruled by immigrants from Scandinavia known to us today as Anglo-Saxons. And there were other similar ship-burials in Suffolk, at Snape near the head of the Ore/Alde estuary and at Ashby in the Lothingland peninsula near Lowestoft;

One of the mounds at Sutton Hoo, said at the time to be a 'Roman barrow', was opened up in 1860 by a party of Victorian antiquaries who might well have travelled to Suffolk by train along the line that had opened the previous year. A report that appeared in a local newspaper[2] stated that 'a considerable number (nearly two bushels) of iron screw bolts were found, all of which were sent to the blacksmith to be converted into horse shoes'. Although described as 'screw bolts' these rusty relics must have been the clench nails and roves from the planking of a ship; what the blacksmith said on being told to turn

Opposite: A half-size replica of the Sutton Hoo ship, the *Soe Wulfing*, under sail on the River Deben. Although the replica boat sailed moderately well there is no evidence that the original ship had any means of propulsion other than oars. Crucially no sign of a mast step was found during the excavation.

From the ship burial mounds at Sutton Hoo, we look down to the river Deben. The magnificence of the grave goods found with the ship can be viewed at the British Museum: the original mask on the left and the beautiful replica on the right are either side of the Saul and Paul spoons, evidence of Christian influence.

them into horseshoes is not recorded, but no doubt his remarks included an interesting selection of good 'Anglo-Saxon' expletives.[3]

The newspaper report reveals nothing about the other finds that might have been made, but adds that 'it is hoped, when leave is granted to open the others, some more important antiquities may be discovered'. All the mounds at Sutton Hoo except two were robbed in antiquity, a trench being driven into the mound to reveal the burial pit. Fortunately in two cases the robbers missed their target and the contents survived to be recorded in modern times. In the case of one of the pits the grave-robbers, for they were nothing more, had been sent packing by a deluge of rain, abandoning their loot in the resulting mud. When those forsaken bits and pieces were eventually recovered by archaeologists they revealed that without doubt the person buried in that barrow, Mound fourteen, was a woman.[4]

It might be that the attention of the unknown antiquaries was called to the mounds above the Deben by their having been shown on a chart made by Captain Stanley, of the paddle sloop HMS *Blazer*,[5] when carrying out a survey of the river in 1845.

What was lost in that campaign of grave robbery nobody knows; the treasures that were almost certainly looted from the opened barrows have never been traced. Fortunately in antiquity, almost certainly about the time of King Alfred, or perhaps just before (c.850), a farmer dug the end off what is known today to archaeologists as Mound one to make his field boundary, altering the mound's shape and crucially moving the centre of the tumulus away from the king's burial chamber. 'In the sordid and profane history of British heritage management, such preservation from the hands of looters, treasure-hunters, and acquisitive royal agents must be counted a miraculous deliverance,' says Professor Martin Carver, who was to lead a meticulous and wide-ranging investigation of the Sutton Hoo site and its context towards the end of the twentieth century.[6]

Thus it came about that when Suffolk archaeologist Basil Brown was employed by landowner Mrs Edith Pretty to investigate the cemetery in 1939 the boat that lay deep in Mound one was still untouched, and so was the fabulous and historically important treasure that lay in the burial chamber

The discovery of the Sutton Hoo ship and its treasure remained a secret until on 29th July 1939 the East Anglian Daily Times printed a story written, anonymously, by chief reporter Alf Bowden telling of the excavation; then the sightseers arrived. These interested visitors in naval uniform, seen in a photograph taken by Barbara Wagstaff, are thought to be pupils of the Royal Hospital School at Holbrook.

The Sutton Hoo replica under oars on the River Deben. It was almost certainly in this fashion that the original Sutton Hoo ship made its voyage from Scandinavia to Suffolk

within that boat. Although it was experts from the British Museum and the Office of Works who stepped in when the remarkable nature of the find became known and others who took much of the credit for the excavation, it should be remembered that it was Suffolk's Basil Brown who was primarily responsible for the discovery. Charles Phillips, the Fellow of Selwyn College, Cambridge, who took a leading part in the latter stages of the excavation, gave Brown the credit he deserved in a letter to Guy Maynard of Ipswich Museum: 'I thought that Basil Brown showed great competence in what he had done when I visited the site'.[7]

The wood of which the boat was built had completely gone, rotted by the acid soil of the heath, but it had left a clear impression in the sand; the clench nails that had fastened the edges of the strakes remained in place, mere nodules of rust. Yet, thanks to the skill and good sense of Basil Brown and those who joined him in the digging, it was possible not only to recover the mould that those timbers had left in the sand but to produce careful measured drawings of the vessel.

Clinker built with overlapping strakes fastened to each other with nails clenched over diamond-shaped roves,[8] the boat was a little over 88ft long. The frames had been secured to the planking with trenails, wooden fastenings driven into holes drilled in the timbers, and the narrow strakes, nine to each side, rose at each end where they were fastened to the stem and sternpost. The spine of the boat was a horizontal keel plank; the vertical keel such as was possessed by the Viking ships was a later development. Although a scaled-down replica of the Sutton Hoo boat has been sailed on the Deben and elsewhere, it is thought that the original vessel was propelled solely by oars; there was no sign of a mast step.

A fifth-century Roman nobleman named Sidonius seems to have had some experience of the Saxons and of their seamanship. Writing to a friend, he remarked that 'to these men a shipwreck is capital practice rather than an object of terror'. They were well used to seafaring, he said. 'The dangers of the deep are to them not casual acquaintances, but intimate friends…'.

Such were the people who came to the Deben in the boat that has become known as the Sutton Hoo ship.

A Viking trading vessel and a longship at the Roskilde museum, Denmark, where archaeological recreation is developing the understanding of the North Sea vessels of the first millennium. From a period several centuries after Saxon vessels, they both show the development of the keel, improving the sailing ability of the clinker-built North Sea vessels. Doubtless such longships struck fear as they went up river to Gipeswic.

Galleys and warfare 2

In response to the French occupation of Gascony, an English possession on the Biscay coast, and to the burning of Dover and raids on Hythe and Winchelsea, Edward I ordered in 1294 that twenty-six towns on the east and south coasts, including Ipswich, Dunwich and Yarmouth, should share in the task of providing a score of galleys for the French wars. Some of those towns were to be jointly responsible for the building, but in the case of Ipswich it was thought the town could, on its own, produce both the galley and its attendant barge, which was much more than a mere ship's boat.

From time to time the town of Ipswich had been required to supply merchant ships when the king needed to gather a fleet for operations against the Scots or the French; they would either be used as transports and supply ships or would be temporarily equipped as warships, with raised forecastle and aftercastle and a fighting top on the mainmast. The galleys, on the other hand, were purpose-built warships.

Very little is known of their construction and appearance, but they were quite different craft from the Mediterranean galley, of which a replica may be seen in the Drassanes, the historic dockyard in Barcelona. The thirteenth-century English galley was very much in the tradition of the Viking longship, an oared vessel of considerable size, with a single mast on which a square sail might be set in suitable conditions, and with a crew that was not chained to the thwarts and was not composed of convicted criminals, however ruffianly the men might have been.

Galleys seem to have been the maids-of-all-work of the medieval navy, employed in convoy duty when impressed merchant ships were conveying English soldiers across the Channel, in stopping and searching ships at sea and in enforcing customs regulations. They were used during the Hundred Years War (1337-1453) for cross-Channel raiding by both the English and the French.

In some of the towns chosen for the building of the royal galleys there were problems in enrolling a skilled workforce and it was found necessary to bring together teams from different parts of the country and even abroad; at Southampton a master builder of Bayonne in Gascony was fetched from Portsmouth to supervise the construction of the galley. There is no mention in the Ipswich accounts of any such difficulties, nor is there any mention of having to rent the land on which the vessels were laid down and of enclosing the building site with a fence of hurdles and thorns to keep out pilferers, as proved necessary at Southampton. One is led to consider the possibility that

Opposite: A document in the Ipswich Corporation archive recording the building in 1294-95 of a galley and its attendant barge.

at the end of the thirteenth century Ipswich was an established shipbuilding centre capable of taking such a contract as this in its stride.

We are most fortunate in having among the Ipswich Corporation records the accounts for the building of the two vessels, the galley and the barge, rendered to the Exchequer by the bailiffs, John de Causton and John Lew.[1] It is written in Latin; I am indebted to John Fairclough for a translation of the printed version which appears in the Historic Manuscripts Commission report of 1883 on the Ipswich Corporation records; he also provided a translation of the Exchequer record.

The account is for the building of a new galley and a barge for it, 'for the defence of the realm and the security of the seas against the enemies of King and kingdom, by the King's writ and by order of William de Marchia, Bishop of Bath and Wells, the King's Treasurer, on behalf of the King in his 23rd year [of his reign], under the inspection and taxation of Philip Harneys and Thomas Aylred, assigned to this work by the said writ'.

These two men, Harneys and Aylred, were prominent inhabitants of the town, but there is no evidence that they were shipbuilders. So far as can be seen they were in the nature of managers, obtaining the necessary materials, arranging the employment of skilled shipwrights, and organising the payment of the workers at the appropriate times. Philip Harneys is said to have been the second richest man in Ipswich in 1282, when he had corn and malt, timber and wood, cattle and pigs, horses, millstones, salt, iron, steel, pitch, boards, plate and jewellery and all kinds of other things worth the very considerable sum of £117. He was, shall we say, very comfortably off. And Thomas Aylred was not exactly a poor man either. It was hardly likely to have been shipbuilding alone that made their fortunes.

Total cost of building the galley was £195 4s. 11½d. and of the barge £23 7s. ¼d. A detailed account includes items for 'timber bought from various sources for building the galley £19 9s. 6d. and in felling the said timber and transporting it by land and water from various places with ropes bought for dragging the said timber £6 14s. 9d.; and for 1,097 planks, 32 pieces of timber to be sawn into planks and various items for the said galley with carriage of the same £29 4s. 6d.; and for 9,300 of iron bought for the said galley with the wages of smiths working the said iron £24 4s. ½d.; and for 13,000 nails bought for the said galley 52s. 6d.'

That strange figure of 9,300 'somethings' of iron is rendered in Latin figures, ixm iiic , and one wonders if it is not 9,300 but in fact 9003 cwt.

This was clearly a sizable vessel with a mast and sail that together cost £8 7s. 4d. Once the timber and all the other materials had been assembled the building of the vessel occupied some five months—the master carpenter was paid 6d. a day for 21 weeks and one day, and the other shipwrights working on the galley received £54 1s. 4d. for the same period. Needless to say, an attempt to add up the costs of the individual items does not produce the answer given at the foot of the account.

Unfortunately the Ipswich accounts do not name the men employed in building the two vessels, nor do they reveal the number of workers. The accounts for the London galley name the shipwrights employed; there were fifty of them. At York there were sixty-nine employed on the building of the galley. Ian Friel, who worked for some years as medieval historian at the National Maritime Museum and was later exhibition manager for the Mary

Rose Trust, suggests that the average number of shipwrights employed at the various sites was thirty-nine.[2]

He points out that the manpower involved in the great castle-building projects of the time make the shipbuilding effort look puny – he quotes the number of men thought to have been employed in the building of Edward I's castle at Beaumaris as some 1,800. Shipbuilding does not seem to have been a major employer of men. It is interesting to note that when there was a great round-up of shipwrights, caulkers and other shipbuilding specialists to work on the construction of Henry VIII's massive 1,000-ton *Henri Grace a Dieu* and three galleys at Woolwich in 1512 a total of 252 men were conscripted from as far afield as Cornwall and Yorkshire. Only four places – Smallhythe in Kent, Dartmouth, the Exe estuary ports, and Ipswich – could muster twenty or more men each to send to Woolwich.[3]

On completion the galley was taken down the Orwell and out of Harwich harbour for its sea trials. Unfortunately the trials were interrupted by a storm in which the vessel was quite badly damaged; it was, say the accounts, 'torn apart and broken by the fury of the sea'. An additional £5 6s. 6d. had to be expended on repairs which occupied seven men for eight days. It has been suggested that the damage was the result of bad workmanship by the shipwrights employed, but this cannot be so as the Exchequer accepted the cost of repair as well as the costs of building; there is ample evidence in medieval records that where bad workmanship had to be made good the Exchequer took steps to ensure that it was done at the expense of those responsible and not at the king's.

The barge was a much smaller vessel requiring only thirty oars compared with the hundred bought for the galley, but it was still much more than a mere ship's boat, even if the thirty oars included an allocation of spares to replace breakages; it too had a mast and sail. The total amount spent on the barge was £23 7s. ¼d., which when added to the £195 4s. 11½d. spent on the building of the galley and the £5 6s. 6d. for repairing storm damage came to a grand total of £223 18s. 6d. One is a little surprised to find that in this case the simple addition is no more than a farthing out.

The Ipswich accounts, together with the accounts for the galleys built at Newcastle and Southampton, indicate that these galleys were above 100ft. in length on the keel – one authority postulates an overall length of as much as 140ft – with a probable beam of 20-25ft. Both in their construction and in rig they were quite different from the galleys of the Mediterranean. It seems likely that they were of double-skin clinker construction, with each strake overlapping the adjoining strake and fastened to it with clench nails. Evidence of clinker construction is to be found in the accounts, which mention *clenchatores*, *clynkeres* or *cleyncherers* and *tenences contra clenchatores* or *holderes*.

The *clenchatores* were clearly the men who clenched the nails over roves, convex washers that had been used in the Sutton Hoo ship and are still used in wooden boatbuilding today. As the end of the nail is being clenched it is necessary to hold a 'dolly' or perhaps a hammer firmly on the head of the nail to prevent it being driven out by the hammering, and the job of holding the 'dolly' was equally clearly that of the *holderes*.

Clinker building was largely a northern technique, while Mediterranean vessels were usually carvel built, with the strakes or planks butted up against each other. The configuration of the strakes was not the most significant difference between the two building methods, however. In carvel building it is usual for a skeleton or frame to be erected first, and the planking is then fastened to the frames. In the other method, sometimes termed the shell technique, the strakes are always fastened to each other before any internal structure is set up. It is the way in which the strakes are formed and manipulated that gives the shape to the vessel under construction; only when the shell is complete are frames inserted to strengthen the vessel and to ensure that that shape is retained for the life of the boat.

Both the galley and the barge had a single mast and square sail. Doubtless sail was used when cruising with a fair wind, but the essence of a galley was that it was an oared vessel. When it was necessary to intercept an enemy vessel, or to make rapid progress to windward, out would come the oars.

It is not easy to see how the hundred oars purchased for the Ipswich galley could have been utilised in a craft of a mere 130ft. or so. Contemporary pictures show the oars arranged in pairs, and the varying dimensions of the oars suggests that they might indeed have been fitted in pairs, with the rower of the longer oar sitting inboard of the second rower. Effective use of oars in this way would require considerable practice as well as the natural skill of the seaman. One wonders if the numbers of oars stipulated for each galley included a generous allowance for spares to replace breakages.

Considering the special skills needed by the galley crews it is likely that these men were retained in rather more permanent service than was usual at that time. The Pipe Rolls tell of preparations in 1205 for a great expedition to France that never took place, but nevertheless the fleet assembled at Portsmouth. The total recorded expenses of the planned expedition were at least £2,222, of which some £968 was spent on galleys.

What became of those galleys when the expedition was abandoned? On the reverse of Close Roll 33 (for 1205) is a list of fifty-one galleys allocated to fifteen different ports, and this could be a distribution of the galleys intended for this abortive expedition. Two of them were sent to Ipswich (Gipewiz) and five to Dunwich (Dunnewiz). There is also a note to a writ of 17th April that year that one galley is entrusted to the men of Ipswich and three to the men of Dunwich, while a writ of 20th May to the Bailiffs of Ipswich stated that 20 marks of silver seized of the men of Ipswich from men of Rouen and Caen could be lent to the men of Ipswich towards the cost of preparing ships taken at Ipswich for the King's service. Did the towns of Ipswich and Dunwich have to pay to keep the crews ready for service?

When ships were commandeered for the king's service the costs of fitting them out and maintaining them normally fell on the owners or on the towns from which they came. Compensation for loss while on royal service was not normally forthcoming. When eleven Dunwich ships were taken up for an expedition to Gascony in the winter of 1296-97 and four of them were lost the men of Dunwich petitioned for recompense; Edward I ordered an inquiry into their claims, but the wheels of the civil service turned with a remarkable lack of speed then as now. It was only twenty-three years later that a report into the matter appeared; the lost ships were valued at £200, and the wages for the thirteen weeks that the crews of the Dunwich ships went unpaid were assessed at £1220 10s. Another seven years went by before the government of Edward III ordered that the sum be allowed against the town's tax obligations.[4]

Suffolk was the setting for events that had a great impact on English history in the early part of the fourteenth century. Edward II, who proved to be a weak and politically inept monarch, had succeeded to the throne in 1307; his troubled twenty-year reign was nearing its violent end when on 24th September 1326 his estranged wife, Queen Isabella, and her lover Roger Mortimer landed either at the port of Orwell, an anchorage downriver from the town of Ipswich, or, as some historians believe, elsewhere on the Suffolk coast. Sir William Laird Clowes points out in his history of the Royal Navy that the ships had been driven off course by a storm and the mariners were lost, and there is every chance that the landfall was made further north; preparations had been made to defend the Orwell with twelve ships from Ipswich and Harwich, so it is very likely that those in charge of the fleet changed their original plans to land in the Orwell.

Isabella and Mortimer had with them only a relatively small force of some 1,500 men, of whom about half were mercenaries from Hainault, but such was the unpopularity of Edward II and his favourites, the Despensers, by then that few in England would obey the king's orders. The campaign that began on the Suffolk coast resulted in Isabella's son Edward of Caernarfon being proclaimed king. No doubt it was Queen Isabella's need for support at that time that at last brought a favourable answer to the Dunwich petition.

Whenever it was necessary for the king to assemble a fleet on the east coast ships from ports between London and the Humber were ordered to assemble at the port of Orwell. When in 1336 Flanders took offensive action against English mercantile interests it was at Orwell that one of the two convoys organised to protect ships trading to and from Gascony was ordered to make rendezvous.

With the death of Charles IV of France in 1328 Edward III of England, his nephew, was able to make a plausible claim to be his heir. In 1337 Edward formally lay claim to the Crown of France and began preparations for a campaign against Philip VI, who had succeeded Charles. During the following two years Edward spent a good deal of time at Walton Manor, close to the Suffolk coast and conveniently situated between the port of Goseford on the Deben and the port of Orwell as he planned his campaign on the continent. Did he perhaps stride around the Suffolk countryside wearing the red and blue surcoat sewn with English leopards and French lilies with which he had furnished himself as a sign of his claim to the French Crown?[5]

The war had not gone well for England thus far. In 1336 French galleys had taken prizes off the Suffolk coast, and in 1338 a raiding party burnt Portsmouth; five English ships, the king's own biggest ships among them, were captured in Arnemuiden harbour on the island of Walcheren; and then on 5th October that year French and Genoese galleys captured and burnt Southampton.[6] Panic gripped residents of coastal areas as enemy forces ranged England's south coast virtually unchallenged. Things were little better the next year, when Ayton Doria's Genoese galleys, operating under French control, attacked Harwich but were beaten off.

In April 1339, however, Robert Lord Morley, admiral of the northern fleet, sailed from Orwell with a convoy of sixty-three ships for Flanders and captured many ships from an enemy convoy escorted by Genoese galleys which they chased into the Flemish port of Sluys. The English success was marred by the behaviour of the undisciplined English seamen, who plundered neutral Flemish and Spanish ships and then quarrelled over their booty when the fleet returned to the Orwell; at that point some of the ships deserted the fleet.[7] Far from aiding Edward's campaign, the unruly actions of the English seamen caused great harm to his efforts to construct an anti-French alliance.

The French also had their troubles. The Genoese men of Doria's galleys were discontented, because for one thing they had not received their pay; they mutinied and sailed for home. In September the remainder of the Franco-Genoese galley force moved to Sluys with the intention of raiding the English herring fishery off Yarmouth, but when the galleys put to sea on 2nd October they were dispersed by an autumn gale.

Then in January 1340 the men of the Cinque Ports, that confederation of south coast ports that controlled the important Yarmouth autumn herring fishery, learnt that eighteen galleys, part of a fleet that had been gathered in the Mediterranean by Philip VI for a crusade that never took place, were lying in Boulogne with only shipkeepers on board; they had been transferred to the Channel with the idea of supporting an invasion of England. Undeterred by a fog that hid their approach as much as it hindered their navigation, the Cinque Ports men sailed into Boulogne and burnt them all, along with twenty-four merchant ships and a large part of the lower town.

In February Edward III returned from Flanders, where he had been attempting to persuade various rulers to join him in an anti-French confederation, and began assembling a fleet in the Orwell. After celebrating Pentecost at Ipswich, the king belatedly sailed from Orwell haven on 22nd June, by which time the French had occupied the Flemish seaports in support of Philip's invading army. On the afternoon of the following day Edward's fleet was off the coast of Flanders and the English seamen sighted the enemy fleet anchored in the Swyn, a channel between the island of Cadzand and the Flemish mainland leading to the town of Sluys and to Damme, then the port for Bruges. It should not be confused with the Swin off the Essex coast, used in more recent times by barges and other small vessels bound to or from London.

Ignoring the good advice of the Genoese commander, Pietro Barbavera, to attack the English ships as they approached the coast, the Frenchmen moored their vessels in three lines across the channel, chaining each ship to its neighbours to present a solid barrier to the approaching English. The

The coast of Flanders and Zeeland as it was at the time of the Battle of Sluys. The French ships were moored to form a barrier across the Swyn, but Edward's fleet took them in the rear by spending the night before the battle in the Wester Scheldt and sailing south-west through the Zwarte Gat, with the morning sun behind them. The map is after N.A.M.Rodger.

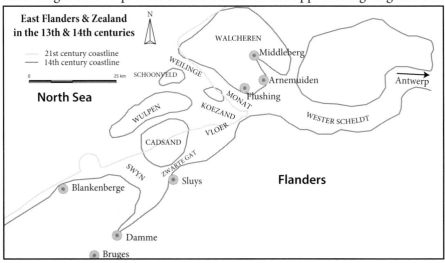

The Battle of Sluys as depicted in Jean Froissart's fifteenth-century *Chronicles*. While it is of course only an impression, it does correctly show what was essentially a land war fought from 'castles' at sea.

chronicler Jean Froissart wrote that from his vessel, the cog *Thomas*, Edward III saw 'so great a number of ships that their masts seemed to be like a great wood'.[8] Neither French nor English had any idea of naval tactics: the approaching fight was to be a normal land battle fought on the water.

Instead of tackling the French headlong the English fleet seems to have worked its way northwards to enter the Wester Schelde. Accounts of the battle that took place the following morning are contradictory and confusing, but all seem to agree that the English ships approached with the morning sun behind them; that can only mean that they sailed south-west from the Wester Schelde through the Zwarte Gat to approach the French from the landward side;[9] there is some evidence that the French endeavoured at the last moment to reorganise their formation to meet the advancing English fleet.

It would seem that the French fleet consisted of 202 ships, six galleys and twenty-two barges; the English had only between 120 and 160 ships, but the French superiority in numbers was outweighed by their inability to manoeuvre. As their ships neared the French fleet the English archers loosed a hail of arrows on to the stationary French. The archers with their longbows proved quite as devastating afloat as they did against the French at the land battle of Crecy later in the war.

As the ships came together English seamen and soldiers boarded the moored French ships; few if any prisoners were taken, and those Frenchmen who did not die in the hand-to-hand fighting were forced overboard and drowned; a man in armour had little chance in the water. The slaughter continued for hours: the French lost between 16,000 and 18,000 men, the English far fewer.

It was a crushing defeat for the French, and it established the reputation of the young Edward III as a warrior. It did not, however, give the English command of the narrow seas, for Philip VI had a far better appreciation of the uses of naval power than did Edward.

Fishermen and traders 3

Among the multitude of cargoes carried coastwise coal and corn were undoubtedly the most prolific. Coal had been shipped from the Tyne since at least the fifteenth century, and while most of the corn went to London not a few cargoes went to Newcastle in the same ships that brought coal to Suffolk ports.

It is apparent from the Newcastle chamberlains' accounts that Suffolk ships were prominent among the vessels loading coal in the Tyne in the early years of the sixteenth century, when the trade was perhaps in its infancy.[1] The majority of them were from Dunwich and Aldeburgh; others were from Covehithe, Easton, Iken, Ipswich, Kirkley, Lowestoft, Orford, Orwell, Pakefield, Sizewell, Southwold, Thorpe, Walberswick and Woodbridge.

The most frequent Suffolk visitors to Newcastle to load coal in the period 1508-1511 were undoubtedly ships from Dunwich, which paid 198 visits to the Tyne in those four years. Of those it is recorded that on 138 occasions the ships entered 'empty', fifty times they were in ballast and on ten occasions they were loaded with stones, which attracted the modest toll of fourpence a cargo. Perhaps those stones were flint cobbles off Dunwich beach, which might well have been in demand for paving the Newcastle streets. Second to Dunwich was Aldeburgh, whose ships called forty-nine times 'empty' for coal and seventeen times in ballast;[2] three times Dunwich ships carried cargoes of malmsey wine and once a ship brought fish.

Vessels arriving in the Tyne in ballast had to unload their ballast into the 'ballast shore', described in 1524 as made of timber, 360ft long; its upkeep came to 40 marks (£26.67p) a year. The chamberlains of Newcastle levied ballast dues comprising a fixed impost of 12d and a toll calculated at the rate of 1½d a ton on all ships discharging ballast, except those owned in Newcastle.

The earliest formal statement of the tolls charged at Newcastle seems to be in the answer of the mayor and burgesses of Newcastle to the Aldeburgh shipmasters' complaint of 1524. They affirmed that every ship or boat not free of the town paid an impost of 20d with a further impost of 12d on every ship discharging ballast and another 12d on every ship let to freight or hire. In addition to these imposts there were tolls levied at the rate of 3d a ton on ballast discharged, of 2d a chaldron on coal shipped, and of 3d a chaldron on grindstones. The Newcastle authorities further claimed that they farmed these tolls from the Crown for £100 a year, and that the surplus to this rent was used to repair and maintain the town walls and pavements, the Tyne bridge and the ballast shore, these costs being estimated at £300 per annum. The shipmasters

Opposite: 'A whistle that was his father's' – a memorial brass from Beeston Regis Church portraying John Deynes, who has, hung around his neck, a boatswain's whistle, somewhat magnified by the brasier.

had objected to the imposts and had claimed that they were actually charged at the rate of 3d a chaldron on coal, 12d a chaldron on grindstones, and as much for any other merchandise.[3]

While ships owned by freemen of Newcastle were free of these imposts and tolls, there was a second class of favoured ships and shippers who paid no impost and a toll on the outgoing cargo of coal at the beneficial rate of 1d a chaldron. Among these were ships owned in Dunwich and Ipswich. If individual merchants who shipped goods in a 'free' ship were not themselves free, however, while there would be no impost charged on the ship the 'unfree' goods would be charged at the higher rate of 3d a chaldron – a measure that was the amount carried by one of the local coal wagons.

Thus the *Clement* of Dunwich when leaving Newcastle on 24th April 1510 with a cargo of twenty chaldrons of 'unfree' coal paid 60d.[4] Such a 'free' ship of Dunwich would normally have paid a toll of only 20d on a cargo of twenty chaldrons, while an 'unfree' ship would have paid 80d – an impost of 20d plus 60d toll at the rate of 3d a chaldron. In another case the Dunwich ship *Petter* sailed on 26th April 1509 with a cargo of 27 chaldrons of coal which was chargeable 6s 2½d; it was recorded as 'one half unfree of Aldeburgh and a quarter belonging to Walberswick'.[5] The same ship carried a similar cargo assigned to the same three places just a month later, and also on other occasions.

Master of the *Petter* at that time was Edmund Freman, who had earlier had the *Trinite* of Dunwich and later transferred to the *Kattrin* of 'Albroughe', the larger of two ships with that name belonging to the Suffolk port. It is fascinating to endeavour to work out the sequence of voyages for particular ships, but it is a task that is complicated by the duplication of names; there were at least three ships belonging to Dunwich with the name *Petter* at the same time, Freman's ship carrying 26 or 27 chaldrons and the others between 15 and 18.

The *Nicolles* (Nicholas?) of Dunwich left Newcastle laden with coal three times in June and July 1508 under Robert Mower and then five times between April and the end of August the following year under John Wynssent (Vincent?). John Freman, who might have been closely related to Edmund, took her over in 1510, when she left Newcastle on 16th March carrying 22 chaldrons of coal. There was a smaller vessel also named the *Nicolles* of Dunwich that carried only 13 chaldrons and made five trips to Newcastle for coal under John Gudwen (Goodwin?) in the summer of 1510; in 1511 Robert Kyng had charge of her and she made three trips in June, July and August.

A final confusion may be noted with John and Robert Tongg, who both sailed the *Mawdlen* of Aldeburgh. When both ships were in the port of Newcastle at the same time, as they often were, John's ship was named as the *Little Mawdlen*; it carried only 20 chaldrons against the larger ship's 36 or 38. In contrast with other skippers, who changed ships from time to time, the Tonggs remained in the two *Mawdlens* throughout the period, and no doubt for longer. Between them they made twenty-two visits to the Tyne in those four years studied by Dr Fraser.

The Newcastle records show that for the most part the Suffolk ships restricted their sailings to the less stormy months, though the *Gorge* of Dunwich left her last voyage of 1508 until the early part of December and began 1510 with a departure from the Tyne on 27th January; she was not, however, one of the regular Newcastle traders. Aldeburgh fishmonger Thomas Bench knew what he was about when he reminded his executors to purchase his gift of coals for the poor of his home town 'when they may be had best cheape, in the somer time'.

The *Mary Anne* of Aldeburgh was making her way slowly across the North Sea on 30th June 1559. We know little or nothing about the *Mary Anne*; she was probably a small vessel, no more than 50ft in length, with square sails set on her mainmast and possibly another sail on a mizzen, and she might have been bringing a cargo of coal from the Tyne or carrying barley or wheat grown on the fields of Suffolk to some port in northern England, or to a port in the Low Countries.

Cutbert Watson, a member of her small crew, was nearing the end of his voyage through life. He was nearing harbour, but the *Mary Anne* was not; she was rolling her way across the North Sea, out of sight of land, the helmsman steering her by the stars towards her destined port. John More, master of the *Mary Anne*, and Cutbert's other shipmates, those who were watch below, gathered round his bunk – or was he lying in a hammock swinging from the deck beams above? It was very dark below deck and hard to see anything, but his shipmates could see clearly enough that his end was nigh.

Leaning down to speak into Cutbert's ear, the skipper asked him, 'D'ye wanta mearke yer will, booy?'

'But there en't nobody te wroite it down.'

'Dun't ye worry 'bout thet, Bert, jus' tell us what ye want and we'll get that writ down when we get hoom.'

'Oh!' There was a pause. 'Well, I bequeath my soul te Almighty God 'n' all that . . .'

'Yis, 'n' what about the money for this 'ere viage?'

'Ah, better give thet to my ol' woman at hoom, she'll want thet.'

'Who's goin' te hev thet bo't o' yours, Bert?' broke in one of the crew. 'Who'd ye want te hev yer nets?'

When at home between voyages Cutbert went fishing off the beach at Thorpe, a few miles north of Aldeburgh.

'Ah, thet bo't, thet en't mine,' muttered Cutbert. 'Do yew give them flews te moi gal Margery, oh, and that linen I had offa thet man . . .'

A fit of coughing interrupted Cutbert's words. 'She'd better hev moi clothes, they'll do fer her husband, and a kettle – ah, no, Tom, I tell him he c'n hev that good coat o' mine, and a hat too.

'The gal, she c'n hev all the rest onet.'

'Yis, an' who's a-goin' te look arter all this fer yew?'

'Whoi, my brother Tom, o' course.

'Oh God! Yis, moi body, oh thet hurt, that do! I leave thet – oh God!'

The ship lurched over to larboard as the watch on deck put her about on the other tack. No good saying bury me in the chu'chyard, we're at sea. The words 'committed to the deep' came into the dying man's mind. Oh ah, thass what they'll do, they'll commit me te the deep – stitch me up in a bit o' old sailcloth 'n' throw me uvver the side.

'Ah, do you tell my ol' lady te give, te give suffin te them poor folks, them in Thorpe. An' come Michaelmas – Oh God! Oh!' He coughed again, and fell silent.

Captain More looked round at his crew. 'Du yew remember what he say,' he ordered.

'Dun't yew fergit nothin', not a dene onet.'

True to his word, John More sought out a clerk to set out Cutbert's will when they eventually reached their home port. The nuncupative (verbal, unwritten) will of Cutbert Watson as dictated to the clerk is among those transcribed by Suffolk historian Peter Northeast:

Cutbert Watson of Thorpe by Leyston, lyng upon his deathbed in the said ship.

Dated 30 June 1559, before John More, master of the *Mary Anne* of Aldeburghe, Robert Swetman, John Palmer, Thomas Fysher, John Cordell and others present in the said ship.

my soul unto the pleasure of almighty god and I hope to have forgiveness of my sins and everlasting life through the merits of Christ's precious death and passion

my body to the pleasure of almighty god

to my child Margery 4 flewes, 8 yards of fine linen cloth, 6 yards of coarse linen cloth, a kettle or else the price thereof and £3 in money out of the house's payments and all my clothing except a coat and a hat which I give to Thomas Hanbye

my wages which is due unto me for this voyage to Christian my wife except 3s.4d. thereof, which shall be distributed and given to the poor people in Thorpe by my exors.

All the rest of my other goods, which appear by a bill inventory remaining in the hands of Thomas Potler, to my child Margery

exors: my brother Thomas Hanbye, to execute the same testament which was not put in writing for defect of a clerk and brevity of time.

The above named are ready to testify this to be of very truth.[6]

Farmer-fishermen

Other medieval wills tell us a little about life along the Suffolk coast at that time. Richard Cotyngham the younger of Thorpethe (Thorpe hythe) left to his wife in 1475 'from the ship called le *Mart* a manfare of Fissyngur' and 'a half part of the Sparlyngebote'; he also left other nets as well as sheep, lambs and his barley to various people. He was clearly a farmer as well as a fisherman.[7]

A manfare was a pair of drift nets, one man's contribution to the gear of the vessel in which he served, or possibly more generally a similar share of other fishing gear such as longlines; the word Fissyngur is probably simply translated as fishing gear. A sparlingbote or sperlingbote was a small boat employed in fishing for sprats, known in medieval times as sperling; many were the bequests of sperlingnets or spernets used in spratting.

In spite of the farming influence seen in Richard's will the Cotynghams were clearly a seafaring family. His widowed mother Elizabeth in 1560 had left to him 'a manfare of flewes, a manfare of deep sea nets and a warrope [the warp to which the nets were attached], ready to the sea'. Possibly Richard's father had been a man of some standing, for his mother also left him 'a whistle that was his father's'; it seems likely that it was a boatswain's pipe, used to pass orders at sea.

'Half a boat's flete of flewes' or drift nets was among the bequests left to his wife Elizabeth by John Cordwell of Thorpe in 1599. He also left her 'one half of my fortyll boat, with the half of all the tackling that belongeth to it', with the other half of the boat and its tackling going to his sons John and Raynold. A fartyll, fertyll or fortyll boat was a small longshore fishing boat propelled by oars, used in the inshore herring fishery that took place in the autumn, one that was of great importance to the economy of the coastal communities. The word fartyll possibly derives from the Middle English fardel, meaning 'a small bundle' or 'a pack', an indication of the boat's limited carrying capacity.[8]

Thorpe hythe was not then a parish; it was a coastal settlement within the parish of Aldringham, a fact that is indicated in many wills by bequests split between the church of St Andrew at Aldringham and the subsidiary chapel of St Mary at Thorpe. John Codyngham of Thorphithe directed that 'my part of le *George* to be sold by my exors and Richard my son to have 20s. out of it and Robert my son 20s.', while another part of the proceeds of sale was to be divided between the parish church and the chapel.

There would have been no difficulty in beaching the smaller boats at a place like Thorpe, but one does wonder where the larger vessels found a haven. There is a clue in the will of John Jackeson 'of Aldringham Thorpe, mariner', who in 1570 left 'to my son William my great boat that is now at Orforde, he to pay the workmen and suffer his mother to have a quarter venture with him, if she will towards her living, as long as she liveth'. It would seem that the vessel was under repair at Orford.

A rather sad family story is revealed by the will of Joan Cantell, widow of Woodbridge, who in 1533 left to her son John Cantell 'my ship and all that belongs to it when it shall please god to find him his perfect wit, and until that time, Thos Mariot my son-in-law to have the overseeing of the ship.' Son John was clearly suffering from some mental disability.[9]

'If John die without reason, wit or issue, the said Thos Mariot to have the ship to his use. To John Cantell my son all my other lands, whatever they may be, if he come to his right wits, otherwise . . .'.

Wills made by some Lowestoft people indicate clearly the maritime nature of that town in the fifteenth century. John Heygham (probably pronounced Ham), a Lowestoft merchant, was just about to set off on a journey – 'destined for foreign parts' – when he made his will on 4th February 1442, and in case he did not return he directed that he was 'to be buried in Christian burial where god so disposes'.

Agnes, late wife of William Whyte, was also about to set off from her Lowestoft home when she made her will on 3rd May 1479; she was undertaking a pilgrimage to the shrine of St James at Compostella in northern Spain and she wanted to ensure the wellbeing of her second husband, Everard Wresteler, should she not come back. 'My husband Everard, during his lifetime, to have my tenement and after his death, it to be sold. Nevertheless, if Everard should be reduced to poverty and is unable [to] avoid indigence, he may sell my tenement and have from it 20 marks. As soon as my death be learned of with reasonable certainty, then my feoffees to release estate in the said tenement to Everard, my husband. . .'.[10]

If it is a surprise to find a woman setting off on such a pilgrimage and leaving her husband at home, that is not the only surprising thing about Agnes Wresteler. She owned the family house, and it would appear that it was quite a substantial property. And she had taken for her second husband a foreigner – Everard Wresteler, a blacksmith by trade, was an immigrant from the Continent who had settled in Lowestoft.[11] Agnes did return home safely; that is apparent from her appearing in her husband's will, which he made in 1486.

It is obvious from the frequent mention of nets of one kind and another in wills that many people along the coast were engaged in fishing, but information regarding medieval fishermen and their work is somewhat sparse. It might be expected that William the Conqueror's great list of customary taxes and fees would contain much detail about sea fisheries off the Norfolk and Suffolk coasts, but in fact the Domesday Book gives little or no information on the subject; the fisheries mentioned are almost entirely inland freshwater fisheries. The herring fishery does however find an echo in the Suffolk survey, for in the hundreds of Blything, Lothingland and Wangford (those in the north-east of the county) there are eighteen places which paid levies of herring. Southwold returned 25,000 herrings and Beccles 60,000, while Dunwich returned 68,000.[12]

Historians have contended on the strength of the payment to Bury Abbey of those 60,000 herrings that Beccles was at the time a significant fishing port lying at the head of a deep inlet, but it seems much more likely that it was a market for fish brought in from the coastal fishing settlements. By the eleventh century the Great Estuary of Roman times had silted up and flocks of sheep were being kept on the marshes of that area.[13] While Domesday Book records a market at Beccles that was three parts owned by the Abbey of St Edmund and one part by the king, there is no mention of a market at Yarmouth, later to become one of the main herring ports. Strangely, the Norfolk folios have nothing to say about the Yarmouth fishery, although in the Suffolk section of the Little Domesday Book, that more detailed version covering the eastern counties, there is an entry stating that twenty-four fishermen in Yarmouth belonged to the manor of Gorleston; Professor H. C. Darby observes that 'from this hint we must imagine the rest'.[14]

A holding in Kessingland, a village that was centuries later to become an important centre of the herring industry, was 'then worth 10 shillings now 22 shillings and 1,000 herrings'; 'then' was of course in the time of King Edward the Confessor, 'now' was the year 1086 when the survey was being compiled.

Professor Darby was as mystified as we are by all these rather vague references, and could only observe that 'it is impossible to say exactly what activity all these references imply, and we can only note the existence of Yarmouth with its fishermen just across the county boundary, and the mysterious reference to a seaport (portus maris) at Frostenden in Blything'.

There were also other references to activity along the seashore, as Professor Darby puts it. At Southwold there was the moiety of a sea-weir and the fourth part of the other moiety, but there is no reference anywhere to the remaining three-eighths. One is reminded of the division of the ownership of seagoing vessels into sixty-fourths in a later period.

There also belonged to the manor of Blythburgh the fourth penny from the rent of the haye or hedge of Riseburc, though we are not told what kind of haye this was. It could well have been some kind of fish-trap erected in the River Blyth; fish weirs in Morecambe Bay, Lancashire, were constructed of wattle fencing and known as hedge baulks. The remains of such a fish trap, dating from Saxon times, have been investigated in the River Stour at Holbrook, and timbers together with wattle panels that are almost certainly part of fish weirs have been found in the Alde by members of the Aldeburgh and District Local History Society in the course of their excavation of the Roman and Saxon site at Barber's Point, inundated by a tidal surge in 2013.[15]

The use of fish weirs and keddle or kettle nets, stake nets and baulk nets has been recorded in considerable detail by a fisheries scientist from the laboratory at Lowestoft, Mr F.M. Davis.[16] The weirs that he saw in use were certainly very ancient in design, and his book, first issued in 1923, has great value in showing us how the medieval shore fisherman operated.

One of the devices he records is the splash or peter net, also known historically as a flue net, used widely around the south-east coast and in the Thames estuary. The net, held by an anchor at each end, was shot in shallow water in a segment of a circle, with the concave side facing the flow of the tide. When the net was set a boat was rowed up towards it, the fisherman banging an oar on the surface to frighten the fish towards it – hence the name splash net. The name peter net was doubtless a transference from St Peter, one of the fishermen who abandoned their boats to follow Jesus; whether Peter actually used such a net is somewhat doubtful.

Fortunately there is information to be found in documents relating to Leiston Abbey's right to all wrecked goods washed up along the Suffolk coast between the Minsmere and Hundred rivers, to the north of Aldeburgh. The abbey monitored this potentially lucrative right through a special court, known as the Hethewarmoot, held each year on 6th December. Two bailiffs were appointed each year, one each from the coastal hamlets of Sizewell and Thorpe, and these bailiffs would swear in a jury from each village to deal with the year's business.

Every shipmaster who was operating from the beaches of Sizewell and Thorpe was compelled to serve as a juror in that year's court, so we have a reliable tally of the masters operating from these hamlets between 1378 and 1409. The churchwardens' accounts of Walberswick and the town records of Dunwich also provide a useful insight into the scale and organisation of the fishing industry in those two ports, and can be usefully compared with the Hethewarmoot evidence.

Privilege and piracy

Manorial rights to wreck cast up on the shore might have provided an excellent source of income for those who possessed such rights; they also constituted a privilege that could be manipulated to their advantage by unscrupulous title holders as well as a source of fees for lawyers who endeavoured to unravel the resulting disputes between the original merchant owners and the claimants.

A large piece of wreckage from a vessel of uncertain age which came ashore at Dunwich in 1955.

In the course of his research into the early history of Lowestoft and the half-hundreds of Mutford and Lothingland in the north-east of Suffolk David Butcher has unearthed an intriguing and somewhat puzzling episode in 1352 when the crews of ships run ashore in the vicinity of Lowestoft were attacked by Sir Edmund de Hemgrave, who was lord of the half-hundred of Mutford and as such was entitled to wreck of the shore, Edmund de Thorpe and others under the pretence that the shipwrecked men were Scottish. It was claimed that some men had been killed as they swam ashore or saved themselves on pieces of wood, and others had been wounded and left for dead on the sand.[17]

The cargoes of these ships had been claimed as wreck and had been sold to Mary, the widow of Thomas de Brotherton, Earl of Norfolk, to prevent recovery of the goods by the rightful owners, merchants of Newcastle-upon-Tyne and Berwick-on-Tweed, who petitioned the King for redress.

That was not the only such incident under investigation at the time. Three Flemish ships, the *Marie* from Nieuport, the *Nicholas* from the same place and *Le Godberade* belonging to and commanded by William Ladman from la Scluse (Sluys), had been wrecked between Kessingland and Old Kirkley mill on 1st November 1352 and the cargoes of the three ships had been seized on the orders of Joan de Hemgrave and Edmund de Thorpe on behalf of Edmund de Hemgrave. In this case as well the excuse for the seizure was that the owners were Scottish; while it is conceivable that men from Berwick might have been mistaken by their accent for Scotsmen, it is hard to believe that Flemings might have been misidentified in that way.

All of those in the Flemish ships – including a merchant named Christopher de Coloyne (Cologne) – appear to have got ashore safely, but one man, Johan Wollore, was killed by two Suffolk men and his finger was cut off to obtain a ring he was wearing. Whatever happened that November day, it seems to have been a pretty violent affair.

The presence of Christopher from Cologne is not without interest; Nicholas Amor has remarked on the major part played by merchants from the Rhineland city in the trade of medieval Ipswich.[18] Even in the fourteenth and fifteenth centuries Suffolk seaports were somewhat cosmopolitan communities, with immigrants from the Low Countries and elsewhere in Europe numbered among their inhabitants. In the early 1400s incomers such as Rumbald Herreyssone in Ipswich and the Fleming William Berbrewer in Lowestoft introduced the brewing of beer using hops – as opposed to ale, which is not hopped.

A near view of the closely spaced timbers of the ancient ship whose remains came ashore at Dunwich in 1955.

Among the European immigrants listed by David Butcher in his book on medieval Lowestoft are Gerard Ducheman, Jacobus Ducheman, Helewyse Duchewoman, Janyn Frensheman and Joan Frenshewoman, and Walter Skotman who hailed from north of the Tweed. Another was Joceus Couper, a cooper by trade, who no doubt made the barrels for his fellow immigrants William Berbrewer and Tymon Brewer.[19]

Cogs and hulks

Just what were the ships that sailed from Suffolk ports in the Middle Ages? Until relatively recently the only clues we had to the appearance of medieval shipping were the somewhat distorted images on the seals of towns such as

A model of the Hanseatic cog that was discovered in the River Weser in 1962 in the Deutsches Schiffartsmuseum at Bremerhaven, where the vessel herself has been conserved and put on display.

Sandwich, Stralsund, Dover or Ipswich, whose seal bears one of the earliest depictions of a vessel with a stern rudder rather than the steering oar attached to the quarter. Those images suffered from the necessity to contain them within a circular inscription.

It was only when in October 1962 the dredging of a new channel in the port of Bremen revealed the wreck of a medieval Hanseatic cog that maritime

A replica of the cog that was found near Kampen in the Netherlands, making her way along the Kiel Canal under her 'iron tops'l, a device unknown to the men who sailed the original vessel..

Looking down on the deck of the replica cog. Vessels similar to this sailed from the Suffolk ports in the Middle Ages.

researchers were able to examine an actual ship from that period. The vessel was apparently still incomplete when about 1380 it was swept away by a severe storm from the shipbuilding yard in which it had been constructed. The wreckage of the cog was carefully salvaged from the sandbank on which it had been stranded almost six hundred years earlier and taken to the Deutsches Schiffartsmuseum for conservation. Since then a number of other wrecks have been discovered in the Baltic and in the Netherlands, adding immeasurably to our knowledge of medieval trading vessels, and several replicas have been built in order to gain knowledge of the sailing qualities of those craft.

Sailing tests of the replicas disproved once and for all the oft-quoted assertion that a craft with a single square sail could only make progress before the wind; it was quickly found that with the yard well braced up the cog would sail well to windward.[20]

The borough seal of Ipswich, thought to date from soon after the granting of borough status in 1200, showing a cog.

The cog, which is so intimately linked with the trading activities of the Hanseatic League, was very different from the various earlier traders developed directly from the double-ended Viking ships such as those excavated from Roskilde Fjord and now displayed in the Viking ship museum in that Danish city. The Bremen cog and the smaller vessel found in the newly drained polder near Nijkerk in the Netherlands reveal that the North Sea cog was a rather flat-bottomed vessel with high freeboard and a raking stem and sternpost. The bottom strakes were butted edge to edge carvel fashion, but above the turn of the bilge the planking was overlapped in clinker fashion.

Other wrecks found in recent years in the Baltic show that those built in that area were different in various ways from their North Sea counterparts. For one thing the planking of both bottom and sides was clinker, with rather narrower planks.

Model of a mid-fourteenth-century cog from the Baltic port of Elbing, now the Polish city of Elblag.

It is impossible to say how closely contemporary vessels built in the Aldeburgh and Ipswich shipyards resembled their continental counterparts; the seamen who might have told us about the distinctive features of hull and rigging that differentiated their Suffolk ships from those built in other places left no record, not merely for defect of a clerk and brevity of time but because they saw no necessity for doing so.

However, the borough seal of Ipswich, which is thought to have been made quite soon after the town received its first charter from King John in 1200, provides us with a very adequate depiction of a cog. She is clinker built, with a raking stem and a hefty rudder attached to the sternpost, a single mast with a squaresail furled to a yard, and an aftercastle that appears to be an appendage rather than an integral part of the structure. Unlike the Bremen cog, she does not have transverse beams that penetrate the planking.

The seal of the bailiffs of Ipswich, on the other hand, shows an entirely different craft. It has a single mast with a square sail furled to the yard, but at both bow and stern the clinker planking is swept up almost to the vertical and there is neither stem nor sternpost, the ends of the planking apparently being fastened to a horizontal collar; both fo'c'stle and aftercastle appear to be very much part of the hull structure. This is a hulk, a type of craft that is also known from the seal of the south coast town of New Shoreham, also known in the Middle Ages as Hulksmouth.

It is probably too much to claim, as some have, that these stylised depictions are portraits of Ipswich-built ships, but the appearance of these two vessels on the seals is surely an indication that these were the types of craft using the Suffolk ports at the time the seals were created.

The port of Orwell 4

The only satisfactory landlocked haven between the Humber and the Thames is Harwich harbour, formed by the estuary of the rivers Stour and Orwell and sheltered from north-easterly winds by the shingle promontory of Landguard Point. Often pronounced in the local vernacular 'Arryjarber', it provided a safe anchorage for large numbers of ships in the days of sail, offering not only refuge for vessels seeking shelter from bad weather but a convenient haven for those awaiting a fair wind for their destined passage.

While the harbour and the River Stour have for a thousand years and more formed a boundary between East Anglia and the territory of the East Saxons, it is convenient to treat the history of this stretch of tidal water as being Suffolk history. In justification of this it can be pointed out that until the formation of the Harwich Harbour Conservancy Board in 1863 it was the Corporation of Ipswich that claimed jurisdiction over the harbour – though this claim was for centuries disputed by the inhabitants of Harwich.

Lying on the Essex side of the harbour, the town of Harwich was for many years a packet port with links to the near Continent and was the site of a minor naval dockyard established in the seventeenth century. On the Suffolk side was built the stronghold known as Landguard Fort that protected the harbour from enemies who over the centuries threatened the security of the realm.

Of the two rivers, the Stour gives access to the small ports of Mistley and Manningtree and for a time carried lighters up to the town of Sudbury. The Orwell has carried shipping to the much larger port of Ipswich for more than a thousand years.

Situated at the lowest crossing point of the river, where a Roman road forded the stream, and at the head of the Orwell estuary, Ipswich, or Gipeswic as it was first known, was established at the beginning of the seventh century by the Wuffingas, the Anglo-Saxon rulers of East Anglia, as a trading entrepot. The contents of the burial ship excavated in 1939 at Sutton Hoo provide an indication of the far-flung trading links of this embryonic seaport: items in that fabulous treasure, now on display in the British Museum in London, came not only from the Wuffings' Scandinavian homeland but also from as far away as Constantinople.

The Orwell was undoubtedly wider when the Saxons set up their settlement on its north bank, and it is likely that the small ships that traded with the Rhineland were grounded on the shelving shore to unload their cargoes; there might have been timber jetties projecting into the river to facilitate the work of

Opposite: If one closes one's eyes to the giant container ship and the lofty cranes one can look over the lower reaches of the Orwell and imagine little ships loading wool fells or Suffolk broadcloth at the Port of Orwell.

moving goods. Archaeologists have found evidence of the import of Rhenish wine as well as whet-stones and Neidermendig lava quernstones that came from the Cologne area.[1]

The Saxon settlement of Gipeswic produced a wheel-thrown form of pottery known to archaeologists as Ipswich Ware, and a distribution map of finds of this characteristic grey ware indicates that it was traded widely in eastern England by sea and inland waterway. Find spots are almost invariably on the coast or along navigable rivers, indicating that there was a thriving coastal trade in Saxon times.

The Anglo-Saxon Chronicles tell of a battle at 'Stourmouth' in the Orwell-Stour estuary in AD 885 in which a 'ship-force' sent from Kent by King Alfred defeated sixteen Danish ships. The ships were seized and the crews all killed.[2] It has often been said that the battle took place where the two rivers merge off Shotley and that the slaughter gave Bloody Point its name; it is more likely that the name is derived from an old word meaning 'an empty place'.

While they were on the way back to Kent with their spoils the Saxons came up with a large Danish fleet. There was a second battle and, we are told, 'the Danes had the victory'. The story of the fight off Shotley is to be found in all the guidebooks; the return match is less frequently mentioned.

The estuary was probably very different at that time from how it is today. It has been surmised that in prehistoric times the two rivers entered the sea to the northward of where Landguard – or Langer – Point is now and close under Bulls Cliff, the edge of the high land on which the town of Felixstowe was developed in the nineteenth century. It was the gradual deposition of a shingle spit that diverted the two rivers some two miles to the southward.[3]

Possibly in the Roman period the now-submerged Saxon Shore fort known as Walton Castle – it contained a motte and bailey castle in the centuries after the Norman Conquest – lay close to the northern shore of the estuary when it was first constructed. There is certainly a suggestion that another Saxon Shore fort or even a Roman port lay in the vicinity of the West Rocks, some two miles to seaward of the Naze.[4]

The growth of the town of Harwich on its peninsula at the mouth of the estuary in the years after the Norman takeover proved something of a threat to the upriver port of Ipswich, the new settlement being in a position to control the flow of shipping up and down the rivers. It was part of the manor of Dovercourt, and that manor was held by that powerful magnate Roger Bigod, Earl of Norfolk and Earl Marshal.

The Bigods had a house and quay in Ipswich, but they were by no means averse to using their extensive landholdings to their own profit even when this had an adverse effect on the wellbeing of Ipswich. Besides Dovercourt they held estates on the Suffolk side of the estuary, including the stronghold of Walton Castle, and also the port of Orford. Roger Bigod was indeed in a position both politically and geographically to make life very difficult for the merchants of Ipswich. In 1274, four years after his death, there were complaints that Roger had been interfering seriously with the trade of Ipswich.

It was alleged 'that the Earl Marshall, late deceased, made purpressure [an illegal takeover] upon the water of the King in the Port of Orwell, which is a port of the King and common to all persons for buying and selling, extending from the sea as far as the town of Ipswich. And neither the said Earl nor

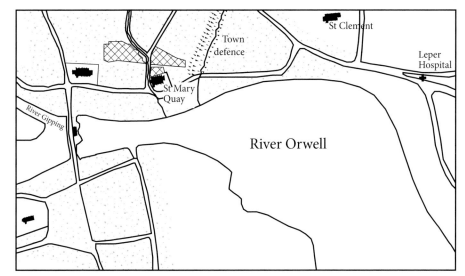

A sketch map of the port area of Ipswich in the medieval period showing Stoke Bridge and, just below the bridge, the site of the ford that had been in use in Roman times.

his men of Oreford allow the merchants, who wish, to put in at the town of Ipswich with their merchandise, but against their will he compels them by force to put in at Herwiz, which is a town of the said Earl's, taking their sails, anchors, and steering gear and drawing their ships to dry land, taking their merchandise at will, and they pay what pleases them for the said merchandise, whereby the town of Ipswich is much depreciated'.[5]

If that sounds like piracy, it has to be said that there was plenty of that going on in medieval times, in the harbour as well as elsewhere. An inquiry was held in 1399 into the alleged seizure in Harwich harbour of a vessel belonging to William Fuller, of Nacton, together with a priest, Dominus Johannes Brygge. The assailants, 'having boarded it by force of arms removed from it the said priest, with a boy and other things, viz a fardel[6] packed with fourteen pieces of cloth worth thirty marks' and took from the priest two purses containing money.[7]

While at Walton planning his expedition to Flanders in 1338 Edward III made the mistake of granting jurisdiction over the haven to the town of Harwich. Kings do not err, of course, but the burgesses of Ipswich immediately appealed against his decision, pointing out to him that 'the whole Haven of Erewell in the arme of the sea there to the said Towne of Ipswich dothe belong, and from all times passed hathe belonged'.[8]

It was true enough that Ipswich had obtained jurisdiction over the Orwell down to Poll Head – a somewhat indeterminate position to seaward of Landguard Point – as a result of the charter given by King John in 1200, but that was something the men of Harwich repeatedly attempted to wrest from the upriver town.

Endeavouring to convince the king of his error, the burgesses of Ipswich cleverly hinted that his granting of rights to Harwich would have a bad effect on his Treasury. They averred that because of the interference of the Harwich men they were prevented from raising the fee farm, the sum of money that they paid to the Crown each year. Edward consulted his advisers.

The result was that notification was issued from Walton on 11th July 1338 'that the king has revoked his late grant to the bailiffs and men of Herewicz of a murage [a toll to pay for building a wall around the town] for four years at the said town and the port of Orewell as pertaining to the town, at the prosecution of the burgesses of Ipswich setting forth that the whole port of Orewell ought to belong, and has belonged in the past, to the town, and that none but their bailiffs and ministers ought to make distraints or attachments or levy toll or other custom there.'[9]

That was by no means the end of the story. In 1379 Ipswich petitioned Richard II that they might have the haven to Poll Head, 'w[ch] they have time out of memory belonging to them', officially and clearly assigned to the town. The thirteen-year-old king gave directions for an inquiry to be held, and at an inquest held at Shotley on 3rd November 1379 a dozen witnesses declared under oath that the port of Ipswich extended downriver to the Poll Head, 'and soe hathe donne time out of minde, and remaineth soe …'[10]

Succeeding monarchs confirmed the charter and extended the privileges enjoyed by the citizens of Ipswich, but the disputes with Harwich continued. In his charter Henry VIII more particularly stressed the maritime nature of Ipswich by specifically confirming the Corporation's jurisdiction over the Orwell and granting that body admiralty jurisdiction: 'That the Bailives of the said Town, for the Time Being, shall be Our Admirals, and the Admirals of Our Heirs, for and within the whole Town, Precincts, Suburbs, Water, and Course of Water.'[11]

As the remarkable series of letters that passed between members of the Paston family bear witness, the fifteenth century was a tumultuous one. It had begun with the success of Henry V and the English archers, commanded by a Norfolk man, Sir Thomas Erpingham,[12] at Agincourt, but the calamitous reign of Henry VI (1422-61 and 1470-71) brought little but discontent and strife. The struggle between the houses of York and Lancaster, each with a rose as its badge, brought in its wake a breakdown of law and order at home, while on the Continent the final phase of the Hundred Years War saw the English driven out of Normandy and Aquitaine.

It was all too easy for the ordinary people to link the parlous state of affairs abroad with the breakdown of government at home, and to blame prominent personalities for both, however unjust this might in fact have been. One who suffered great unpopularity was William de la Pole, 1st Duke of Suffolk, who had in 1445 stood proxy for Henry VI at the king's marriage with Margaret of Anjou.

Committed to the Tower of London in 1450 on charges of treasonable dealings with the French, de la Pole was banished by Henry VI not only from England but from all his dominions for five years.[13] Having spent six weeks at Wingfield or elsewhere in Suffolk while arrangements were made for ships to carry him and his servants overseas, he moved to Ipswich towards the end of April. On 30th April he took the sacrament and, watched by some of the leading county gentry, swore on the sacrament that he was innocent of treason.[14] Later that same day he and his retinue left Ipswich in two ships and a pinnace.

As the little fleet sailed through the Straits of Dover it was intercepted by an English vessel, the *Nicholas of the Tower*, whose master sent a boat across with orders that the duke must come and speak to the captain. Suffolk must have known the game was up as soon as he stepped aboard and was greeted by the master with the words 'Welcome, traitor!' He had a safe-conduct from the king, but it proved of no use to him; the seamen of the *Nicholas of the Tower* simply

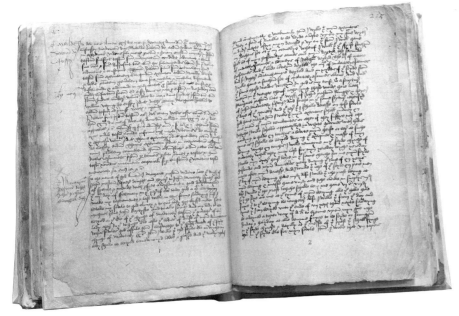

The remarkable Paston letters, many written by Margaret Paston whose will we see here, provide us with the story of an East Anglian family in the 15th century. The first of the letters dates from 1418. One of the Clement Pastons would become an Admiral.

tore it up. Next day he was transferred to a small boat and executed by one of the seamen, who hacked his head off on the gunwale with a rusty sword.[15]

Can it have been mere chance that the *Nicholas of the Tower*, a Bristol ship that seems to have been engaged in privateering and semi-piratical activities in the Channel, came on de la Pole's ships in the way that it did? And was the murder of the duke simply the act of a disgruntled ship's crew whose hatred for the 'traitor' was such that they scorned the king's safe-conduct? Could it be that the interception was planned by some of the Duke of Suffolk's enemies and carried out on their orders?

We shall probably never know. It could, however, be relevant that in February 1453 a number of the followers of the Duke of York and John Howard, Duke of Norfolk, were indicted before a grand jury of the county of Suffolk accused of plotting to raise a rebellion, conspiring to put the Duke of York on the throne, and planning the murder of the Duke of Suffolk.[16] The conspiracy was alleged to have taken place at Bury St Edmunds, where the conspirators would have been in a position to have kept a close watch on de la Pole's movements. The conspirators could have provided information that enabled the *Nicholas of the Tower* to be in the right place at the right time to intercept the duke's ships.

In other ways, too, Ipswich was at the heart of maritime and naval affairs, as is shown by the career of one of the town's leading burgesses, Richard Felaw, eight times bailiff and twice the town's representative in Parliament. An exporter of woollen cloth, he carried pilgrims to Santiago de Compostella in Spain in 1445.[17] The Patent Rolls reveal his activities on behalf of the Crown during the reign of Edward IV, who came to the throne in 1461 after defeating the Lancastrian forces at the battle of Mortimer's Cross.

In the year of Edward's accession Felaw and three other men were appointed to provide wheat, malt, mutton, fish, salt and other things required for victualling the king's ships. In June of that same year he was among the commissioners raising a fleet for the king's use against his French and Scottish enemies, providing six ships with 700 men-at-arms and archers. Three years later Felaw was one of the men appointed to assist the Duke of Norfolk in an inquiry into Lancastrian activities in East Anglia.

At a time when England was divided by the struggle between the houses of York and Lancaster there can be no doubt of where Felaw's sympathies lay; he was a Yorkist. He acted as local agent for Sir John Howard, of Stoke-by-Nayland,[18] who served as vice-admiral for Norfolk and Suffolk and was involved in 'furnishing forth ships for the wars' following the outbreak of hostilities with France in 1468. Sir John became Duke of Norfolk and Earl Marshal of England in 1483, and died with Richard III on Bosworth field.

The Howard accounts for 1462-69, which were published in 1841, throw considerable light on Felaw's work with Sir John, who in 1463 visited 'Richard Felawys howse' and in 1466 'did recken with Herman berebrewer of Yipswyche' there. The accounts also describe Felaw's lading of the *Mary Talbot* of Lynn, carried out on Sir John's instructions; among other things he supplied corn, hides, tallow, iron, salt and that staple Ipswich product, beer.

While a Member of Parliament in 1449 Felaw served on a commission of inquiry into the evasion of customs duties, and about 1458 he became Comptroller of Customs and Subsidies for the port, his task being to keep an account of the customs duties paid by vessels entering and leaving the Orwell.

Over the years many people have done their utmost to avoid paying tolls and customs. In 1438 the Ipswich bailiffs heard a case at the Wardmote court concerning a cargo of wool and woolskins landed by a vessel from the Low Countries at the quay of John Cadon of Ipswich. The cargo was put into a warehouse belonging to Thomas Cadon, but some time later 'on the night of Saturday next after the feast of St Mark the Evangelist' (26th April) William Horald and Thomas Ingram took the cargo from the warehouse and loaded it into Ingram's boat. Notwithstanding the intervention of one of the serjeants-at-mace the two men, with John Cadon's consent, spirited the

The port area of Ipswich at the beginning of the seventeenth century, from John Speed's map of Suffolk which first appeared in 1610. The structure on the Common Quay that looks rather like a post windmill without its sails is the Crane; the use of the capital initial indicates that it was at the time the only one in the port.

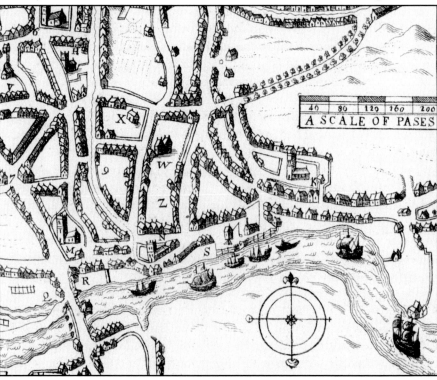

The Common Quay at Ipswich, with the Crane on the left and the Custom House at right.

boat and its cargo away to Woolverstone, 'with intent to defraud the king of customs pertaining to him'.[19] There were occasions when the customs that were paid were somehow diverted before they reached the king's treasury. In 1401 Thomas Godeston, John Arnald and John Bernard, the collectors and controller of customs at Ipswich, had been charged with frauds upon the customs. Professor Geoffrey Martin, who made so careful a study of the early town records of Ipswich, has described the elaborate organisation that existed by the beginning of Henry IV's reign (1399-1413) for the collection of the king's customs.

At the centre of this organisation was the Exchequer at Westminster, where a permanent staff supervised the work and audited the accounts of an army of part-time officials in the principal ports. In each of the chief ports were two collectors who kept a joint account and a controller, who kept a separate account, of each ship, the name of its master and the date of sailing, together with the amounts of cargo shipped and the sums paid for customs and subsidies. The controller's task was to verify the accounts of the two collectors, but to ensure honesty—or at least to detect fraud—there was a somewhat elaborate system of checking the documents.

So far as the wool trade was concerned, all shipments of wool from England had to be handled at a single mart, the staple. This arrangement ensured that the king could control the trade, not only for purposes of collecting revenue but also to enable him to use the trade as a means of bargaining with the Flemings. One is reminded of Geoffrey Chaucer's merchant, who was so anxious that the sea 'were kept for anything Betwixte Middelburgh and Orwelle'. Professor Martin has a list of forty-five sailings between December 1399 and September 1402 between the port of Orwell and Calais, where the staple then was.

Ships sometimes loaded at the downriver moorings, perhaps because they could not move from the quays on neap tides when fully laden. An account of the expenses incurred in handling the king's wool in 1337-38, when the government attempted to manage the entire trade for its own profit, details the money spent in carrying the wool by small boat from Ipswich downriver 'to the port of Orwell'.

Professor Martin's research on the customs documents suggests that in favourable conditions vessels could sail the seventy-odd nautical miles (82 statute miles) from the Orwell to Calais in as little as twenty-four hours, as when the *Goodeyere* and the *Trinite* cleared customs at Ipswich on 10th December 1399 and apparently arrived at Calais on the 12th. On the other hand, the *Cokjohn*, *le Peter*, the *Godeffrend*, the *Seintmariship* and another vessel that cleared customs on 31st January 1400 all took between a week and ten days to make the passage; they were probably overtaken by bad weather and foul winds and spent much of that time swinging at their anchors in the Colne or in some other sheltered anchorage.[20]

It is tempting to use Professor Martin's list to assess the number of ships engaged in the Ipswich wool trade at that time, but there are too many pitfalls. There were numerous ships with the same name, or similar names, and the spellings adopted in the documents vary widely. There are, for instance, three different spellings for the name *Goodyear* (to adopt the modern spelling), whose master was J. Genewe; and in one entry this vessel is named only as 'Ship of W Meye', though it seems reasonable to assume that the same vessel is being referred to in each entry. She left Ipswich on 10th December 1399, on

Old houses in Duck Lane, or Duke Street as it is now named, that had been built to accommodate the growing population attracted to the area by the employment generated by the port activities. All have long since been swept away.

Merchants' houses in St Clement's Fore Street, with the entrance to one of the yards in the middle of the picture. Almost all have now gone.

31st January 1400, 1st April 1400, and 6th October 1400, her shortest passage being two days and the longest nineteen.

It might not be entirely irrelevant that there are frequent mentions of a John Genewe and a John Mey in the Dunwich records at the beginning of the fifteenth century.[21] Possibly both the master and the owner of the *Goodyear* hailed from the port of Dunwich.

Then there is the *Trinite* already mentioned. A vessel of this name commanded by J. Whitton sailed between Ipswich and Calais 10th-12th December 1399; what is probably the same vessel, described as 'of Gosford' but under another master whose name is decipherable only as Rob. Be-, cleared from Ipswich in March or early April 1400. Then, two months later, the *Trinite*, master Rob. Pette, makes another trip from Ipswich to Calais. It looks very much like the same vessel that clears from Ipswich on 8th June 1401, but if the '*Trinite of Gosseford*' is indeed the same vessel she has a new master, J. Stavele, under whom she makes two further voyages in August-September and October-November. Fascinating, but as clear as Orwell mud.

The National Archives contain many references to 'the bailiffs of Gosford' as well as to 'the bailiffs of Orwell', but it is clear that neither of these places was a corporate town in which one would expect bailiffs to be heading a corporation. While Orwell was a somewhat amorphous anchorage or port in the lower reaches of the river of that name, perhaps synonymous with Harwich harbour or some part of it, Gosford was a broad stretch of water in the estuary of the Deben between Kirton and Falkenham on the west and Bawdsey on the east; today marshes occupy the area that was open water in the Middle Ages. The watercourse known as King's Fleet, draining a valley between Kirton and Trimley St Martin, might be a survival of the haven in which the monarch gathered his fleet in the fifteenth century.

A study of the Registers of the Constable of Bordeaux from 1303 to 1420 reveals that Goseford was by no means an insignificant port, having a considerable number of ships engaged in trade and military operations, much larger than most other east coast ports. Between 1303 and 1311 Goseford had a total of ninety-four ships, 14.9 per cent. of the total owned in the ports between Newcastle and London and a figure exceeded only by Great Yarmouth.[22]

A narrow lane in Ipswich not far from the Orwell and the quays, seen in a drawing by John Shewell Corder. The lane with its houses dating from the early days of the port has been obliterated by subsequent development.

Merchants and adventurers   5

Seafaring in the sixteenth century was a perilous business, the natural hazards of rock and tempest being compounded both by the risks of war with other nations and by attacks from pirates, including those from the Barbary States and the Ottoman Empire who ravaged English trade in the Mediterranean and enslaved Christian seamen, many of whom became the power source in their wide-ranging galleys. Those captives who did not become oarsmen in the galleys were sold into other forms of slavery in the North African slave markets.

One man who suffered years of captivity was John Fox, of Woodbridge, who was gunner of the *Three Half Moons* on a voyage from Portsmouth bound for Seville in 1563. He was taken prisoner with other members of the crew after a gallant fight against overwhelming odds when surrounded by a fleet of Turkish galleys as they approached the Straits of Gibraltar.

He and other survivors of the crew of the *Three Half Moons* were incarcerated in a prison near Alexandria when not actually pulling the oars of the Turkish galleys, which were regularly hauled out and refitted each year. During the winter refits the unfortunate oarsmen were kept in chains in the prison in conditions that were harsh indeed. Starved and ill-treated, those unhappy captives had little hope of any relief until death ended their misery, unless, like the owner of the *Three Half Moons* and the master, they were ransomed by friends in England.

The story of Fox's fourteen years as a galley slave and of his eventual escape to freedom was set down by an English parson, Richard Hakluyt, who was for some twelve years rector of the Suffolk parish of Wetheringsett. Hakluyt's monumental work *The Principal Navigations Voyages Traffiques & Discoveries of the English Nation Made by Sea or Overland to the Remote & Farthest Quarters of the Earth* is probably the most quoted and least read piece of English literature, and is certainly our main source of information on sea travel during the early age of exploration.[1]

Hakluyt tells how Fox was one of those men who always manage to withstand hardships better than others and who by one means or another contrive to overcome any adverse situation. In the Turkish prison he made use of his skills as a barber to serve not only his fellow-prisoners but also the Turkish gaolers, thereby gaining for himself both an additional meal here and there and small privileges from the Turks, to whom he made himself useful whenever he could.

Eventually Fox and a half-dozen other trusted prisoners were permitted to come and go much as they pleased during the time the galleys were laid

Opposite: Thomas Cavendish, or Candish as he was often known to his contemporaries, who made the second circumnavigation by an Englishman.

up. Among the small number thus privileged were two other Englishmen, Robert Moore of Harwich and William Wickney of Portsmouth. They were hampered with leg-irons, nonetheless, and had to return by nightfall, 'paying a certaine stipend unto the keeper,' as Hakluyt put it, but they were able to visit a 'victualling house' kept by Peter Unticaro, a Spanish Christian who had been a prisoner for some thirty years and had over those years gained a degree of freedom.

For these few life in the Turkish prison must have been at least bearable, but for the other three-hundred-and-more Christian prisoners, chained, often beaten and well-nigh starved, it was intolerable. After thirteen years and more of captivity John Fox hatched a plan for a mass escape from the prison, seizure of a galley and a desperate voyage to freedom.

With Unticaro's help he and his co-conspirators obtained a large quantity of files that were surreptitiously distributed to the prisoners with instructions to cut through their irons and be ready by a certain time the following day, 3rd January 1577. The prison governor was tricked into leaving the prison and killed by Fox with a 'bright sword of tenne yeeres rust' which he had found in Unticaro's house; his keys were taken, the prisoners released and the Turkish warders slaughtered.

A graphic depiction of European captives being driven back to prison by their Turkish jailer after a hard day's labour.

While some of the freed prisoners held off a counter-attack by the Turks others quickly prepared and launched a fast galley in which they somehow ran the gauntlet of cannon fire from two fortresses at either side of the bay. The Turkish gunners must have been poor gunlayers, because the vessel was not hit as it made for the open sea.

The ship was crowded with no fewer than 266 escapees, and provisions ran out long before they reached the island of Crete, where they were welcomed most hospitably by a house of Dominican friars; eight men died on that month-long voyage, but the rest had won their freedom.

John Fox seems not to have returned home until 1579, having served the king of Spain for some time as a gunner on the recommendation of no less a person then the Pope, to whom Fox was introduced after his escape. If Hakluyt is to be believed he was granted a pension by Queen Elizabeth 'to helpe to maintaine him now in age . . . and to the incouragement of all true hearted Christians'.

Circumnavigation

Richard Hakluyt, the parson of Wetheringsett, lost his first wife in 1597. The parish register records that 'Duglasse Hackluytt ye wieff of Mr Richard

Hackluytt p'son of Wetheringsett was buryed ye 8 day of August 1597'. Duglasse, or Douglas to use the modern spelling, was the sister of Thomas Cavendish, or Candish, of Trimley St Martin on the Orwell, the second Englishman to circumnavigate the world.

That being so, one might have expected that Hakluyt would have had his account of 'The admirable and prosperous voyage of the Worshipful Master Thomas Candish of Trimley in the Countie of Suffolk Esquire, into the South sea, and from thence round about the circumference of the whole earth, begun in the yeere of our Lord 1586, and finished 1588' direct from the mouth of his brother-in-law.[2] He did not: instead he used an account written by Francis Pretty, 'a gentleman employed in the same action,' who came from Eye, a small town some five miles north of Wetheringsett. Pretty had also sailed as a man-at-arms with Drake on his round-the-world voyage, and had written a first-hand account of that as well.

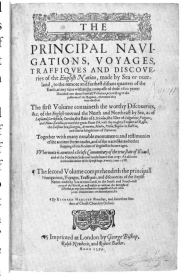

Born at Grimston Hall, Trimley, in 1560, Cavendish inherited his father's fortune at the age of twelve and two years later went to Corpus Christi College, Cambridge, but did not take a degree. His mother was a Wentworth, from Nettlestead Hall near Ipswich, and he was related by marriage to the Cecils and to the Seckford, Tollemache, Tyrrell and other prominent Suffolk families; at the age of twenty he went to the court of Queen Elizabeth I, where his sister Anne was one of the Queen's ladies-in-waiting. There he became a friend of Walter Raleigh.

In 1585 Cavendish commanded the *Elizabeth* in Richard Grenville's expedition to plant an English settlement on Roanoke Island off the coast of what is now North Carolina. The little fleet ran into bad weather on the way to the Canaries, from where it was planned to strike out for the West Indies, and the ships became separated. Cavendish did, however, rejoin Grenville at a pre-arranged rendezvous off Puerto Rico, where on the island of St John, one of the Virgin Isles, Grenville had erected a small temporary fort and also set to work to build a new pinnace to replace one that had been lost in the storm off the Portuguese coast. The arrival of the *Elizabeth* was greeted by Grenville's *Tyger* with a gun salute 'according to the manner of the Seas'.[3]

Leaving the mosquito-ridden island of St John, Grenville's little fleet captured a number of Spanish vessels, one of which was carrying some high-ranking Spanish officials who were 'ransomed for good round summes'. It seems that young Cavendish was more interested in such piratical activity than in the avowed object of the voyage, the colonisation of America. On returning from the voyage Grenville complained of Cavendish's behaviour; it seems that Thomas might already have been showing signs of the fatal weakness that blighted his final voyage and led to his own death in 1592 at the age of no more than thirty-two.

Having returned from that transatlantic voyage, Cavendish began making plans to emulate Francis Drake, who had made the first circumnavigation

A three-masted armed ship probably very similar to Cavendish's *Desire*.

by an Englishman between 1577 and 1580. Cavendish's plan was to raid Spanish ports and settlements on the Pacific coast of America and then to sail across the Pacific and return to England by way of the Cape of Good Hope. For this project he had a 120-ton ship, the *Desire*, built for him and armed her with 18 guns.

By the time the *Desire* made her departure from Plymouth on 21st July 1586 in company with the smaller 60-ton 10-gun ship *Content* and the 40-ton bark *Hugh Gallant* with a total complement of 123 men England was at war with Spain, whose King Philip was already planning an invasion of the Protestant country. The three ships headed southwards, and by 18th August they were to the westward of Sierra Leone, into which harbour they made their way a week later. Learning that there was a Portuguese ship further up the harbour, Cavendish laid plans to capture it, but because he had no pilot he dared not take the risk of sending the *Hugh Gallant* into unknown waters. Instead about seventy men went on shore and set fire to some of the mud-walled houses of the town.

The little fleet left Sierra Leone on 6th September and crossed to the South American coast, where on 17th December they put into a harbour which ran inland some twenty miles and which Cavendish named Port Desire after his ship. Today that Argentinian port is named Puerto Deseado, which is the Spanish translation of the name given it by Cavendish; and the point at the harbour mouth is still Punta Cavendish.[4]

From Port Desire the three ships coasted southwards to reach the Straits of Magellan, by which they passed into the Pacific, which they reached on 24th February 1587 after spending some seven weeks on the passage through the straits. Francis Pretty was embarked in the *Hugh Gallant*, the smallest of the three ships, which suffered severely in a storm lasting three or four days at the beginning of March: 'for that time we in the *Hugh Gallant* being separated from the other ships, looked every houre to sinke, our barke was so leake, and ourselves so dilvered and weakened with freeing it of water, that we slept not in three days and three nights,' the man-at-arms wrote afterwards.

On the morning of 15th March the *Hugh Gallant* came in between the island of Santa Maria and the mainland to discover the *Desire* and the *Content*, which had spent two days sheltering behind the offshore island of La Mocha, where some of the crews had been in a fight with local Indians who had taken them for Spaniards.

At other times the English adventurers benefited from being mistaken for Spaniards, for on more than one occasion the inhabitants brought them supplies which had been intended for their Spanish overlords. Continuing on their way northwards, Cavendish's expedition burnt several small towns and collected supplies where they could, and by the end of March they had reached the Bay of Quintero, where they anchored and filled their water barrels; fresh water was something they needed to replenish at every opportunity.

On 1st April 1587 men were ashore filling their barrels at a pit a quarter of a mile from the shore when they were surprised by nearly two hundred horsemen who came powering down from the hills, to use Pretty's own words. Twelve men were killed before the English soldiers could drive the Spaniards off.

It was not the only time the expedition suffered casualties. While lying in the harbour on the island of Puna, in the Gulf of Guayaquil, a foraging party of sixteen or twenty men was attacked by a hundred Spanish soldiers who had landed on the other side of the island. Five men were 'slaine by the enemie', one died when his own musket went off as he clambered on board a boat, and others were drowned as they tried to escape, while three were captured; it is said that the prisoners were later hanged by the Spaniards. In retaliation the English landed in force and burnt the town to the ground, and then 'made havocke of their fieldes, orchards and gardens, and burnt foure great ships more which were in building on the stockes'.

Leaving Puna on 5th July, the little fleet sailed to Rio Dolce, where they again watered.[5] Such had been their losses that they no longer had sufficient personnel to man the three ships, and at Rio Dolce the decision was made to sink the *Hugh Gallant* and divide her complement between the *Desire* and the *Content*; Francis Pretty went to the *Desire*. They left the Rio Dolce on 11th June and crossed the Equator next day.

For the rest of June they sailed northwards out of sight of land, and then on 1st July they sighted the coast of Nueva Espana – a Spanish province consisting basically of Mexico and Central America. Just over a week later they took a new 120-ton ship, which was set on fire after the sails and rigging and anything else that would 'serve our turnes' had been removed. The seven men taken from this ship included a Frenchman born in Marseilles, Michael Sancius, who was a most valuable acquisition because he was said to be one of the best pilots in the area; he it was who first told them of the likely arrival from Manila in the Philippines of the 'great ship called the *Santa Ana*' with a rich cargo bound eventually for Spain.

Towards the end of the month they spoiled and burnt the town of Aguatulco, and a few weeks later did the same to Puerto de Natividad, where they also destroyed two large ships that were under construction. As time went on the great object was to intercept the *Santa Ana*, and for that purpose the *Desire* and the *Content* patrolled up and down off Cabo San Lucas, at the southern tip of Baja California. Then between seven and eight o'clock on the morning of 4th November the lookout in the *Desire*, who happened to be the ship's trumpeter, saw a vessel coming in from sea and heading for the cape, 'whereupon he cryed out with no small joy to himself and the whole company,' as Francis Pretty recorded. Hearing his shout of 'A sail, a sail!' the master of the *Desire*, Thomas Fuller, an Ipswich man, and others of the crew hurried aloft to see what ship it was.

Capture of the *Santa Ana*

The English ships immediately gave chase, trimming the sails to get the best possible advantage from the wind and at the same time preparing for the fight to come. The *Santa Ana* was one of two galleons that had left Manila, but they were caught in a typhoon and the other ship, the *San Francisco*, was wrecked. The *Santa Ana* also received considerable damage, but she was able to resume her voyage after being repaired.

The chase went on for several hours before the *Desire* came up with the Spanish ship, a very large vessel thought to be of about 700 tons burthen. As they drew alongside the English ship fired a broadside into the *Santa Ana*, and the crew, not more than fifty or sixty men, prepared for boarding. The Spanish ship was not armed with cannon, but the crew of the *Santa Ana* were well prepared to repel any attempt at boarding, both with lances, javelins and other personal weapons and with a supply of large stones which they hurled down at the Englishmen in their much smaller vessel.

When the English scrambled up the side of the Spanish ship they were repulsed, with the loss of two men killed and several wounded. The *Desire* stood off and fired her heavy guns into the Spanish ship, holing her below the waterline as well as doing a good deal of damage to the upper decks. 'We gave them a fresh encounter with our great ordinance [sic} and also with our small shot, raking them through and through, to the killing and maiming of many of their men,' Pretty declared, though he did not enumerate the casualties. The battle lasted for some five or six hours, but at last, with their ship taking in water fast, the men of the *Santa Ana* surrendered.

'Our General [Cavendish] of his goodnes promised them mercy, and willed them to strike their sayles, and to hoyse out their boate and to come aboord: which newes they were ful glad to heare of, and presently strooke their sailes, hoysed their boate out, and one of their cheife marchants came aboord unto our General,' Pretty continued.

Cavendish 'most graciously pardoned him' – presumably for being Spanish – apparently on condition that he revealed honestly all the treasures that were in the galleon's cargo. Besides a great quantity of gold the ship was laden with silks, satins and damasks, musk and a great store of 'al maner of victuals with the choyse of many conserves of all sortes for to eate, and of sundry sorts of very good wines'.

The shattered *Santa Ana* was escorted to a haven behind Cabo San Lucas known as Aguada Segura – easily translated as 'secure watering place' – where the 190 people captured with the galleon, including a number of women passengers, were put on shore while the work of transferring as much of the cargo as possible went ahead. Cavendish, who earlier had shown little humanity towards Spaniards, 'Portugals' and others with whom he came into contact and showed a great willingness to torture prisoners in order to obtain the information he wanted, seems to have treated these people with considerable kindness, putting ashore the sails from the *Santa Ana* for use as tents and giving them timber with which they could construct a small vessel to take them back to civilisation together with a plentiful supply of food as well as weapons, powder and shot to protect themselves against the natives.

When as much of the galleon's cargo as could be accommodated in the two English ships had been removed from the *Santa Ana* Cavendish prepared to leave for the voyage across the Pacific towards home. He took into the *Desire* two young men from Japan, Christopher who was about twenty and Cosmus who was rather younger, both of whom were educated men, able to both read and write in their own language, and three boys from the Philippines, fifteen-year-old Alphonso and two younger companions. He also took a Portuguese, Nicholas Roderigo, who had been to both Japan and China and was able to give much information about those two countries. At the same time he chose to take with him Tomas de Ersola, a Spanish pilot who was very knowledgeable regarding the route across the Pacific and, most important, where fresh water might be taken in on the way.

As so often happens when riches are shared out, as they were following the unloading of the *Santa Ana*, dissension arose over the apportioning of the spoils; those in the *Content* seem to have been of the opinion that the crew of the *Desire* were more favoured than they were, and a mutiny ensued. The men were pacified in some way or other, but it would seem that the rift was not entirely healed. When on the afternoon of 19th November the *Desire* set sail, after the battered *Santa Ana* had been set on fire with what was left of her cargo, the discontented *Content* lagged behind. The men of the *Desire* looked back at the flames devouring the galleon and saw the *Content* following slowly in their wake; they never saw her again.

Perhaps she foundered in a storm; perhaps she turned south to return to England by way of the Straits of Magellan and was cast on the rocky shores of that difficult waterway; perhaps – but the sea keeps its mysteries.

As for the *Santa Ana*, the flames did not entirely consume her as Cavendish had intended. The fire severed the anchor cables, which at that period were of course of rope, not chain, the burning galleon drifted ashore and the Spanish crewmen were able to board her and extinguish the blaze. Using the materials which Cavendish had seen fit to provide for them, the Spaniards contrived to restore the ship sufficiently to carry all the survivors to the port of Acapulco, a voyage of some 800 miles.[6]

The *Desire* crossed the Pacific alone, making use of the equatorial current and the favourable wind belt, to what were known at the time as the Lodores – 'the islands of thieves' from the acquisitive tendencies of the natives; today they are known as the Marianas, the largest of these islands being Guam, where they were met by by a large number of sailing outrigger canoes whose occupants were happy to trade potatoes, plantains and fresh fish for pieces of old iron which the crew of the *Desire* lowered to them on fishing lines. The natives in their canoes followed the *Desire* for so long that Cavendish tired of them and ordered his men to fire at them with their harquebuses, 'but they were so yare and nimble, that we could not discerne whether they were killed or no, because they could fall backward into the sea and prevent us by diving,' Pretty declared. On 14th January 1588 they sighted the Philippines, and next day came to anchor off one of the islands, trading with the inhabitants for food supplies. 'Thus we rode at anker all that day, doing nothing but buying rootes, cocos, hennes, hogges, and such things as they brought, refreshing our selves marvellously well,' as the man-at-arms wrote in his account of the voyage.

All seemed to be going well, but there was trouble brewing, as Nicolas Roderigo, the Portuguese gentleman they had taken out of the *Santa Ana*, revealed privately to Cavendish. Tomas de Ersola, the Spanish pilot, had written a letter revealing that the English ship had only a small complement and suggesting that the Spanish authorities in Manila take action forthwith to attack the intruder; he planned to pass it to the local inhabitants with instructions to send it on at once to Manila. The plot having been foiled, de Ersola was hanged next day.

Undeterred by the possible threat from the Spaniards in Manila, Cavendish and his crew remained at anchor in the same place for nine days, with 'diverse kindes of fresh victuals, with excellent fresh water in every bay, and great store of wood'. Then, on 24th January, they set sail; they were on the way home, but their company was getting smaller. Not only had they lost men in fighting the Spaniards but the hardships of life afloat were taking their toll; many were sick, the inadequacy of their diet while at sea contributing to the problems they faced. Scurvy and similar afflictions affected many of the men.

John Gameford, a cooper, who had been ill for some time, died on 17th February; and then on 21st February Captain Havers, who had been in command of the *Hugh Gallant*, died 'of a most fervent and pestilent ague'. Captain Havers was a most respected and popular man, and his death was greatly mourned by the whole company; he was buried at sea 'with great lamentation of us all'.

They spent some two months 'traversing that mightie and vaste Sea, betweene the yle of Java and the maine of Africa' and then after several days becalmed the *Desire* met with 'a very stiffe gale' from the east that carried her around the Cape de Buena Esperanza (Good Hope) into the Atlantic. They made a call at the island of St Helena, where they took in wood and water, and then on 20th June set sail once more towards England. For a time they had little or no wind, but at last they were in the north-east trades and making good headway towards the Azores.

On 3rd September they met a Flemish hulk, a trading craft out of Lisbon, whose crew told them of the overthrowing of the Spanish fleet, 'to the singular rejoicing and comfort of us all'. Nearly home, and wonderful news! But a week later the *Desire* was in the midst of a 'terrible tempest' which carried away many of her sails. Nevertheless, on 9th September 1588 she entered Plymouth at the end of a voyage that had made history and had paid good dividends.

Not quite the end, perhaps. She sailed from Plymouth later for the Thames, up which she sailed, according to one account – not Francis Pretty's – with new sails made of blue damask from the cargo of the *Santa Ana*. Believe that if you can.

During his voyage across the Pacific Cavendish had learnt all he could about China and Japan, not only from Nicolas Roderigo and the Japanese lads he removed from the *Santa Ana* but from other sources as well. When in the Philippines he had announced to the inhabitants that he intended to return to trade with them and to turn out the Spaniards, and to that end he soon began to plan an expedition that would, like his first, access the Pacific through the Straits of Magellan and would then aim for China.

Much of his fortune must have gone into fitting out the new expedition, but there are some who claim that he frittered away his riches by high living and unwise generosity. The five ships that made up the fleet sailed in August 1591; had all gone well they should have passed through the Straits of Magellan in the south hemisphere summer, but things did not go well, one disaster following another. Supplies ran short, a storm separated the ships from one another, and Cavendish quarrelled with those on whom he should have depended for support; there are indications that he might have been suffering from mental problems, and there is no doubt that by the time he died in May or June 1592, probably somewhere in the vicinity of Ascension Island, he was deeply depressed. In a letter he wrote in his last days he blamed the failure of the expedition on the shortcomings, nay, the treachery of his subordinates, a charge which the survivors of them naturally strongly denied.

After more than four hundred years it is impossible to assess the responsibility with any degree of certainty. The one thing that is certain is that the voyage was an unmitigated disaster, not for Cavendish alone but for all who set out on the expedition. Those who returned were few in number.

Among the 123 men who accompanied Cavendish on his circumnavigation was an Ipswich mariner and merchant, Thomas Eldred, whose house in St Clement's Fore Street in Ipswich contained a delightful reminder of that epic voyage. In the main room of that house Eldred installed an overmantel containing three oil-painted panels showing him, a ship and a globe; an inscription commemorating the voyage declares that 'He that travels the world about, Seeth God's wonders and God's works'. Typically of Ipswich, Eldred's house has been demolished, but the overmantel is preserved in Christchurch Mansion, now a museum.

Nothing is known of Eldred's position in Cavendish's company, but thanks to the researches of Dr John Blatchly we do know something of Eldred's family.[7] He was the second, and eldest surviving, of the six sons of Thomas Eldred and his wife Margery Studd. Both his father and his grandfather were tallow chandlers, but young Thomas preferred to go to sea, though he was merchant as well as seafarer. The family certainly had close maritime links; Thomas married Susan, the daughter of Henry Aldham (c.1530-1608), mariner, of St Mary Quay parish, who later kept the Angel Inn on Ipswich quay, while his sister Sara married Richard Burlingham, another Ipswich mariner. Thomas was certainly quite a prominent citizen of Ipswich, being elected to various town offices, none of which he took up; he seems to have preferred to pay fines to avoid serving, perhaps because he was often away at sea.

In 1600 Thomas was recommended by John Eldred of Great Saxham, near Bury St Edmunds, who might have been a distant relative, to the East India Company as a suitable man to serve in a venture to develop trade with the East Indies. He was described as 'a man of good report who hath been employed with Capt. Caundish' [sic} and was said to be 'willing to be employed as captain or master of one of our ships'. It is uncertain whether Eldred did take service with the East India Company, but it would seem that by about 1608 when he was shipping cloth to Bordeaux in other men's ships he had come ashore and was resident in Ipswich. In that year he accepted election as a twenty-four-man, a member of the town council in modern terms; he was town treasurer in 1613-14, and in 1620 he became one of the twelve portmen. He died in 1624, a wealthy man, and was buried in St Clement's Church, close to his Fore Street home.

Henry Tooley, merchant

Among the merchants of Tudor Ipswich one name stands out; Henry Tooley was perhaps the most successful and certainly the richest of them all. Almost five hundred years after his death the generosity of 'Great Tooley of Ipswich' is still commemorated in the almshouses in Foundation Street that were set up under the terms of his will following his demise in 1551.

Tooley did not have the family connections of Cavendish, but he certainly enjoyed a degree of ability that the young Thomas seems to have lacked. It was clearly to Henry's advantage that he acquired a wife, Alice Purpet, whose father John Purpet had had the good sense to ensure that she learnt not only to look after the usual household arrangements but also to read and write, an ability that was by no means universal in Tudor England; she would have been able to aid her husband in his business activities, particularly when that business took him away from home.[8] Henry and Alice set up home in a substantial house close to the quay, with a cellar in which wine and merchandise could be stored and no doubt with warehouses surrounding the yard between the house and the river.

Most of the fine merchants' houses that once lined the river in the parishes of St Mary-at-the-Quay and St Clement were in later centuries downgraded into purely commercial premises such as maltings[9] and have long since been cleared away. In Fore Street, though, there still survives a complex of buildings from the late sixteenth century and the early seventeenth that is probably very similar to that occupied by the Tooleys. The house fronts the street, with a wagon entry from Fore Street giving access to a yard surrounded by storehouses and beyond them to the quay; the entrance to the house is from the yard, there being no front door opening to the street.

A cross-wing bridging the yard appears from its superior timbering and the herringbone brick nogging to have been a showroom in which the merchant's wares might have been laid out for inspection. In later days the warehouses were turned into maltings, and the complex now bears the name of its twentieth-century occupier, Isaac Lord, maltster and corn and coal merchant. The malt kiln is now a public house and the former warehouses-cum-maltings have been turned into an entertainment complex. In a town more attuned to the tourist potential it would probably have become a maritime museum.

From his home in Ipswich Tooley traded widely. Among the goods he sent overseas were bales of Suffolk cloth, woven in places such as East Bergholt, Lavenham, Long Melford and Sudbury; the southern part of Suffolk was in his time the most populous and prosperous area of the kingdom thanks to the woollen trade. He also imported wine from Bordeaux, along with woad which was in demand from the dyers who had an important part in that trade, and also iron from the north of Spain. He appointed Simon Cowper as his factor in the Biscayan ports in 1520 with instructions to sell goods that were sent from Ipswich and in return to obtain for Tooley iron, wax and commodities and to dispatch them to England. In 1522 Cowper bought a large ship from the son of a certain John of Koretto on Tooley's behalf; it seems likely that the ship was renamed on acquisition, because under Tooley's ownership it was the *Mary Walsingham*, after the East Anglian shrine of Our Lady of Walsingham, a few miles inland from the port of Wells.

The street frontage of a fine merchant's house of the late sixteenth and early seventeenth century still standing in Fore Street, Ipswich. With the commercial premises at the rear running down to the river it is a rare survival from the great days of the town's trading heyday.

On at least five occasions between 1526 and 1536 the *Mary Walsingham* sailed 'by the Grace of God Icelandward' in search of cod. In 1533 Tooley joined with his friend and fellow Ipswich merchant Robert Daundy in freighting the *Mary Imperial*. The manner in which the Iceland voyage was managed is interesting; from his study of Tooley's surviving account book John Webb discovered that at least twice the *Mary Walsingham* was hired by groups of fishermen on a complicated contractual basis. It would seem that the owner, besides providing the ship, contributed the greater part of the ship's lading of salt, fishing gear and sufficient provisions for the crew for a voyage lasting several months.

It was vital that the provisions should not only be sufficient but that they should be of good quality. Nicholas Humble of Orford deposed before the bailiffs of Ipswich in 1551 that he had been steward of the *George Saxcye* of London and that the crew could not drink the beer that had been taken to Iceland 'for that it was soo thicke that it colde nott run out of the vessells as well for the gret quantitie of lees and grapes as also for dyvers and sundry shepes guttes and netes guttes whiche were within the seide vessells whiche did stynke more lykar to have poysened men then otherwise'.[10]

While it proved impossible to discover quite how the profits of the voyage were distributed when a ship was hired out, it is apparent that in the case of the *Mary Walsingham* they were divided up under a share system of some kind.

The appointment of Simon Cowper as his factor in the Biscayan ports seems to have been one that Tooley later regretted, because when Cowper returned to England and came to Ipswich to settle his affairs his angry employer had him thrown into gaol, accusing him of not having paid over a large sum of money due to Tooley. The imprisoned Cowper complained that because of Tooley's 'Cruell mynde' he was deprived of access to his business papers which had been seized by Tooley and so was unable to prepare a defence to the charges against him.

The lawsuit against Cowper went on for some time, and with the passage of time it is impossible to judge whether his complaint of ill-treatment by Tooley was justified. There were other times when the merchant proved obdurate; in 1539 he was disfranchised after refusing to pay a fine of £40 for some offence against the town authorities, the nature of which is now forgotten. Deprived of his rights as a burgess, he became a 'foreigner' in his own town, liable to pay the tolls and dues from which a freeman was exempt and excluded from trading within the borough. Only in March 1541 did he repent of his obstinacy and obtain admission to his freedom and liberty on payment of a fine.

Like Thomas Eldred he refused public office and paid to be relieved of it when he was building up his business, but in 1523 he was elected 'into the number of Twenty-four' and a few years later became a portman. He served as bailiff on at least three occasions, on one of those occasions sharing the duties of office with his close friend Robert Daundy.

When he died Tooley was buried in the church of St Mary-at-the-Quay, his wife Alice being laid alongside him when she died in 1566. The town authorities had a suitable memorial made in London; and it is surely appropriate that it was brought to Ipswich by sea for erection in the church.

To the New World   6

The east coast ports were not ideally placed for communication with America, yet in the early days of colonisation Ipswich and Harwich played a considerable role in the carriage of settlers to the New World. The legitimate claims of these ports to have been the port of origin of various transatlantic voyages have been obscured and even denied by the pretensions of various ports on the south coast and in the west country which were in fact no more than ports of call.

In 1611 the corporation of Ipswich 'adventured' £100 towards the cost of ships to carry settlers to Virginia, where the Virginia Company had founded the port of Jamestown four years earlier. Just possibly the corporation's interest had been aroused in part by the involvement of locally owned ships; when in 1609 the Virginia Company sent a fleet of seven ships and two pinnaces with supplies and further settlers the leading ship was the *Sea Venture*, probably a Harwich vessel and, according to one report, the product of an Aldeburgh shipyard.

A vessel with this rather unusual name received the bounty given to builders of ships 'fit for service' as naval auxiliaries in 1606; she was recorded as being of 240 tons and having Harwich as her home port.[1] The ships of the Third Supply, as this little fleet was named, assembled at Plymouth in May 1609 and weighed anchor on 2nd June. The fleet was, however, forced back by unfavourable winds and obliged to remain at anchor until 8th June, when it made its departure. All went reasonably well until at the end of the month the fleet was struck by an Atlantic hurricane that scattered the ships and caused serious damage to the *Sea Venture*, severely straining her hull and causing leaks that necessitated continuous pumping and bailing. With the *Sea Venture* separated by the storm from the rest of the fleet, the men on board, crew and passengers alike, were soon engaged in a desperate fight for survival.

Thanks to the inspiring and intelligent leadership of the expedition's commander, Sir George Somers, and of the newly appointed governor of the Virginia colony, Sir Thomas Gates, ably backed by the ship's captain, Christopher Newport, a Harwich man, they succeeded in keeping the ship afloat for four days. In spite of their efforts the ship appeared to be doomed; those at the pumps and those who had been bailing with buckets were exhausted, and it seemed they could do no more. Just as all hope seemed to be gone Sir George Gates, standing on the poop as he had done without intermission for three days and nights, saw land ahead and called for a final effort to keep the water down and enable the ship to reach land.[2]

Opposite: The *Mayflower II*, a suggested replica of the ship that took the Pilgrim Fathers to America, on display at Plymouth, Massachusetts.

Two of the replica vessels, the *Susan Constant* and the *Godspeed,* that can be seen at Jamestown today The *Sea Venture* would have been a very similar vessel.

The *Sea Venture* did not come to a safe anchorage; she ran hard aground on one of the dangerous reefs that had given the islands now known as the Bermudas the seamen's title of Isle of Devils. Firmly wedged between two protruding rocks, she remained complete long enough not only for the 150 men, women and children who had come in her to be landed in safety but for many of the stores she carried to be salvaged. Those 150 people became the first settlers in the Bermudas, and after two boats had been built from the wreckage of the *Sea Venture* most of them went on to Jamestown after a ten-month stay on the island.[3]

It is believed that it was another Harwich vessel that carried the Pilgrim Fathers to New England in 1620. Christopher Jones, the owner and master of the *Mayflower,* was a Harwich man, the son of a mariner who when he died in 1578 left 'all that my part of the Shippe called the *Marie Fortune* with the stock belonging unto the same to my eldest son Christofer Jones at 18 years'. The senior Christopher Jones also bequeathed 'to my youngest son Roger Jones and to the child which my wife now goeth with, both at 18 years, all that my eight part and stock of ye newe shipp called the *Centurian* to be equally divided between them'.

To his wife Sibill he left 'my house in ye High Street at Harwich next ye water with ye keye and all other appurtenances to the same together with ymplements and household stuff in the same for life. . .'. That house with its twin gables facing the street survives and is pointed out to visitors as the birthplace of Christopher Jones, captain of the *Mayflower*; it is now 21 King's Head Street, 'ye High Street' having acquired a new name since his time.[4]

It has been suggested that the young Christopher Jones might well have served in one of the three ships, the *William*, *Katherine* and *Primrose*, sent from Harwich to fight the Armada in 1588. There were Harwich men in others of the English ships that served to defend England from the would-be invaders; Thomas Gray was master of the flagship *Ark Royal* and his brother John was master of Drake's ship, the *Revenge*.[5] We have no information on Jones's activities at that time, but we do know that in 1593 he married Sara Twitt, the seventeen-year-old daughter of Harwich merchant and shipowner Thomas Twitt; the marriage is recorded in the St Nicholas parish register, and so is the baptism of their son Thomas, whose burial is also recorded only five months later in 1596. Sara's father and his family lived opposite the Joneses in what is now the Alma Inn, and had earlier been occupied by shipbuilder Peter Pett, who had died in 1553.

Todays' Historic Jamestown makes a lively place to visit, with reenactment being a key part of the presentation.

Sara died in 1603, and later that year Christopher Jones married Josian Gray, the twenty-year-old widow of Richard Gray; Josian's father was Thomas Thompson, who had been master of the *Dainty* when in 1591 that Harwich ship took part in an expedition to the West Indies during which the mighty Portuguese carrack *Madre de Dios* was captured and plundered.

Two years before his second marriage Christopher had been admitted a freeman of the borough of Harwich, giving him a certain standing in his home town. Then in 1605 he had the 240-ton *Josan* built for him with the help of the government bounty, naming her after his wife. In the *Josan* he voyaged to Bordeaux and no doubt other continental ports, and from 1609 onwards he was master of the *Mayflower*, a ship of which much has been written and rather little is known.

In 1957 a three-masted vessel, the *Mayflower II*, was built at Brixham in Devon and crossed the Atlantic under the command of Captain Alan Villiers, but she was not truly a replica of the original ship. She could not be a true replica, because nobody knows for sure just what the first transatlantic *Mayflower* was like. The designer of the *Mayflower II*, William A. Baker, a naval architect by training and a ship historian by inclination, could do no more than reconstruct as accurately as he could a typical merchantman of the first half of the seventeenth century

Whereas the *Sea Venture* had a quite unusual name, the name *Mayflower* was extremely popular and there were many vessels given that name, making it impossible to discover much about the history of the particular vessel captained by Christopher Jones. In 1611 it was described as the *Mayflower* of Harwich, but in that same year Jones sold his Harwich house and moved with his family to Rotherhithe on the Thames. From that time on the ship was described as the *Mayflower* of London and was engaged in trade with various parts of Europe until in 1620 she was chosen to carry those Puritan settlers who later acquired the name of Pilgrim Fathers to a new home in America.

When she left London in July 1620 with some sixty-five passengers Christopher Jones was expecting to return before the end of the year; unlike some who set off on such voyages he did not trouble to make his will before setting off, though he did take his wife Josian and their growing family back to Harwich to stay with members of her family still living in the town. Mrs Winifred Cooper, who made a close study of Jones's links with Harwich, believed that they sailed from the Thames to Harwich in the *Mayflower*.

Archaeology at the
Jamestown, Virginia, site
is an on-going process,
alongside the costume
reenactment of life of the
first settlers.

Captain John Smith, himself
a Lincolnshire man, was
the first Governor of the
Virginian settlement.

The transatlantic voyage did not go according to plan. At Southampton the *Mayflower* met up with the smaller *Speedwell*, which had brought a contingent of would-be settlers from Leyden in the Netherlands. They left Southampton together, but the *Speedwell* was leaking like a sieve and they were forced to put into Dartmouth, where the smaller ship underwent repairs. More time was lost when Captain Reinolds reported that the *Speedwell* was 'so leakie as he must bear up or sink at sea, for they could scarce free her from much pumping' and the two ships had to turn back to Plymouth. Doubtless Christopher Jones feared that he would have to pick up survivors if the little *Speedwell* foundered before they could reach the Devon port.

In the event it was decided that the larger vessel should go on alone after some of the *Speedwell* passengers had transferred; the *Mayflower* eventually sailed from Plymouth with 102 passengers at the beginning of September. The delay meant that she was crossing the Atlantic at a time of year when gales were to be expected, and the ship suffered considerable storm damage during the passage; she did not anchor inside Cape Cod until 11th November, with many of the passengers and some of the crew very ill. More than twenty crew members as well as many of the settlers died during the winter.

It was not until 5th April 1621 that the *Mayflower*, ballasted with stones gathered from the shore, set out on her return voyage, which she accomplished in sixty-six days. It might be that Christopher Jones had suffered severely from illness and from the deprivations suffered that winter; he died in March 1622 shortly after arriving back from a voyage to France, and was buried in the churchyard of St Mary the Virgin, Rotherhithe. He had still not made a will, and his widow Josian had to obtain letters of administration, granted on 26th May 1622.

Eleven ships carried almost 700 passengers from Ipswich in 1630 in what became known as the Winthrop fleet, since the leader of the party and the inspiration behind the whole operation was John Winthrop, of Groton, who became the first Governor of Massachusetts. Of those passengers, no fewer than 324 were from south Suffolk and north Essex, a great many of them linked by family ties. One of the settlements founded by the Winthrops and those who went with them was given the name of Ipswich 'in acknowledgment of the great honour and kindness done to our people who took shipping there'.

It was religious intolerance that had persuaded the Pilgrim Fathers to seek settlement in New England, and it was very largely religious views that differed strongly from those of King Charles I and the hierarchy of the Church of England that created a wave of emigration from Puritan Suffolk in the 1630s. As the tide of emigration began to flow strongly Henry Dade, the commissary of the Bishop of Norwich for the Archdeaconry of Suffolk, complained to the Archbishop of Canterbury in 1634 about the increasing emigration of people 'whom he supposes are either indebted persons or persons discontented with the government of the Church of England'. He attributed this largely to the discontent created by the preaching of the Ipswich town preacher, Samuel Ward, against the Prayer Book and set prayer, and to fears expressed by him of changes in the national religion. Another on whom Dade heaped the blame for the spate of emigration was the parson of Woolverstone, 'who is a great stickler for transporting these people'.[6]

Dade said that he heard 'that as many are expected not long after to go as altogether will amount to six hundred persons. If suffered to go in such swarms it will be a decrease of the King's people here, an increase of the adversaries to the Episcopal state and will also be an overthrow of trade,' he declared.

Dade's complaints to Archbishop Laud led to the Privy Council preventing the departure of two vessels which were to have sailed from Ipswich early in March 1634 for New England with some eighty emigrants in each. It was reported about that time that 'two ships are to sail from Ipswich with men and provision for their abiding in New England, in each of which ships are appointed to go about six score passengers'. These ships, the *Elizabeth*, William Andrews, master, and the *Francis*, John Cutting, master, both of Ipswich, sailed down the Orwell 'bound for New England the last of Aprill', so it seems that the Privy Council did no more than delay their departure.

In the *Elizabeth* were fifty-five adults, the oldest of them sixty-year-old Martha Scott from Rattlesden, and forty-seven children and youngsters under sixteen. Many were in family groups, including Thurston Raynor and his wife Elizabeth from Elmsett near Ipswich and their six children, varying in age from one to thirteen; they were bound for the settlement of Watertown, along with miller Richard Woodward, his wife Rose and their thirteen-year-old sons George and John. Other passengers were from Dedham and from Capel St Mary and elsewhere in Suffolk.

The *Elizabeth* and *Francis* were followed across the Atlantic by the 400-ton *Great Hope* of Ipswich, which arrived in America in the middle of August, 1635, after weathering a storm that had wrecked the Bristol ship *Angel Gabriel* and nearly wrecked another vessel. Three more ships, the *Mary Anne* of Yarmouth, the *John and Dorothy* of Ipswich, and the *Rose* of Yarmouth, sailed from Ipswich in May 1637 with 360 passengers, arriving at Boston towards the end of June.[7] The master of the *John and Dorothy* was William Andrews, possibly he who had had the *Elizabeth* two years earlier, and the master of the *Rose* was William Andrews jnr., presumably his son. About the same time the *Mary Anne* of Yarmouth sailed from Ipswich and landed more emigrants in Boston; among them was William Cockram, mariner, of Southwold.

The following year the *Diligent* of Ipswich, John Martin, master, was among no fewer than twenty ships which crossed the Atlantic with at least 3,000 men, women and children, arriving at Boston on 10th August with about a hundred people, most of whom had left Hingham in Norfolk for its namesake settlement in Massachusetts.

It is unfortunate that the Ipswich port books for that period have disappeared, making it difficult to discover more about the contribution made by the port to the colonisation of North America. One wonders if at some time those records might have followed the emigrants across the Atlantic and been lodged in the library of some American university. If they did, they are now well hidden.

The Dutch Wars   7

There is a very distinct affinity between Suffolk and the Netherlands that began somewhere way back, probably long before the Flemings settled in Norwich and Colchester and introduced the manufacture of the New Draperies. The very dialect of East Anglia is replete with words of Dutch origin; we use a dwile to mop the floor when we spill something, and if we are in a hurry we are liable to go loping down the street.

In 1345 a William de Ipre was granted property adjacent to the town rampart next to 'le Shirehouse' in Ipswich. And an earlier generation of the same family, John de Irpe [sic}, was among the leading townsmen of Ipswich at the time of the granting of the town's charter in 1200.[1] Surely they came from Ypres in Flanders, that place that Tommies of 1914-18 knew as Wipers. Were they also distant ancestors of a certain western marshal, Wyatt Earp?

When in the reign of the first Elizabeth the Protestant Dutch were having such a very hard time under the domination of Catholic Spain refugees sought religious freedom in this country. The Queen gave special permission for thirty families to settle in Yarmouth, just across the river from the Suffolk town of Gorleston, on condition that those thirty families should not number more than 300 men, women and children – and servants. Another condition, imposed by the town authorities, was that the fishermen – they were mainly fishermen – should share their secrets with the Yarmouth men; and that is how the English fishermen came to learn the vital secret of the Dutch cure of herring.[2]

The Order in Council allowing the settlement of those thirty families was issued in 1569, and the Dutch community stayed in Yarmouth for almost a hundred years. During those hundred years there had been extraordinary developments in their homeland.

Perhaps we should set the scene by considering how the Netherlands fell under the rule of Spain. In 1364 the French king invested his younger son Philip the Bold with the Duchy of Burgundy. Through his marriage with Margaret of Flanders and his excellent relations with the Duchess of Brabant Philip obtained for his dynasty both those wealthy states. From that base his House was able to acquire, in the early fifteenth century, the whole of the west coast, with Zeeland and Holland as well as Hainaut, Namur and Luxemburg.

A century later Philip's descendant Charles V conquered the Duchy of Gelderland, and in 1548 he put the seal on his achievements by granting the Low Countries a privileged and virtually autonomous position in the German Empire. Common pride at being the homeland of the greatest emperor since

Opposite: The Dutch assault on Landguard Fort in July 1667, a detail from the grisaille by Willem van de Velde the Elder showing Jan Roetering's ship *Het Huis te Oosterwijk*. It is thought that the picture, which was produced two years after the action, might have been commissioned by Captain Roetering.

Charlemagne – Charles V was born at Ghent – and at having in Antwerp the most advanced business centre of the world reflected a growing sense of unity as much as did the common distrust of endeavours on the part of their rulers to centralise government and to increase taxes to provide the capital needed for carrying out policies of truly global dimensions.

Charles V abdicated in 1555, leaving his sovereignty over Spain and the Low Countries to his son, Philip II. A few years later the Low Countries entered into the long and complicated series of wars and disturbances commonly called the Revolt of the Netherlands – an upheaval that led to a group of fishermen quitting their homeland for a port on the east coast of England.

At the Peace of Munster in 1648 the Spanish king, while retaining sovereignty of the southern Netherlands, recognized the independence of the so-called Seven United Provinces, de Zeven Provincien, otherwise known as the Dutch Republic. The Seven Provinces were Holland, Zeeland, Utrecht, Gelderland, Overijssel, Friesland and Groningen, but the territory ruled by the States General was somewhat larger.

The Netherlands were at the forefront of industrial development in mainland Europe. In the south the cloth trade was booming, at the same time that the Suffolk broadcloth woollen trade was in terminal decline. In the North, and especially along the River Zaan, north-west of Amsterdam, shipbuilding and many another industry were growing apace, some of them making use of a natural source of power, that of the wind. One could forgive the out-of-work weavers of Lavenham and Sudbury if they clamoured noisily for war with the Dutch.

On the other side of the North Sea there were many who favoured war with the English, who were interfering with Dutch interests not only in Europe but in the East Indies and in North America. As English shipping and trade grew apace in the seventeenth century the merchants and shipowners of the Seven Provinces found the competition increasingly irksome. Tromp's refusal to dip his flag in salute to English warships was no more than an expression of a far wider rivalry that poisoned relations between Holland and England. As it became clear on both sides of the North Sea that hostilities were likely to break out the Dutch community that had settled in Yarmouth some eighty years earlier took to their fishing boats and left for a home some of them had never known.

With the passing in 1651 of Cromwell's Navigation Act a direct attempt was made by Parliament to restrict trade with British ports – both at home and in the 'plantations' – to English ships; that is, British-built vessels owned by British subjects and of which the master and three-quarters of the crew belonged to this country. By this Act the prosperity of Holland was dealt a most serious blow, and it was of course deeply resented by the Dutch.

With war fever building up on both sides it was the English demand that Dutch ships struck their topsails and dipped their flags to English warships in the narrow seas that prompted the first conflict at sea, not off the Suffolk coast but in the Downs, the anchorage off the coast of Kent that is sheltered by the Goodwin Sands. To put it simply, when an English fleet and a Dutch fleet commanded by Marten Tromp in the *Brederode* met off the South Foreland on 19th May 1652 the English commander fired a gun for Tromp to strike his flag. As this had no effect, it was followed by another, and then by a third which Tromp promptly answered with a broadside. The English had rather the better of the battle that followed, but a fleet of Dutch merchant ships, homeward bound with a variety of rich cargoes, slipped past while the two fleets were slogging it out.

Before very long Robert Blake was dealing with the Dutch herring fleet in the North Sea. Of thirteen small warships guarding the fishing boats he captured or sank twelve; he also took about a hundred of the herring busses. The busses, with some 1,500 men on board, were set free; however unpopular the news might have been in England that so many prisoners had been allowed their freedom, to have brought that number of Dutchmen ashore might have proved embarrassing in terms of providing accommodation and guarding them.

With the rival fleets, English and Dutch, in the same vicinity a battle might have been anticipated, but on 26th July a heavy gale sprang up and, blowing hard all night, scattered the Dutch fleet across a wide area; Blake's fleet was able to find shelter and escaped with little damage.

War at sea in the seventeenth century was as horrible a business as war has ever been. Ships lay close to one another and sought with broadside after broadside to batter one another into submission. Men died on deck, struck by grapeshot or chainshot that was intended to tear their bodies to pieces, and down below on the gun decks there was no protection from the bombardment. A 32-pound roundshot would smash its way into if not through the oak of which the ship was built; in doing so it would shatter the timber into splinters that would cause death or terrible injury as they flew around the confined space below decks. The common view of a veteran seaman as a man with a wooden leg had a firm basis in fact.

Casualties in a fleet action would be numbered not in dozens but in hundreds and even thousands. After a battle in June 1653 between the evenly matched English and Dutch fleets off the Gabbard – an area almost due east of Harwich in which a large windfarm is now being developed – a number of wounded men were taken to Ipswich in the *Tenth Whelp*, the last of ten 14-gun sloops built in 1627, all of them named *Lions Whelp* and differentiated from one another by numbers. At the same time other sick and wounded seamen were landed at Harwich.

The Ipswich bailiffs, Richard Puplett and Nicholas Phillips, received a letter dated 5th June 1653 from Major Nicholas Bourne, a Navy Commissioner and Rear Admiral in the fourth-rate *Tyger* at Harwich, asking them to make provision for some of the many sick men from the warships ordered into Harwich. At about the same time the Generals-at-Sea, Robert Blake and George Monck, wrote ordering the bailiffs to look after the wounded sent up to the town, adding that the bailiffs would be reimbursed what they laid out on this. The bailiffs duly appointed surgeons to treat the seamen and spent £80 a week on the men's care, but the promised reimbursement was very slow in coming.[3]

A naval doctor, Dr Daniel Whistler, was sent down to Ipswich to care for the sick and wounded men, who numbered at least eighty at Ipswich alone. Dr Whistler, whom Samuel Pepys found 'good company and a very ingenious man', had studied medicine at a famous Dutch university, Leyden, and was the author of the first book on rickets; some years later he assured Pepys over

Amputation of shattered limbs was a common enough follow-up to seventeenth-century naval actions: one of the veterans in this detail from a picture by the brothers Buck has lost both legs, the other is missing just his right leg.

dinner that experiments carried out on dogs concerning blood transfusions were likely to be found of great use to men.

The doctor wrote from Ipswich that the number of sick and wounded was 165, presumably at both Ipswich and Harwich, and that sixty more had come since his arrival. 'Harwich is no place for sick men, the air being as bad as at sea . . . I wish all the sick were sent here, there being very good accommodation'. Most likely some of that accommodation was in Lord Curson's House in Silent Street, which was turned into a makeshift naval hospital at that time.[4]

George Monck, an officer with an unfailing concern for his men's welfare, ordered that the bailiffs of Ipswich and those of Aldeburgh, Dunwich and Southwold should be reimbursed for their outlay on behalf of the sick and wounded men, but still the money remained unpaid. Readers of Pepys's diary will know that this was not untypical of the period.

Eventually there were so many wounded men at Ipswich that it became necessary to send some to Woodbridge and to other neighbouring towns and villages. Monck wrote that he was 'very unwilling to overcharge yor Towne with sick men, no more than needs must', and gave permission for the bailiffs to 'dispose of some of them into the neighbouring Villages which you say bears none of ye burden provided the like Care bee taken of them as where they now are'.

In August 1653 one of the Bailiffs, Nicholas Phillips, wrote to Monck that there were 'neere a thousand sick and wounded soldiers and seamen in the towne' and spoke of the town's 'inability of relieving them, wee have expended all the moneys we could command. . .sent to London and received noe Returnes. We are likelie to see these poore people perish for want of support'.

At the end of their year of office the two bailiffs rendered an account to the Admiralty and the Commissioners for the Sick and Wounded showing that they had spent £3,838 9s.8d. on the sick and wounded between 11th July and 29th September and claiming the balance due of £738 9s.8d. Their successors as bailiffs had spent another £141 12s.8d. up to 8th December.[5] The town was having to find a great deal of money for this humanitarian work, and there must have been times when the two bailiffs were worried men indeed as they sought repayment.

The war came to an end in 1654, but this did not remove many of the problems that beset Ipswich, in common with the country at large. In the summer of 1659 the town was still occupied in looking after sick seamen sent upriver by Edward Montagu (created Earl of Sandwich the following year). There were still difficulties in obtaining reimbursement of the money spent in caring for the seamen, and in September 1660 John Maidston, clerk to that most redoubtable town clerk, Nathaniell Bacon, was told to continue his efforts in London to obtain payment.

There were many who were concerned at the increasing part being played by the military in the government of the country, and this concern was reflected at Ipswich in the deliberations of the Assembly, which in 1659 ordered a fast 'to seeke God for the Establishmt of A Governmt that maie be an Incouragemt to trueth righteousnes & Peace'. One concern of the local authorities was to recover local control of the militia and the trained bands.

Early the following year the Assembly decided to write to General Monck pointing out that Ipswich was suffering from having so many troops quartered in the town and asking that the unfortunate innkeepers on whom they were billeted should be paid the money due to them. Monck, who believed firmly in the subordination of the military to the civil power, was already engaged in moves that would result in the restoration both of a free parliament and of the monarchy. The same day that they agreed to send a letter to Monck in Scotland the town's leaders ordered that a day of thanksgiving be held 'for returninge of thanks to the Lord for his Mercies to the Nation in restoreinge of the Parliament to their settinge & soe many changes without blood sheddinge. . .'.

There is little doubt that there were those in Ipswich who secretly wished for the return of the king. The arms of the Commonwealth had replaced the Royal Arms in the churches, but both at St Margaret's and at St Stephen's someone had painted the Prince of Wales's feathers on the back of the panel bearing the Commonwealth Arms, where they remained unseen until the day of Charles's coming, or perhaps rather earlier; Pepys tells how the king's arms were being set up in London churches in April 1660.[6] Not until 25th May did Charles land at Dover, and only on 10th July did the Ipswich Assembly give orders for the painting of the Royal Arms for display in the Moot Hall, an instruction that was ratified by the Great Court on the 23rd. John Brame, limner, was next year paid £20 for painting the arms and other similar work done at the same time.

It is hardly to be supposed that there would have been universal rejoicing at the king's return to the throne in a town with such a reputation as Ipswich, but the authorities gave instructions for the gallery of the Town Hall and the Market Cross to be decorated and for wine and food to be made available on the day the king was proclaimed. Powder was made available to the seamen to fire a salute on the Common Quay and the Trained Bands were to muster, the musketeers being provided with powder and a yard and a half of match so that they too could add to the general rejoicing; their arms were matchlocks in which the smouldering match ignited the charge of powder.

As a token of their allegiance the town decided to send a gift of £300 to the king, but had to borrow £250 from four townsmen, who were given a lease of Portmen's Meadow as security. One of those nominated to go to London to present the gift was Robert Sparrow, who was later to demonstrate his loyalty by including the arms of Charles II in the new plaster front of his house in the Buttermarket.

Among the peers deputed to invite Charles to return was Leicester Devereux, 6th Viscount Hereford, of Christchurch, Ipswich, and Sudbourne. Throughout the period of the Commonwealth Lord Hereford had been active as a government servant, but it could well be that by 1660 he, like others who had served the Commonwealth, was prepared to seek the restoration of the monarchy.

The anniversary of the Restoration was annually celebrated in the town with gun salutes and parades by the Trained Bands. In 1665 the Corporation ordered that eleven guns should be fired three times each and two men were 'desired to take Care to gitt the Great Gunns Ready'; the town records show many signs of having been written by speakers of the Suffolk dialect.

Anglo-Dutch maritime rivalry continued unabated, yet in spite of the increasing tension the opposing navies maintained an air of cordiality even as late as 26th September 1664. Vice-Admiral Sir Thomas Allin, a Lowestoft man who after his wartime service retired to Somerleyton Hall, records in his journal that on that day he and Vice-Admiral Sir John Lawson happened to meet Lieutenant Admiral Michiel de Ruyter at sea. 'De Ruyter came under our sterns and asked how I did and saluted me with 7 gunnes and dranke to me and I dranke to him and answered him 7; he thanked me in 3 the which I answered,' wrote Allin.

Little more than two months later Allin and his squadron fell in with about thirty Dutch ships off Cadiz. The merchant ships, homeward bound from Smyrna, were convoyed by three frigates under the command of Captain Pieter van Brakel. When Captain van Brakel sailed towards the English squadron and fired a complimentary salute he was met not with an answering salute but with a full broadside; in the sharp engagement that followed van Brakel was killed and Allin took two merchantmen and sank one of the frigates.

That was not the only incident, but it was perhaps the one that precipitated the declaration of war by the Dutch on 14th January 1665. Already by the time Charles II responded by declaring war on the Dutch on 4th March more than a hundred prizes had been taken by the English fleet. It was a war that was to affect Ipswich even more than the earlier struggle with the Dutch, the conflict being brought very close to home when a Dutch force landed on Felixstowe beach in 1667.

The English certainly had good reason to be optimistic about the outcome, for they had the superior fleet, numerically and in terms of quality. They had some 160 warships mounting five thousand guns against the 135 of the United Provinces, and the English first rates were bigger, better gunned and better manned. But morale on the Dutch side was at least as good as on the English, and Sir George Downing reported from the Hague 'Tis not to be imagined how infinitely high all sorts of people are here, as if they had victory in their laps; and the commanders of their fleet say that they will not make any long business with their great guns, but clap board on board and conquer or be conquered'. That was the Dutch answer to England's superiority in ships and gunnery; they would board the English ships and fight hand to hand.

There was great activity at the Navy Yard at Harwich, which had been established in the time of the Commonwealth. It had been leased to Thomas King in 1662, but the Commissioners of the Navy took possession again two years later and sent Captain John Taylor to take charge. On 15th October 1664 Anthony Deane, destined to become the most eminent shipbuilder of his generation, was transferred from Woolwich to his native town to be master shipwright at the yard. Commissioner Taylor impressed shipwrights and Deane bought timber and stores, and work began to fit out existing ships and to build new ones.

A list of thirty-two Ipswich ships 'fit for the King's service' was prepared in January 1665, twenty-seven of them being of 280 to 300 tons. To begin with, however, local involvement was restricted to the impressment of seamen and to caring for wounded men brought ashore from the fleet. Some of those being cared for in Ipswich were buried in town churchyards. The register of St Mary Stoke records the burial in April and May 1665 of men belonging to the *Royal James*, *Royal Oak* and *Henry* and later in the year of men belonging to the *Lyon*, *Monck* and *St Andrew*; that of St Stephen's refers to the burial of fifteen seamen who had 'died at the ospele in this parish'. Faced with the extreme difficulty of getting money from official sources the Corporation made use of the proceeds from land bequeathed for the maintenance of the poor to pay for the care of the wounded seamen.[7]

While in Ipswich the authorities did their best to look after the sick and wounded, people on the coast were all too aware of what was going on at sea. With both countries making energetic preparations for hostilities, the British fleet was the first to be ready. It consisted of 109 men-of-war and twenty-eight fireships and smaller vessels with more than four thousand guns. There were 21,000 seamen, marines and soldiers on board those ships. 'We have lain a good while with a good fleet at Harwich,' Samuel Pepys wrote in his diary on 8th April 1665. 'The Dutch not said yet to be out.'[8]

Pepys was much concerned with the cost of that fleet. On 12th April he was in Whitehall, 'where I lose most of my time nowadays, to my great trouble, charge, and loss of time and benefit. And there I did give them a large account of the charge of the Navy, and want of money. But strange, to see how they held up their hands, crying, "What shall we do?"'

And what did our Samuel do? 'So home, vexed,' he wrote. 'And going to my Lady Battens, there found a great many women with her in her chamber, merry – my Lady Pen and her daughter, among others; where my Lady Pen flung me down upon the bed, and herself and others, one after another, upon me, and very merry we were. . .'.[9]

On the 21st Pepys heard that the Duke of York and the fleet had sailed from Harwich the day before; 'pray God go along with them – that they have good speed in the beginning of their work,' he wrote in his diary.[10]

The even larger Dutch fleet did not put to sea until May, but it had an early success when a convoy of merchantmen from Hamburg bound for England was captured in its entirety near the Dogger Bank. Among the cargoes taken were pitch, hemp, tar, cables, and other essential naval stores, a very serious loss not just to the merchants concerned but also to the English government.

Not surprisingly, this disaster caused an outcry in England. The English fleet weighed from the Gunfleet anchorage off the north Essex coast on 29th May and lay for the night off Aldeburgh, where the Duke of York seems to have received news that the Dutch were not far off. The fleet proceeded to Sole Bay and anchored there on the morning of 1st June.

About midday the Duke learnt that the enemy was about six miles away to the east-south-east, so he led the way in the *Royal Charles* – formerly the *Naseby* in which Charles II had returned to England in 1660. The Dutch fleet, under Jacob Van Wassenaer, Lord of Obdam, kept away to seaward that afternoon and night, perhaps to enable his scattered ships to assemble. Next day the Dutch were seen five miles to the south-east, with Lowestoft eight miles to the north-west, which would mean the English were somewhere off Covehithe.

Nothing much happened that day, but come the morning the two fleets were some fourteen miles nor'nor'east of Lowestoft and the English had the weather-gauge. The two met at about half past three in the morning, sailing on opposite tacks; as they passed each ship fired a broadside at its counterpart on the other side, and great slaughter was caused.

Towards the middle of the day the two fleets were in confusion, and there seem to have been moments when ships narrowly avoided firing into friendly vessels; heavy smoke from the guns cloaked the sea and visibility became extremely poor. At one point Obdam in the *Eendracht* engaged the Duke of York in the *Royal Charles*, the Dutch crew endeavouring to board the English flagship, but without success. Three officers were killed at the Duke's side by a single chainshot, Pepys telling later how their blood and brains were thrown in the Duke's face.

The *Royal Charles* was in danger of being overwhelmed by the enemy when the *Eendracht* suddenly blew up, probably owing to some loose cartridges igniting and the resulting flames reaching the powder room. More than four hundred men, including Obdam, died; only five survived out of the *Eendracht's* crew.

The fact that this is called the Battle of Lowestoft is somewhat misleading. Those ashore could see nothing of the fighting, they could only hear the noise of the guns. 'All this day, by all people upon the River and almost everywhere else hereabout, were heard the Guns, our two fleets for certain being engaged,' Pepys wrote on 3rd June; 'which was confirmed by letters from Harwich, but nothing perticular; and all our hearts full of concernment for the Duke, and I perticularly for my Lord Sandwich and Mr. Coventry after his Royal Highness.'[11] Next day Pepys knew little more. He ended his diary entry 'and so to bed – news being come that our fleet is pursuing the Duch [sic}, who, either by cunning or by being worsted, do give ground; but nothing more for certain.'

The authorities in London were as anxious for news as was Pepys. They sent messengers to Yarmouth to gain the earliest intelligence. On 6th June the government agents were able to report that a battle had successfully taken place, and that 'the bells are ringing and colours flying, which displeases some in this town who are friends of the Dutch and have grown impudent through the negligence of the king's friends'. Could there have been some in Yarmouth who remembered favourably their Dutch neighbours of past years?

Only on 8th June, after 'the hottest day that ever I felt in my life,' did Pepys go to the Lord Treasurer's 'where I met with the great news, at last newly come, brought by Bab May from the Duke of York, that we have totally routed the Dutch. That the Duke himself, the Prince, my Lord Sandwich and Mr. Coventry are all well. Which did put me into such a joy, that I forgot almost all other thoughts' – including the two or three houses in Drury Lane he had seen the day before 'marked with a red cross upon the doors, and "Lord have mercy upon us" writ there'.[12]

Pepys was indeed joyful as he wrote of 'our having taken and sunk, as is believed, about 24 of their best ships. Killed and taken near 8 or 10,000 men; and lost, we believe, not above 700. A great victory, never known in the world.' Later Coventry told him the Dutch could not have lost fewer than 6,000 men 'and we not dead above 200, and wounded abut 400; in all, about 600.'

Those four hundred wounded men needed looking after. Sir William Doyly was the Commissioner for the Sick and Wounded with responsibility for the eastern counties and was active in dealing with the situation in Ipswich. Pepys met him at Viscount Brouncker's over a good venison pasty on 9th September 1665, 'lately come from Ipswich about the sick and wounded'. That evening he met Sir William again at Captain Cocke's, 'full of discourse of the neglect of our masters, the great officers of State, about all businesses, and especially that of money—having now some thousands prisoners kept to no purpose, at a great charge, and no money provided almost for the doing of it'. The authorities at Ipswich were not alone in finding it well nigh impossible to get the money needed for looking after the sick seamen.

One of the Commissioners for the Sick and Wounded and Prisoners of War, the diarist John Evelyn, wrote from Greenwich to Sir William Coventry on 30th September 1665 complaining bitterly that more than two thousand sick seamen and an even larger number of prisoners of war were without food and medicine. Saying that he had run out of credit to pay for supplies, Evelyn told Sir William that men 'perish by the hundreds' and pleaded with him 'let us not be thought barbarians'.

A correspondent wrote from Ipswich to Sir Roger L'Estrange's *Public Intelligencer* on 31st August 1665 that

> Our Townsmen here have a very remarquable tenderness for the Sick and wounded Seamen, and many of the Principals have propounded the depositing good summes of money in order to their further relief if there should be occasion; divers Tradesmen also offering their commodities without profit to be employed upon that service.

Such altruism seems scarcely credible, and even if the report is correct the Town Clerk continued his attempts to get money from the Commission for Sick and Wounded Seamen. In a reply sent to the Town Clerk in March 1666 Sir William Doyly complained that the inhabitants of Ipswich had made unreasonable demands, and offered to make payment only if they moderated their demands by a half. Possibly that was a desperate attempt on his part to make the available money go further; the Treasurer to the Commission, Captain George Cocke, a man whom Pepys seems to have regarded as untrustworthy, ran into trouble with his accounts and had to face trial in 1670.[13]

English casualties in the Four Days' Battle which began off Ostend on 1st June 1666 were horrific, and Ipswich had to redouble its efforts to care for the wounded. One of those who died in the fight was Captain Philip Bacon, second son of Nicholas Bacon of Shrubland Hall, whose ship, the 52-gun fourth rate *Bristol*, was brought into Harwich with her masts and rigging gone and as many as 180 enemy shot in her hull. The captain's body was brought upriver to Ipswich, where the members of the Corporation, with the Trained Bands and the county gentry, paid their respects as it was taken to Coddenham for burial.[14]

Another casualty was Sir William Clarke, Secretary at War and the Duke of Albemarle's secretary, who was buried in old Harwich church. The memorial, transferred to the new St Nicholas built in 1820, bears a lengthy inscription in Latin telling us that 'as he fought by the admiral's side, on the second day he lost his right leg by a cannon ball, on the fourth his life. Yet notwithstanding his wound, he would not suffer himself to be moved from the danger of the battle but whilst the rest of the wounded were carried ashore he remained in the ship which was shattered and exposed to the fire of the enemy, and with surprising constancy awaited the doubtful issue of the battle and his own life.

Part of the panorama of
Chatham Dockyard by
Samuel and Nathaniel Buck
showing the establishment
some years after the Dutch
attack on the Medway.

His wounded body, having for several days been tossed on the sea, was at length cast into this haven, whilst his soul retired to its native heaven. . .'.

Perhaps his insistence on remaining in the danger of battle is partly explained by the fact that at Harwich limbless men, casualties of the battle, were left lying in the streets. The Navy Yard was a scene of great activity as near a score of disabled ships were refitted for sea; such were the efforts made that they were all ready for service within three weeks.

Samuel Pepys, who had clearly heard the gunfire while walking in London's St James's Park, arrived home on 4th June just in time to be told of two men who had arrived from Harwich and had news for him. The stark realities of naval warfare are made plain in Pepys' description of the men's appearance as they stood before him.

'So I down, and who should it be but Mr. Daniel [Lieutenant John Daniel, of the *Royal Charles*], all muffled up, and his face as black as the chimney and all covered with dirt, pitch and tar, and powder, and muffled with dirty clouts and his right eye stopped with Okum. He is come last night at 5 a-clock from the fleet, with a comrade of his that hath endangered another eye. They were set on shore at Harwich this morning at 2 a-clock in a ketch, with about twenty more wounded men from the Royal Charles.

'They being able to ride, took post about 3 this morning and was here between 11 and 12. I went presently into the coach with them, and carried them to Sumersett-house and there took water (all the world gazing upon us and concluding it to be news from the fleet; and everybody's face appeared expecting of news) . . .'[15]

The English fleet had received something of a drubbing, and a Dutch fleet was soon to be seen off the Suffolk coast, bent on operations that were intended to bring the war to a speedy end. The Council of State, startled out of its complacency, responded to the threat of invasion by giving orders for 'the Plateforms of Landguard Fort' to be repaired and for 'pallisados from Ipswich or Harwich or anywhere else' to be sent to the fort without delay.[16]

The dangers of sending large warships, even those of shallow draught as the Dutch ships were, close inshore, and the fact that the Dutch found the English 'well awake and in a position to put up a good defence' caused operations against the Thames and an alternative assault on Harwich to be abandoned, or at least postponed. Nevertheless, a letter from Ipswich on 5th July stated that '30 of De Ruyter's men in his boat landed on the marshes about Bardsey [Bawdsey] for fresh meat for their general but boat and men were all taken as was some wine going to him'; a couple of days later Edward Suckley reported from Landguard Fort that the appearance of the Dutch fleet had 'put the whole County into armes to attend their motion'.

Alarm turned to rejoicing when at the end of July the Dutch were soundly defeated in the St James's Day Fight, which moved slowly across the North Sea from off the North Foreland almost to the Dutch coast. As the surviving Dutch ships straggled into the Texel there were 'bonfires, guns and bells' of celebration in Ipswich, by order of the Earl of Suffolk, while Harwich fired a victory salute.

Considering the close links between eastern England and the Netherlands it is not altogether surprising to learn that considerable numbers of disaffected English seamen were serving in the Dutch fleet, nor that there were people in Ipswich who were suspected of a degree of treachery. In June 1666 Samuel Stannard was elected one of the 24 but was considered unfit to serve on the grounds that he was 'under suspition of holdinge correspondence with our enemies the dutch'.

It was not only the Corporation of Ipswich who suffered from the shortage of money at the time. Money for the navy was so short that it was rumoured that the king had decided not to fit his ships out after their normal winter lay-up. The Dutch, on the other hand, seem to have spent the winter refitting their ships and building new ones, and when the spring came plans were made to attack the Thames and Medway. In the State Archives at The Hague is a letter from the Special Commissioners for Naval Affairs instructing someone in Rotterdam to 'transport yourself towards the respective Prisons of these

Another section of the dockyard as recorded by the Buck brothers, showing the long ropery and cable store towards the left.

The Dutch attack on
Landguard Fort: a grisaille
by the elder Willem van de
Velde showing the attacking
ships lying offshore as the
landing operation
goes ahead.

Lands, where English seamen are held, to enquire among them, whether there are among them no accomplished Pilots or Steersmen who possess pertinent knowledge of the English sands … And finding such people to dispose them in some way or another, to go in the State's Fleet in the service of the State …'. It has been alleged that when the Dutch sailed up the Medway and attacked Chatham the ships were piloted up by English seamen.

The Dutch penetration of the Medway in June has gone down in history as possibly the worst disaster to strike the Royal Navy until the Second World War. Not only did the Dutch overcome the local defences and burn a number of English warships but they also boldly made off with the *Royal Charles*. When Pepys recorded that he went to bed 'full of fear and fright; hardly slept all night' he was almost certainly not the only Londoner to have a sleepless night that 12th of June.

Much nearer home, a Dutch fleet spread alarm along the Suffolk coast, and at Harwich Captain Anthony Deane, Master Shipwright of the Naval Yard, was hurriedly fitting out fireships, of which thirteen were merchant vessels belonging to Ipswich that had been impressed by an Order in Council of 16th June. Fireships were relatively small vessels well packed with inflammable materials whose crews endeavoured to attach their ship to a large warship and destroy it by setting it on fire; such ships were expendable.

On the last day of June there were no fewer than seventy Dutch warships in the Gunfleet anchorage to the south of Harwich, and when the whole fleet weighed anchor at dawn on 1st July it was expected that an attack was to be mounted on Harwich. Frank Hussey tells how their progress with a north-westerly wind and an adverse tide was painfully slow, 'stretching jangled nerves ashore to limits heretofore unreached'.[17]

Instead of turning towards the harbour the enemy sailed away northwards, and they spent the night at anchor some two miles off Aldeburgh. There was much movement of troops to counter the expected landing, and a hundred 'brave seamen' were sent from Ipswich to reinforce the garrison of Landguard Fort, at the entrance to Harwich harbour and the Orwell.

Next morning the Dutch ships all weighed anchor and, after standing to the northward for about an hour, tacked on to a southerly course towards Harwich. Watchers on Beacon Cliff and other vantage points saw a number of the vessels come to an anchor in the outer part of the Rolling Grounds, abreast of where the town of Felixstowe is now.

They watched anxiously as more than forty boats and barges were rowed towards the shore with a landing force estimated by one observer at a thousand men. The intention of the Dutch commanders was to take Landguard Fort and so gain control of Harwich harbour and the Orwell, thus putting pressure on the English to sue for peace.

The plan might have succeeded if one of the Dutch ships which was to have bombarded the fort from the harbour entrance had not gone aground on the Ridge shoal on the way in and if the fort garrison had not been reinforced beyond the expectations of the attackers. As it was the Dutch were repulsed by the Landguard garrison, commanded by Nathaniel Darrell; they returned to their boats in the evening and, with some difficulty because of the ebbing tide, rowed off back to their ships.

There must have been enormous relief in Ipswich when the news came through that the Dutch attack had failed. In London Pepys went to the Council Chamber to deliver a letter and found 'the King and a whole tableful of Lords' considering a case in which an old man complained that his son did not allow him enough to live on. 'This cause lasted them near two hours; which methinks, at this time to be the work of the Council-board of England, is a scandalous thing. . .' he wrote in his diary. 'Here I find all the news is the enemy's landing 3000 men near Harwich, and attacquing Langnerfort and being beat off thence with our great guns, killing some of their men and they leaving their lathers [ladders] behind them; but we had no Horse in the way on Suffolke side, otherwise we might have galled their Foot.'

From Harwich Lord Oxford sent a dispatch to Lord Arlington, the Secretary of State: 'My Lord, This night with the young flood, the enemy shipped the

The red-brick fort which in 1716 replaced the Landguard Fort that had been attacked by the Dutch, seen from the harbour.

remainder of their beaten party, and this morning the fleet have turned their backs, and are driving away as fast as the dead calm will suffer them.'[18]

Proud sentiments, but in fact the Dutch fleet had not gone away, and the port of Ipswich suffered because the colliers did not dare come further south than Yarmouth. One result of the blockade was to inflate the price of coal by a multiplier of five in only three weeks.

A peace treaty was signed before the month was out, but nobody either in Suffolk or at Court was in any doubt as to the consequences had the Dutch taken Landguard Fort and established a foothold on the Suffolk shore. It is not overstating the facts to say that the future of the monarchy would have been in doubt.

Very likely that thought was in the King's mind when he visited Landguard Fort on 3rd October, 1668, having come over from Newmarket by way of Ipswich. It was a belated acknowledgement of the bravery of the defenders, who had since been sorely neglected. Major Nathaniel Darell, who had been wounded while defending the fort fifteen months earlier, took the opportunity to present a petition to the king stating that 'his Company of his Royall Highness the Duke of York's regiment in ye said fort doe only fall sick for want of Bedds, Blanketts, & other accomodation wch he humbly prayed may be forthwith provided'. The king and his brother, the Duke of York, graciously ordered that the fort's requirements 'bee immediately sent and delivered'.[19]

After visiting the fort and crossing to Harwich to see what had been done there the king sailed in the yacht *Henrietta* up the coast to Aldeburgh, where he disembarked next morning and whence he rode immediately back to Ipswich to dine with Leicester Devereux, Viscount Hereford, at Christchurch. A letter written from Ipswich the following day says that in the town 'they had all the expressions of joy possible, ringing of bells, discharging of guns, the steeples adorned with flags and streamers, the streets strewn with herbs and flowers, and echoing with the acclamations of the people, and prayers for his Majesty's health and prosperity. The bailiffs, portmen, and commoners attended his Majesty, and presented their mace, which they immediately received again, and after dinner, attended him on horseback with the trained bands, out of the town'.

The Treaty of Breda that brought the second Dutch war to an end has been described as an honourable compromise. The English accepted the Dutch definition of contraband as restricted to weapons and munitions of war and the Navigation Act was clarified in one important respect in favour of the Dutch, who were to be allowed to import into England in their own ships not only commodities of Dutch growth, production and manufacture but also those of Germany and the southern Netherlands as well. And the Dutch promised to render the honours of the flag to English warships 'in the British Seas, in the same manner as was used in former times'.

That treaty was followed six months later by the conclusion of a Triple Alliance between the two maritime powers and Sweden, temporarily checking the designs of Louis XIV on the Spanish Netherlands. The Triple Alliance, fragile as it proved to be in practice, was warmly welcomed in both England and the United Provinces, to whom the French advance into the Spanish Netherlands posed a definite threat.

However, within months of signing the Triple Alliance Charles II was engaged in secret negotiations with Louis XIV leading to the Treaty of Dover in which he promised to join France in an unprovoked attack on the Seven Provinces.[20] One particularly secret clause of the treaty signed in 1670, made known only to an intimate group of ministers, promised that the King would at some stage become a Roman Catholic, a conversion that would certainly not have been acceptable to popular opinion at home. The Earl of Arlington, who had been Secretary of State since 1662, manipulated the commercial and maritime disputes which inevitably arose with the Dutch to bring about an outbreak of war. 'Our business is to break with them and yet lay the breache at their door,' he said.[21]

The war which broke out in March 1672 was different from the earlier Dutch wars. For one thing England was not the chief opponent of the Dutch, and this time it was not primarily a war at sea; the French invasion of the Netherlands which came near to destroying their independence was for them paramount. While the landward provinces were soon overrun by the invaders Holland and Zeeland were saved from a similar fate by breaching the dykes that defended them from flooding, and at sea only the skill and courage of De Ruyter saved the Dutch Republic from defeat. As William Laird Clowes wrote in his history of the Royal Navy, had it not been for the naval genius of De Ruyter and for the masterly manner in which he utilised the sea power of

The smoke of battle hangs over Landguard Point as Dutch gunners bombard the fort; a re-enactment on the 350th anniversary of the last landing by a hostile force on English soil.

Michiel Adriaenszoon de Ruyter, defender of the Dutch Republic.

his sorely-tried country, Holland must have collapsed under the terrible ordeal to which she was exposed.[22]

A French fleet of thirty-three ships, eight fireships and four storeships mounting nearly two thousand guns and with almost 11,000 officers and men commanded by Vice-Admiral Jean d'Estrees was sent to join the English fleet on the east coast. Commanded by the Duke of York, the English fleet consisted of sixty-five ships and twenty-two fireships as well as a considerable number of smaller craft.

There seems to have been a distinct problem in that the English did not trust the French, whom they despised as seamen, and that the French, besides being jealous of each other, were jealous of the English. Dutch writers told how English prisoners declared after the battle that they had no ill-feeling against the Hollanders, but would have been delighted to fight the French. Such attitudes did not bode well for the decisive victory that was hoped for by the allies.

The Dutch fleet, on the other hand, was united and disciplined as it had never been during the previous war. It consisted of seventy-five ships and thirty-six fireships mounting almost four thousand five hundred guns, as well as smaller vessels. There were more than twenty thousand officers and men.

De Ruyter fell in with the combined English and French fleets on 19th May about twenty-four miles east south east of the Gunfleet but lost sight of them in thick weather. The allied fleets anchored in Sole Bay, where the Duke of York is said to have taken lodgings ashore in Southwold. The ships were anchored more or less parallel with the coast, the French squadron being to the south. On 27th May the wind was blowing stiffly from the north east. It is said that at a council of war in the flagship the Earl of Sandwich, Pepys' patron and friend, pointed out that the fleet was in danger of being surprised on a lee shore and suggested they ought to weigh anchor and put to sea. The Duke, instead of taking his advice, seems to have hinted that the Earl's caution was the effect not so much of prudence as of apprehension.[23]

A little before three the following morning the sound of gunfire was heard and soon afterwards a French vessel, which had been on lookout in the north east, was seen running before the wind under full sail to report the approach of the enemy from that direction. The allied fleets were taken by surprise; many ships had their boats ashore and their men filling water barrels, and it is said that the Duke of York was in bed at Sutherland House when the alarm was given.

There was no time to weigh anchors, with the seamen treading round the capstans hauling in the lengthy cables; out came axes and the cables were cut even as men were aloft setting the sails. Sandwich's Blue squadron, which lay to windward, cut its cables and stood out to sea on the starboard tack to meet the oncoming Dutch fleet, arranged in two divisions line abreast. Had the wind not dropped as they did so the enemy's fireships would almost certainly have got in among the allied fleet before it could gain searoom and great would have been the destruction.

While the Duke of York's squadron followed rather tardily in Sandwich's wake on the starboard tack towards the north the French squadron, for reasons that remain obscure, set off on the port tack, sailing towards the south east. While French historians have given their countrymen full support, saying that they bore a very important share of the action and greatly distinguished themselves, Laird Clowes describes much of their account as 'pure imagination'.[24]

Edward Montagu, Earl of Sandwich, was a most likeable man. When he died in battle a Dutch newspaper described him as 'so friendly that it was tragic such a gallant gentleman came to such a pitiful end.'

The Earl of Sandwich in the *Royal James* was closely attacked by Captain Jan Van Brakel in the *Groot Hollandia*, a much less powerful ship. Van Brakel eventually lost no fewer than 150 killed and fifty wounded out of his crew of three hundred, and his vessel would undoubtedly have been overwhelmed by the *Royal James* had that ship not been attacked by two fireships and by another large vessel. Sandwich defended himself bravely for two hours, but about noon a third fireship grappled the *Royal James* and set her on fire. Sandwich held his ship to the last, and was lost with her. His body was picked up several days later off the Essex coast, was brought into Harwich, and was later buried with great ceremony in Westminster Abbey.

As the little *Fanfan* left harbour with his body on its way to London the governor of Landguard Fort ordered a guard of honour to fire a volley of small shot and followed that with a 24-gun salute, considering it 'undecent to part without some such'.[25]

It is perhaps significant that the greatest tribute to Sandwich appeared in a Dutch newspaper, the *Hollandtse Mercurius*: 'He was one of the handsomest men of our century, with long blond hair, well made, politely mannered, and so friendly that it was tragic such a gallant gentleman came to such a pitiful end.'

The battle continued until near nightfall, when the Dutch withdrew to the northward. Though both sides claimed victory, the Battle of Sole Bay was in reality a drawn fight. The losses on both sides had been heavy; some of the casualties were landed at Southwold.

The war went on for another two years, but the sympathies of people in England were with the Dutch rather than with the French, who it was felt had proved untrustworthy, if not treacherous, allies. The accession of the House of Orange in the Netherlands contributed greatly towards removing the differences that had estranged the governments of the two great maritime nations, and peace negotiations were concluded in February 1674. Before the end of that year a commercial treaty had been made between the two countries, and in 1677 the Anglo-Dutch alliance was cemented by the marriage of the Princess Mary of York to William, Prince of Orange. How they became William and Mary, King and Queen of England, is another story.

The Dunkirk menace   8

When Charles II sold the town of Dunkirk to the French for a mere £320,000 in 1662 there were fears among many people, notably the merchants of London, that it would again become 'the Harbour of all the Privateers'. That fortified harbour and town had been garrisoned by English soldiers since being taken from the Spaniards in 1658 by a Cromwellian army fighting with the French.

The Flemish port had been developed by the Duke of Parma from 1583 onwards, when it was a part of the Spanish Netherlands, as a base for a fleet of fast-sailing warships whose primary purpose was to prey on Dutch shipping and fishing boats. That fleet was in time expanded by privateers issued by the Habsburg authorities with letters of marque whose semi-piratical exploits in time of peace as well as in wartime spread fear and loathing not only among English seamen but among the inhabitants of the English east coast.

In 1585, at a time when England and France were nominally at peace, the master of the ship *Nightingall* of Harwich reported on his return to Ipswich that he had been robbed by the crews of two French warships he had met with off Cape Finisterre, the north-westerly tip of the Iberian peninsula. He was probably on the way home from a voyage to the Mediterranean and had on board payment for a cargo delivered on behalf of some Ipswich merchants. The French sailors not only stole seventeen bags of money, one belonging to him and the others to various Ipswich merchants, but violently assaulted him and members of his crew and took their clothes from them. The larger of the French ships was, he said, a very new ship with a stern gallery; the smaller one was equipped with six or seven oars on each side. And both of them bore the arms of the King of France on their sterns, suggesting that they were the King's ships rather than privateers.

Little more than ten years later six or seven Dunkirkers were said to be blockading Harwich harbour, and some thirty traders had been taken by them. Those privateers from the northern French ports – Dunkirk was not alone in fitting out those marauders – remained a potent threat to shipping from Ipswich, Yarmouth, Lynn and other east coast ports when in the early years of the seventeenth century James VI of Scotland ascended the throne of England following the death of the first Queen Elizabeth. James's autocratic rule and the machinations of George Villiers, 1st Duke of Buckingham, created discontent at home while their foreign policy aroused antagonism abroad. The King's determination to assist his son-in-law Frederick, the Elector Palatine and champion of militant Calvinism, who was assailed by Catholic enemies intent on driving him from power, set England on a course towards war in Europe.

Opposite: One nation's admiral might be another nation's privateer. Jean Bart entered service with the Dutch navy, then fought against them and the British, commanding a small fleet of privateers. His statue stands in Dunkirk and a French frigate carries his name.

'Privateers are vessels which an individual arms in time of war, by authority of government, to take merchant ships and others belonging to the enemy,' wrote the Swedish shipbuilder Fredrik af Chapman in his treatise on shipbuilding, first published in 1775.[1]

Having thus succinctly defined the purpose and nature of those craft, Chapman went on to describe the requirements for a successful privateer. 'If ships of superior force were not to be feared at sea, all sorts of ships might be employed in privateering, provided they were well armed with guns and men. But as a privateer may possibly meet with ships of the line, which are always of greater force, to escape in the chase, it should carry sail well, and sail fast in bad weather.'

He advocated that to defend itself against frigates, which were specifically intended to counter privateering, the privateer should carry heavy guns 'rather of a large caliber than in great number'. This was advantageous not only because of the greater effect of the heavier guns but 'because there is a greater interval between the guns, so that the men at the oars and guns are not too much in the way of each other . . . these oars serve during a battle to present the privateer in an advantageous position, and in a calm to retire from a superior enemy'.

The navy had long suffered from incompetence and corruption, the fleet deteriorating in both quality and size as the annual cost of its upkeep soared.[2] When Buckingham became Lord High Admiral he sought both to create greater efficiency and to reduce costs, but it is apparent from the many complaints made by captains of inadequate supplies and lack of funds that he was not entirely successful.

Captain John Pennington on board the *Garland* in the Downs wrote to Buckingham on 23rd October 1625 stating that twenty-two privateers had left Dunkirk the previous week. He proposed to sail with five ships in pursuit of them, but complained of want of stores and provisions, arising from shortage of money. And just the following day it was stated that 'Ships are making ready, but want of money is the chief let'.[3]

When war did break out between England and Spain in 1625 the Dunkirkers wreaked havoc among English shipping, and an expedition planned by Buckingham against the port of Cadiz in south-western Spain was a dismal failure. The merchant ships, including a number from Ipswich, that had been pressed into service for the attack on the Spanish town were intended to have bombarded the fort guarding the approach to Cadiz, but their crews proved timid, if not downright cowardly, and took refuge behind the king's ships, succeeding only in putting a cannonball through the stern windows of one of those warships. When the fort eventually capitulated and the soldiers advanced towards Cadiz they discovered that their knapsacks were empty, and the countryside provided them with no food but with plenty of wine. With their stomachs empty and the semi-tropical sun beating down on their heads the men soon became hopelessly drunk; the march on Cadiz had to be abandoned.

Sir John Eliot, who had been George Villiers' companion in foreign travel in earlier years, commented bitterly that 'our honour is ruined, our ships are sunk, our men perished; not by the sword, not by the enemy, not by chance, but, as the strongest predictions had discerned and made it appear beforehand, by those we trust'.[4]

The following year the shipowners and merchants of Ipswich complained to the Privy Council of the dire effects the war was having on the town's economy. In their petition they told how twenty-four Ipswich ships had been taken up for Buckingham's abortive expedition to Cadiz, for which their owners had not been paid; one of the ships, the *Long Robert*, had been lost with all hands, 'to the utter undoing of many poor mariners' wives and loss to the owners of £1,200, for which they have not received any recompense'.

Once their ships were returned they had hoped to have resumed trading, but they dared not go to sea for fear of the Dunkirkers, who had taken two of their ships. It was said that no fewer than fifty-eight ships were laid up in the Orwell for fear of attack, and the Iceland and Northern Seas fisheries had been 'given over'. Not only that, the town's important shipbuilding industry had been at a standstill for some time.[5]

The Admiral of the Narrow Seas, Sir Henry Palmer, had twelve ships under his command, four of which were based in Harwich harbour and were charged with 'scouring' the coast from there to Yarmouth.[6] In February 1626, however, there were complaints that the Harwich ships lay in harbour and allowed the

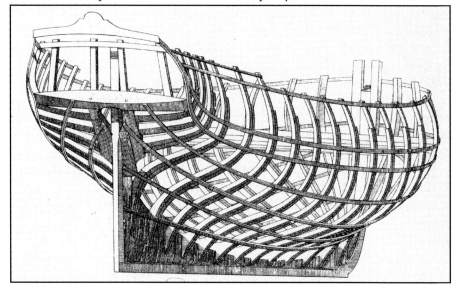

A privateer in frame, shown in Fredrik af Chapman's *Architectura Navalis Mercatoria* of 1775. Such a vessel had a length between perpendiculars of 85ft and carried a crew of ninety men, including officers.

Dunkirkers a free run of the coast; Buckingham sent orders to Sir Henry 'to quicken and awake them'.[7] Not only were the French privateers faster ships under sail than the English warships sent against them but many of them were also equipped with oars, giving them a great advantage in light weather.

It is uncertain whether Buckingham's orders had any effect, but within weeks he was telling Sir Henry to take the war to the enemy's lair. His instructions were for ships to ply up and down off Dunkirk to meet the Dunkirkers 'and hinder and annoy them' as much as he could.[8] An excellent idea in principle, but with the ships as ill-provisioned and the men as demoralised as they were it is hardly likely that the order had any beneficial effect.

When it became time for ships to set sail from the Suffolk ports for the annual voyage to the Westmann Islands and Iceland Captain Richard Harris of the *Hector* and Captain Edward Button of the *Aletheia* were given instructions to convoy the ships and to see them safe as far as 'the Gattes of Scotland'; beyond that they were expected to look after themselves.[9] The northern voyage was an important one for the merchants of Ipswich and Southwold as well as those of Yarmouth and other places on the East Anglian coast.

The Ipswich shipowners renewed their complaint in March 1627 in a petition to King Charles I, who had succeeded his father in 1625, saying that the Dunkirkers had taken five ships with their lading, worth £5,000, and had carried their crews captive to Dunkirk. They declared that two of the ships had been taken on 24th February that year by 'a great Dunkirker with 150 men and 20 pieces of brass ordnance.' And then they cleverly remarked on the detrimental effect all this was likely to have on the King's navy. 'No ship can go to sea, and the livelihood of all seafaring men is taken from them, with the means of training men for the King's service.'[10]

An Ipswich ship, the *Return*, played a somewhat inglorious part in another of the Duke of Buckingham's expeditions, that to the Ilé de Re in 1627 after England had gone to war against France as well as Spain. The purpose of the landing on this island in the Bay of Biscay was to support the Huguenots in La Rochelle, to defend English commerce and to destroy French and Spanish ships, but the Rochellese proved unwilling to accept the English intervention on their behalf and the expedition failed in its other objectives also.

The *Return*, with 160 troops, set out for the Bay of Biscay with the rest of the fleet engaged in the operation, but she somehow became separated from the other ships, was caught in a severe storm and was eventually forced to return to Dartmouth when her provisions ran out; there is a hint in the official reports that she might have been rather too small for the service in which she was engaged. One of the king's ships of this period was named the *Happy Return*, but it is clear that the *Return* of Ipswich was not a happy ship.

Her master, Captain Thomas Dowrich, expressed a willingness to sail when his ship had been provisioned, but some of the crew were mutinous and it seems that he had to put back once more. Many in both the sea service and the army were mutinous at that time, not only for want of pay but also for detestation of Buckingham's authority.[11]

King Charles is said to have been infuriated by the return from the fleet of the Ipswich ship, and to have expressed the view that the men who caused it to turn back should be harshly dealt with. 'His Majesty thinks the fault so foul as that some of the men deserve death,' we are told.[12]

Whatever happened to the men of the *Return*, the expedition returned to England 'with no little dishonour to our nation, excessive charge to our treasury, and great slaughter of our men', as a contemporary comment had it. In spite of this disaster the Duke planned yet another expedition; he was at Portsmouth making preparations for it when he was assassinated by a naval officer, John Felton, a deed that was widely likened to David's slaying of Goliath.[13]

The French privateers ranged the English coast in the most brazen fashion. A Dunkirker of 160 tons captured a 100-ton ship off Southwold in full view of the townsmen, and when the townspeople attempted to drive the Dunkirker from her prey they were 'beaten from their ordnance by the enemy, who shot into the town in contempt'.[14]

It was not only the merchants who suffered, and it was not only the Dunkirkers that caused trouble. In 1632 three fishing busses were captured 'by Hollanders and Dunkirkers'; the *Experience* was taken by the *Flying Horse* of Groningen in Friesland in August that year, the *Flower* by a man-of-war from Enkhuizen and the *Concord* by a Dunkirk ship in September.[15]

The simple fact was that the Suffolk coast was virtually defenceless, and there were fears that Harwich and even Ipswich were open to attack, the 1626 fort at Landguard being then incomplete and vulnerable. There was no money in the King's coffers to pay for fortifications at places like Aldeburgh and Southwold, and when appeals were made by the coastal communities for help they were told to look after themselves.

It is, perhaps, not entirely surprising that when, faced with a dire shortage of cash, Charles I demanded 'voluntary gifts' from all those who could afford to pay there was considerable opposition in Suffolk to the levy. The Earl of Suffolk called an assembly at Bury St Edmunds in August 1626 with the object of raising money for the King, but instead of being offered cash he was answered with loud cries from those who lived along the coast. Rather than pay up, they complained that 'their ships were taken and fired in the havens before their faces, insomuch that they durst not look out of their ports'.[16]

Small wonder that the London merchants went to Whitehall in 1662 to protest at the surrender of Dunkirk, a nest of vipers if ever there was one. During the eighteenth-century wars with France the privateers operating from Dunkirk and Ostend inflicted serious losses on the English coasting trade; it is said that between 1656 and 1783 English prize goods worth almost six million pounds were sold in the Dunkirk prize courts alone.

In the French ports privateering was serious business, bringing good returns for those who financed what were in effect private warships. Some of those vessels had very large crews, sufficient to allow prize crews to be put aboard captured ships to take them into a French port: in 1758 the Dunkirker *Vandanger*, taken by the sloops *Hound*, *Peggy* and *Ranger*, was found to have a crew of forty-nine men.[17]

Not all the privateers were so well manned, however. One day in March 1745 Captain Stringer of HM Sloop *Tavistock*, built at Gosport only the year before, was off the Suffolk coast when he saw a small sailing boat which he thought had an unfamiliar look about her, so he gave chase to her and drove her ashore somewhere in Harwich harbour. The boat's crew of six were taken prisoner and found to be Frenchmen from Calais armed only with pistols and cutlasses; 'the design of these desperadoes,' the *Ipswich Journal* reported, 'was to cut out one of the Dutch packets from Harwich and make a privateer of her.'[18]

It was not only the larger vessels like the Harwich packets that suffered from the attention of the Dunkirkers. A small vessel laden with what was described as chalk-rubbish was lying off Woodbridge Haven waiting for the tide one day in 1744 when she was taken by a privateer; the master, Richard Byard of Bawdsey, and his crew escaped ashore in their small boat. And an Aldeburgh pilot, John Newell, was killed and another Aldeburgh man, Thomas Norton, was mortally wounded that same year when a yawl in which they had put off to a Danish ship was fired into by the crew of a French privateer that had attracted them by flying an English ensign, understood by them as a signal for a pilot.[19] The other five men in the yawl threw themselves down in the bottom of the boat and let her drift away from the privateer, which went in pursuit of

An account in the *London Gazette* of 17th October 1747 which includes the sloop *Tavistock* among those receiving an award for an action off the coast of France. All of the crew would be interested in such award announcements, as there would be a return for everyone – albeit heavily weighted in favour of the senior officers.

thence all the Tea, which had been lately seized by Capt. Johnson, Commander of the Swift Privateer, being upwards of Four Thousand Two Hundred Weight, and carried the same to a Place in the said Town, where their Horses waited; obliging the Watchmen to go and remain with them, till they had loaded them: That they were upwards of Sixty in Number, with about Thirty Horses; and that they left behind them, in their Hurry, a Crow Bar of a new and uncommon Make; His Majesty, for the better discovering and bringing to Justice the Persons concerned therein, is pleased to promise his most gracious Pardon to any one of the Offenders, who shall discover any one, or more of his Accomplices, so that he or they may be apprehended and convicted thereof.

HOLLES NEWCASTLE.

Custom-house, London, October 16, 1747. And as a further Encouragement for bringing the Offenders to Justice, the Commissioners of the Customs do hereby promise a Reward of Two Hundred Pounds for the discovering and apprehending each of the Persons concerned in breaking open the said Warehouse, and carrying off the Tea; to be paid by the Receiver-General of the Customs, upon the Conviction of each Offender respectively: And if any of the Persons, who were concerned in the Offence above-mentioned, will discover any of his Accomplices, so that any one or more of them, may be apprehended, he shall receive the like Reward of Two Hundred Pounds; to be paid upon the Conviction of each Offender; and will also be entituled to his Majesty's most gracious Pardon, as above declared.

By Order of the Commissioners,
William Wood, Secretary.

Office of Ordnance, October 27, 1747. The Principal Officers of his Majesty's Ordnance do hereby give Notice, that they intend to sell by publick Auction, at their Office in the Tower, on Wednesday the 2d of December next, several Lots of Waggons, Parchment and Paper Cartridges, Tann'd Hides, Sword Belts, Lanthorns, Junk, Match, Sheepskins, Horse and Mens Harness, Blocks, Bedding, Intrenching Tools, Handscrews, Swords, Bayonets, Rope, Woolpacks, Gun Barrels, and other old and unserviceable Stores, which may be viewed at the Tower of London; where printed Lists of the Lots will be delivered to such Persons as apply for the same.

By Command of the Board,
Charles Bush.

Mine Office, October 28, 1747. This is to give Notice, That a General Court of the Governor and Company of the Mine Adventurers of England, will be held at their Office on Thursday the 12th of November next, at Twelve at Noon, for the Election of a Governor, Deputy Governor, and Twelve Directors for the Year ensuing, pursuant to the Charter and Act of Parliament, concerning the Affairs of the said Company; and that the Transfer Books will be shut from and after Thursday the 5th, and opened again on Thursday the 19th of the said Month of November next.

Assurance Office, Serjeants-Inn, Oct. 27, 1747. A General Quarterly Court of the Corporation of the Amicable Society, for a perpetual Assurance Office,

will be held at their House in Serjeants Inn, Fleet street, on Tuesday the 3d of November next, at Eleven of the Clock in the Forenoon.

Robert Michel, Register.

Charitable Corporation, October 30, 1747. This is to give Notice, that a General Court of the said Corporation will be held at the House of Mr. Church, the Cardigan's Head Tavern, facing the Meuse Gate Charing Cross, on Monday the 9th of November next, at Eleven of the Clock in the Forenoon.

J. Innes, Secretary.

Notice is hereby given to the Captains, Officers and Companies of his Majesty's Ships Exeter and Poole, and Fly and Tavistock Sloops, who destroyed the L'Ardent, a French Ship of War, on the Coast of France, and to whom the said Prize was legally condemned, that they may receive their respective Shares of the said Prize, at Mr. Gyles Lones Office in Birchin-lane, London, the first Wednesday in every Month, for the Space of three Years, to begin and be accounted from the 9th Day of September last, and not at the Crown Tavern behind the Royal Exchange, as advertised in several former Gazettes.

Whereas his Majesty's Ship the Oxford is fitting for a Foreign Voyage, Notice is hereby given to the Officers and Company of said Ship, who were on board at the taking the Nostra Dame De Grace, that their respective Shares of the neat Produce of said Ship and Cargo, will be paid on board the Oxford at Plymouth, on or about the 13th of November next, before she proceeds to Sea. The Recalls will be at the House of Mr. Bruce, in Mark-lane, London, the first Wednesday in every Month for three Years.

Notice is hereby given to the Officers and Company of his Majesty's Ship Prince Frederick, who were on board at the taking of several Prizes on the 3d of May last, by a Squadron under the Command of the Right Honourable Lord Anson, that they will be paid their respective Shares of the Bullion on board the Prince Frederick, on the Day she comes out of Portsmouth Harbour to Spithead.

Advertisements.

Dr. ANDERSON's, or,
The Famous SCOTS PILLS;

ARE faithfully prepared only by JAMES INGLISH, Son of DAVID INGLISH, deceased, at the Unicorn, over-against the New Church in the Strand, London; and to prevent Counterfeits from Scotland, as well as in and about London, you are desired to take Notice, That the true Pills have their Boxes sealed on the Top (in black Wax) with a Lyon Rampant, and Three Mullets Argent, Dr. Anderson's Head betwixt I. I. with his Name round it, and Isabella Inglish underneath the Shield in a Scroll. They are of excellent Use in all Cases where Purging is necessary, and may be taken with Epsom, Tunbridge, or other Medicinal Waters.

NOtice is hereby given, (pursuant to the Statute made in the Eighth Year of his present Majesty's Reign) that William Gresham, of St. George's Parish Hanover-square, on the 15th Day of October instant, between the Hours of Three and Four in the Afternoon, in the Parish of Flampsted, Hundred

the Danish ship to which they had been bound. Once they were well clear of the privateer they managed to set sail and reach Southwold beach in safety.

Not long afterwards the 14-gun sloop *Hound* captured the privateer involved in that incident and took her into Hellevoetsluis, the continental end of the Harwich packet service on the island of Veere. It was found that she had a crew of ninety-one men and was armed with ten carriage guns and ten swivel guns, a quite formidable armament.[20] Twenty of her men were killed and wounded in the encounter, which occurred twenty days into what had been planned as a sixty-day cruise; she had already taken four English ships and sent them into Dunkirk.

One of the most notorious Suffolk smugglers, John Pixley, who had a few years earlier been sentenced to transportation for his exploits but had somehow escaped, was living at that time in Flushing, or Vlissingen to give it its Dutch spelling, with other fugitives from English law. When an English collier was taken by a French privateer off the coast of Zeeland in 1744 Pixley sallied out from Flushing in a cutter and retook the ship after what was described as 'a sharp engagement' with the Frenchmen who had been put on board.[21]

Sometimes captured ships were ransomed by the Dunkirkers, to the considerable benefit of their French owners and backers. In the autumn of 1745 a Harwich codsmack 'with a sea-fare of fish on board' was taken off Cromer by a small lugger privateer, and she was ransomed.[22] The same thing happened when the Ipswich brig *Providence* was taken by a privateer on Christmas Day the same year; the master, John Terry of Ipswich, managed to ransom his ship for a payment of £135.[23]

The Harwich packets were not immune from attack by the Dunkirkers. In 1762 one of the packets on its way to Hellevoetsluis was chased by a schooner privateer and took refuge in Flushing.[24]

French privateers were active in the North Sea throughout the Revolutionary and Napoleonic wars, continuing to sap British trade in a way that the French regular navy proved incapable of doing. Their crews were sometimes as diverse as the crews of merchant vessels at the time, not a few Americans being found in Dunkirkers that were taken by British warships.

The American crew members sometimes proved unreliable, however. When in November 1804 the collier *Eve* was captured off Hartlepool by a privateer from Flushing two Americans were among the prize crew put on board the collier to sail her to a French port. The crew of the *Eve* were taken on board the privateer, only the mate and a boy being allowed to remain on board their own ship. Just what passed between the Englishmen and the Americans is not on record, but English and Americans acted together to overcome the three Frenchmen of the prize crew and sailed the *Eve* into her home port of Yarmouth.[25]

The first Woodbridge shipping register, which dates back to 1786 when the registration of British ships was initiated by the Shipping and Navigation Act of that year,[26] records seven vessels captured by the French during the Napoleonic Wars, at least five of them by privateers. The brigantines *Sally* and *Industry*, the schooner *Deben*, the smack *Success* and the sloop *Margarett* were all taken by privateers, while the lugger *I.O.* is said simply to have been 'taken by the French'.

Another little sloop, the *Kingston*, was re-registered in 1804, the entry bearing the enigmatic note 'Memo. This vessel was taken by the Enemy in the year 1804 and the Certificate of Registry with her', which suggests that she might have been ransomed.

The scourge of the Dunkirk privateers was ended when the Napoleonic War came to an end in 1815, but the enmity that had existed for so long between seamen from that part of the European coast and British seamen and fishermen seems to have remained. In 1880 an inquiry was held at Lowestoft and Yarmouth into the depredations perpetrated by continental fishermen, mainly from Ostend, who employed grapnels known by the English fishermen as 'Belgian devils' to play havoc with the English drift nets.[27] Was that, perhaps, a survival of the Dunkirker spirit?

New harbours for old   9

The nineteenth century was a time of change. The Industrial Revolution did not entirely pass Suffolk by, and the establishment of Richard Garrett's engineering works at Leiston in 1778 and Robert Ransome's at Ipswich in 1789 paved the way for an expansion of the county's industrial base that was to have an effect on the maritime trade of its ports.

The Garrett family owned their own small ships in which they sent their products to customers around the country, while James Smyth at Peasenhall sent his seed drills to Slaughden to be loaded into coasting vessels for delivery to farmers in other parts; Ransomes and other firms in Ipswich imported raw materials such as pigiron and coal by sea. As new industries blossomed, so did maritime trade.

It was the desire of the merchants and manufacturers of Norwich to break away from their dependence on the port of Yarmouth that led to the construction of a harbour at Lowestoft in the 1820s. For many years textiles woven in Norwich had gone downriver in keels and wherries to be loaded into seagoing craft for export, and supplies destined for the city had also to be transhipped at Yarmouth, but there came a time when it was suggested that seagoing ships might sail up the Yare and right into the city. Not only was Yarmouth harbour prone to blockage as a result of a bar being formed in certain weather conditions, leading to ships being held up for quite long periods, but the losses that resulted from transhipment caused the Norwich merchants great concern.

Norwich Corporation appointed a committee in 1762 'to enquire into the abuses committed in the measurement of coals from on board ships', and twelve people were nominated as coal meters. That was evidence of subtle abuse. There was also piracy, not on the high seas but on the river between Yarmouth and Norwich; coal was shovelled out at some isolated staithe into carts which disappeared into the marshes.

In 1778 several merchants, keel owners and wherry owners formed an association 'for the better discovering, apprehending, prosecuting and bringing to Justice all such person or persons who have or hath stolen, purloined or embezzled, or may at any time or times hereafter steal, purloin or embezzle any of their goods, wares, or merchandize. . .'. It could be dangerous to provide information on such miscreants, however. One waterman, Henry Scarle of Bungay, was murdered by three men he had discovered plundering his wherry and had given away to his employer, Matthias Kerrison, the Bungay merchant. Perhaps it was Kerrison who provided the gravestone in Bungay Holy Trinity

Opposite: Lowestoft harbour in the closing years of the nineteenth century showing Peto's north pier. The three harbour tugs, *Imperial* nearest, are lying alongside what had been the south pier of the 1830s harbour.

The distinctive lighthouses at the outer ends of the two piers that were part of Morton Peto's outer harbour.

The paddle tug *Powerful*, built at Poplar in 1857, and a cutter in the outer harbour; note the length of the cutter's boom. The buildings are the cattle sheds provided by Morton Peto for cattle imported from Denmark during the 1850s.

churchyard describing poor Scarle as 'valued when alive, and respected now dead'.

As time went on things only got worse, and in the second decade of the nineteenth century it was claimed by one Norwich merchant that in five years goods worth £25,000 had been stolen from wherries on the Yare. Led by Crisp Brown, an alderman of the city and a leading maltster and merchant, a group of Norwich businessmen sought to promote a scheme for the making of a navigation for seagoing ships up to Norwich. This required the dredging of certain shoals at the west end of Breydon and the deepening and straightening of the upper parts of the River Yare and the Wensum.

As early as 1814 William Cubitt, who had two years earlier taken a position with Ransomes, the Ipswich firm of agricultural engineers, and was to project them into the field of civil engineering, had undertaken a survey of the River Yare on behalf of the Norwich merchants with a view to making it navigable up to the city for small seagoing vessels. In a report issued in 1818 he proposed a three-and-a-half-mile channel from the confluence of the Yare and Waveney to the Knowl where the Bure enters the Yare, avoiding the shallow channel across Breydon; he estimated the cost of this project as £35,626. It was Cubitt's first involvement with waterways; in later years he was to work on improvements to the Oxford Canal and to succeed Thomas Telford as engineer to two other canal undertakings.

Faced with the implacable opposition of Yarmouth Corporation to his scheme, Cubitt prepared alternative plans for a harbour at Lowestoft and a ship canal linking the Waveney at Haddiscoe to the Yare at Reedham. The results of that change of plan were to have a resounding impact on the future of the town of Lowestoft, which at the time of the first Census in 1801 had a population of no more than 2,332. The built-up area of the town was then confined to the High Street and a small number of thoroughfares immediately to the west of that main street, with only fishermen's stores and smokehouses below the cliff that fell away sharply on the seaward side of the highway.

The parish church of St Margaret's lay a mile inland, where it had once served the farming settlement of Akethorpe. A mile or so to the south of the town was Lake Lothing, a stretch of freshwater that was connected with Oulton Broad at its west end and separated from the sea at the other end by a causeway of sand and shingle that carried the London road southward from Great Yarmouth. Despite the fact that it had no harbour Lowestoft had enjoyed a modest maritime trade for very many years, employing small ships that landed their cargoes on the beach; ships had even been built on the beach and launched into the sea in the eighteenth century.

Undeterred by the assurance that the Corporation of Yarmouth would do everything in its power to oppose an undertaking 'which was pregnant with the most ruinous consequences to the interests of the town and neighbourhood', the Norwich a Port party opened a subscription in 1822 to defray the costs of obtaining Parliamentary sanction to William Cubitt's scheme. There was great rejoicing at Yarmouth when the Norwich and Lowestoft Navigation Bill was thrown out in the 1826 session, but it was the men of Norwich and Lowestoft who had the last laugh; a new Bill passed safely through all its stages the following year, and the way was clear to build the navigation and the new harbour that went with it.

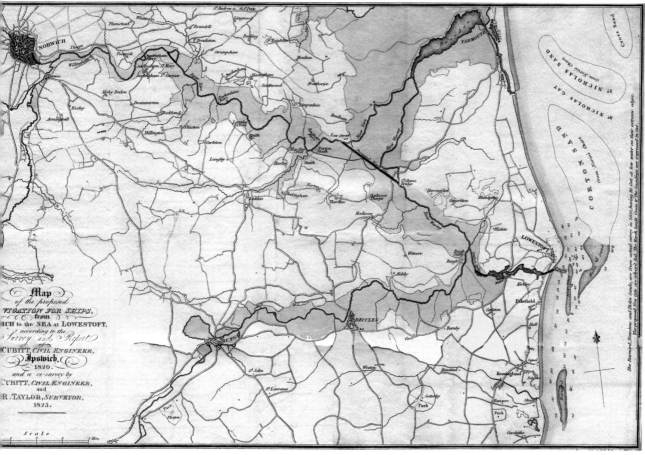

The *Times* coach, in which the promoters of the Bill had travelled down from London, was met by a procession at Harford Bridges on the outskirts of Norwich and was dragged in triumph through the streets by a crowd of excited men after the horses had been removed at St Stephen's Gates, where the London road entered the city. That evening there were great celebrations in the city, and as so often happens matters got out of hand. Wooden palings and watch boxes fed the celebration bonfire in the market place, and when the ringleaders of the mob were lodged in clink their comrades rescued them and added the clink doors to the fire.

The promoters did not allow the grass to grow under their feet, and work began in the early autumn of 1827. A dinner and 'aquatic sports' were held to celebrate the digging of the first spadeful of earth by Mr Crisp Brown on 4th September of that year, and the lock between Oulton Broad and Lake Lothing was completed in 1828; seagoing vessels did not use it until 1830, when the little sloop *Rose* arrived by way of Yarmouth with parts for a swing bridge to carry the London road over the harbour.[1]

The *Rose* had had to come up the Waveney and through Oulton Dyke because the cut from Lake Lothing to the sea was not then in existence. It was not until the beginning of April 1831 that a local newspaper announced that the sea lock had been filled from Lake Lothing and the sluices had been opened to allow the water to run into the cut leading to the sea. The short harbour piers were still under construction, but on 3rd June 1831 the directors of the Norwich and Lowestoft Navigation Company watched the lock gates

William Cubitt's plan for the Norwich and Lowestoft Navigation, including the New Cut across the marshes between Haddiscoe and Reedham.

Formal commencement of work on the Norwich and Lowestoft Navigation at Mutford Bridge on 4th September 1827, portrayed by Norwich School artist James Stark.

being opened to scour out the entrance channel. As the freshwater ran out a counter-current brought saltwater into the harbour, killing all the freshwater fish 'which were seen floating by myriads into the ocean'; next day the beach was littered with dead fish, many of them 'bitten in twain' by dogfish.[2]

Just five days later, with the wind blowing hard from WNW, ships anchored in Yarmouth Roads were forced to seek a more sheltered berth off Lowestoft. The master of a schooner from Goole, seeing that there were no breakers on the new entrance, decided to run into the harbour for shelter. Next day a sloop entered harbour to be hauled up on the patent slip that had been installed by Jabez Bayley, the Ipswich shipbuilder who had been awarded several contracts by the navigation company. Bayley was entrusted with the construction of the massive gates for the sea lock, and in 1828 built a steam dredger for the company. That early bucket dredger was, as Hugh Moffat remarked, 'an interesting piece of naval architecture' – with a sash window and a pedimented doorway or entry port.[3]

A brig making for the entrance to Lowestoft harbour, seen in a picture by Norwich School artist James Stark. Kirkley Church is visible just ahead of the vessel.

The swing bridge installed over the sea lock at Lowestoft in 1833, seen in a print of about 1855 which also shows the outer harbour and fish market constructed by Morton Peto following his takeover of the navigation company.

The people of Lowestoft watched with interest as work went ahead on the new harbour. On 25th June 1831 the Yarmouth-registered *Little Mary* arrived with a cargo of coal from Newcastle which was 'soon disposed of in the town and neighbourhood'. The same day the brigantine *Lady Anne*, launched at Wells in 1827, came in with a cargo of chalk from the Thames and the schooner *Providence*, of Boston, arrived with a cargo of culm or small coal, both these cargoes being consigned to Beccles, to the account of the maltster Patrick Stead, who had maltings in Bridge Street at Beccles as well as others in Halesworth.[4] As work on deepening and straightening Oulton Dyke had not then been completed one assumes that the two cargoes were transhipped into wherries for onward delivery, although by that time there were plans to allow seagoing ships up to Beccles.

The Corporation of Beccles played a leading part in obtaining an Act of Parliament for deepening the Waveney from the town down to Oulton Dyke, making it possible for seagoing vessels to reach Beccles by way of Lowestoft. The

The steam dredger built by Jabez Bayley for the construction of the Norwich and Lowestoft Navigation. It survived until 1916, when it was struck by a German shell during the bombardment of Lowestoft.

Mutford lock as drawn by James Stark for the book *Scenery of the Rivers of Norfolk*. Work on the construction of the lock had not begun when he made the drawing.

river was duly improved, and in July 1831 there appeared an advertisement for the London, Lowestoft, Norwich and Beccles Shipping Company which had been set up to operate a shipping service to London. For the time being it was proposed that one vessel a week should sail between London and Lowestoft, and that wherries should be provided to carry the goods on to Beccles, Bungay, Norwich and other places, but the advertisement promised that 'as soon as the Navigation to Norwich and Beccles is completed, the vessels will proceed direct to those places'.

The company had a number of Lowestoft men as its principals, and when faced with competition from the New and Direct Beccles and London Shipping

The lock between the harbour and Oulton Broad had four pairs of gates to allow for the tidal changes with which it had to cope. The tide rose and fell on both sides of the lock at different times.

and Trading Company in 1832 claimed public support 'from their local situation and knowledge of the trade'. The schooner *Sally* was bought from King's Lynn in 1831, and the company also owned a second schooner, the *Orion*, which was sold to Wells in 1834; the latter was replaced by the schooner *Sarah*, built at Wells the previous year. In that same year it had the 80-ton schooners *Lowestoft Merchant* and *Norwich Trader* built by Thomas Branford, one of the Yarmouth shipbuilders.

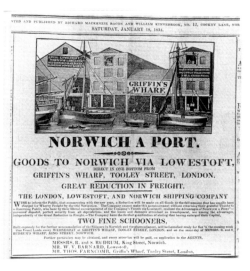

An advertisement for the London, Lowestoft and Norwich Shipping Company from the *Norwich Mercury* of 18th January 1834

Confusingly, the company also owned a sloop called the *Sarah*; the register contained many vessels with such popular names as *Sarah* and *Mary Ann*. In 1838 the sloop *Ocean*, built at Wells in 1831, was acquired.

In March 1832 Captain John Moon took his billyboy, aptly named the *Luna*, upriver to Beccles with the first cargo of coal to reach the town without having to be transhipped at Lowestoft. By 1834 several ships were coming to Beccles each week with coal from Goole, goods from London, tiles from Hull and timber and deals from London and taking away cargoes of ale and grain, or ale and malt. It seemed that trade was thriving, but the navigation to Beccles did not prove a financial success in the long term. Small coasting vessels did, however, continue to sail upriver to the quays below Beccles bridge, where they unloaded coal or grain for the local mills and loaded malt produced in the town's maltings or agricultural produce from farms in the vicinity.

Besides the quays on the town side of the river the development of a maritime trade encouraged the laying out of quays and the excavation of two small docks on the Gillingham side by Richard Thornton, a Beccles coal merchant and corn chandler. Besides laying out a wharf with some 500ft of quayheading he built two large timber and slated granaries with stabling and coal bins just on the downstream side of the bridge – 'at the bridge foot', as it was described when sold at the King's Head Inn on 6th December 1839. Either at that sale or a little later the site and buildings were acquired by Samuel Darby, a timber merchant, whose family continued to operate on the site for more than a hundred years.

The new harbour at Lowestoft was publicly opened on 10th August 1831, in the presence of 'an immense concourse of spectators of the most respectable description'. The steam packet *Lowther*, which had inaugurated a service between Selby on the Yorkshire Ouse and Yarmouth in 1824, brought the directors of the Norwich and Lowestoft Navigation Company into the harbour and towed in the local shipping company's schooner *Orion*, just arrived from London with a general cargo, and the little sloop *Carrow*, which had been built by Thomas Batley at Norwich not long before.

For the people of Lowestoft it was a day of general rejoicing. Guns were fired in salute, nearly drowning the music of the two bands that had been brought in to enliven the proceedings, and the crews of the little ships cheered

A billyboy ketch on its way up the River Waveney to Beccles in 1884.

A billyboy at Beccles Quay .

A billyboy lying at Beccles,
seen in a photograph taken
by George Christopher
Davies in 1884.

lustily as they entered the lock. Later in the morning the *Union* of London came in under sail, and then about noon Captain Moon brought the *Luna* into the harbour.

The wharves on the north shore of Lake Lothing saw quite a lot of activity as trade got under way. Irregular shipping lists in the local newspapers tell of vessels bringing coal from Newcastle, Shields and Sunderland and of others arriving from London with goods. And, as a foretaste of what was to come, an occasional fishing smack from the Thames put in for shelter, and perhaps to land its catch.

The New Cut linking the Waveney to the Yare was opened in January 1833, and a month later the indefatigable Captain Moon took the *Luna* up to Norwich with about 80 tons of coal, but the navigation company was in trouble. The work was costing much more than had been expected; in fact the lock and bridge at Lowestoft had cost twice as much as had been estimated. In 1832 the company had borrowed £50,000 from the Exchequer Loan Commissioners, and later it had to return for two further loans of £2,000 each.

In the three months of August to October 1834 some 170 vessels entered the harbour with cargo, about half of them going upriver either to Norwich or to Beccles, but the income was not nearly enough to enable the company to pay off its debts. The Exchequer Loan Commissioners took possession of the harbour and navigation, and in due course put them up for sale;[5] perhaps unsurprisingly no buyers came forward.[6]

Equally unsurprisingly the Exchequer Loan Commissioners were unwilling to throw more money into the pot and the still unfinished harbour began to deteriorate due to lack of maintenance; it was said that all they did was pay a resident engineer, George Edwards, for doing nothing. A particular problem was that the wooden piles of the piers and the gates of the sea lock were attacked by teredo worm and gribble, which together seem to have caused considerable damage.

It was only in 1843 that the undertaking was sold to six local men for a mere £4,935. Those six, James Cleveland, George Everitt and his brother William Everitt, brewers and maltsters, John Salter Lincoln, James Wigg Hickling, a local lawyer, and William Bradley, invested £2,000 in repairs to the harbour before selling it on to Morton Peto, the railway contractor who gave Lowestoft its first railway link with the Norfolk Railway at Reedham, laying part of his line alongside the Haddiscoe New Cut.

Peto not only provided the fishermen of Lowestoft with a means of getting their fish to inland markets but provided an outer harbour incorporating a fish market and developed a trade with Denmark, setting up the North of Europe Steam Navigation Company for that purpose. The company failed and the trade came to an end within a few years, but nevertheless the future of Lowestoft as a port was assured.

Ten miles to the south the little port of Southwold, which had prospered when Dunwich succumbed to the sea centuries earlier, was faced with a struggle with the same enemy that had overwhelmed its neighbour. When the men of Southwold and Walberswick made a new haven in 1590 they found themselves in conflict with the men of Dunwich, who took the matter to the Court of Exchequer. It was a dispute that was not easily settled, and as James Maggs neatly observed the case dragged on until 1598 'to the great satisfaction of oyster-loving lawyers'. [7]

Maintaining the harbour proved both difficult and costly; in 1714 the charge of 'digging and making a new haven' came to £37 10s. 11¼d., and when only nine years later it became necessary to 'stop the haven and make a new one' Southwold Corporation had to seek 'aid from the gentlemen in the country'. The harbour entrance tended to wander from place to place according to the direction of storm-force winds, and from time to time working parties were gathered in the town by sending a drummer around the streets to lead

The Norwich and Lowestoft NAVIGATION.
TO BE SOLD,

At the Auction Mart, London, on Wednesday, October 21 (unless previously disposed of by Private Contract, by order of the Commissioners for the Issue of Exchequer Bills in Aid of Public Works, appointed by the Act of 1st and 2nd of William IV. chap. 24, and the Acts therein referred to, and the Acts subsequently passed for amending the same, and authorizing a further issue of Exchequer Bills,

THE NORWICH and LOWESTOFT NAVI-GATION, and all Works and Property belonging thereto, and all Rates, Tolls, and Receipts to arise therefrom and made payable to the Company of Proprietors of the Norwich and Lowestoft Navigation, by the Act of 7 and 8 George IV. chap. 42, together with the corporate rights of the said Company under the said Act, and a subsequent Act to amend the same. This public work in its present state opens a communication from Norwich to the Sea, at Lowestoft, by which Sea-borne Vessels, without breaking bulk, are enabled to navigate to Norwich and Beccles, instead of discharging their cargoes into small craft, as heretofore, at Yarmouth. The receipts for tonnage on this Navigation have progressively increased as follow:—

To 10th of August, 1832, £743. 9s. 7d.
    To ditto, 1833, ... £1371. 16s.
    To ditto, 1834, ... £2007. 17s. 5d.
    To ditto, 1835, ... £2246. 9s. 5d.
    For further particulars apply to Winstanley and Sons, Paternoster-row, London, or to Mr. John Winter, Solicitor to the above Commissioners. N. B.—All communications requiring particulars, per post, are requested o be directed, under cover, to the Commissioners for the Issue of Exchequer Bills, South Sea House, London.

The Norwich and Lowestoft Navigation for sale in 1836, an advertisement in the *Norwich Mercury*. There were no bidders.

The wooden piers at Southwold about 1880 and the accretion of shingle that was threatening to block the harbour mouth.

A wherry apparently converted into a simple dredger lying on the mud in Southwold harbour. The *Good Intent*, converted by the harbour commissioners in 1815, was probably very similar.

them down to the harbour; 'to drum up support' as the saying goes. Such a procedure was by no means confined to Southwold; at Redcar at the mouth of the Tees a drummer marched around the town to call the crew of the lifeboat *Zetland*, built in 1802 and now the oldest surviving rescue boat in existence.

The building of a north pier in 1749 and a south pier three years later helped to stabilise the harbour but did not solve all the problems faced by shipping using the haven. The north pier had to be rebuilt in 1780 and both piers had then to be extended inland to prevent heavy seas throwing shingle into the river during bad weather. Unfortunately the piers did not prevent the accretion of sand and shingle in the entrance, which had to be dug out by hand in 1776, in 1784 and again in 1792.

The importance of the harbour to the town of Southwold may be judged from figures given by Maggs in his handbook of the number of men employed in the vessels belonging to the town. In 1819 there were forty-two vessels with an aggregate tonnage of almost 3,000 tons, and no fewer than 235 men employed at sea; the population of Southwold at that time was no more than 1,600.[8]

In 1815 the harbour commissioners converted the little *Good Intent*, possibly a wherry, into a makeshift dredger to deal with silting of the river, and when that proved inadequate they spent some £1,500 on a steam dredger in 1833. Somewhat unwisely they sold the dredger once it had dealt with the shoals between the harbour entrance and Blackshore Quay, and when silting again

The fish market provided by Morton Peto as part of his outer harbour project, seen in a carte de visite photograph of about 1860.

became a problem in 1838 they hired the Lowestoft dredger that had been built by Jabez Bayley ten years earlier.

At various times in the nineteenth century

A proposed harbour entrance at Slaughden which never materialised is illustrated in this watercolour by George Chambers, dated 1834. The position of the proposed cut through the shingle bank is clearly shown as just to the south of the Martello tower CC, which can be seen in the background with the houses of Slaughden beyond.

proposals were made to form a harbour of refuge at Slaughden or further downstream on the River Ore, but nothing came of any of them. The first scheme, put forward in 1813, was for a cut through the shingle of Orfordness directly opposite the easternmost point of Havergate Island, about a mile below the town of Orford. In 1836 a Lieutenant Wise chose a point further downriver for a cut to the sea, and then in 1847 the Tidal Harbour Commissioners ordered a survey of the river by an officer from the steam paddle sloop HMS *Blazer*, but again no new harbour entrance was made. Neither Aldeburgh nor Orford was considered significant enough by that time to be worth the expenditure.

Ipswich, on the other hand, was, or had been, a flourishing port when a group of businessmen and industrialists formed a Committee of Subscribers for the Improvement of the Port of Ipswich and called in a Newcastle engineer, William Chapman, to advise them how to make necessary alterations to the port's approaches. In the course of the eighteenth century the Orwell had silted up so badly, probably because of the embanking of the Corporation Marshes, that it was impossible for vessels drawing more than eight feet to reach the town's dilapidated quays; they had to anchor in Downham Reach, some three miles below the town, and be unloaded into lighters that carried their cargoes up to the town. Not only was this an expensive process but there was inevitable damage and pilferage involved; the annual loss was estimated at no less than £3,000, a very substantial sum at that time.

Chapman had been assistant to William Jessop on the Grand Canal in Ireland and had been involved in the improvement of the River Hull in Yorkshire; he had considerable experience of waterway projects.[9] In his report, made in 1797, he proposed a ship canal avoiding the shallows at Downham Bridge – not a bridge at all but an enigmatic causeway that might once have been a paved ford – leading to what he called a 'proposed bason or floating dock' eleven acres in extent; alternatively he suggested a new river channel that would cut out such meanderings as Back-again Reach. Alas, his ideas were thought to be too costly, and over the following eight years he came up with various other schemes, all of which proved too ambitious and too expensive for the people concerned. Eventually, in 1803, having scaled down one plan after another, he realised that they would pay only for the dredging of a deeper channel and the cutting off of some of the worst bends; but he warned that in the long run such economies would prove costly.

There followed a conflict between the river users and Ipswich Corporation, which was anxious to preserve its rights and privileges and to retain control of the income from shipping dues and the sale of ballast, necessary when ships sailed without cargo; the monopoly of the supply of ballast had in the past provided the corporation with a steady income, little or none of which they spent on maintaining the navigation. An Act for 'improving and rendering more commodious the Port of Ipswich' received Royal Assent from King George III in 1805, and work began on deepening and improving the river to enable ships to reach the quays.

Though the parsimony of the Ipswich committee had caused him great frustration, Chapman stayed to advise the new body of River Commissioners as they set about their work. At his suggestion they acquired a steam dredger, only the fourth to be put to work in England. Much of the money for the purchase of the dredger and for the work on the river was provided by individual river commissioners, Samuel Alexander alone subscribing £3,150 during the first year. As with all new technology, the dredger suffered from teething troubles, but once these had been overcome it proved its worth.

While they awaited the arrival of the dredger, the River Commissioners gave instructions to the harbourmaster to 'engage any number of men he can to excavate the mud in the intended new cut between the Carpenters Quays and the Cliff to such a depth as may be necessary to enable the steam engine dredge barge to work at half flood tide'.[10] What a horrible job the 'mud men' must have had preparing the way for the dredger, floundering in the slippery ooze as they wielded their spades and shovels.

By 1830 the River Commissioners had paid off the original loan of £8,000, borrowed on security of the rates to be levied on goods entering the port, and by dint of good housekeeping they also accumulated a surplus of £25,000. That credit balance proved an advantage when in 1836 a meeting was called in Ipswich under the chairmanship of banker Dykes Alexander to consider forming a wet dock in which ships might lay afloat at all states of the tide.

Towards the end of the nineteenth century the River Blyth had a rather bleak look, although as can be seen from this photograph it was well used both by trading vessels and fishing craft.

Chapman had died in 1832; did his ghost stalk the Moot Hall on the day of the meeting saying 'Told you so!'?

It was William Lane, the Collector of Customs for the port and a former bailiff of the town, who suggested damming off a section of the Orwell to form a large dock and excavating a new cut to carry the natural flow of the river. He estimated that the work would cost between £25,000 and £30,000, and proposed that an Act of Parliament be sought allowing the River Commissioners' £25,000 to be used to finance the scheme. Together with the Alexanders, brewer and shipowner John Cobbold, James and Robert Ransome, the ironfounders, shipbuilder William Bayley and engineer George Hurwood, Lane was elected to a committee that promptly sought the advice of a prominent civil engineer, Henry Palmer.

The scheme that Palmer put before the committee was an ambitious one. He proposed a dock of 33 acres that would be by far the largest on the east coast and would provide facilities that would enable the town to meet the challenges that lay ahead. At the same time that he drew up his far-sighted proposals the dock committee prepared a Bill for submission to Parliament.

There was, however, a diehard group of River Commissioners headed by Welham Clarke that was strongly opposed to the dock project. This group proposed at a meeting of the River Commissioners that they should pay out of their funds 'all expenses the gentlemen of the dock committee had incurred up to the present time, provided they throw the Dock Bill overboard into deep water'. When put to a meeting of the River Commissioners, however, that proposal was convincingly defeated. On 30th June 1837, just ten days after Victoria's accession to the throne, the Ipswich Dock Act[11] received Royal Assent. And it was to the new body of Dock Commissioners that Henry Palmer presented his report later that year. His estimate for the construction of the dock and the necessary improvement of the river approach was £58,100.

That proved to be a considerable underestimate. The lowest tender received, from David Thornbory of King's Lynn, was for £65,178, and that was accepted in March 1838. As is so often the case, the lowest tender was not in fact the most economical, for not only did the commissioners have to foot many a bill for extra work during the construction of the dock but Thornbory proved a thorn in the side of the engineer throughout the period of the work.

A very early steam dredger pictured by E.W. Cooke, probably very similar to the dredger acquired by the Ipswich River Commissioners in 1807.

The ferryman at Walberswick about 1880. A ferry was operating between Walberswick and Southwold as early as the thirteenth century, and in the early twentieth century there was a steam chain ferry providing the link across the Blyth.

At one stage Thornbory and Palmer came into conflict over the construction of the lower dam that was to separate the dock from the Orwell. The contract stipulated that this was to be composed of gravel and clay uniformly mixed, and that within the bank there was to be a wall of puddled chalk or clay and gravel or sand 10ft in thickness.[12] The specifications left no room for argument; the contractor was to carry the work out to the engineer's entire satisfaction, and the engineer's decision was to be final and binding.

Yet when the work was complete it was discovered that the contractor had omitted the wall of puddled clay from the lower dam, and instead of using gravel and clay uniformly mixed as stipulated in the contract he had merely heaped up material dredged from the river. Palmer tried to insist that the contractor should put right the faulty construction, but Thornbory had ingratiated himself with all and sundry by hosting lavish celebrations both for the workmen and for civic dignitaries and the townsfolk in general, and he insisted that what he had done was good enough. The unfortunate engineer found himself quite unable to make any headway against the wily contractor, who somewhat incredibly organised his own appointment as a Dock Commissioner.

To make matters worse, it seems that Palmer was at loggerheads with some of the commissioners, who more than once accused him of exceeding his authority by giving instructions to the workmen that had not been authorised by the commissioners. In vain did he point out that it was not normally considered necessary for an engineer to consult on 'a matter of purely mechanical arrangement'.[13]

There was indeed a faction in the town that opposed the dock scheme and considered it to be an unwarrantable waste of money. This opposition was given voice by the *Ipswich Journal*, which lost no opportunity to denigrate

One of William Chapman's proposals for improving the navigation of the Orwell. His earlier schemes had been more ambitious, with a ship canal leading to an eleven-acre dock in the parish of St Mary-at-the-Quay.

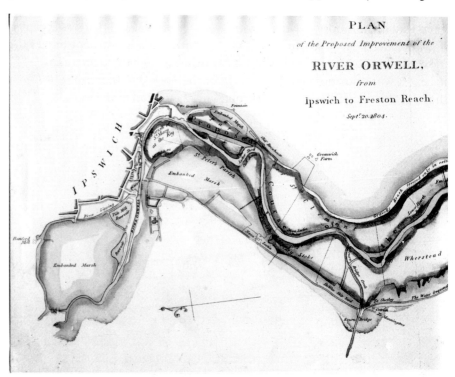

every aspect of the work. When at last on 17th January 1842 the lock gates at the entrance to the dock were operated for the first time to allow the little sloop *Director* to leave for Rochester with the mayor, Dock Commissioner John Chevallier Cobbold, on board the newspaper gave its verdict: 'Thus, after no inconsiderable bungling and delay, the town may be said to enjoy the advantages of a Wet Dock.'[14]

The early steam dredger acquired by the Ipswich River Commissioners in 1807 at work near the Cliff, as portrayed by the Revd Richard Cobbold in one of his paintings. It was one of the first steam-powered dredgers to enter service.

Whatever the sneers of the Tory newspaper, there can be not the slightest doubt that the construction of the Ipswich Wet Dock had a most beneficial effect on the town's trade and on its industries. In 1844 the navigation dues received by the Dock Commissioners doubled, and by 1855 they had increased to £10,000 a year. More significantly, perhaps, between 1843 and 1845 the number of vessels arriving from and leaving for foreign ports more than doubled, and before the end of the decade it had doubled again. Above all, the new facilities gave Ipswich the ability to face the challenges and to grasp the opportunities presented by the Victorian era.

In order to ensure that the entrance to the dock was in a sheltered position Palmer chose to place the lock some distance along the New Cut, as the cut-off channel is known to this day. To access the lock ships had to turn almost at right angles across the channel, easy enough at slack high water but potentially hazardous when the tide was running either up or down the New Cut. The result was a number of accidents when vessels were driven into the abutments of the lock or struck the lock gates, causing damage both to the lock and to the ship. The problem was compounded as the size of ships trading to the town increased, and in 1877 an Act of Parliament was obtained for major improvements, including the construction of a new lock 300ft long and 50ft wide placed at the southern end of the dock.

In spite of difficulties caused by the geology of the area construction of the lock began in 1879 and was completed by 1881. On 27th July of that year the paddle steamer *Glen Rosa* with the President of the Board of Trade, Joseph Chamberlain, and other VIPs on board made a ceremonial entry into the new lock chamber just at high water; with both inner and outer gates open, the steamer passed straight through into the dock as cannon boomed out in salute.

Downriver in Harwich harbour there were other developments going ahead in the 1880s. At Felixstowe landowner George Tomline, having already opened a railway line from Westerfield to a pier on the north side of the harbour, began the excavation of a dock that he planned should initiate a trade with northern Europe.[15] On the Essex side of the harbour the Great Eastern Railway was developing a new rail-served quay, Parkeston Quay, from which its steamers were to sail to the near continent.

Colliers, billyboys and barges   10

In the seventeenth century Ipswich was, as Daniel Defoe noted in his oft-quoted travel book, 'the greatest town in England for large colliers or coal ships employed between Newcastle and London; also they built the biggest ships and the best for the said fetching of coals of any that were employed in that trade'.[1]

At that time Ipswich had a great reputation for shipbuilding, Defoe noting that 'They built there so prodigious strong that it was an ordinary thing for an Ipswich collier, if no disaster happened to him, to reign (as the seamen call it) forty or fifty years and more'.

Defoe paints a wonderful word picture of the town of Ipswich at a time when the colliers laid up in the Orwell each winter, sheltered by a high woody shore, 'where they lie as safe as in a wet dock, and it was a very agreeable sight to see; perhaps two hundred sail of ships of all sizes lie in that posture every winter; all this while, which was usually from Michaelmas to Lady Day [29th September to 25th March], the masters lived calm and secure with their families in Ipswich, and enjoying plentifully what in the summer they got laboriously at sea, and this made the town of Ipswich very populous in the winter… so that in the winter there might be perhaps a thousand men in the town more than in the summer, and perhaps a greater number'.

Thus did Defoe write of the Ipswich colliers in 1724. It would seem that the glories of the old coasting trade were in the past as far as Ipswich was concerned, for he told how 'the ships wore out, the masters died off, the trade took a new turn, Dutch fly boats taken in the war and made free ships by Act of Parliament thrust themselves into the coal trade for the interest of the captors, such as the Yarmouth and London merchants, and others, and the Ipswich men gradually dropped out of it.' Certainly the port of Ipswich was facing a long period of depression which would come to an end only with the advent of the nineteenth century and the construction of a wet dock that was the biggest on the east coast.

The coasting trade went on, however. In 1743 an Ipswich-built catt, described in the advertisement as *The Good Ship Humphry* of 300 tons, was for sale at Lloyd's Coffee House in Lombard Street, London, that gathering-place of merchants and shipowners that was to give rise to a great marine insurance organisation. The *Humphry* was said to carry about twenty keels of coals, meaning that her spacious hold would take the cargoes of twenty of the Tyne keels that brought the coal downriver from the collieries.[2]

Opposite: A sloop-rigged barge depicted by E.W. Cooke in 1828. Instead of having a sprit like many of the later barges she has a boom to the mainsail.

Daniel Defoe blamed the introduction into the coal trade of captured Dutch 'flyboats' taken during the Dutch wars for what he termed 'the present pretended decay of the town of Ipswich'.[3] Later in the century during the long-sustained hostilities with France and countries subjugated by Napoleon Bonaparte British warships took as prizes many small trading vessels that were acquired by British owners and registered as British ships; not a few came on to the Ipswich and Woodbridge registers with names that did not betray their foreign origin.

A fairly typical case was that of the brigantine *Gunilde Maria*, taken by the 18-gun sloop HMS *Calypso* on 7th July 1812 and soon afterwards registered at Woodbridge as the *Friends Goodwill*. In 1819 she was rebuilt, being lengthened by ten feet, and appeared in the register as a snow, that is a two-masted vessel square-rigged on both masts similar to a brig but with a secondary mast attached to the mainmast carrying the fore-and-aft spanker. She was later re-registered at Ipswich and was described as a schooner when sold to William Boutland, shipbuilder, of Bill Quay, County Durham, in 1851.

The port of Ipswich seen from Stoke Hill at the time of which Defoe was writing: a section of the well-known prospect published by the brothers Samuel and Nathaniel Buck in 1741.

The billyboy *Eva* of Lowestoft, built at Allerton in Yorkshire in 1872, anchored in the lower part of the Deben. At extreme right another billyboy lies on the shingle, possibly loading ballast.

She was re-registered at Newcastle the following year, and lost with her crew in the North Sea in November 1861.[4]

Another vessel bearing the name *Friends Goodwill* – there were four of that name in the Ipswich register at the same time – was a sloop of 47 tons, formerly known as the *Springeren*, taken by HM hired armed cutter *Princess of Wales* on 10th July 1810. Registered at Woodbridge in that year and later at Ipswich, she was lost off Orfordness on 23rd June 1847.

Then there was the sloop *Dolphin*, which came on to the Ipswich register after being taken by the hired armed cutter *Swan* and condemned as a prize in 1810. The *Swan* was herself captured by the French in 1811, and the *Dolphin* was lost on the Yorkshire coast near Flamborough Head in 1828 after springing a leak; happily the crew survived.

The snow *Hoppet*, renamed *Avis* under British ownership, was captured in 1811 by the 44-gun 5th rate HMS *Fisgard*, formerly the French *Resistance*, captured off Brest in March 1797 by the *San Fiorenzo* and *Nymphe*, both of them also captured French ships.

Several of the prizes were described in the register as schoots, no doubt an anglicised rendering of the Dutch schuyt, and another was said to be a galliot. A number of them had a feature not common among English coasting vessels, a raised quarterdeck which doubtless provided accommodation for the master, perhaps his family, and some at least of the crew.

Following the opening up of the South Yorkshire coalfield and the development of the new port of Goole at the confluence of the rivers Don and Ouse numerous cargoes of coal came south from there, many of them in craft with the resounding name of billyboys. A seagoing version of the Humber keel, the billyboy was a bluff-bowed, flat-bottomed vessel whose sailing qualities were notoriously poor; early examples were usually sloop rigged, later ones often being rigged as ketches or schooners. A pair of billyboys is said once to have taken three weeks to sail from the Humber to Yarmouth with their cargoes of Yorkshire coal.

A billyboy moored in the River Blyth awaiting the tide to enable her to reach her intended berth at Blackshore. In the right background can be seen the harbour entrance, later greatly improved.

Their bluff bows and rounded sterns, their flat bottoms and their use of leeboards[5] have led some people to claim a Dutch ancestry for the billyboys, but it is a claim that cannot stand up to inspection. While their lineage might stretch back into the Middle Ages, there is little doubt that their origin is to be found on the east coast of Britain and not on the far side of the North Sea.

Many of the earlier billyboys were, like some of the fishing luggers built in Yarmouth and Lowestoft, clinker-built up to the wales, with the topsides constructed carvel fashion. The reason for this seems to have been that the old builders, accustomed to build in the northern tradition of setting out the planking and afterwards fitting the timbers when planking up was completed, found it simpler to achieve the required form of the ship's bottom by the old method than by setting up the frames before planking up. Once the bottom was formed to their satisfaction the frames could be set in place and the topside planking of heavier scantling offered up to the frames.

The name of this type of coasting vessel appears to have originated in the port of Kingston-upon-Hull, where many of them were owned. In the seventeenth century the men of Hull were great adherents of Dutch William, who with his wife Mary ascended the English throne in 1688; his statue, covered with gold leaf, is to be seen in the town's market place to this day. This loyalty to William III led to the town's inhabitants being nicknamed Billy Boys; as has happened elsewhere, the men's nickname became transferred to the craft in which they sailed.

The fact that the majority of these vessels were built in Yorkshire and Lincolnshire should not blind us to the fact that some were built and owned in Suffolk ports. The *Heart of Oak* was built at Southwold in 1836 and traded to that port for many years, and William Taylor at Woodbridge built the billyboy sloop *Charlotte* in 1843 and the *Laura* the following year. One of the later steel-hulled billyboys, the ketch *Halcyon*, built at Hessle on the Humber in

A sloop-rigged billyboy with square foresail and topsail making four or five knots off the Suffolk coast, as portrayed by Roger Finch. It used to be said of the billyboys that 'you'll starve afore ye drown in them'.

1903, was owned in the 1930s by Edward Pudney of Beccles; she and the ketch *Mavis*, built of iron at Beverley in 1896, traded on the east coast as motor vessels when the era of sail was at an end.

With their somewhat ungainly hulls and inefficient sailplan the billyboys proved no match for the spritsail barges and ketch barges that developed in Suffolk and the area of the Thames Estuary. Whereas the billyboys had flat bottoms and round bilges, the barges had flat bottoms meeting the side planking at a chine, a very different form of construction. The term sailing barge covers a variety of different types from little ditch-crawlers no more than 40ft or 50ft long to three-masted schooners and even barquentines three times the size. The craft seen racing today on the Orwell, Colne and Blackwater each summer are all spritsail barges, rigged with a sprit mainsail; that is, instead of the gaff and boom of most vessels the sail is extended by a sprit running diagonally from foot to peak. The sail is not lowered when not in use but is brailed up rather in the nature of a theatre curtain.

The barge as we know it seems to have been born in the eighteenth century, although it undoubtedly has an ancestry going back to Roman times. A barge of the Roman occupation period discovered in the mud of the Thames between the bridges at Blackfriars was excavated by Peter Marsden, then of the Guildhall Museum in London. He found that like another discovered in Bermondsey in 1958 it did not fit into the same scheme of development as other ships investigated in northern Europe.

As Peter Marsden says, there is every reason to believe that these two sailing vessels found in different parts of London were built by native shipwrights according to a local tradition that survived into the occupation period.[6] It might be fanciful to suggest such a thing, but these two seagoing cargo-carriers – the Blackfriars ship had a cargo of Kentish ragstone apparently brought from the Maidstone area – look surprisingly like the far-distant ancestors of the Thames and Medway barges of the nineteenth and twentieth centuries; both had the side strakes meeting the bottom at a chine.

However that might be, rather box-like spritsail barges were certainly employed on the Thames, and on the coast of Essex, in the eighteenth century. Edward Cooke shows several such vessels in his *Shipping and Craft*, published in 1828, and Philip Kershaw discovered in the library of the National Maritime Museum a certificate of registry of a barge built at Chelsea in 1788 and subsequently registered at Colchester. This vessel, the *Betsey*, of which Adam Glendining Jnr. was master and part-owner when she was re-registered at Colchester in 1825, was described on the certificate in the following terms:

> That the said Ship or Vessel has One Deck and One Mast, that her length from the fore part of the Main Stem to the after part of the Stern Post is Fifty seven feet five inches her breadth at the broadest part taken above the Main Wales is Seventeen feet five inches her Depth in the Hold is Five feet three inches that she is Barge rigged, with a Standing Bowsprit, and Lee Boards; is Square sterned Carvel built; has neither Galleries, nor figurehead.[7]

There is a typical spritsail barge of the eighteenth-century pattern, sloop rigged, though from the description on the certificate we cannot say whether

A swim-headed sailing barge of the 1820s seen in an etching by E.W. Cooke. Her bowsprit is steeved up when working the confined and crowded waters of the Thames. The hemp rigging appears much more bulky than wire rigging such as William Read fitted to the *Mary*, which he built at Ipswich in 1848.

she had a sprit or the more standard gaff; both were employed by the barges shown in Cooke's etchings.

Frank Carr in his classic book *Sailing Barges* quotes Charles Woodruff, who was born in 1842 and went to sea at the age of twelve. 'There were no boomies when I was a boy. Billyboys, smacks, brigs and schooners came to Woodbridge in those days. Later on, little barges started to creep round. We called them ditch-crawlers.' However, places like Maldon were building barges in the 1830s, when the *Rogue in Grain* (did ever a barge have a more charming name? asks Frank Carr), a swim-headed spritty, was built there. The 45-ton *Rogue in Grain* had a long life; launched in 1838, she was still in the register at the end of the century when she was owned by Jonah Chambers, of Poplar.

A swim-headed spritsail barge of the first half of the nineteenth century running before the wind, seen in an etching by Edward William Cooke. She sets a large squaresail and square tops'l and the bowsprit has been steeved up, the setting of a jib being unnecessary in such circumstances. The usual crew of a barge of this size was two men; in this case there appear to be three, but one might be a 'passenger'.

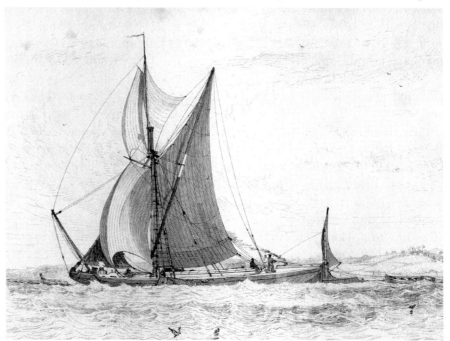

During the 1840s and 1850s great improvements were made in the hull design of barges, and the stem head began to take the place of the swim, that blunt sloping bow that later characterised the steel lighters seen in their hundreds in London River. The run was hollowed out and the lines of the vessel improved all round. A factor in this development was the introduction of barge racing at Harwich during the 1840s and some years later on the Thames, where the enthusiasm of Henry Dodd, 'The Golden Dustman' as he was nicknamed, led to the holding of annual matches, in the second of which no fewer than forty barges competed.

There were only three entries in the first recorded barge race, organised as part of the Eastern Coast Regatta at Harwich on 18th September 1844. The first prize of £5 was won by the *Ironsides*, of Ipswich, with the *Victoria* of London coming a close second and the *Ceres* of London coming in third after a very spirited race.

The name *Ironsides*, today carried by a barge built in 1899, was an appropriate one, for the winner of that first barge match was one of the earliest barges to be built of the new material, iron. She was also one of the barges employed on the Stowmarket Navigation, which had been opened in 1793.

The navigation is described in the Admiralty *North Sea Pilot* of 1905: 'From Ipswich the inland navigation is continued by Gipping river to Stowmarket a distance of nearly 16 miles. Three quarters of a mile above Ipswich the Orwell is connected with the Gipping by a lock. The Gipping has been canalized and has 15 locks; it is used by barges having a maximum length of 55 feet, width 14 feet, and draught 3 feet; the headway under bridges 7 feet'.

Those early barges were towed up and down the river by horse, but on arrival below Stoke Bridge at Ipswich they were able to raise their masts and sails and proceed down the Orwell to the open sea. It is clear that around the middle of the nineteenth century a direct trade was being carried on between Stowmarket and London in these small sailing barges.

The *Ironsides* was built by Read & Page at Ipswich, where a number of iron vessels were launched in the early 1840s. Her master was killed when he fell overboard and was crushed between the barge's hull and a bridge on the

The first barge match taking place off Harwich in 1844, with the iron-built Ipswich barge *Ironsides* in the lead.

Stowmarket quay as it was in 1838, seen in an etching by Henry Davy. In the foreground a crane is being used to unload the salt barge *Friends*.

The little sailing barge *Cygnet* at Palace Quay on the Stour about 1910.

Stowmarket Navigation as the barge came downriver with a cargo of ale; by an evil twist of fate the man's son was washed off the deck of the same barge in the Swin only a month later on Christmas Eve 1841.[8]

Another barge working up to Stowmarket was the *Gipping*, also an iron vessel built at Ipswich in 1842 by Read & Page and said when advertised for sale in 1847 to have been 'constantly employed in conveying goods between London and Stowmarket'; her first owner was the Stowmarket brewer John Stevens, who used barges to carry his India pale ale[9] to London. She was lost off Orfordness in 1870.

The partners in the firm of Read & Page were William Read, who had earlier been shipbuilder Jabez Bayley's foreman, and blockmaker Enos Page. Besides building the two iron sailing barges the firm built the iron steamer *Orion* for the Ipswich Steam Navigation Company in 1840. The introduction of new technology is always fraught with a certain amount of difficulty, and it was reported at the time that the *Orion* 'would have been launched much earlier had the men employed upon the iron part of the vessel been more disposed to hard work. Some of them, strangers to the town and neighbourhood, were, in consequence of not giving satisfaction, discharged, and others left of their own accord.'[10]

Read was most certainly an innovator. When he built the barge *Mary* at Halifax yard in 1848 he gave her wire rigging, something new at that time for a small vessel. Two years later he disposed of his business to Thomas Harvey & Son, a firm that had been building on the Colne in Essex since 1832.

The owners of the Stowmarket barges complained strongly at the failure of the Ipswich Dock Commissioners to provide a second lock at the north end of the new Wet Dock as a short cut for barges coming down from Stowmarket or leaving the dock to proceed up the navigation. The Trustees of the Stowmarket Navigation had made representations to the Commissioners in 1836, when the dock was first proposed, asking them to 'admit the Stowmarket Trade into the Dock at the Bridge end. . .otherwise a serious injury will be sustained by those whose interests we are bound to protect', and in 1841 they even offered to contribute a moderate sum 'to meet the expenses attending its accomplishment'. Their entreaties fell on deaf ears, and in 1842 the barge owners complained that the new lock, half way along the New Cut, was regularly causing the barges to miss a tide. Whereas they had formerly been able to reach the Ipswich quays, discharge their cargo and return upriver on the same tide, they were now often forced to wait until the next tide. Even when they were able to leave the dock on the same tide they could not get up to the first river lock at Handford Bridge because of the fast-ebbing tidal current.[11]

Apart from being built of iron, these sailing barges working on the Gipping were fairly typical of the smaller barges working along the Suffolk coast and into the Deben, Orwell and Stour. One of the smallest barges in trade was the 25-ton *Fairy*, built at Limehouse on the Thames in 1861 and owned by William Groom of Harwich, which made regular trips from Harwich into the Walton Backwaters and was often to be seen in Ipswich Dock. A surviving example of the small barge that made use of the farm wharves on the Orwell and Stour is the *Cygnet* of Harwich, built at Frindsbury on the Medway in 1881 and of only 16 tons; she was owned for many years by the Wrinches of

Erwarton, on the Shotley peninsula, who used her to carry grain from their farm to Marriages' mill at Felixstowe and Cranfield Brothers' mills at Ipswich, from where she usually returned with cattle feed.

At a time when transport in London was largely dependent on the horse the stack trade from Suffolk and Essex was vital to London's economy. Without a constant supply of fodder and straw for bedding in the stables life in the City and its expanding suburbs, Southwark, Chelsea, Elephant and Castle and the rest, would have ground to a halt. A whole fleet of barges, many of them specially built for the stack work, went up through the London bridges to Vauxhall and other upriver wharves with hay and straw and returned with an equally vital cargo, London muck. The sweepings of the London streets and the soiled straw from the stables provided the Essex and Suffolk farmers with a valuable source of manure for their fields.

It was an old-established trade, for when Richard Rigby, the swashbuckling politician who at his death in 1788 was said to have 'left near half a million of public money', began to develop the village of Mistley a part of the quay was set aside for the heaps of manure brought coastwise from the great city. The steaming muckheaps can be seen in an eighteenth-century print of 'Mr. Rigby's seat', the new Mistley Hall built by the politician's father, also Richard.

In the middle of the nineteenth century a report to the General Board of Health revealed that the manure then cost about £10 per barge-load of 40 tons when it was unloaded at Mistley. Unfortunately it sometimes lay on the quay for weeks before being removed by the farmers, and the stench was said to be well-nigh intolerable.

Cargoes of hay and straw were despatched from, and return cargoes of 'muck' were unloaded at, a number of places on the north bank of the Stour between Stutton and Shotley. An old painting shows a little ship lying alongside a quay beside Stutton New Mill, and there was a landing place below Crowe Hall at Stutton, marked as Graham's Wharf on the OS map; it apparently took its name from William Isaac Graham, who farmed nearby Crepping Hall in the 1890s. At the head of Holbrook Creek was a busy quay that sent away cargoes of bricks from the nearby Holbrook Creek Brick Works as well as many a cargo of hay, and further downriver barges loaded at Erwarton Ness, where the 1881 Ordnance Survey first edition 25-inch map shows a hardway

The little barge *Fairy*, owned by William Groom of Harwich, seen in Ipswich Dock. Built at Limehouse by Surridge and Hartnell in 1861, she was of only 25 registered tons. She was sold to the Great Eastern Railway in 1920 to be sunk as a breakwater.

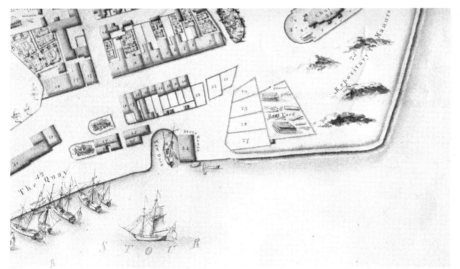

Mistley quay and the manure heaps next door to the deal yard.

Two stackie barges that
have just come through the
London bridges; one of them
is already hoisting its mast –
it is possible to see the gap in
the deck cargo where bales
have been removed to allow
the mast to be lowered. In
the background can be seen
the Bankside shot towers.

running out across the mudflats with two mooring posts at the foot of a lane from Ness Farm. Later there was a timber jetty at this point.

The 1881 map shows a solitary habitation at the foot of Dawson's Lane, Erwarton, which it names John All Alone's, some 200 yards north of the site of St Clement's Chapel. The creek which once ran up to Beaumont Hall but had been dammed by the time of the map is marked as John All Alone's Creek, and it was this creek that was used by the stackie barges belonging to Walter Wrinch.

A little further downriver is Waterhouse Creek, in which is another barge quay paved with chalk and stoutly revetted with timber. Here Harwich fishing boats and other craft called to fill their water casks from the stream flowing down from the fish ponds near Erwarton Hall – the *er* is pronounced as in *clerk* and the name was formerly written with a capital *A*. In the eighteenth century there was a pump in close proximity to the quay, apparently installed by Sir Philip Parker, Bart., who was at the beginning of the century MP for Harwich;

A laden stackie barge,
possibly Wrinch's *Bluebell*,
and the little *Cygnet* at
Erwarton quay.

at that pump 'water shoots' – an anglicisation of the Dutch word schuyts – filled their tanks for transfer to Harwich, whose own water supply was brackish.[12] The 'shoots' were also employed by brewer Thomas Cobbold to supply his Harwich brewery, and it might have been Cobbold who had them built.

There were other places at which barges loaded and unloaded their cargoes within the parish of Shotley, including Hare's Creek in the Orwell; it took its name from Joseph Hare, who farmed nearby in the 1850s. There was a quay at the head of the creek, and close to that quay was a small brickfield that contributed the occasional load of new bricks.

The Wrinches were, and still are, prominent members of the farming community in the Shotley peninsula, Charles Edward at Freston, Robert at Nether Hall, Harkstead, and Walter at Ness Farm, Erwarton. As well as being a farmer Walter Wrinch was a considerable bargeowner, with a fleet of barges largely employed in the hay and straw trade. Besides the little *Cygnet* he had the *Bluebell*, *Butterfly*, *Havelock*, *Primrose*, *Snowdrop* and *Victoria*; the last-named was the oldest of the fleet, having been built at Faversham in 1864.

Another of Walter Wrinch's barges was the *Farmer's Boy* of Harwich, which Frank Carr tells us in his *Sailing Barges* was reputed to have carried fifty-two cargoes of hay to the Thames and brought back the same number of cargoes of manure within fifty-two weeks when commanded by Ben Keeble. Considering that during the period the *Farmer's Boy* had spent two weeks on the yard refitting, that is an average of rather more than one round trip a week.

Frank Carr says it was a record that was never equalled. This is not surprising when one realises that the barge took its cargoes upriver to Vauxhall, and before it could pass under the Thames bridges the mast and gear had to be lowered; trusses of hay had to be removed from the middle of the stack and put aside to make a space into which the mast and sprit could be dropped. Once alongside the wharf the mast and gear had to be laboriously raised so that unloading could commence, and then had to be lowered again so that the barge could shoot the bridges on the way down.

One might have thought that a ten or twelve-foot stack above the deck did nothing to improve the sailing qualities of a small vessel, but the stackies proved quite capable of turning to windward up the crowded Thames; their masters knew how to get the best out of a barge. Chubb Horlock in his book *Mistleyman's Log* recalls seeing the *Farmer's Boy* 'gallantly battling her way up to the Mud Hole at Wapping to lower down her gear'.

And back in Suffolk the cargo of 'muck' had to be shovelled out into carts, a laborious task that might take more than a day. Occasionally the men shovelling out the odiferous manure would obtain a welcome bonus in the form of lost coins among the muck. From the quay the 'London mixture' would be taken to the fields and deposited in heaps that could be spread out over the land and later ploughed in.

A particular style of barge was developed for the stack trade, wide in the beam and with little sheer; a wide, flat deck provided the best foundation for a stack. John Howard, the Maldon shipbuilder, excelled in designing stackies that were shapely little craft. Hervey Benham records that one of Howard's stackies, Walter Wrinch's *Butterfly*, had a song written in her honour:

> As dainty as a butterfly, as fair as a queen,
> The prettiest little stack barge that ever was seen.[13]

Unloading a stackie at a London wharf.

A sailing barge with a stack just loaded at Waldringfield on the Deben. A little further upstream another barge lies close to the cement works, which both received cargoes of chalk from Kent and mud from the river and sent bags of cement away by barge.

A hay baling press in use preparing bales for loading into a stackie barge.

A laden stackie barge, thought to be Wrinch's *Bluebell*, about to set out from the Stour for the voyage to London. The mainsail and foresail have both been reefed so that they clear the stack,

Captain Hazell Polley, who was for many years chairman of Brightlingsea Town Council and came of a long line of coastal seamen, told a chauvinist bargemen's joke about the stackies. If a skipper quarrelled with his mate, or if the mate left him for a better berth, he was in trouble because a stackie cannot be sailed single handed; someone must keep a lookout from the top of the stack. One skipper found the answer; when his mate walked out on him he took his wife for a trip, put her on the tiller while he conned the ship from the top of the stack, and placed the broom on one side and the mop on the other. His helm orders, shouted from aloft on the stack, were 'Hard-a-mop!' or 'Hard-a-broom!'[14]

A stackie barge makes its way up the Thames, with St Paul's Cathedral in the background. Instead of the normal sprit mizzen this barge sets a standing lug on the mizzen.

John Cann with a skeleton half-model of a bawley built on the J. & H. Cann yard at Harwich. Such half-models were an essential part of the design process, but the belief that ships and boats were built direct from the half-model is in many cases erroneous. This style of half-model, consisting of a backboard on which the outline of the profile was drawn and wooden sections cut to the shape of the sections drawn on the plan were erected on the board at the correct positions on the profile, was made after the hull lines had been draughted. The wooden stem, keel, deadwood and transom were then added and longitudinal battens, representing ribbands, were bent around the sections and fastened at stem and stern rebates. The model gave an experienced eye a good idea of the final form of the hull.

In 1937 Sydney W. Wrinch still had two barges at work, the *Bluebell* and the *Cygnet*. It was the *Bluebell* that took away the last stack from the Stour in 1936 or 1937; she was later sold for conversion to a yacht barge, but the conversion did not take place. On the outbreak of the Second World War she was requisitioned by the Admiralty and became a degaussing vessel under the name of HMS *Torchbearer*, with the task of 'wiping' ships to render them immune to magnetic mines.

The Ipswich-registered *Bluebell* was built at Rochester in 1888, but many barges were built at Ipswich and at Harwich. At that Essex port the Cann family had a yard at the head of Gashouse Creek from which were launched, among others, the *Florence* in 1877, *Haste Away* in 1886, *Freston Tower* in 1889, *May* and *Marjorie* in 1891, *Felix* in 1893, *Centaur* in 1895, *Kimberley* in 1900, *Memory* in 1904 and the little *Leofleda* in 1914. The business was started about 1868 by George Cann, who had served his time with Robert Aldous at Brightlingsea.

Besides building spritsail barges the firm produced a number of bawleys both for Harwich fishermen and for those at Leigh, on Canvey Island; Cann's also built the Norfolk and Suffolk type lifeboat *Sailors' Friend* for Frinton. About thirty men worked on the yard, including father and son sawyers

A barge in Holbrook Creek loading a cargo for London.

The sailing barge *Kimberley* being launched sideways from the yard of J. & H. Cann at Harwich in 1900.

Stephen and Jim Ainger and the Pennicks, also father and son, who made sails in a loft above the sawpit. The yard's steamchest in which planks were placed to make them supple was supplied with waste steam from the adjacent gasworks.

John Cann and his brother Herbert took over the business when their father George died in 1889 from injuries sustained in an accident while unloading timber from a railway truck. John, who was an able shipwright and naval architect but knew little of business, consulted his uncle Garling Cann, and as a result Herbert, who was then a corporal serving at the Curragh in Ireland, was bought out of the Army to manage the business. Besides doing the bookkeeping Herbert was responsible for the production of 14ft clinker barge boats, of which one was turned out each week on spec. and sold to the Horlocks and other bargeowners both locally and on the Thames.

Cann barges were always fitted out on the yard right down to pots and pans, cutlery and everything in the cabin. The last things put in were a cigar and a box of matches on the cabin table – for the skipper.

John and Herbert were men of uncompromising conscientiousness. The story is told of how John noticed a

A spritsail barge sailing into the French port of Boulogne. The barges, including some from Ipswich, did well in the continental trade during the First World War carrying coal and coke at very profitable rates.

tiny spot of sap in a pitchpine keelson being put into the Faversham barge *Orion*, later renamed *Gold Belt*; the owners were quite satisfied, but John was not, and he had it cut up into planks that went into a new ceiling for her hold.

The boomie barge *Pearl*, built at Ipswich by Orvis and Fuller in 1889 and owned at the time this picture was painted by shipbuilder William Harvey Orvis. The painting is by Reuben Chappell, who originated in Goole but continued to sign his pictures 'R. Chappell of Goole' after moving to Par in Cornwall.

It was not often that an owner found fault with a barge built by J. & H. Cann. Once, though, an owner brought back his new barge, complaining that she was leaking. She was put on the blocks in the creek and nothing much was found wrong with her, so the owner was told that wherever possible the seams had been caulked and she should be all right. But back he came at the end of the next voyage with a story that the barge was still leaking.

John, who was young and inexperienced at that time, went to Uncle Garling for advice. Uncle told him to put it on the blocks and carry out a thorough inspection. 'Tell me what you find wrong – don't tell the owner,' were his instructions. John could find nothing wrong, and told his uncle so.

When the owner turned up he was told 'You'd better go along and see Uncle Garling.' On his arrival Uncle Garling gave him the choice: 'There's your barge, here's her value,' and held out a cheque. The owner chose the barge.[15]

Barges were also built on the old Navy Yard at Harwich by two generations of the Vaux family and then by the McLearons, who struggled on into the bad years after the First World War, losing money year by year until bankruptcy closed the yard.[16]

The sprit rig is a very handy one for river work and for comparatively short coastal voyages such as from London to Ipswich or Yarmouth, and a very economical one. It was these qualities that enabled the spritties to remain in trade long after almost all other sailing vessels had gone out of use; it was still possible to see a small fleet of sailing barges loading or unloading their

Two sailing barges, one a ketch barge and the other a smaller spritsail barge, at Remagen on the Rhine above Cologne to load Apollinaris water before the 1914-18 war, the outbreak of which trapped the ketch barge *Carisbrooke Castle* and the sprittie *Tintara*, both of which were interned along with their crews.

Seen here newly launched, the ketch barge *Lord Tennyson* was built by Orvis and Fuller at Ipswich in 1891 for London owners.

cargoes in Ipswich Dock in the 1950s. It is, though, less suitable for longer coastwise and continental trading, the weight of gear aloft making the spritty an uncomfortable craft when lying at anchor in the Downs or some other exposed anchorage.

Although during the 1914-18 war spritties traded regularly to the French Channel ports[17] and many of the bigger spritties like the Yarmouth-built quartet of *Everard* barges engaged in the coal trade from Keadby and Goole, the boomie with a gaffsail that was lowered to the deck when furled was more suitable for long-distance coastal and continental work. Some owners reverted in the 1840s to the sloop rig, with a big gaff mainsail and a jackyard tops'l. Then in 1857 Hartnell & Surridge at Limehouse built the *Flower of Essex*, probably for John Watts of Harwich, with a small mizzen converting what would otherwise have been a sloop-rigged barge into what seamen termed a dandy. It was at that same period that the big fishing smacks working from East Anglian ports were in many cases being lengthened and turned from cutters into dandies.

The east coast owners were looking for shallow-draught vessels as a substitute for the schooners like the *Bernard Barton* that had predominated in the coasting trade up to then. They found what they wanted in the boomie barge, the first of which, the *Stour*, was built by John Vaux at Harwich in the same year that the *Flower of Essex* was built on the Thames, possibly by no mere coincidence for a Harwich owner. The *Stour* was to all intents and purposes a flat-bottomed schooner, with a clipper bow and counter stern, and high bulwarks – what old seamen termed 'a schooner with the bottom cut orf'.

Before long many such craft, mainly ketch rigged but including a number of schooners, were being turned out by shipbuilders at Brightlingsea, Maldon, Harwich, Ipswich and Yarmouth, where the *Garson* was launched by Mills & Blake in 1864. Ipswich builders launched a whole line of graceful ketch barges such as the *Lothair*, built for a Rye owner in 1872, the *Alice Watts*, 1875, *Lucy Richmond*, 1875, and *Pearl*, 1889. They also built the *Lord Shaftesbury* in 1886, *Lord Hartington*, 1887, *Lord Iddesleigh*, 1888, and *Lord Tennyson*, 1891, all of them owned by the English and Continental Shipping Company of London, who also had a number of boomies with the names of other noble lords built at Littlehampton on the south coast in the same period.

Undoubtedly the handsomest of all the ketch barges was the *Record Reign* of Maldon, built at Maldon in the year of Queen Victoria's diamond jubilee by Howard & Son for Joseph Sadler of that town. She was designed to be of the largest dimensions to allow her to work into Heybridge Basin, where timber was unloaded into canal barges that took it up the Chelmer and Blackwater Navigation to Chelmsford, but John Howard had drawn out her beautiful counter to such an extent that it proved impossible to close the lock gates behind her when she was deep loaded. She was taken into the Royal Navy for conversion into a Q-ship during the First World War.

One of the last boomies to be launched and the last to continue trading was the *Martinet*, built at Rye in 1912. A barge with a somewhat evil reputation, she foundered off Aldeburgh in 1941 while under the command of Bob Roberts, well known as a resident of Pin Mill on the Orwell in the 1950s and 60s. The last boomie of all to be built, the *Moultonian*, was launched from the

Looking very much like an early nineteenth century trading barge, the *Montreal* making her way downriver during a Pin Mill Sailing Club Barge Match, followed by the *Scone*, which was built as late as 1919. In fact the *Montreal* is a swim-headed London River lighter converted by enthusiasts into a sailing barge.

Littlehampton yard of J. & W.B. Harvey in 1919; by that time no fewer than twenty-nine such barges had been built there.

The boomies could go almost anywhere. They went up the Rhine to Remagen to load Apollinaris water, a once-popular mineral water; they brought coal from the Tyne to gasworks at Harwich and Ipswich; they carried Portland stone for building work in London and elsewhere; and three of them even sailed out to British Guiana between 1920 and 1930 to work out of Georgetown, Demerara.[18]

When working on the second edition of his book *Sailing Barges* Frank Carr compiled a list of more than 150 barges trading under sail in June 1949, not a few of them being fitted with auxiliary engines. In succeeding years many of them lost their sailing gear and were operated as fully-powered motor barges, and by 1970 the big mulie *Cambria* was the only barge trading under sail. In that year her skipper-owner, Bob Roberts, brought a cargo to the Eastern Counties Farmers' premises in Ipswich Dock and announced that he had decided to hand her over to the Maritime Trust for preservation.

That was the end of trading under sail, but barges can still be seen on the Orwell and Stour. Instead of cargo they are now fitted to carry a limited number of passengers, and each summer some of them take part in barge races at Pin Mill and elsewhere, providing spectators with a welcome reminder of days when sailing barges were an important part of the British merchant fleet.

Schooner.

The coasting trade   11

To a great extent the coasting trade was a trade with London, that Great Wen that according to Defoe sucked the vitals of the surrounding counties. Defoe comments that 'this whole kingdom, as well the people as the land, and even the sea. . .are employed to furnish something, and I may add, the best of everything, to supply the city of London with provisions'.[1] Many of those provisions reached London by sea.

Golding Constable, artist John's father, the miller of Dedham and East Bergholt, owned a little sloop, the *Telegraph*, in which he oftentimes sent the flour ground in his mills from Mistley to London; the sacks of flour had been taken down the Stour in the river barges shown to such good effect in John's paintings and transhipped into coasting vessels at Mistley Quay.

At Ipswich a whole community of windmills and watermills turned out flour not just for local consumption but for export to London and elsewhere. When a postmill at Halifax, on the west bank of the Orwell not far from Bourne Bridge at Ipswich, was for sale in 1843 the advertisement noted how conveniently situated it was for the 'export trade'.[2]

Malt made in the maltings of Mistley, Ipswich, Snape and other places went by coasting vessel to supply the London breweries, while grain grown in the Suffolk fields went not only to London but to many other ports around the British coasts. When in the nineteenth century the expansion of the malting trade in East Anglia outstripped the supply of home-grown barley sailing barges brought imported barley loaded overside from ships in the London docks to fill the garners of the riverside maltings.

The coal trade remained an important one and continued in the nineteenth century to employ a good many of the craft registered and owned in East Anglian ports. In 1847 no fewer than forty-seven vessels arrived at Ipswich with coal in a single week; the cargoes probably totalled little more than 5,000 tons, an average of only a little over 100 tons a ship. When the barque *Ruth* of Ipswich brought 450 tons in one trip in 1848 her arrival excited comment because of the unusual size of the cargo. This vessel was lost off the Irish coast in 1849 when on her way from Ipswich to New Brunswick for a cargo of Canadian timber – a reminder that those same vessels that sailed week by week in the coasting trade might at suitable times set off for ports in Europe or in the Mediterranean, in North America or some other far-flung part of the world.

In that year, 1849, no fewer than 1,312 coasting vessels totalling 97,350 tons were recorded inwards at Ipswich and 718 vessels totalling 38,320 tons

Opposite: A schooner of about 1830 seen in one of E.W. Cooke's incomparable etchings. The *Perseverance*, which was built at Walberswick on the Blythe in 1803, was probably very similar.

A watercolour by H.W. Hart of the schooners *Bernard Barton* and *Ramson* at Woodbridge in 1886.

Unloading a collier by whipping out, portrayed by Edward William Cooke in 1828. The coal is being shot over the side into a lighter.

outwards. The discrepancy is explained by the fact that almost six hundred of the vessels recorded inwards left in ballast, that is, without cargo. The number of vessels owned in Ipswich in 1850 was 186, with a total tonnage of 15,012; the average tonnage of each ship was therefore no more than eighty.

These relatively small ships were greatly dependent on the weather; not only was stormy weather a handicap to trade but a contrary wind might hold up great fleets of sailing vessels in Harwich harbour or Lowestoft Roads. In January 1847 it was reported at Ipswich that the number of vessels in the newly-constructed dock was 'unusually small, the prevailing south-easterly winds having prevented the arrival of much shipping. At the present period about 500 vessels are wind-bound in the Humber – most of them being colliers. The price of coal in Ipswich has in consequence advanced. . .'.[3]

Later in the month the price of coal dropped as the first of the delayed colliers sailed up the Orwell, and then at the beginning of February it was announced that 'there has been a larger number of vessels entered the port this week than at any previous period, there being no less than 41 colliers arrived since our last, out of which number about 30 arrived within the past two days. On Sunday there were not less than 40 sail of vessels under way between the Dock and Downham Reach at tide time.'

It was not only the big ports like Ipswich whose trade fluctuated with the weather; much smaller places like Woodbridge, Aldeburgh and Orford were equally dependent on the strength and direction of the wind. A remarkable

archive of letters, cargo books and business papers in the Suffolk Record Office at Ipswich provides a fascinating insight into the operation of a family firm in the nineteenth century; the collection of documents pertaining to the Mingays and their little fleet of ships operating from Orford is probably unique in the light it sheds on the work of the coasting trade in the days of sail.

George Mingay, who was born at Orford in 1758, became master of the *Enid May*, which belonged to his father, and later took over his father's business. By the time he died at Quay House, Orford, in 1827 he was described as a merchant and gentleman; his grave is to be found in Orford churchyard. His eldest son, another George Mingay, born at Orford in 1783, inherited the business in his turn.

About the time of his father's death the younger George Mingay took into his employ his thirteen-year-old nephew George Rope, who had been born in 1814. George Rope was one of three brothers who all played a significant part in local commerce. His elder brother Samuel, four years his senior, went into the grocery and drapery trade in the town, while his younger brother Edward is described in 1855 as shipowner and wine, spirit, malt, hop, ale, porter and coal merchant; he seems to have done everything, including running the brewery in Quay Street that is now a private house. Both the Ropes and the Mingays were much involved with the corporation, which 'having but a small and unimportant jurisdiction. . .was left untouched by the Municipal Reform Act of 1835';[4] neither family would have agreed with that assessment of the local authority.

At some stage George Rope became George Mingay's partner; in the 1844 directory Mingay & Rope are shown as corn and coal merchants. In that year George Rope acquired shares in several of the Mingay ships, including the sloop *Sophia* and the schooners *Queen Adelaide*, *Dorothea* and *Clementina*. It would seem that George Mingay spent some time in London, and in the 1840s he moved to Croydon, into a newly built dwelling that he named Ore House. From then on a stream of letters passed between him and George Rope, who remained in charge at Orford, though living and farming in the village of Blaxhall, some six miles from the town.[5]

The family firm had diverse business interests, importing coal that was sold from coalyards both in Orford and at Iken Cliff, some miles upriver beyond Slaughden, and acting as corn merchants, besides operating a lime kiln at Orford which supplied local builders and also the area's many farmers. As corn merchants the firm bought at corn markets over a wide area of East Suffolk and sent consignments of grain mainly up to Mark Lane, the London corn market, but also to Newcastle and to Yorkshire markets. At Mark Lane the selling of the corn was overseen by the Woodleys, the Mingays' London agents, with whom the Orford merchants had friendly personal as well as business relations.

Some of the ships were employed very

Laid-up cod smacks at Slaughden Quay, where the Hunt family operated a boatyard throughout the nineteenth century.

largely in the trade with London, sometimes returning with chalk from Kent to supply the Orford lime kiln after unloading corn for Mark Lane. Vessels engaged in the London trade regularly returned also with parcels for shopkeepers in Orford, Aldeburgh and Saxmundham and for well-to-do residents of the area; on occasions furniture was carried from London addressed to local residents. In February 1833 George Rope wrote to Woodleys saying that 'a piano is to go to the wharf shortly for our Rector's Lady will you be good enough to request one of the Capns to ask Mr. Barber to have it taken particular care of'.

One might have hoped that the grain trade would have been a relatively lucrative one, but George Mingay too often found it otherwise. All too frequently, it would seem, prices at Mark Lane failed to provide a profit, sometimes not even reaching the price at which the corn had been bought in Suffolk. Mingay was at times greatly upset by the antics of the London merchants, who were apt to buy grain and then to refuse it on the pretext that it was not up to the sample, in the hopes of acquiring it at a knock-down price.

'I am vexed at the purport of your favor of yesterday viz refusal of Barley,' wrote George Mingay to one of the Woodleys in 1827. 'I wish you could Hang half your buyers probably it might in some measure shy the others. The system is most rascally.

'Herewith are acc of Corn by *Gainsbro*, *Ann & Idas* and a precious acct I fear the Barley one will be. I really dread it. The Corn Trade is just like "Licking Money off Thorns". I am quite sick of it.'[6]

At times his ire was aroused also by the local farmers and graziers who refused to pay the price for linseed oil cake which he imported in his own ships from Rotterdam, where he had regular contact with several firms of merchants. In one letter he complained that the graziers would not take his cakes at £8 10s. a ton, but some of them were prepared to pay him £7; 'I suppose they imagine I stole them,' he added acidly.

Between about 1820 and 1850 the Mingays, father and son, were involved in the ownership and operation of at least fifteen vessels, mainly sloops with a

A schooner and, on the outside, a smack at a wharf on the River Thames. The Mingay vessels regularly traded to such a wharf, where they discharged their cargoes of grain and loaded a variety of goods for tradesmen and residents of Orford and nearby towns and villages.

single mast and two-masted brigantines and schooners. It is notable that they never owned any barges,[7] and when looking for new purchases the younger Mingay did not favour the double-ended billy-boys, of which so many traded from Hull and other ports on the Humber.

The pattern of ownership was typical of nineteenth-century practice, with other members of the family and acquaintances owning varying numbers of shares. Under the 1824 Registration Act the ownership of a vessel was broken down into sixty-four shares which might be divided among several owners in unequal proportions. In the case of the 54-ton sloop *Enterprize*, a prize taken in 1810 during the Napoleonic Wars, the ownership was divided between George Mingay, sen., George Mingay, jun. and Mary Ann Mingay, each having sixteen shares, and William Woodley and Thomas Burrows, the Mingays' London agents, who had sixteen between them.

In 1829 the *Enterprize* underwent an overhaul, the details of which are not recorded. With typical humour George Mingay informed his London agent that the ship had 'had a thorough overhale, a similar operation must be done to the Captain and Mate'.

The *Enterprize* was engaged mainly in the corn trade from Iken Cliff and Orford Quay to London, and each year the owners received a payout varying between £9 15s. and £37 10s. each. By the time she was sold to Thomas Francis, mariner, of Maldon for £105 in 1844 there were only two owners; George Mingay held three-quarters (forty-eight shares) and his sister the other quarter (sixteen shares).

Another sloop, the Woodbridge-built *Idas*, was owned by George Mingay, jun., thirty-six shares, and his cousin George Edward Mingay, sixteen; the other dozen shares were held by Iken farmer Philip French, John Hunt, the Orford baker, and widow Elizabeth Beeden, whose connection to the Mingay family has not been traced.

Only five of the Mingay vessels exceeded 100 tons, the largest of them being the brigantine *Coaster*, built at Southtown, Yarmouth, in 1812 and acquired by George Mingay in 1839 from Mary Barnes of Aldeburgh, John Barnes of Knodishall and William Jessup of Leiston, 'one of those men called Quakers' as he is described in the Aldeburgh shipping register. A brigantine had two masts, the mainmast with square sails and the other with fore-and-aft sails. The brigantine *Gainsborough*, built in 1813 on the Trent in the town whose name she took, was next in terms of size at 112 tons. A third brigantine, the *Œconomy*, of 105 tons, had been built at Whitby in 1788. She was owned by George Mingay jun. and William Woodley until sold to Whitby owners in 1826.

The other two vessels of over 100 tons were both schooners. The older of these, the *Perseverance* of 106 tons, had been built at Walberswick on the River Blyth in 1803 and in 1825 was owned by George Mingay jun, Edward Crisp of Rendlesham, a farmer, John Potter, a Yoxford maltster, and three others who held only eight shares between them. By 1837 Mingay held fifty-six shares, the other eight belonging to Crisp's widow Mary. In 1846 George Rope reported that 'I have given Gibbs orders to broom the Perseverance'; a broom at the masthead was a common indication that a vessel was for sale. The schooner was sold to William Adamson of Sunderland, who sold her on to Robert Alexander of Carrickfergus in the north of Ireland.

From 1830 to 1835 George Mingay owned a half share of the schooner *Commercial Packet*. This vessel had been built at Ferry Port on Craigs in Fife in 1818 and when first registered at Aldeburgh in 1826 she was described as a sloop with a running bowsprit and square stern measuring 70 tons; in 1828, however, she was re-registered after apparently being rebuilt and was then described as a schooner with a standing bowsprit measuring 89 tons. The rebuilding almost certainly involved lengthening the vessel, giving her a greater cargo capacity and thus, hopefully, making her more profitable. Another schooner, the 79-ton *Providence*, had been built at Barton-on-Humber in 1814 and was owned by George Mingay sen, George Mingay jun and William Woodley until sold to Colchester in 1834.

Possibly the expense of maintaining such old vessels persuaded Mingay to have a new vessel built for him, and in 1829 he was casting around for a shipbuilder to build him a schooner. He found what he was seeking in William Bayley, who had moved from Woodbridge to Ipswich in 1826. Bayley built the schooner *Dorothea* of 95 tons for him in 1830 and four years later launched the *Clementina*, another schooner, for him.

The other vessels in the Mingay fleet were all sloops. Newest of them was the *Sophia*, built for George Mingay by William Bayley in 1836. The builder's bill came to £716, but other bills, including two from Ipswich innkeepers, brought the total cost to some £916; the launching was apparently a convivial occasion for her owner's friends. Bayley did not build only little craft like the *Sophia*, which was of only 54 tons, for in the same year that she was launched he also built the snow *Hannah* of 146 tons for Harwich owners.

The *Sophia* got in three voyages to London with corn in the latter months of 1836, producing a net income of £47 13s. 2d, and in the following year made twelve corn voyages and one to Newcastle for coal, producing a net income that year of £236 0s. 3d. It is unlikely that she ever made so much again. Between 1838 and 1841 she paid to her owner an average of £152 a year, but in succeeding years the balance paid to the owner at the end of each year

Shipping, some of it probably arriving from Suffolk ports, in Blackwall Reach in the Thames seen in an etching by E.W. Cooke.

fell markedly, some years actually ending in debt. While always hoping for a payout at the end of a profitable year, those who held shares in a ship needed sufficient capital to meet a proportion of any loss that might be incurred.

In 1844 George Mingay sold twenty-eight of his sixty-four shares in the *Sophia* to his nephew and partner George Rope, who seems to have become sole owner when Mingay died about 1853. There are indications in one of the books[8] that she was re-rigged as a schooner in the earlier part of 1867. In 1869 the *Sophia* was in collision with a ship named in the correspondence the *Nelly*, which necessitated a journey to Shoreham to settle damages. That and the associated shipwright's bill might have contributed to the loss of £48 1s. 2d on the year. There is in Clayton's register of 1865 a barque *Neilly* of Shoreham, 205 tons, built 1855, owned by R.H. Penney of Southwick; possibly this is the vessel with which the *Sophia* collided.

The *Sophia* was still trading for George Rope in 1870. In May that year she took 89 tons of shingle to Hull and 86 tons of salt to Middlesbrough, and brought 20 tons of coal to Orford Quay and 60 tons to Iken Cliff, presumably in one trip; also that year she took coal to Boyton Dock near the mouth of the Butley River, a minor tributary of the Ore.

The other sloops were already more than twenty years old when the *Sophia* was launched from Bayley's yard in 'Carpenter's Row'. The *Ann* had been built at Southtown in 1814 and was broken up at Orford in 1851, while the *Idas* had been built at Woodbridge in the same year. The 53-ton *Plough* was built at Southtown in 1817.

While the correspondence reveals that neither Mingay nor his nephew was overkeen on spending money on their ships, some of which were quite elderly vessels when acquired by them – the *Coaster* was twenty-seven years old when bought by George Mingay in 1839 – there were certainly no 'coffin ships' in the Mingay fleet. Those little vessels sailing from the Ore were well found and well looked after.

Despite the many risks run by vessels using the busy channels of the east coast George Mingay lost only one vessel, the 84-ton schooner *Lucy*, built at Woodbridge in 1816 and owned jointly by George Mingay and William Woodley. She went down with all hands in a severe storm off the Norfolk coast in May 1836. The Marquis of Hertford, who lived at nearby Sudbourne Hall and from time to time made use of the services offered by the Mingay concern, headed the subscription raised for the widows and families of the crew of the *Lucy*, giving £25. The owners of two Tyneside collieries also featured in the list of subscriptions, which in total amounted to £136. In January 1837 one of the widows, Sarah Hunt, made her mark on a receipt for £15 10s. 6d., her share of the amount.[9]

The North Sea weather certainly made life hard and uncertain for those navigating the east coast. In January 1845 George Rope reported the arrival of the *Dorothea* after having had a bad passage up from the North. 'Nottage says she was as near as could be a lost ship on Sunday evening; he brought up under the Barnard [a sandbank off Benacre Ness] in the night, the wind flew round and blowd so he was obliged to let his second anchor go and ride both cables at an end, and was fearful every minute to see the anchors come home or that they would snap as there was so much sea on, but thanks to the almighty she is home safe and nothing but her anchor stock broke, the wood one'. It is interesting to see that in 1845 she was still using a wooden-stocked anchor.

Among the letters George Rope sent on to his uncle is one from Jonathan Simpson, the master of one of the Mingay and Rope ships which had been sheltering in the Yorkshire port of Bridlington. Written in the broadest Suffolk, it is worth quoting in full. The spelling of haraken exactly replicates the Suffolk pronunciation of hurricane.

> Bridlington April 11
>
> Sir I Enform you that I got satled this evening   I should lick to goten the other 10 powns for the Ship they were quit Agreabel to pay for All the damage But they want to have the Ship pay sum of the Salvage   They would goo to law A Bout that but if they had they would af lawst the caws   but I thought it would cawst nearly as much to git off   the Agent sayed it would cawst money And trubel so I thought for the sak of 10 powns I had Beater satel   As I have the Balance left from the Agent's   12 15 0 I have paid for what I have had hear Bakes and Groces   And I gave the hands sumthen Extry for the Trobel.
>
> So I have mearde A Bill of All   And the Balance I Have kept for I want a new Tow Rope very Bad I am A fraid   Of my one it have Broaken three tims. If I had got Towse theas strong winds it would not towed me In   I hop We shall soan git Away Now whe Are All Ready But it have blowed A Haraken hear to day And there have not Bean nothen But gals of wind since I have been hear   the Ships have Bean beaten back to the Bay All moast Every day
>
> I am very tired of Laying hear but I Hop I shall have a fair wind down for owr Ship Rowl very heavy With this stuf in   And She Mearke A Litel Water But nothen searius But I hop I shal soan git to Newcastle
>
> > I Reamain Sir
> > you obedient
> > > Sarvint
> > > J. Simpson
>
> Friday Morning the wheather Is finer I am
> A goan to sea to day If I can git

In the light of evidence from the accounts of the schooner *Queen Adelaide* it appears this letter might be dated 1853 and might relate to that vessel. The accounts of the first voyage in that year include the entry 'To Readhead & others assisting ship into Bridlington Harbour 25.2.6.' A later entry relates to 'Garrod & Turners Bill 1.11.6' which suggests she might have been sold at Ipswich; Garrod & Turner were well-known Ipswich auctioneers, and the *Queen Adelaide* was re-registered at Ipswich in 1854. One of the larger units of the Mingay fleet, the *Queen Adelaide* had been built at Wells in 1830 and initially registered there, but was transferred to the Aldeburgh register in 1834, presumably on being acquired by George Mingay.

In April 1827 George Mingay wrote to a Newcastle shipbuilder, William Boutland, giving him instructions 'to have the Anns main Decks raised which

The ketch barge *Mystery* and other shipping at Snape about 1905. Built at Milton in Kent in 1875, the *Mystery* was owned by Charles Stone of Mistley.

I trust you will do in the best & most reasonable way you are able as the Ann is very flat in the floor'. He adds several suggestions for improving the sloop, which had been built in Southtown, Yarmouth, in 1814, and after leaving it to the ship's master, Captain James Nottage, to superintend the work he ends his letter with the admonition 'Let it be done well'.

In May he wrote again to the shipbuilder approving of the work he had done on the *Ann* and asking 'What will be the expence to Double the providence with Dantzic Fir up to her Bens'. In his letters he often failed to give a ship's name a capital letter. The answer seems to have been satisfactory, and the sloop *Providence*, built at Barton-on-Humber in 1814, was duly attended to, as was the *Idas*, which required caulking and a part new covering board. After having all that work done Mingay seems to have been running short of money; 'pray dont do any thing but what is absolutely essential,' he told the shipbuilder.

Upriver trading

Besides trading to the little quay at the bottom of the street below the church at Orford the Mingay ships took cargoes to a wharf at Iken Cliff, on the Alde midway between Aldeburgh and Snape, which was the head of navigation. The Ore and the Alde are in fact the same river; it is the Ore from its mouth at Shingle Street up past Havergate Island to Orford and beyond, but above Slaughden where the river turns sharply to port it is known as the Alde. Opposite the marshy Cob Island was the brickworks jetty where bricks produced at the Aldeburgh brickworks were loaded for 'export' to Ipswich and London, and above that point the channel becomes narrower and the chances of grounding on the wide mudflats were greater.

It was no easy passage upriver to Iken Cliff and Snape: the naming of Lower Troublesome Reach beyond Iken's isolated church and of Upper Troublesome Reach gives some indication of the difficulties facing those trading to such places. From Upper Troublesome Reach one turned into Cliff Reach, and on the south side was Iken Cliff Wharf, from which at high water one could

A section of an old chart showing the course of the river sailed so often by the Mingay ships to Orford and to Iken. What it does not indicate is the confined channel and shallow water of the upper reaches.

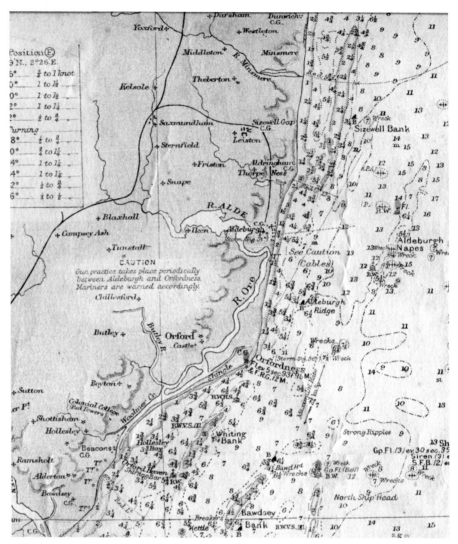

look over half a mile of shallow river; but the shipping channel was only a few yards wide. And it became narrower still as it approached Snape Wharf, where Newson Garrett, brother of ironfounder Richard Garrett of Leiston, was established as merchant and maltster.

Newson Garrett was vice-consul for Norway and Sweden at Aldeburgh, superintendent of pilots and Lloyd's agent. His interests at Snape extended beyond the ownership of the extensive maltings; he was a corn, coal and lime merchant and also brick and whiting manufacturer. He was also a shipowner with a small fleet working from the Alde. That fleet consisted of the sloops *Argo*, *Bengall*, *Endeavour*, *Hope*, *Margaret*, *Ouse* and *Resolution* and the schooners *Percy*, built at Snape in 1860, *Robert & William*, *Salamander* and *Wallace*, plus the smack *Triune*.

Today all trace of the wharf at Iken Cliff has gone, and it is hard to believe that ships once unloaded their cargoes of coal and oilcake and took in cargoes of Suffolk grain destined for London's Mark Lane corn market in such a place. Nor is it easy to visualise the scene at Orford quay as the Mingay ships discharged their cargoes into carts drawn up alongside. There were strict rules governing the use of the quay, the first being that 'Any Vessel that shall arrive *coal laden*, or with any other *heavy* cargo, shall land the same at the Quay. . .'.

The second of the thirteen regulations aimed at facilitating the use of the port was that 'vessels laden with *light goods* will deliver their cargoes at the Quay, and will be allowed to retain the same berth for the space of *two days*, if necessary. . .' And the third was that all vessels that had landed their freight should give up their berths to vessels that had cargoes on board to deliver. Should there be any argument over the rules it was stipulated that the word of the harbourmaster was law.

One November day in 1850 the *Coaster* was alongside the quay and had unloaded some 61 tons of coal, but trade was slow and George Rope was inclined to use her as a floating coal warehouse for the remaining part of her cargo, which did not meet with the approval of other users of the quay. 'Mr. Markin has had to deliver all his cargo over her – at which he is not well pleased,' George reported to his uncle. 'James tells me that about 10 or 15 tons will be wanted tomorrow – and then I will have her go off and moored in the stream again. . .'. Saunders Markin, who was aggrieved at having to cross the decks of the *Coaster* with his goods, was the Orford grocer and draper.

Industrial links

The regular trade of these little ships was down to the north for coal and up to London with Suffolk grain, either wheat or barley, but that was by no means the extent of their trading. After unloading a cargo of coal they would sometimes take in coprolites, those phosphatic nodules that were the raw material of the artificial fertiliser industry, for a Tyneside chemical works.

The cargo book of the *Clementina* reveals intriguing links with local tradesmen and industrialists. In March 1847 she carried a thrashing machine and a seed drill to the Tyne for James Smyth and Son, of Peasenhall. The thrasher went on by rail to the customer in Cumberland, to a farm called Sleightholme, about four miles north-west of Wigtown station, while the drill was 'to be landed at Elleron Quay', wherever that might have been. On the return voyage she carried 100 carboys of vitriol (sulphuric acid) from the Jarrow Chemical Company for Edward Packard, who was at that time producing artificial manure at Snape; he used the acid to break down the coprolites he ground in a steam mill hired from Richard Garrett of Leiston. Also stacked on top of the 65 tons of coal and eight chaldron of coke in the hold were twenty casks of 'soder' (soda) for Joseph Till, the Orford shopkeeper, and four gross of bottles for Mr Rope – presumably Edward Rope rather than George.

Consignments of sulphuric acid were regularly carried on top of the coal as the *Clementina* shuttled back and forth between the Ore and the Tyne; the empty carboys were returned on her trips down to the north. She completed six round trips by the end of July, and on the last of these she brought not just 98 tons of coal for Mr Rope but '2 creats of erthinware' for Robert Turner, glass, china and toy dealer of Aldeburgh.

Returning from Newcastle at the end of October she brought 98 tons of coal, fifty carboys of vitriol for Packard and ten firkins of butter consigned to 'Markin Orford'. In December she went to Hartlepool in ballast and returned

The engineering firm of
Richard Garrett of Leiston
used their own ships to
take employees to the
Great Exhibition in 1851,
utilising them as hostels
for the period they spent in
London. This contemporary
print shows the Suffolk
workers marching off to
Hyde Park behind a brass
band to spend the day
looking around the displays.

with 98 tons of coal for George Rope, then sailed to Newcastle in ballast. Instead of returning to the Ore she took 98 tons of coal to Folkestone for railway use, sailed back to Hartlepool in ballast and took 106 tons of small coal from there to Whitstable.

In 1851 the *Clementina* took a thrashing machine to Newcastle for Richard Garrett's, but that firm had its own vessel, the schooner *Jane*. She was built by William Hunt at Aldeburgh in 1840 to replace another schooner, the *Richard & Sarah*, named after the second Richard Garrett of Leiston and his wife, which was sold that year to Thomas Capon, a Dennington farmer.

When the coalyards at Orford and Iken Cliff were adequately supplied the *Clementina* took her cargoes of coal elsewhere. On more than one voyage she took coal to Folkestone 'for the rail way company', and at other times she sailed to St Valery at the mouth of the Somme or to London, Rochester or Whitstable. Sometimes she and other Mingay vessels were chartered to Tabor & Rankin of Stambridge Mills on the River Roach in Essex to fetch coal from the Tyne for supplying their coalyard.

Arrangements with Tabor & Rankin and other firms elsewhere in Essex were usually made from Orford by letter, but the master of a Mingay vessel was often left to fix a freight for himself when he was away from his home port. When William Bantoft was master of the *Clementina* – he took her over from James Burrows in September or October 1851 – he roamed all around the British coasts seeking cargoes. In March 1854 he fixed a cargo of coal from Newcastle to Par in Cornwall, from where he took china clay in casks to Runcorn on the Mersey, returning from there with 100 tons of white salt for Yarmouth, no doubt to be used in curing herring.

After that he went back into the coal trade, delivering at Orford, Rochford or wherever was wanted. At the beginning of 1855 he fixed a cargo of coal from Newcastle for 'Pettylun' – probably Porthleven in Mounts Bay, on the south coast of Cornwall; from there he took the ship light to Bo'ness on the Firth of Forth near Linlithgow, where he loaded 105 tons of pigiron for Dunkirk. Leaving Dunkirk in ballast, he sailed to Middlesbrough to load railway iron (rails) for London. It seems that he made a useful contact with the big iron and steelmaking firm of Bolckow Vaughan & Company, because he had several cargoes of railway iron, pigiron and similar materials in succeeding months. We would know more of his enterprise had two sheets not been torn out of the *Clementina's* cargo book.

In the summer of 1857 he fixed a cargo of coal, bricks and two casks of clay from Newcastle for Ryde, in the Isle of Wight, where he must have put his vessel on the beach to unload. He then went to Poole in Dorset in ballast, and there loaded 105 tons of clay for Dysart, in Fife, from where he sailed to Bo'ness to load 51 tons of coal and 55 tons of pigiron. He took that cargo to Rotterdam, and from there he sailed in ballast to Hartlepool, whence he brought two cargoes of coal to Orford. Then in November he loaded 'copperlite' (coprolite, probably from pits at Boyton on the Butley River) for Newcastle, returning with coal. One would imagine he was making a good enough return for his owners.

Almost all the masters of the Mingay fleet could read and write, up to a point at least. They had to be able to do that, because even before Rowland Hill's introduction of the penny post in 1840 the principals at Orford were controlling the movements of the ships by means of the postal service. The skippers were expected to send in letters providing information on their arrival in port, be it Hartlepool or Newcastle, Rotterdam or Par, on the loading of a cargo of coal or on the prospects of another homeward cargo, and on the progress of any necessary repairs.

For instance, on 15th November 1850 Henry Gibbs, master of the *Dorothea*, wrote from East Cowes in the Isle of Wight:

> Sir
> This is to inform you that I arrived here last night and all well with us on board after a long passage. Sir we shall begin to work to day and I expect that we shall be all out on Monday and I am a going to write to poole by this post for an answer by return Sir I received your letter this Morning and if I cannot get a fraight here any where I shall go to Hartlepool and load upon your account, Sir if you or Mr. Mingay is a going to sail the *Coaster* if you have not engaged a Master for her I should like for to take her if it would be a greeable to you and Mr. Mingay as she is larger Sir I will write you a gain as soon as we are ready for sea and send you what Money that I have, Sir I hope this will find you Mrs. Rope and all in good health.
> Sir I remain your most Humble
> and Obedient Servant
> H. Gibbs

Poor Gibbs had problems, however. On 28th November George Rope informed his uncle at Croydon that 'I have rec'd a letter from Gibbs who states that his Merchant has gone to London without settling with him or any of his tradesmen or workmen being a builder – but he is assured by a Gentleman who is [supplying ?] him that he is to return as today and will settle with him. I hope this will be the case. he has engaged to take a cargo of pipe Clay from Poole to Goole – @ 9/6 – but 1/6 of which he has to pay by Cheque to Leeds – I have written him to load Coals for me there and come home – the *Queen* I hear at Orford was ready to sail on Friday last from Stambridge Mills. . .'.

It was decided that Gibbs should sail from the Isle of Wight and that perhaps matters should be put in the hands of Henry and James Southwell, the Saxmundham solicitors. Instead George Rope asked the London agents, Messrs. Woodley, to take the matter up there as the defaulting recipient of the cargo was said to be in London. A further difficulty arose when it was found that the charter party, the legal document concerning the shipment, was not signed with a sixpenny stamp as it should have been.

On 12th December Gibbs wrote from Yarmouth, Isle of Wight, saying he was held up there by lack of wind, but he was soon at Poole and loading pipeclay for Goole. Two days after Christmas George Rope wrote to his uncle 'I have much pleasure in announcing the safe arrival of the *Dorothea* yesterday afternoon after a fine passage – and I am also glad to say I this morning recd a check for the remainder of the *Dorothea's* freight from Mr Morgan – Gibbs did not make so good a freight to Goole as he expected for he chartered to deliver the Clay to Hull @ 9/- and the party told him the expenses up the Canal was about 1/6 pr ton and it turned out to be 3/6 per ton.'

When it became necessary to choose a new master for the brigantine *Coaster* in 1845 George Rope told his uncle that he thought Robert Butcher would be very suitable, and his view was backed up by G.W. Mingay (another George), who said that so far as seamanship was concerned he thought him quite capable of taking command. 'The greatest drawback is his not being able to write,' said George Rope, 'but that might in some cases not be an objection for it is likely to keep him honest, for if he did wrong those who kept his accounts must know it – I will endeavour to find out a good mate for him.' Robert Butcher was appointed.

A succession of apprentices, usually local lads of fourteen upwards, were assigned to various vessels to learn seamanship and navigation at the hands of the skippers. No fewer than twenty-three youngsters are listed in a small notebook containing the names and rates of pay of apprentices from 1835 to 1856. It seems likely that at least two of the apprentices went on to command Mingay ships: William Bantoft became master of the *Clementina* in 1851, and Henry Gibbs became master of the *Perseverance* in 1843 and of the *Dorothea* four years later, eventually coming ashore to serve as the Orford harbourmaster.

One of the former apprentices earned censure in January 1845 when he put the *Coaster* ashore at the entrance to the Ore. 'It was Lucock again who had charge of the helm, I think he ought not to have charge of another vessel in or out of the Harbour,' George Rope observed in a letter of 17th January to his uncle in Croydon. And in another letter the next day he complained that 'Lucock got him ashore entirely through carelessness for there never was a finer chance to take her in, plenty of water and a fair wind, and just enough to fill the sails.' Fortunately the ship was refloated after being lightened.

The relative mildness of George Rope's reaction to this near-disaster is noteworthy: he merely recommended that Lucock not be given charge of a vessel when entering or leaving the harbour. The same good nature was evident when one of the masters, James Nottage of the *Dorothea*, showed signs of a mild mental breakdown apparently caused by a quarrel between his wife

The snow *Celerity*, one of the last sailing colliers in trade, wrecked near Lowestoft in 1905. She had been built at Middlesbrough in 1867.

and the mate's wife. When the crew refused to sail with Nottage because of his behaviour Rope wrote to his uncle saying that he had sorted the matter out.

'I have had Nottage and his men into the Compting House this morning and have given all a good talking to. The men have agreed to go again. . .I hope this matter will rouse Nottage and do him a great deal of good – he is a good fellow and I hope it will.'

George Rope's forbearance was remarkable in an age when many employers would have dismissed a man for much milder misbehaviour. His grandson, the Revd H.E.G. Rope, recalled that he would lie awake on stormy nights full of anxiety for his men at sea.

George's grandson also recalled that he had attributed the decline of the coasting trade to the coming of the railways, which rapidly drove the little schooners and brigantines off the seas. Peter Bruff brought the Eastern Union Railway to Ipswich in 1846, and the line was extended to Bury St Edmunds and to Norwich thereafter; the arrival of the iron road at Snape Maltings is still marked by the date 1859 on the keystone of an arch through which the line entered the maltings complex.

No longer did the maltings find it essential to send its malt to the London breweries by sea; no longer did Saxmundham gasworks need to have its coal transported in waggons from the wharf at Iken Cliff when a railway siding brought it right into the works. The sloop *Sophia* was still trading to Orford Quay, to Iken Cliff and to Boyton Dock in 1870, as we can see from her cargo book, but the trade to the little ports was by then almost at an end.

The last of the sailing vessels in the coal trade like the snow *Celerity*, owned by Lowestoft coal merchant J.S. Sterry, were still bringing their cargoes to Suffolk ports at the beginning of the twentieth century, but by then steam was supreme. The end came for the *Celerity* when she was wrecked on the Suffolk coast in a south-easterly gale in January 1905, the crew being taken out of her with great difficulty by the steam lifeboat *James Stevens No.3* from Gorleston.

The life of a river 12

For more than a thousand years the Orwell was not only a channel of trade but also a background to the life of people living along its banks. For many residents of the town of Ipswich and of the surrounding villages the estuary was also a source of employment and a working environment.

Fishing provided a livelihood for some men living in places like Pin Mill and Shotley, and until well into the twentieth century there was a small oyster fishery operated mainly from Wherstead, on the southern side of Ipswich. The main fishing ports in the area were, however, Manningtree on the Stour, where the Howard family owned a fleet of smacks in the first half of the nineteenth century, and Harwich; James Howard moved eight of his larger boats, the *British Rover, Emma, Howard, Laurel, Liberty, Marquis, Mary* and *Success*, to Grimsby on the Humber.[1] With Howard's little fleet went two brothers, William and Harrison Mudd from the Suffolk village of Holbrook, who became leading figures in Grimsby and the booming Humber fishing industry; Harrison Mudd was Mayor of Great Grimsby in 1900.

For a few years in the eighteenth century Ipswich sent out whalers to the Arctic seas to the east of Greenland. It was in 1786 that banker Emerson Cornwell and Captain Timothy Mangles, a Londoner, formed a company which operated the Yarmouth-built *Ipswich* and the chartered *Orwell* and constructed a try works in which the whale blubber was to be rendered down at Nova Scotia, on the Stoke side of the river some way below the town quays.[2]

The *Orwell* arrived in the river with seven 'fish' on 30th July 1787, but because the channel was so badly silted up she was unable to proceed beyond Downham Bridge, a mile or so downriver, and the blubber had to be brought to Nova Scotia by lighter. The rendering of the blubber was an extremely noisome business, but according to the *Ipswich Journal* 'the inhabitants of this town were released from the apprehension of being very much incommoded by the nauseous smell that arises in the process of extracting the oil. The stench did not reach any part of the town, neither was it scarcely to be smelled within 100 yards of the place'.[3] Possibly a nor'east breeze wafted the stench out into the countryside; how else could the townspeople have failed to be sickened by such a stink? The *Ipswich* arrived in the river on 24th August, with no whales but with 1½ butts of blubber obtained from fifty-four seals.

In subsequent years the whale fishery proved unprofitable and the whaling ships forsook the Orwell. G.R. Clarke said in 1830 that some of the buildings used for extracting the whale oil – used in street and other lamps – were

Opposite: Sailmaker 'Percy' Gladwell at work in Whitmore's sail loft on Neptune Quay at Ipswich about 1975.

Harrison Mudd, born in the
Suffolk village of Holbrook,
who founded H. Mudd &
Son, of Grimsby, one of the
biggest fish processing and
distribution companies
in Britain.

still standing at that time, presumably then used in connection with the
shipbuilding that was carried on at Nova Scotia.[4]

The launching of a new ship from one of the Ipswich yards was always an
event that brought out the spectators, often in their hundreds and sometimes
in their thousands; it is said that when Jabez Bayley launched the Indiaman
Orwell from the Halifax Yard on 28th August 1817 no fewer than 20,000
people turned out to watch the event. And after the arrival of the railway the
Eastern Union even ran excursion trains to bring country people to see the
launching of a large vessel. After all, there was no cinema, no television, and
there was always a chance the owner would invite some of the closer watchers
to partake in the celebrations; the expenses of building a new vessel often
included payments to the landlords of certain riverside hostelries for beer and
victuals at the time of the launching.

While shipbuilding was an important source of employment in Ipswich,
there were also mast and sparmakers, shipsmiths, sailmakers and ropemakers
and other tradesmen providing a backup to the shipwrights and others
working in the shipyards. There were several ropewalks around the town in
addition to the one that gave its name to the street now called Rope Walk.

Emigration to Canada

At a time of serious agricultural depression in the 1830s Ipswich became a port
of embarkation for men and women seeking a better life in the New World.
With Napoleon despatched to St Helena and his endeavours to starve Britain
into submission thwarted, the farming community was no longer essential to
the country's survival and it became cheaper to import food from overseas
than to grow it at home; many farmers found themselves facing ruin, while
their workers were 'thrown on the parish'.

In 1836 the Churchwardens and Overseers of Redgrave, a Suffolk village
close to the source of the rivers Little Ouse and Waveney, borrowed £250,
to be repaid from the Poor Rates, 'as a fund for defraying the expences of

The site of the whaling
station at Nova Scotia,
Ipswich, seen about 1970. It
disappeared under the West
Bank Terminal not long
after this photograph was
taken by Hugh Moffat.

The East Indiaman *Orwell* nearing completion on Jabez Bayley's Halifax Yard at Ipswich. It is said that her launching was watched by a crowd of 20,000.

several poor persons having Settlements in the said Parish and being willing to emigrate'.[5] That same year an advertisement in one of the local newspapers showed that some Suffolk authorities were seeking a larger-scale solution to the problem of paupers.

Blything Union
Notice to Shipowners and Shipbrokers
Wanted to charter, a Ship or Ships, with Emigrants, for Quebec, Montreal, &c., to sail from Great Yarmouth, Lowestoft or Southwold about the 2nd or 3rd week in April.

All Persons having Ships to offer for the above Service are requested to send in sealed Tenders for the same on or before the 4th day of April next, addressed to Mr. Harry White, Solicitor, Halesworth, free of expence.
HARRY WHITE
Clerk to the Board of Guardians.
Halesworth 21st March 1836

That year thirteen ships from Yarmouth alone took out to Canada no fewer than 3,057 emigrants in the months of April and May. One of those ships, the *Morning Star*, left with 212 emigrants, all of them agricultural labourers from Suffolk, most of them intending to settle on the estates of the British American Land Company which had been advertising 'ONE MILLION ACRES OF LAND' on the south side of the St Lawrence between Quebec and Montreal. The company's advertisements advised that the best way to reach the Eastern Townships, as the area was called, was to take a river steamer from Quebec, but another ship that sailed from Yarmouth at about the same time, the *Brunswick*, was taking 447 emigrants direct to Port St Francis, the main port for the Eastern Townships. Such was the number of people emigrating from Suffolk that emigration agent Samuel Noller, of Debenham, had the idea of embarking emigrants in the Orwell.

Sam Noller was an enterprising man, and a busy one. He was a farmer, tilling that heavy clay land that grew prodigious crops at a time when high yields and excellent quality were by no means universal. Besides that he was a carrier, operating a weekly service with waggons to London by way of Ipswich, Chelmsford and Romford;[6] his waggon left Debenham each

Wednesday afternoon, taking several days to reach the Metropolis and several more to return home; in December 1836 a heavy fall of snow seriously delayed the service and the waggon failed to return within the week.[7] In the 1840s he replaced the waggons with horse-drawn vans running between Great Yarmouth and London, by way of Debenham, of course.

In addition he acted as an emigration agent, arranging passage for individuals and groups seeking a new life in far-away places, advising on the opportunities, and liaising with the various shipmwasters. Throughout the 1830s the Suffolk newspapers carried advertisements inserted by him extolling the opportunities to be found in Canada and the United States. A typical advertisement was that which appeared in one of the Norwich newspapers:

> Fourth Spring Ship To Sail positively on the 10th June for Quebec and Montreal. The fine fast-sailing Teak-built Ship Brightman, coppered and copper-fastened, C.W. Nockells, Commander, 500 tons burthen, lying in the London Dock. This fine ship has a splendid poop and excellent accommodation for passengers.
>
> For freight or passage apply to Samuel Noller, Debenham, Suffolk, or P. Saunders, No. 5 Crescent, Minories.[8]

Noller was also involved in a scheme involving the settlement of emigrants on the east coast of Central America in what is now Guatemala, at a place then known as New Liverpool, on the south bank of the Cujabon, a river running into the Bay of Honduras.[9]

A large ship outward bound from Ipswich with a tug assisting astern passes Redgate Hard at Wherstead where emigrants embarked for Canada in the 1830s. On the far side of the river is John's Ness where warships had been built a century earlier.

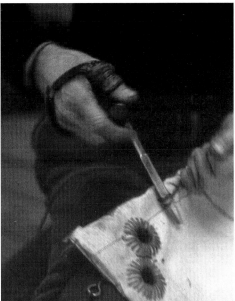

Sailmakers in J.O. Whitmore's sail loft on Neptune Quay, Ipswich, were busily occupied in the 1970s not only in making new sails for spritsail barges but also in producing sails for Dutch traditional craft whose owners took advantage of the then-current economic situation to obtain new sails on this side of the North Sea. At far left 'Percy' Gladwell is stitching the boltrope of a sail and at left he is using a stitch mallet to tighten the stitching. In the lower picture a barge sail is laid out in the spacious sail loft.

Sparmakers wield their adzes in George Overy's workshop on Battery Green at Lowestoft.

The first intimation that Noller was planning to send emigrants to Canada from the Orwell came in an advertisement in the *Ipswich Journal* in May 1836:

> Wanted on board the Ship *Venus* (which Sails on the 13th instant from the River Orwell, Ipswich, to Upper Canada), a Medical Man to take charge of the sick &c. Immediate application to be made to Mr. S. Noller, Debenham.
>
> The public are respectfully informed that on the 27th instant another Ship will Sail to the above place. Any Union wishing to contract for the conveyance of Emigrants may meet with every attention to their respective interests by applying as above.[10]

The *Venus* carried between one and two hundred men, women and children who were being shipped out by the Hoxne Union, the Board of Guardians clearly being of the opinion that this would relieve pressure on the £5,500 workhouse then being built at Stradbroke. The vessel had not sailed up to the town quay but was lying off Redgate Hard, half way along Wherstead Strand and a little below where the Orwell Bridge now carries the A14 trunk road over the river. Possibly the *Venus*, a barque of 300 tons owned by George Danby Palmer of Yarmouth, was too large to reach the town quay; the Wet Dock was not then in existence. On the other hand embarkation a mile and more below the town might have been arranged to avoid interference by troublemakers who might try to deter the countrymen and their families from leaving their homeland at the behest of the Poor Law Guardians.

As it was their arrival in the town in a number of carts and waggons and their subsequent progress along Wherstead Road and over Bourne Bridge did attract a crowd of agitators from Ipswich, described in a local newspaper as 'disreputable characters', who 'by inflammatory language endeavoured to dissuade them from embarking'.[11]

The chairman of the Hoxne Union, the Revd Henry Owen, and several of the Guardians of the Poor had gone down to the Red Gate Hard to see the party embark. Mr Owen, a magistrate, took quick action to quell what he feared might become something of a riot and 'caused two of the most turbulent to be taken into custody'. According to a contemporary report 'this had the effect of subduing the excitement, and the emigrants embarked, with the exception of two families' who returned home to Stradbroke.

The members of one of those families changed their minds again and joined the *Venus* before she sailed in the third week of May, but one man was obdurate and refused to do so. Mr Owen committed him to the county gaol for twelve calendar months 'for using inflammatory and profane language and thereby exciting others. . .to a breach of the peace'.[12] One can sympathise with these people, leaving their homes for what they hoped might be a better, yet still an unknown, country, and being faced with a noisy demonstration aimed at putting them off their venture. One wonders what became of them all?

The *Venus* was not the only vessel to take passengers from the Orwell that year, at least three vessels taking out 667 emigrants, more than half of whom were children.[13] The *Mary Stewart* embarked her passengers at Red Gate Hard and another vessel, the full-rigged ship *Lochiel*, embarked hers at Pin Mill, afterwards calling at Harwich to embark an Essex contingent.

The following year another vessel, the brig *Mariner*, was advertised to sail from Ipswich with emigrants for Quebec, but that appears to have been the last such sailing from the Orwell. Any later passages, if any there were, seem to have gone unrecorded.

The wherries

At a time when waterways were considered the most convenient channel of communication for both passengers and goods there was a regular service of wherries operating between Ipswich and Harwich, and also between Harwich and Manningtree. These were neither the cargo wherries that sailed up the Waveney to Beccles and Bungay nor the rowing wherries of the Thames used by Samuel Pepys when going about his official business as a naval administrator; they were a purely local type, 20-30ft long with gaff sails on two masts. Although in the eighteenth century they worked from the Common Quay at Ipswich they later gave their name to a Wherry Quay, and there is still a Wherry Lane leading from the dockside to Salthouse Street in Ipswich.

There is no record of just when the wherries began to run downriver to Harwich on the ebb tide and up to Ipswich on the flood, but we do know that

An Orwell wherry on the left, with a sprit mainsail, and a large sloop.

A successor to the wherries,
the Great Eastern Railway
paddle steamer *Norfolk*
heading downriver before a
fresh following wind.

in 1624 a wherry with five people on board was run down by a ship in the Orwell.[14] In 1708 a wherry bound for Ipswich was struck by lightning, killing the master, John Woollard, and three passengers. Woollard was buried in St Clement's churchyard at Ipswich under a stone that described him as 'master of the wherry', the apparent implication being that there was only one wherry operating at that time. The probate inventory of Woollard's effects, however, includes '2 Wherrys with masts, sails, anchors and cables' as well as '2 small boats with oars'.

Later members of the Woollard family kept up the connection with the wherries, and in 1761 James Woolward (a variation of spelling, but the same name) went into partnership with Joseph Cole, who eight years earlier had advertised the building of a new 'swift and commodious' wherry for the service between Ipswich and Harwich.[15]

Other wherries ran a similar service on the Stour between Harwich and Manningtree, where there is a Wherry Corner at the east end of the High Street – named from a former hostelry and only indirectly from the rivercraft. In 1760 wherryman John Norman, of Manningtree, built a new wherry for the service to Harwich; in 1839 John Moor, licensee of the Wherry public house, was owner and captain of the *Sally* and ran a daily service to meet the London packets at Harwich.[16]

Not only did the wherries carry passengers on the Orwell and Stour but they operated what would today be termed a parcels service, carrying small packages of goods from one town to another. During the French wars towards the end of the eighteenth century, when the area was crowded with troops

The *Norfolk* going astern in
Harwich harbour, with a
naval vessel at her moorings
in the background.

preparing to repel a threatened French invasion, the wherries were extremely busy; it was reported in 1793 that the wherries sailing to Harwich were so crowded that every day would-be passengers were left behind on the quay. The historian G.R. Clarke tells us that at that period between twenty and thirty open boats had been known to leave Ipswich in a single day with passengers for the Essex seaport.[17]

The wherries survived the introduction in 1815 of the first steamer to run between Ipswich and Harwich, the steam packet Orwell, built at Great Yarmouth by James Lepingwell. Perhaps the wherrymen laughed scornfully when the steam packet's engine, made in the Norwich foundry of Aggs and Curr, proved to have insufficient power to drive a ship on the tideway; a more powerful engine was ordered from London, but all the same the Orwell lasted only a few weeks before being withdrawn. Nevertheless, steam did take over in due course, and the surviving wherries were employed in very different trades.

A view of Harwich from the Redoubt with the kilns of the Board of Ordnance cement works pouring out smoke on the right.

In 1841 the wherry *Generous Friends*, which had been built at Ipswich in 1807 and was 'long known as a favourite wherry between this town and Harwich', was lost on the Pye Sand in the Harwich approaches. Recording her loss, the *Ipswich Journal* revealed that 'since the introduction of steam she had been employed in the fisheries and stone dredging'.[18]

The stone boats

The establishment of Roman cement factories at Ipswich and Harwich in the early part of the nineteenth century provided an alternative occupation for fishermen both on the Orwell and on the Essex side of Harwich harbour. Ever on the lookout for a more profitable line of business, they turned to 'stone dredging', bringing up the septaria that was the raw material from which the so-called Roman cement was manufactured

Roman cement was patented in 1796 by James Parker, who set up a works at Northfleet in Kent, and production of this useful quick-drying material was taken up elsewhere soon afterwards. The Board of Ordnance set up a works in the Angel Gate area of Harwich in 1818;[19] the kilns in which the septaria was burnt can be seen in the background of a print published in 1837 of the Redoubt, a monster version of a martello tower, in the construction of which the Roman cement is said to have played a significant part. Thomas Wright told how 'the septaria on the south of Walton, on the coast of Essex, are . . . collected into heaps and shipped to Harwich, where they are manufactured by government into a cement'.[20] One suspects that it might in fact be Walton in Suffolk, on the north shore of Harwich harbour, rather than Walton-on-the-Naze to which Wright refers.

Main base for the stone boats, as they were called, was the riverside hamlet of Pin Mill, an outlying part of the village of Chelmondiston, with Shotley and the town of Harwich itself also adding their quota. In 1845 Pin Mill had about thirty boats 'employed chiefly in getting stone on the rocks near Harwich, for the manufacture of Roman Cement at the works in Ipswich and other places'.[21] A directory of that year listed John, Charles, Henry and Samuel Howlett as cement stone merchants and dressers and William Howlett as shopkeeper and stone dresser in Chelmondiston. Of Shotley the directory says merely that 'Several boats are employed here in collecting stone for the manufacture of Roman cement'.

Ten years later the number of boats working in the stone trade out of Pin Mill had increased to fifty and another family, the Kings, had entered the business – three of them were among the twenty-two men described as boatowners;[22] a hundred years later a member of that same family, Harry King, was a boatbuilder at Pin Mill.

The smaller pieces of septaria, a sedimentary rock akin to sandstone, were hauled up in dredges similar to those used elsewhere for obtaining oysters. It would seem, though, that other means might have been used for obtaining larger pieces of the rock since an advertisement[23] for three boats being sold at Harwich in 1838 includes in a brief list of gear not only dredges but tongs and cromes, the latter being an implement similar to an agricultural fork but with the tines at right angles to the shaft. These three boats, the *Swan*, the *Bee* and the *Prosperous*, all of Harwich, could each carry between five and nine tons and were what would today be described as cutter rigged, with gaff topsails – or as the advertisement was worded, gaft-topsails, using the east coast vernacular.[24]

With a length of 40.3ft. and a beam of 11.7ft., the *Providence*, owned by Edward Shilling of Chelmondiston, was among the largest of the stone boats; she was built by the Ipswich firm of William Read and Enos Page in 1841. Launched from the same yard in 1840 were the *Anne*, owned by Henry Hayward of Pin Mill, the *Celerity*, owned by Edward Goodman of Chelmondiston, and Joseph Pinner's *Agenoria*, which passed to Harwich registry in 1858. A rather smaller smack, the *Silvan*, owned by James Cook of Pin Mill, had a length of 33.9ft. and a beam of 10.1ft.; she was built by William Bayley at Ipswich in 1840. Bayley also built Mark Crane's *Ranger* in the same year.[25]

Clearly the stone trade was booming, if one is to judge from the number of new boats being launched. An item in a local newspaper in 1840 states

A plan of George Tovell's cement mill beside the Wet Dock at Ipswich.

that 'there are at this time about 80 boats and small vessels employed here [Harwich] in dredging for cement stone and nearly £400 a week is paid to the persons employed. The competition . . . in sailing for the first turn to deliver the stone gives us a daily illustration of the excitement of a regatta . . .'.[26] The boats did not race only in the course of their work: the Shotley Regatta of 1842 offered a prize to be sailed for by the stone and fishing boats of the local ports,[27] and in a report of the Harwich Regatta of 1860 it was stated that 'the boats of fishermen and stone dredgers, lying opposite the town, formed in themselves a great fleet of several hundred sail'. One of the races at that regatta was for stone dredgers of below 10 tons, won by the *Edith* of Ipswich, with the Harwich boat *Victor* in second place.

No doubt the prosperity of the cement stone trade made it possible for owners to have new boats built for them. It is, however, noticeable that in

Shotley was not only a base for the stone boats but had a thriving barge trade. In this picture a ketch barge and two spritties lie near the bottom of Bristol Hill at Shotley.

many cases the new boats were immediately mortgaged either to the builder or to some tradesman in Chelmondiston or Ipswich.

It would seem that the dredgermen, like the fishermen, were not averse to participation in the 'free trade' that was so prosperous an occupation for those who were able to avoid or outrun the Revenue cutters. It was only the unsuccessful smugglers who found their exploits recorded in the newspapers, but the number of craft that were caught is surely an indication of the extent of the illegal trade. On 7th March 1841 the Revenue cruiser *Scout* seized the smack *Friends* of Ipswich in 'Ipswich water' with fifty-five tubs of valuable contraband.[28] The *Friends* had been built in Brightlingsea forty years earlier, but this was the end of her career. The Ipswich register tells its own story: 'Condemned and broken up at Harwich, registry closed 12th November 1841'.

Only two months after the capture of the *Friends* the *Scout* took the smack *Rosabelle* of Ipswich, belonging to innkeeper William Bird, with between eighty and ninety packages of tobacco, snuff, spices and other contraband on board.[29] The clench-built cutter had been built in Portsmouth in 1823; she too was condemned and broken up at Harwich. A William Bird, mariner – possibly the same man – was the owner of the smack *Prince of Wales* that had been built at Ipswich in 1791. The Customs House register contains an undated note that she was 'captured by the *Ranger* at Dover with contraband goods on board and condemned at Dover'

A not dissimilar note records the end of another little boat that came on to the Ipswich register in 1828, having previously been registered at Maldon. She was registered at first as the *Pot8oes*, but apparently at the insistence of the registrar was reregistered in September of that year as the *Potoooooooo* (Pot eight Os) 'to agree with the Maldon register'.

It appears that at her launching some years earlier she had been given the name of a famous racehorse, foaled in 1773, that had defeated the greatest of eighteenth-century thoroughbreds and after retirement had become an influential sire of a number of later winners. The story goes that the chestnut colt received his name after a stableboy had been told to write the name on a feed bin and had spelt it with eight Os; the lad's version amused the owner, Willoughby Bertie, fourth Earl of Abingdon, and that was the name entered in the Stud Book. One wonders if the original owner had paid for the building of the boat with his winnings on Potoooooooo.

In August 1830 the then owner, James Wardley, mariner, mortgaged the *Potoooooooo* to Jabez Bayley and Enos Page for £40, and at some later date an entry was made in the register: 'Seized at Woodbridge, condemned and broken up'.

The law decreed that vessels used in defrauding the Revenue should be sawn in two and utterly destroyed, though in some cases they were seized and sold. Matthew Swain, merchant, and James Good, innkeeper, were joint owners of the *Providence*, a smack built at Yarmouth in 1801, which was caught with contraband goods on board. The record of her reregistration at Ipswich in 1831 tells the story: 'the said Vessel having been condemned in His Majesty's Court of Exchequer under Appraisement Indenture B for having on board illicit spirits and having been afterwards sold by order of the Customs and purchased by John Cordingley as Agent for Matthew Swain. . .'. Cordingley was an Ipswich shipbuilder.

The cutter *Neptune*, built at Maldon in 1801 and owned at one time by members of the Howlett family at Pin Mill, seems also to have escaped breaking up after capture. An undated note in the register states that she was 'seized and condemned for smuggling and now reregistered at Chichester'.

In 1842 the Revenue cruiser *Scout* captured the Harwich stone smack *Princess Charlotte* with a ton and a half of tobacco and sixteen boxes of cigars; the two men sailing the smack went to prison for six months.[30] They were probably still 'doing time' when in May 1843 the stone dredgers went on strike seeking higher wages. As so often happens there were those who kept at work and those who were determined to impose their will on the faint-hearted; about fifty men – 'a lawless band' according to the local newspaper – stationed themselves in smacks off the harbour with the intention of preventing others from carrying on their normal trade, a maritime picket line. They boarded those boats that had been out dredging and hove the cargo overboard.[31]

Ashore the strikers paraded the streets of Harwich with drums beating, determined to convince the population of the strength of their cause. Some of the strikers went too far when they boarded the Ipswich-Harwich steamer *River Queen* in pursuit of a passenger 'who was obnoxious to them'. Some of the strikers were thrown overboard by the steamer's crew, and the rest jumped into the water and swam ashore as the vessel cast off from the pier. The tone of the report makes it plain that the Tory newspaper had no sympathy for the dredgermen.

By 1840 intensive dredging off Cobbold's Point at Felixstowe, off the West Rocks in the Harwich approaches, and close in under Beacon Cliff at Harwich together with extraction of septaria from the face of the cliff itself was having a dire effect on the harbour, changing the tidal stream and causing Landguard

The Harwich Low Light which, when kept in line with the high light further inland led ships safely into the harbour, but with the building up of Landguard Point became a 'misleading light'.

One of the pair of screw pile lighthouses at Dovercourt which in 1867 replaced the 'misleading lights' at Harwich.

Point to grow as much as 500yds to the southward across the shipping channel; the upper and lower lighthouses that had led shipping safely into the harbour in the past now led vessels on to the shingle of the expanding promontory.[32]

The dredging off Cobbold's Point had removed a natural breakwater and led directly to the extension of Landguard Point, while the removal of rock from Beacon Hill had caused the cliff to be eaten away to such an extent that the scouring effect of the tides was considerably weakened and the harbour entrance was no longer kept clear by such natural means. Captain John Washington, of the surveying vessel HMS *Shearwater* and a future Hydrographer of the Navy, reported to the Admiralty in 1843 on the effect that the removal of cement stone was having on the harbour, which he regarded as one of the most valuable havens on the east coast, and on the steps he regarded as essential to counter the detrimental effects of the dredging.

Among other things he recommended the construction of a 2,400ft breakwater projecting from the rapidly receding Beacon Cliff and the installation of a new light in order 'to obviate the mischief now of daily occurrence, in consequence of the two lights in one being no longer a safe leading mark to clear Landguard Point'.

In his report Captain Washington suggested that the stone boats might play their part in deepening the shipping channel to a depth of 15ft at low water – 27ft at high water springs. The work would cost little 'as the dredgers now on the spot would gladly undertake the work for a bounty of one shilling a ton on all the cement stone taken away from the different shoals in the harbour'. In an addendum he pointed out that in subsequent dredging the 530 tons of soil removed included 70 tons of cement stone worth five shillings a ton.

Work began in 1846 on the breakwater recommended by Captain Washington, still known in Harwich as the Admiralty breakwater, and on dredging a channel with an 18ft depth at low water; the breakwater was not as long as had been suggested, having a length of only 1,569ft.

Arrest by a Revenue cutter when engaged in a spot of smuggling was by no means the only risk run by the stone boats and their crews. In July 1843 William Glanfield, one of the three-man crew of the *Fox*, was drowned when the stone boat was run down by the iron steamer *Orion* – a product of the Read and Page yard in Ipswich – as she neared the end of her voyage from London.[33] The other two men were picked up.

The Admiralty breakwater at Harwich pictured about 1902.

The brickworks at the head of Holbrook Creek which provided many a cargo for barges working up to the quay there.

There were also other perils. A dredgerman named William Simpson was killed in the Harwich smack *Sea Gull* in 1846 when the dredge came fast on some obstruction as they dredged stone off the West Rocks. The warp tautened suddenly and a wooden buoy, used to mark the position of the dredge if it were slipped, was thrown across the deck, striking Simpson and killing him.[34] The *Sea Gull* had been built at Ipswich in 1843.

The building of the railways, which were creeping up into East Anglia and reached Ipswich and Bury St Edmunds in 1846, brought a soaring demand for cement and so for cement stone from the dredgers. According to a report in a local newspaper in December 1846 the local dredgermen were at that time earning a somewhat incredible £25,000 a year,[35] but the demand was not to continue.

The introduction of Portland cement made from a mixture of chalk and clay brought about a decline in the demand for Roman cement; John Pattrick's works at Dovercourt, by then one of only two cement works in the Harwich area, was making Portland cement by about 1850, giving rise to complaints of 'pestilential effluvia and smoke' from the local inhabitants.[36]

Although there were said to be still thirty stone boats working from Pin Mill in 1879,[37] by the end of the century the stone trade was but a memory.

There remained, however, the trade in bricks from brickyards at the head of Hare's Creek on the Orwell and Shotley and Holbrook on the Stour, many a cargo being carried from these places to Ipswich in sailing barges. Larger barges took cargoes of bricks made at the famous Woolpit brickworks and at the several Ipswich brickyards to London, where they were used in many building projects as the capital expanded.[38]

In so many ways the river played a most significant part in the life of the growing industrial town of Ipswich and of the county of Suffolk.

The Sudbury navigation 13

Harwich Harbour provided access not only to the port of Ipswich but to the minor ports of Mistley and Manningtree and to the River Stour, which was for many years navigable up to Sudbury. One says 'for many years', since it is impossible to put a figure on the period during which the river provided a valuable channel of communication not only for the borough of Sudbury but for other smaller towns such as Bures and Nayland, and not least for the millers such as one Golding Constable who operated watermills employing the power of the river itself.

A merchant who was well known in London's Mark Lane corn market, Golding Constable operated the mills at East Bergholt and Dedham and was the father of a certain John Constable whose predicted career was as a miller to take over his father's business. Instead of carrying on a prosperous business young John was determined to become a painter, and so faced a struggle against adversity and relative poverty, gaining small rewards for his work during his own lifetime. He has, however, left us a fascinating record of life on the river that for much of its course divides Suffolk from Essex.

Having worked in the windmill that his father owned at East Bergholt and also in the little watermill at Dedham, John was as familiar with the construction and working of the mills he sketched and painted as with the 'sound of water escaping from mill-dams, etc., willows, old rotten planks, slimy posts and brickwork,' the things of which he wrote in a letter to his friend and patron Archdeacon Fisher.

Some of John Constable's best-known paintings bear witness of the methods of working the lighters that carried coal, timber and other cargoes up the Stour and show, too, the difficulties faced by the lightermen in navigating the twenty-three miles between Cattawade lock and Sudbury. Though a rather makeshift sail might be set on a short mast for negotiating the tidal section between Mistley Quay and Cattawade, craft depended largely on horse towage on the river. The towpath, or haling path, changed sides from time to time, and no roving bridges were provided at the changeover places, as they were on the Midlands canals. Those in charge of the barges had to bring the bow close to the bank so that the towing horse could step on to the foredeck of the barge, and then pole the barge across to the other side of the river so that the horse could step ashore and resume its work of hauling the barge up or downstream. It was inevitable that the occasional accident occurred, the horse slipping into the river or falling on a slippery towpath as it stepped on to the bank.

Opposite: Goods destined for Sudbury or coming off the Navigation were transhipped at Mistley Quay, seen here in a print published by George Vertue in 1831. What appears to be one of the Stour lighters can be seen coming alongside a coasting sloop.

Equally productive of accidental injury to the horse was the practice of jumping the occasional stiles set up across the towpath by farmers to prevent their cattle from straying into a neighbour's marsh. These were no steeplechasers, and tired horses sometimes failed to clear the fences and were seriously injured as a result.

Constable's paintings, including one of a barge under repair in a dry dock at Flatford, show that these barges were very similar to those in use on the Great Ouse and other Fenland waterways. Clinker built and double ended, they had short decks at bow and stern and a small well amidships for the steersman, the rest of the space being taken up by two large hatches covered over with wooden hatch covers. While on the Fenland waterways trains of up to eight barges operated together, on the Stour they operated in pairs, but the peculiar method of steering was the same in both cases. There was no rudder;

John Constable's painting of a Stour lighter under construction in the dry dock at Flatford. It could be emptied of water by means of a wooden trunk under the riverbed discharging into the delph ditch on the far side, after an earth or timber dam had been installed between dock and river.

a 30ft. pole extended from the second barge over the hatches of the first, long enough to reach the midships well of the leading barge, in which was a short, stout post. The pole, which had a length of rope attached to its fore end, served as a tiller, the second barge of the pair operating in effect as a rudder. The lighter that was lifted from Ballingdon Cut in 1972 and restored by the River Stour Trust is 46ft. 9in. in overall length with a beam of 10ft. 6in. and a depth amidships of 3ft. 2in.

How did such a design become transplanted from the Fens to a waterway with which there is no obvious physical connection? It could only be that a boatbuilder from the Fens was brought in to build the original Stour barges, perhaps by somebody who was involved in making the Stour navigable. And who was this?

The dry dock at Flatford after clearing and repair by volunteers from the River Stour Trust

There is a clue in the accounts of the Mayor of Sudbury, Daniel Biatt, for 1634: it is recorded that he expended two shillings 'at the Chequer in wyne with Mr. Doctor Warren and Mr. Spenser, when did wee meete aboute making the river navigable'.[1] The Mr. Spenser mentioned was Arnold Spencer, who between 1618 and about 1630 made considerable improvements to the Great Ouse between St Ives and St Neots and in 1638 obtained Letters Patent from Charles I for making the Stour navigable. There is no evidence of Spenser doing any work on the Stour, and indeed it is said that no work was carried out, Spenser being ruined at the time of the Civil War,[2] but one suspects that in fact he did manage to do some work on the Stour and that he was the link between Fens and Stour boatbuilding. It seems likely that he brought in a Fenland boatbuilder to produce lighters for use on the Stour. Spenser's Letters Patent were assigned to John Little and Benjamin Dodd,[3] who later stated that they had spent great sums on completing the navigation, which if it is to be believed seems to confirm the supposition that the river was made navigable in the seventeenth century.

Little and Dodd petitioned against the Bill promoted by the mayor and corporation of Sudbury in 1703, but their petition was rejected by Parliament

A number of lighters lying by the Anchor Inn at Nayland, where there was at one time considerable trade. It was the failure in 1895 of Jeremiah Stannard, the Nayland miller, that led to a falling off of the river trade.

A notice issued by the proprietors of the Stour Navigation in 1790 warning 'barge-men, boatmen and others employed in towing or haling boats, barges, keels, lighters or other vessels' not to waste water by operating staunches in a careless manner.

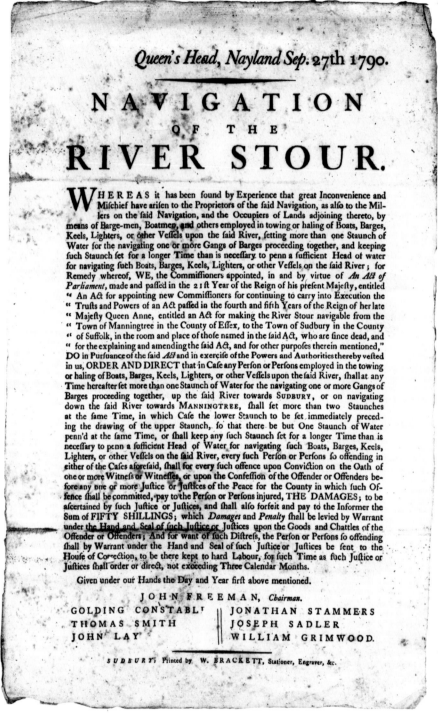

Queen's Head, Nayland Sep. 27th 1790.

NAVIGATION
OF THE
RIVER STOUR.

WHEREAS it has been found by Experience that great Inconvenience and Mischief have arisen to the Proprietors of the said Navigation, as also to the Millers on the said Navigation, and the Occupiers of Lands adjoining thereto, by means of Barge-men, Boatmen, and others employed in towing or haling of Boats, Barges, Keels, Lighters, or other Vessels upon the said River, setting more than one Staunch of Water for the navigating one or more Gangs of Barges proceeding together, and keeping such Staunch set for a longer Time than is necessary to penn a sufficient Head of water for navigating such Boats, Barges, Keels, Lighters, or other Vessels on the said River; for Remedy whereof, WE, the Commissioners appointed, in and by virtue of *An Act of Parliament*, made and passed in the 21st Year of the Reign of his present Majesty, entitled " An Act for appointing new Commissioners for continuing to carry into Execution the " Trusts and Powers of an Act passed in the fourth and fifth Years of the Reign of her late " Majesty Queen Anne, entitled an Act for making the River Stour navigable from the " Town of Manningtree in the County of Essex, to the Town of Sudbury in the County " of Suffolk, in the room and place of those named in the said Act, who are since dead, and " for the explaining and amending the said Act, and for other purposes therein mentioned," DO in Pursuance of the said *Act* and in exercise of the Powers and Authorities thereby vested in us, ORDER AND DIRECT that in Case any Person or Persons employed in the towing or haling of Boats, Barges, Keels, Lighters, or other Vessels upon the said River, shall at any Time hereafter set more than one Staunch of Water for the navigating one or more Gangs of Barges proceeding together, up the said River towards SUDBURY, or on navigating down the said River towards MANNINGTREE, shall set more than two Staunches at the same Time, in which Case the lower Staunch to be set immediately preceding the drawing of the upper Staunch, so that there be but One Staunch of Water penn'd at the same Time, or shall keep any such Staunch set for a longer Time than is necessary to penn a sufficient Head of Water for navigating such Boats, Barges, Keels, Lighters, or other Vessels on the said River, every such Person or Persons so offending in either of the Cases aforesaid, shall for every such offence upon Conviction on the Oath of one or more Witness or Witnesses, or upon the Confession of the Offender or Offenders before any one or more Justice or Justices of the Peace for the County in which such Offence shall be committed, pay to the Person or Persons injured, THE DAMAGES; to be ascertained by such Justice or Justices, and shall also forfeit and pay to the Informer the Sum of FIFTY SHILLINGS; which *Damages* and *Penalty* shall be levied by Warrant under the Hand and Seal of such Justice or Justices upon the Goods and Chattles of the Offender or Offenders; And for want of such Distress, the Person or Persons so offending shall by Warrant under the Hand and Seal of such Justice or Justices be sent to the House of Correction, to be there kept to hard Labour, for such Time as such Justice or Justices shall order or direct, not exceeding Three Calendar Months.

Given under our Hands the Day and Year first above mentioned.

JOHN FREEMAN, *Chairman.*

GOLDING CONSTABLE	JONATHAN STAMMERS
THOMAS SMITH	JOSEPH SADLER
JOHN LAY	WILLIAM GRIMWOOD.

SUDBURY; Printed by W. BRACKETT, Stationer, Engraver, &c.

and the Bill passed all its stages in 1705. When the work was completed there were thirteen flash locks or staunches (a word which in East Anglia was pronounced *staanch*) and the same number of pound locks, with gates at each end of the lock chamber. There is a suggestion that in some cases these were not new constructions but rather were the result of reconstruction of what was there already.[4] Just possibly the navigation was already many years old when it was, according to the published histories, being brought into being for the first time.

The River Stour locks were peculiar in that the gates were hung on pintles rather than being constructed in the same way as on most waterways, with a heel post held at the top by an iron collar anchored to the stonework and with a pin at the foot rotating in a 'pin' or socket in the lock sill. To counteract the tendency of the gateposts to sag inwards they were extended upwards and the tops linked by a substantial 'gallows beam' that held them securely in position. This form of construction is well illustrated in Constable's pictures of the river.

Evidence of the way in which the course of the river has been changed in the interests both of milling and of navigation may be seen between Dedham and the lowest lock at Cattawade. The county boundary between Suffolk and Essex still follows an old course of the river that lies well to the south of Flatford mill and the navigation lock, and is marked on an early edition of the Ordnance Survey map as 'Dedham Old River'.

The promotion of the navigation early in the eighteenth century was not entirely speculative but was intended to relieve pressure on the roads of that part of Suffolk and Essex, if we are to believe the wording of the Act of Parliament.[5] The clearing of the river would be 'very beneficial to trade, advantageous to the poor, convenient for the conveyance of coals, and other goods and merchandises, to and from the said towns and parts adjacent, and will very much tend to the employing and increase of watermen and seamen, and be a means to preserve the highways in and near the said counties and towns.' One might suppose from this that traffic on the local roads was already heavy, and that this was having a most damaging effect on the ill-made and largely unpaved country roads.

There had been a most important woollen industry all along the valley of the Stour in the Middle Ages, making the Babergh Hundred one of the most prosperous areas of the kingdom. At East Bergholt and Dedham, at Nayland and Sudbury and of course at Lavenham there are still many reminders of the woollen spinning and weaving trade and of the prosperity that it brought to the region. At Nayland the church porch was built by a clothier named Abel, who left his rebus (an A and a bell) on the structure to record his benefaction,

Rebuilding a Stour lighter in the Brightlingsea boatyard of the Pioneer Sailing Trust in 2012. Now named the *John Constable*, the lighter is used by the River Stour Trust to carry passengers between Sudbury and Great Cornard.

and nobody needs telling of the splendours of Lavenham and Long Melford churches.

The woollen industry was very largely only a memory by the time the river was being made navigable, or the navigation was being restored, whichever it was. The industry, based on a system of outworkers who spun the wool and wove the cloth in their own homes, from which it was collected periodically by the carts and waggons of the great clothiers, had collapsed in the early seventeenth century, though there were still small pockets of woollen spinning and weaving surviving into the nineteenth. At Lavenham as late as the 1850s there were two woolstaplers who employed outworkers in spinning fine worsted and poplin yarn on domestic wheels, and at Sudbury there were even at that time three manufacturers of bunting, the cloth used for flags. In 1844 there had been four; by the 1870s there were none, though Sudbury did still have a wool merchant in 1879.[6]

The Stour barges brought upriver coal for Sudbury gasworks, which was built adjacent to the quay, on an arm of the river excavated by the proprietors of the navigation in the eighteenth century. The proprietors also built a large warehouse, which became in turn the town's first electricity generating station and the Quay Theatre, and a granary which has become the headquarters of the River Stour Trust.

Perhaps it was the same proprietors who excavated the rather rudimentary dry dock at Flatford that featured in Constable's painting of boatbuilding on the Stour. Large enough to hold one of the barges very comfortably, it could be isolated from the river by a dam of timber and earth and was drained quite simply by pulling out a plug, allowing the water to flow through a 'chunker' – a wooden pipe beneath the river – into the delph ditch on the far side. The ditch discharged into the river below the lock.

With the Sudbury Navigation in full operation the thoughts of people at Hadleigh turned to the making of a branch waterway to that town. John Rennie, a prominent engineer who had been involved in the construction of canals and river navigations in other parts of the country, was called in to prepare a plan for making the Brett navigable from its confluence with the Stour at Higham up to a basin that was to be excavated below Toppesfield Mill. Rennie submitted his report in 1795, but nothing was done.[7]

Though cargo might never have been carried on the Brett an old inhabitant of Boxford has been quoted as saying that small barges used to navigate the Box carrying farm produce to Nayland, where it was transhipped into Stour lighters for taking downriver to Mistley. The skeleton of one of those small barges was still to be seen in about 1970.[8]

On the downriver journey one of the common cargoes was bricks made in the several brickworks in the Sudbury area and particularly Robert Allen's Ballingdon brickworks, which was served by Ballingdon Cut. More than three million bricks were carried down the Stour in 1867 and 1868. Transhipped into seagoing vessels at Mistley quay, those bricks went into the building of many London hotels and public buildings. Allen made much use of the navigation, for as well as being a brickmaker he was head of a firm described also as coal and slate merchants, lime manufacturers and maltsters.

The quantities of bricks carried fell away considerably in the late 1880s and the 1890s. In 1886 the treasurer to the navigation company reported that the brick trade was declining because of the 'opening up all around London of Suburban Railway Stations to which bricks may now be sent direct at a far cheaper rate when the carriage from the wharves in the River Thames is taken into consideration. By means of the East London Railway

Members of the River Stour Trust salvaging one of the Stour lighters from Ballingdon Cut about 1975, She was rebuilt in a simple dry dock cut out of the river bank near Cornard Mill.

under the Thames at the old Thames Tunnel, bricks are now sent direct to the South of London which formerly all went by water to Angerstein's wharf, and were transhipped there for delivery by rail.'

The millers at Sudbury, Great Cornard, Nayland, Bures and Stratford St Mary as well as Golding Constable and his second son Abram, who took over the business that had at one time been intended for John, all made great use of the river, and some of them had their own barges. Golding Constable not only had his own river lighters but owned the little sloop *Telegraph* that took his flour from Mistley to London. The failure of Jeremiah Stannard, who was at Nayland mills for around thirty years from the 1850s, caused a great falling off in the trade of the river, for Stannard was one of only three or four major users of the navigation when he went bankrupt in 1895.

So much had changed since 1781 when Golding Constable and Samuel and John ('Scheming Jack') Gainsborough, brothers of the painter Thomas Gainsborough, were appointed commissioners of the navigation, and since 1826 when a newly erected lime kiln at Stratford St Mary was advertised for sale in the *Ipswich Journal*. Nearly opposite the Swan Inn, the lime kiln was 'rendered highly valuable for the facility afforded for landing Coals, Chalk, Manure, &c. upon its wharf, from the Navigable River Stour, combined with its advantageous situation for Land Carriage, abutting as it does upon the Turnpike-road.'

Trade on the river was brought finally to an end when during the First World War, so it is said, the military authorities ordered that the surviving lighters be sunk in Ballingdon Cut so as to deny their use to an invading army.

It was one of these lighters that was raised by members of the River Stour Trust in 1972 and restored by them in a shallow dock at Great Cornard somewhat reminiscent of the ancient one at Flatford. After restoration the lighter was used for some years for passenger trips, towed by horse in the traditional way, but eventually it became too leaky to be employed in that way. In 2010, however, a grant of £120,000 enabled the barge to be taken to the Pioneer Sailing Trust yard at Brightlingsea for complete rebuilding.

In 2013 the rebuilt lighter, now appropriately named *John Constable*, was returned to service on the Stour, bringing back memories of when the river had been a commercial waterway.

Life and death at sea   14

Those who went to sea formed a distinct class of their own, distinguished from other working people not only by their employment but by their wider experience of the world, however imperfect their understanding of that world might have been. Sailors' stories are renowned as being as tall as the masts of the ships they sailed in.

In the days of sail and oar seafarers faced risks undreamed of by those ashore. Sea monsters like those appearing on early charts had to be contended with, but they posed infinitely lesser dangers than the weather and the many, ever-changing shoals off the east coast that swallowed up so many ships – and men. The deep-sea sailor began to feel uneasy as soon as he came near the coast, and with good reason: an old North Sea Pilot declared that navigation of the east coast south of the Humber was 'rendered difficult by numerous sand banks, forming a series of ridges parallel to the coast, with comparatively deep channels between, and extending in some cases to a distance of thirty miles from the shore'.

These dangers were compounded by the dilapidated state of so many of the ships engaged in trade and the ineptitude and slovenly behaviour of some of the men who had charge of them. While there were many skippers who found their way unerringly about the North Sea without the aid of charts or navigating instruments, using the leadline and their own knowledge gathered over many years to fix their position, there were others who neither knew nor cared about the art of navigation. There were too many like the Russian captain who mistook Blakeney church for Dover Castle; it was by no means unknown for ships to run on to the Kentish Knock or the Longsand off the Esssex coast because the master, having left Hamburg or the Tyne several days earlier, decided blindly that it was time to change course for the run down Channel.

A common cause of collision was the fact that no lookout was being kept by one or both of the vessels involved; it was impossible for the helmsman to see ahead, the sails often masking his view. In one instance a Hull steam trawler ran down a fishing boat because the officer on watch left the bridge for twenty-five minutes, during which the helmsman lashed the wheel and went to sleep under the lee of the weather cloth.[1]

When the weather became really bad even proficient seamen and well-found ships had little chance. A tremendous gale in November 1821 caused havoc all along the East Anglian coast. 'It had been blowing fresh all night from the westward, but between three and four in the afternoon the wind

Opposite: Preceded by the banner presented in 1914, members of the Ipswich Shipwrecked Seamen's Society parade through the streets of Ipswich on an 'anniversary' weekend in the 1920s. Towards the back of the procession is the old banner, also seen in the 1912 photograph.

suddenly shifted to the north and became a hurricane,' reported the *Norfolk Chronicle*. 'At this time the roads were covered with fishing boats, and vessels riding at anchor; many others were seen at a distance coming through the Cockle Gatway. In an instant their sails were shattered to ribbons, and thus were the vessels driven rapidly through the roads by the impetuosity of the wind and tide, whilst those at anchor were obliged to cut their cables and run for shelter. Ten vessels of different descriptions were stranded between the [Gorleston] pier and Lowestoft, some of them went to pieces instantly.'

The loss of the twenty-year-old sloop *Crane* of Aldeburgh[2] in a tremendous gale when on her passage to Newcastle in ballast in May 1830 prompted a letter to the *Suffolk Chronicle* from 'A Suffolk Shipwright' at Deptford, possibly a member of the Barnard family, calling for more attention to the seaworthiness of vessels in the coasting trade. He wrote that 'there are hundreds of vessels … no more fit to go to sea in their usual trade than they would be to go round Cape Horn. It is highly necessary that the legislature of the country should place some controuling power over the constructing and repairing of vessels of this description …'[3]

Referring to 'crazy nail-boxes' which were 'nothing more than a bundle of boards,' he said 'I do hope that some of those powerful advocates of human nature will take this matter up and apply at once to Parliament to adopt some plan whereby a better class of coasting vessels may be produced, giving a greater confidence to our hardy seamen . . . for I will be bold to assert, that looking at the coasting vessels of Great Britain as a whole, they are the worst in the world.'

'Pump for your lives!' A dramatic painting of a crew struggling desperately to keep their leaking ship afloat and looking out for any craft that might come to their aid.

Six years later a Parliamentary Committee that had inquired into 'the increased number of shipwrecks, with a view to ascertaining whether such improvements might not be made in the construction, equipment and navigation of merchant vessels, as would greatly diminish the annual loss of life and property at sea,' published a report setting out its findings.[4] That report contained lurid tales of rotten ships, drunken officers, incompetent seamen, over-insurance and deliberate loss, all matters that were later taken up by a Member of Parliament, Samuel Plimsoll.

A 98-page list of vessels lost in the years 1816-1818 and 1833-1835 showed that during the latter period Yarmouth had lost forty-two ships, Ipswich eighteen, Aldeburgh seven, Harwich and Southwold five each and Woodbridge four. Not such significant numbers of ships, perhaps, when one notes that throughout the British Isles 'about 600 sail have been lost on an average in a year'.

Sometimes, as was pointed out in the Parliamentary report, ships were deliberately sunk in order to obtain an insurance payout. The Ipswich brig *Collina*, owned by William Read and Enos Page, who were shipowners as well as shipbuilders, foundered off the Texel with a cargo of coal in 1841. The two Ipswich men had bought the vessel, which had been built in Prince Edward Island in 1827, only months before her loss.

Three years later Read and the master of the *Collina*, Charles William Simpson, appeared at the Central Criminal Court in London accused of barratry, that is, fraudulently sinking the ship to claim insurance.[5] Reports from the Old Bailey were avidly discussed in Ipswich maritime circles.

In evidence Simpson said that he had complained to Read that the vessel was very leaky. He was, he said, told to 'drop her'. When he told Read that the brig's boat was too old to save the crew he was instructed to buy a new boat. According to Simpson the vessel was worth about £900, but she had been insured for £1,250. He admitted having bored holes in the ship's bottom, insisting that he did so on Read's orders.

Read was, however, acquitted after a number of influential acquaintances had testified to his good character. Simpson was sentenced to transportation for life. Not long afterwards it was announced that he had been granted a royal pardon; justice was seen to be done. It is impossible to know quite what effect the case had on Read, but in June 1844 came the announcement that his partnership with Enos Page had been dissolved and the ships that they jointly owned were for sale.

The *Collina* was, however, just one loss among many. Commenting on the sinking of the seventy-year-old Ipswich schooner *Thomas and Mary* in February 1840, the *Suffolk Chronicle* observed that 'this makes thirty-five belonging to this port lost in seven years, amounting to above 3,500 tons; and the fifth in the present year'.[6] The *Thomas and Mary*, which had been built in one of the Ipswich shipyards in 1769 as a sloop and had later been altered to a schooner, foundered in St George's Channel on passage from Liverpool for London with a general cargo. It was not only such venerable craft that came to grief; in November the same year the Ipswich schooner *George*, launched earlier in the year from the yard of William Bayley, ran on to the Cross Sand off the Norfolk coast while on her passage from the North; she 'fell over into deep water and immediately sank, and, melancholy to relate, every soul on board perished,' the local newspaper reported.[7]

The social conscience of the inhabitants of Britain was rarely pricked by such disasters; the dead men were, after all, only seamen. It was true that they left destitute widows and orphans, but then there were lots of those around everywhere in days when the expectation of life was not much above forty. And it was often said that sailors preferred to be drowned rather than to die in bed; everybody knew that. It was left for the better-off seafarers to look after their own. In 1685, Captain Samuel Green left £50 to be laid out in land for the relief of the widows and children of seamen in St Clement's parish, the port area of Ipswich.[8] The money from the renting of the land acquired at

St Clement's Church, Ipswich, a photograph taken by William Vick about 1890 when the church was the venue for the Ipswich Shipwrecked Seamen's Society 'anniversaries'.

Westerfield, £17 a year, was distributed to the widows and orphans each year on 28th November.

Then in 1719 Robert Cole left £50 in his will to provide for a distribution of bread, once a fortnight at the same church, among poor widows of seamen. The inefficient and slapdash way in which these parochial charities were administered would certainly not satisfy today's Charity Commissioners: Captain Cole's legacy, instead of paying for land from which the income was to be used to buy bread for widows, as he had directed in his will, was laid out in repairing St Clement's Church, the bread that was distributed once a fortnight being paid for out of the church-rates.

Sometimes such legacies were given to commemorate a miraculous escape from death. While in Catholic countries a seaman might have a votive painting done in thanks for such an escape, in Protestant Ipswich the reaction was a little different. In 1722 Captain Edward Larke gave 'ten Shillings yearly for ever for a Sermon to be preached in the Parish Church of St Clement in Ipswich aforesaid, on the 22nd Day of October yearly in Remembrance of the Mercies of God in preserving him on that Day, when all his Men and Ship were lost at Sea: And if that Day fall on a Sunday in any Year, then the Sermon to be on the Monday following'.[9] He also gave 'twenty Shillings yearly for ever to be laid out in Bread, and given to the working Poor of the said Parish of St Clement'.

Shipwreck very often meant ruin for the shipowner, and almost always it meant suffering, hardship and sometimes death for the crews and destitution for their dependants. From time to time special subscriptions were invited from the public to relieve the victims of some particular disaster, but these one-off subscriptions had little or no long-term effect. All too often the money given was frittered away on immediate payments to the sufferers, the widows and orphans, who were later left destitute when the cash ran out.

Quite early in the nineteenth century three organisations were formed, two in Woodbridge and the other in Ipswich, to support local seamen and their dependants. The more senior of these, the Woodbridge Maritime Friendly Society, was a typical nineteenth-century social organisation in which members joined 'for the mutual benefit and support of each other in affliction'.

Members paid an entrance fee of seven shillings, plus sixpence for a copy of the articles of the society, its rule book, and then a monthly contribution of two shillings 'to the stock'. The subscription had to be paid at the monthly meeting at the Boat Inn on the Quay; those who were away at sea had theirs paid by a friend – and there was a rule in the rule book relating to those who failed to pay their debts when they returned. A member became 'free' – that is, eligible for benefit – only after eighteen months' payment of subscriptions, and then he was entitled to twelve shillings a week if he became 'sick, lame, or blind, and thereby rendered incapable of working at his trade or calling'. Members could have the twelve shillings a week benefit for up to twenty-four weeks, and then five shillings – later six shillings – a week for life or as long as they remained incapable of working.

One of the printed rules stipulated that 'No person shall become a member of this society who is not a seafaring man, (except the stewards and clerk.)'. Another rule was designed to deal with unruly behaviour at meetings: 'If any member at any general meeting, quarrels, or abuses another, he for every such offence, shall forfeit one shilling; and the man who first strikes, shall forfeit two shillings and sixpence for every blow.' Clearly a fight could be very expensive.

There was also a rule regarding attendance at funerals: 'At the funeral of any member, or member's wife, of this society, every member (after having notice thereof) shall attend, or forfeit six-pence each, excepting those members whose vessels are finishing loading and upon a tide sail, or who must attend to transport their respective vessels from one quay to another. And it is also agreed, that such members who belong to this society, who are pilots, and fishermen, shall be exempted attending funerals, when down the river after their respective callings. It is also agreed, that women shall not attend the funeral of any free member. . .'

This friendly society was dissolved by an Instrument of Dissolution dated 1st August, 1876, the £439 1s. 9¾d. remaining in the funds being divided among the members according to seniority of membership. Six of the most senior members received £20 2s. 0½d. each and the other thirty members various lesser amounts.

At Ipswich a rather different organisation was proposed in 1826. The idea behind 'An appeal from the Seamen's Shipwreck Society to the Benevolent Inhabitants of Ipswich and its Vicinity', published in the *Ipswich Journal*, was the provision of a permanent fund that would not only look after the men who subscribed to it but would tend to eradicate some of the fraud so often practised by what we today call conmen.

> Whereas many distressing Circumstances have occurred in this and other adjoining Sea Ports, in consequence of Shipwreck, whereby many of our fellow Townsmen have lost their Clothes, and been left entirely dependent upon Petitions and Parishes for their support. Ladies and Gentlemen are frequently appealed to by Seamen from other ports, who in many cases have proved Imposters – and in order that the benevolent may not again be imposed upon, the Seamen of this Port have formed themselves into a Society to assist each other, and respectfully solicit the aid of a benevolent and humane public, to carry their object into effect.

The original idea seems to have been a simple one. Members were to subscribe two shillings each, and the relief given to a shipwrecked member would be dependent on the amount of funds available at the time, the subscriptions hopefully being augmented by the donations from the 'Benevolent Inhabitants of Ipswich'.

That the Ipswich Seamen's Shipwreck Benevolent Society, as it seems to have been known in its early days, was a success seems to be borne out by the figures that appeared in the local paper in 1829 when the anniversary of the society was reported.[10] The number of claiming members was said to have risen from 202 to 250 since the previous anniversary, and the number of honorary subscribers from eighty to ninety-five; presumably they were the 'Benevolent Inhabitants'.

The previous Sunday the members had attended a service at St Mary-le-Tower Church, 'when a most impressive and appropriate sermon was preached by the Rev. Richard Cobbold' – the author of a well-known novel concerning Margaret Catchpole. Next day there was the anniversary dinner at the White Elm Inn on Bishops Hill, attended by about a hundred of the claiming members and quite a few of the honorary subscribers, who might well have subscribed also to the cost of the dinner.

The early title of the society is a little unclear, being rendered variously in the newspaper reports of anniversary services and dinners, but in later days it was The Ipswich Shipwrecked Seamen's Society, as one can see from the banner carried by members in the anniversary processions. The society broadened its objects to embrace the welfare of the widows and orphans of men who were lost at sea; the banner declared proudly 'Here the Widows & Orphans Find a Friend'. Besides the banner a feature of the processions was a large model of a three-masted sailing ship named the *Adela* which was carried shoulder-high by two men on a kind of stretcher; that model is now in the Ipswich Museum collection and is to be seen in the basement of the Old Custom House.

A photograph of the 1912 anniversary shows both the banner and the model ship as well as a large group of youngsters with lifeboat-shaped collecting boxes similar to those used by the RNLI. Two years later the society was presented with a fine new banner, but they continued to carry the old one as well. One of the youngsters, by then a man in his seventies, told me about 1980 how after the anniversary service at St Clement's Church they would all return to the Vine in Grimwade Street or to the White Elm, where they would each receive a bottle of ginger beer and a packet of biscuits. There would be another bottle of pop and packet of biscuits in the evening, together with a shiny shilling for the youngster who collected the most money during the weekend.

The Ipswich Shipwrecked Seamen's Society continued to do good work well into the twentieth century. It operated on quite small subscriptions and on collections which in 1912 totalled only £35 13s. 9½d., including the offertory at the morning and evening services

The Woodbridge Maritime Friendly Society was joined at Woodbridge in 1840 by another society similar to that at Ipswich. At that time the port of Woodbridge was thriving, William White's directory of 1844 telling us that 'the commerce of Woodbridge has much increased of late years, and there are now belonging to the port about 50 vessels, having an aggregate burden of about 3,000 tons'. The winter of 1839-40 was a bad one for the port, the sloop *Emily* and two men being lost and the schooner *Alarm* disappearing

Children of members of the Ipswich Shipwrecked Seamen's Society who carried their collecting boxes on the society's 'anniversary' weekends were rewarded with a bottle of ginger beer and a packet of biscuits. Here they are seen with the society stewards at the 1912 'anniversary'.

on passage from Glasgow Dock to Liverpool with her entire crew of six.[11] It was those two wrecks that led to a 'numerous and respectable meeting' being held at the Anchor Inn at Woodbridge early in February 1840 to consider the formation of what the *Suffolk Chronicle* described as 'a Shipwreck Seaman's Society upon the plan of the one now in such useful operation in the port of Ipswich'. The officers of the Ipswich Shipwrecked Seamen's Society attended the meeting to give their colleagues good advice about the setting up and running of such an organisation.[12] There was no mention of the Woodbridge Maritime Friendly Society.

Hardly had the society got under way than another Woodbridge vessel was lost with all hands on the Cornish coast near Padstow, bringing the number of men lost in less than two months to sixteen. The same issue of the *Suffolk Chronicle* that contained this distressing news also had 'An Appeal to the Benevolent and Reflecting Residents in Woodbridge and its Vicinity'.[13]

> The utter hopelessness of meeting the common demands of humanity on behalf of the sufferers, by any appeals to personal and individual benevolence, under such successive and possibly recurring calamities, has induced several respectable and influential Residents in the Town and Neighbourhood, to suggest the formation of a Society, for the benefit and protection of that class of the community, chiefly exposed to the distressing results of such disastrous casualties; by means of which, their own prudent fore-thought, aided by the contributions of those who may disinterestedly combine with them, may collectively enable such Society to render more efficient aid to the sufferers, than can be reasonably hoped for by a reiterated series of appeals to public benevolence.

By the time the first meeting of the society was held in March it already had fifty-two claimant members and seventy honorary members, and it had received eighty-three donations. The society seems to have sought its support

'Prosperity to the town on the banks of the Deben': a broadsheet issued by the Woodbridge Shipwrecked Seaman's Society with a song to be sung at the annual meeting. Whilst many societies of that era no longer exist, some continue to operate, such as the Spalding Society for Mutual Relief in Case of Shipwreck.

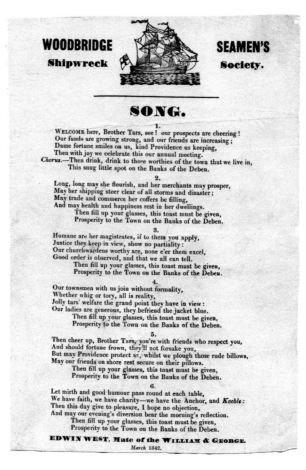

from the big county families, for White's directory of 1855 records that it was 'under the patronage of Lord Henniker, Lord Rendlesham, Sir E.S. Gooch, Major Spink, and many other gentlemen of the neighbourhood. It has upwards of 163 seafaring members, and pays about £94 a year to 22 widows'.

The Rules & Orders for the Government of the Woodbridge Shipwrecked Seamen's Benefit Society, as printed by Loder, the Woodbridge stationer and bookseller, in 1885 state 'That this society consist of seamen of all ages, who shall pay two shillings per quarter, into the box of this society, for the relief of poor shipwrecked seamen, and sixpence per quarter towards defraying the expense of the annual meeting...'[14]

The annual dinner seems to have been as popular an event at Woodbridge as it was at Ipswich. In 1842 Edwin West, mate of the *William & George* of Woodbridge, composed a song which was printed with a woodblock picture of a brig at the head flanked by the words 'Woodbridge Seamen's Shipwreck Society'. West is by no means as well known a poet as his fellow-townsman Bernard Barton. One wonders why? There might be a clue in his song.

> Welcome here, Brother Tars, see! our prospects are cheering!
> Our funds are growing strong, and our friends are increasing;
> Dame fortune smiles on us, kind Providence us keeping,
> Then with joy we celebrate this our annual meeting.
> Chorus. - Then drink, drink to those worthies of the town that we live in,
> This snug little spot on the Banks of the Deben.
>
> Long, long may she flourish, and her merchants may prosper,
> May her shipping steer well clear of all storms and disaster;
> May trade and commerce her coffers be filling,
> And may health and happiness rest in her dwellings.
> Then fill up your glasses, this toast must be given,
> Prosperity to the Town on the Banks of the Deben.

Between 1841 and 1853 inclusive this society received £1,108 15s. in donations and subscriptions and £773 9s. in sailors' subscriptions and spent £334 5s. on shipwrecked seamen. There were also payments of £68 to widows of drowned seamen, £397 19s. 6d. on weekly payments to widows, and £4 8s. 6d. 'Relief to Strangers'.[15] A list issued about 1857 shows twenty-seven widows receiving annual relief of £3 18s. or £5 4s. each. It is not clear why some were drawing the larger amount. A handwritten amendment showed that five had married and two had died.[16]

The Woodbridge Shipwrecked Seamen's Benefit Society survived until 1909, when a proposal was made at the annual meeting at the Crown Hotel in the Thoroughfare 'That in view of the liabilities of the Society and its gradually diminishing assets, it is desirable that steps be taken for its dissolution, with equitable provision for all interests therein'.

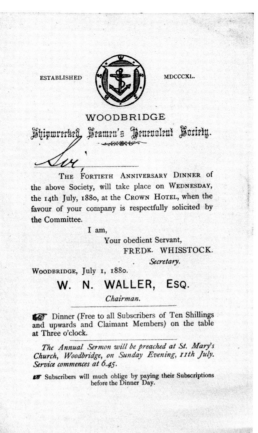

Notice of the fortieth annual dinner of the Woodbridge Shipwrecked Seaman's Society – the wording of the title varied from time to time – at the Crown Hotel in Woodbridge in 1880. The society continued in operation until 1909.

Some of the Woodbridge ships were entitled to wear the numbered flag of the Shipwrecked Fishermen's and Mariners' Society, a national organisation of which the masters were members. The numbered flags enabled the ships to be reported when passing signal stations such as that at the Sailors' Home at Yarmouth, though the captains were told that it was advisable to have the number also painted on a canvas screen or panels that could be exhibited when passing the signal station. Number 325 was Edward Paciful of the schooner *Bernard Barton* of Woodbridge, 644 was Robert Knight of the *Elizabeth*, 645 was J.W. Bromley of the *Alexander* and 646 Robert Barnes of the *Theatres*, all of them Woodbridge ships.

Other captains, including John Magub of the *Pegasus* of Southwold, John Cook of the *Eclipse* of Ipswich, and Samuel Wayth of the *Brothers' Friend* of Southwold, were members of the Master Mariners' Benevolent Society, a London-based organisation with strict rules as to who was eligible for membership. The rulebook stated categorically 'That no one shall be deemed a Master Mariner, or eligible to be elected a member of this Society as such, who is not in actual command of a decked Vessel employed in the Foreign or Coasting Trade, or whose name is not on the Ship's Register as master. And that no master of a Fishing Smack shall be considered eligible to be a member of the Society.'

The Smacksmen   15

No mere fisherman might become a member of the Master Mariners' Benevolent Society, according to the rules of that society, but there were many occasions when the masters and men of highly prestigious vessels owed their lives to the skippers and crews of humble fishing craft. Time after time the men of the trawling smacks used their small boats to save men from sailing vessels that had been swept to destruction amid the terrifying breakers on the Cross Sand, the Haisborough or the Longsand or one of the other banks that line the east coast.

At Harwich and on the Colne in Essex there were first class smacks that interspersed their oyster dredging or other fishing activities with salvaging, and often enough lifesaving when it proved impossible to save a ship or her cargo. Those smacks were fine weatherly cutters of between 55ft and 70ft in length, well able to ride out storms which proved too much for many larger vessels.

Prominent among the Harwich smacksmen were members of the Lewis family, whose exploits in the wild North Sea might easily have provided a Victorian novelist such as the Revd Richard Cobbold with material for a rip-roaring novel. One of them, John Lewis, in the smack of Harwich rescued the three survivors of the crew of the Ramsgate smack *New Maria* in January 1842 after they had spent twenty hours in the rigging of their boat on the Longsand.[1]

In November that same year John went to the aid of the crew of the *Hamilton*, a 'very fine vessel' of upwards of 300 tons that had gone on the Gunfleet in thick weather and a heavy gale. The crew had taken to the rigging, where they hung hoping for rescue. Alas, before the Harwichmen could slack their small boat alongside the mainmast went overboard, taking with it the ten men; only one of them was picked up alive.[2]

The Lewises were undoubtedly professional salvagers first and foremost rather than fishermen, equipping their smacks *Aurora's Increase* of 1839, *Cupid* and *Queen Victoria* with diving equipment. They were employed in 1848 to clear a sunken wreck from the River Welland near Spalding and twenty years later to salvage a steamer off Antwerp.[3] One of their divers, William Porrage, who called himself 'Don the Diver', walked across the harbour from Harwich to Shotley in 1848, confounding those who had taken the announcement of the underwater walk as a probable hoax.

Two of the crew of the *Aurora's Increase* appeared in court at Harwich Town Hall in 1851 accused by the Receiver of Droits of Admiralty of 'unlawfully

Opposite: A cutter-rigged fishing smack of the kind in which members of the Lewis family carried out such good rescue and salvage work from the port of Harwich.

A clinker-built fishing smack of about 1820 rigged as a cutter with her rather badly setting mainsail set loose-footed on the boom. The cloths of the sails were later cut on the diagonal and the sails set much better.

retaining divers stores and materials, viz. the mainsail, a topsail, squaresail and a quantity of rope which had been picked up by them at sea'. They had landed the gear when they came into port and had declared their intention of reporting it as soon as the Receiver's office opened the following morning, yet they were convicted of the offence and fined fifteen guineas each, that being double the value of the articles seized.[4]

The magistrates' decision created a sensation in the court, which was crowded with members of the seafaring community. John Lewis, who told the court that he was both master and owner of the *Aurora's Increase*, said that he had spotted the Sunderland brig *Loyalty* on the Whiting sand off Hollesley and had manned his small boat and boarded her in a gale. 'After being on board about six hours I got her off at dark, with 4½ feet water in her; brought her up, she making water fast; lost one of our boats; took the only remaining one we had to row to the smack to get the crew off, as the ship was sinking; my brother, the captain and crew of the brig remaining for me to take them off. While I was bringing my smack up some had jumped into the ship's longboat and rowed away leaving my brother, the captain and three or four others without a boat or the least means of escape, the brig gradually sinking. I succeeded in the dead of night in reaching the brig; the water was then over her decks, and I took my brother, the captain and others off the rigging, and in five minutes she sank. The next day I recovered the sails. . .'.

The magistrates might have convicted the smacksmen, but a very different view was taken of their behaviour by the Shipwrecked Fishermen's and Mariners' Benevolent Society, who sent £20 for the masters, William and John Lewis and George Barrett, and crews of the smacks *Wonder*, *Tryall*, and *Aurora's Increase* in recognition of their 'brave and humane conduct'. Later the same year the SFMBS awarded the crews of the *Tryall* and the *Aurora's Increase* £5 to be shared among them and voted silver medals to William Lewis, Thomas Tye, William Soder, George Wyatt and Joseph Day after they had rescued the crew of the French brig *Étoile de la Mer*, which had gone on the Longsand while on passage from Archangel to St Valery with a cargo of hemp.[5]

Those men were salvagers; those who went to the aid of the German barque *Titan* in January 1895 were plain fishermen. The *Titan* had left Hamburg with a cargo of cement for an American port when she ran into bad weather on her way up the North Sea, labouring so badly in the heavy seas that she sprang a serious leak. The pumps failed to keep pace with the inrush of water and the vessel was actually beginning to break up when the Lowestoft smack *Legion of Honour*, LT62, largest of the ten smacks owned by James Sladden, came up with her. With little thought of the danger they faced, members of the smack's crew launched their small boat and pulled across to the German vessel. Captain Adolph Hintzpeter and the nine men who made up his crew lost no time in jumping into the little boat, and the smacksmen began the task of regaining their own vessel. As they pulled at the oars they saw the *Titan* go down.

A typical Swin Ranger: Tom Barnard of Rowhedge, of whom many tales are told, not all of them true.

Before another month was out there happened one of the worst disasters ever to occur in the North Sea when the Norddeutscher Lloyd passenger liner *Elbe*, bound for America, sank with the loss of 334 lives after a collision with the steam collier *Crathie*. The only survivors of the 240 passengers and 160 crew were rescued from a lifeboat by the Lowestoft sailing trawler *Wildflower*, LT557.[6] The cause of the disaster was two-fold; both the chief officer and the lookout of the *Crathie* were in the galley at the time of the collision, and the *Elbe* continued on her course at fifteen knots without either slackening her speed or using her siren as a warning when it became clear that the *Crathie* was on a collision course. The little *Crathie* cut into the port side of the much larger ship, which sank in twenty minutes.[7]

The *Crathie* was herself seriously damaged, and her crew had to take urgent action to prevent her from sinking. When this had been done the master looked around and saw what appeared to be the lights of a ship in the distance, and he assumed that the large vessel with which his had collided was little damaged and was sailing away. All unknowing, he continued on to Rotterdam.

The *Wildflower* had been fishing in the vicinity when the two ships collided, and Skipper Billy Wright went to the scene as quickly as he was able. The smack picked up twenty survivors from a lifeboat, the third and last to leave the stricken ship, both the others having capsized as passengers crowded into them. Among those twenty survivors was one young woman, a ladies' maid, Anna Boecker, who had been in one of the boats that overturned; she had swum around in the icy, turbulent water until she was with difficulty dragged into Third Officer Stollberg's lifeboat.

George Vemply Burwood's painting of the rescue of the survivors of the passenger liner *Elbe* by the Lowestoft smack *Wildflower* in the North Sea in 1875. The picture is now in the Lowestoft Maritime Museum at Sparrows Nest.

Once safely on board the smack the soaked and near-frozen survivors were taken down into the cabin and made as comfortable as possible by the smacksmen. They were landed at Lowestoft later the same day. In the Lowestoft maritime museum at Sparrows Nest is a painting by George Vemply Burwood showing the little boat approaching the hove-to *Wildflower*.

The weather was atrocious at the time of the rescue, with snow squalls and high seas, but for Billy Wright and his crew the rescue of a boatload of survivors was a fairly routine operation. It was a rescue that caught the public imagination, however, and Skipper Wright was regarded as a national hero. The German Kaiser presented him with a clock and his four crewmen with silver watches, and a London journalist raised a subscription that was sufficient for Skipper Wright to acquire his own smack, which he named the *Willing Boys*.

The end of November 1897 and the beginning of the following month was a particularly stormy period and the east coast tugs and lifeboats were kept busy for several days in conditions that were just about as bad as they could well be. During the gales of 28th and 29th November no fewer than twenty-nine RNLI lifeboats were launched on service and the lives of 108 people, two of them women, were saved as a result; the majority of these services were carried out on the east coast.

Many lives were lost and an enormous amount of damage was done between the Wash and the Thames. Ashore the damage was considerable; passengers had to be rescued from the Brightlingsea train when it ran into floodwater on its way from Wivenhoe; the bridge between Thorpe and Aldeburgh was washed away, the Aldeburgh railway line was cut and the heart of Slaughden was wrecked by heavy seas that smashed in the doors and walls of houses and filled them with shingle.

At sea matters were far worse. Hewett's Short Blue Fleet, fishing some ninety miles east nor'east of Yarmouth, was scattered by the storm; some

fishing boats were overwhelmed by the vicious seas, men were washed from the decks and drowned, and bigger vessels had their sails carried away and their decks swept clean.

Robert Page, skipper of the smack *Problem*, YH790, a dandy built at Southtown in 1879, was riding out the storm in Botney Gut, a favourite spot not very far from the southern end of the Dogger Bank, when he saw what he thought was a Dutch vessel in distress. He had troubles of his own, for the *Problem* was reefed close down and was in only sixteen fathoms; the sea broke heavily every now and again, and conditions were not just uncomfortable but thoroughly dangerous.

Never a man to hold back when there was work to be done, Skipper Page sailed close to the supposed Dutchman and found that it was another of Hewett's smacks, the *Olive*, YH956, dismasted and with her decks swept clean. He took the *Problem* on to the weather bow of the disabled smack, hove to and asked for volunteers to get the crew out of her.

Smacksmen who worked with the fleets were used to the process of 'boarding', as the work of transferring trunks of fish to the carrier cutters was known; they also knew the risks of this work, and knew of the number of smacksmen who had lost their lives carrying out that operation in bad weather. Today the weather was not merely bad, it was atrocious.

'Are you going to drown yourself?' the crew asked Skipper Page. 'Very well, then,' he told them, 'get the boat out, I'll go alone.'

He did not go alone. Faced with his skipper's determination the third hand agreed to pull an oar with him. They dropped down to leeward across the bows of the helpless *Olive*, but try as they might they could not bring the boat under her lee in order to pull alongside, and it seemed they would be blown away by the gale.

As the two fishermen faced the prospect of being swept out of reach of their goal a huge green sea rose up, broke on the *Olive*, and threw her bodily

The wreck of the 2,898-gross-ton Hamburg-Amerika liner *Deutschland* on the Kentish Knock, some twenty-five miles south-east of Harwich, in December 1875. On the right is the tug *Liverpool*, which rescued 155 people from the wreck thanks to the information given by Harry Mills Cook of the Rowhedge smack *Aquiline*, who was put ashore by his crew in Walton Backwaters and walked to Harwich in seaboots and oilskins to raise the alarm.

towards the little boat. Skipper Page and his third hand saw the wave welling up and thought their end had come; the boat gave what they described as 'an awful swerve', but they managed to keep her head to sea and she righted herself.

The crew of the *Olive* had not been idle. They managed to throw a line to the men in the boat and hauled her alongside. Five smacksmen jumped into the little boat before it was swept away again into the gathering darkness.

During their skipper's absence the crew of the *Problem* knew just what was expected of them. They sailed the smack down to leeward and waited; in spite of the darkness they successfully picked up the boat with her human cargo without mishap, if not entirely without difficulty.

Next morning Skipper Page was still keeping his eyes open. Fifty miles west sou'west of the Leman and Ower he saw a big Norwegian barque, all her sails gone and with a signal for assistance flying in her rigging. This time the skipper did not go in the boat; the third hand was joined by the fourth hand, and together they took the boat over to the barque, the *Dronning Louise*, and picked up ten men. Conditions aboard the *Problem* must have been crowded indeed on the 150-mile voyage back to Gorleston, but nobody seems to have grumbled, even if the extra fifteen hands did make serious inroads into the smack's meagre store of provisions.

Another fishing vessel, the Yarmouth sailing drifter *Verbena*, YH275, found herself in dire trouble in the same gale. Just before daylight on 29th November a large merchant ship, the 214-ton brig *Harriett Wardle*, built at Sunderland in 1862, unmanageable in the conditions then prevailing, drove down on the fishing boat and caused her so much damage that the crew feared she would founder. The fishermen made a scramble for the rail of the bigger vessel; seven succeeded in getting on board the brig, but one of the younkers or country lads shipped as a capstan hand was lost as he misjudged his jump for the brig's rail.

Two men were left on the drifter, which was being swept by tremendous seas. Her masts had been carried away and there was little the two men could do except put an anchor over in an attempt to keep the boat head to wind and

A Ramsgate smack entering Lowestoft harbour watched by holidaymakers on the South Pier; the trawl beam is stowed on the port rail, as was customary. Fishermen from the Kent port were among the first to settle in Lowestoft as the North Sea trawl fishery developed in the mid-nineteenth century, and they were followed by others from the West Country. Several present-day Lowestoft families tell of how they moved to the town with the furniture lashed down on deck and the women and children below in the cabin.

sea. All that day and all the next night the *Verbena* wallowed in the heavy seas, then just before daybreak on 30th November she was sighted by the four-man crew of the Lowestoft smack *Snowdrop*, LT200. Two of the trawlermen launched the small boat to take a rope to the disabled drifter, and then began the long tow which ended at Lowestoft on the morning of 1st December.

Sometimes such rescue operations resulted in long wrangles over salvage payments, but in that case the owners of the two boats, Henry Shepherd and James Jackman, arrived at a mutually satisfactory settlement that same morning. The *Verbena* was towed to Yarmouth for repair in the afternoon even before news arrived of the landing at Harwich of the seven men who had scrambled aboard the *Harriett Wardle*.

Usually such rescues went unremarked. A paragraph in the *Ipswich Journal* or the Lowestoft column of the *Norwich Mercury* might record that survivors from a wrecked ship had been landed by this or that smack on its return from a fishing trip, that would be all. If it had been a particularly dangerous and meritorious rescue the Board of Trade might present the skipper with a pair of binoculars or some foreign ruler might send medals for the crew, but such rewards were exceptional.

So far as the men involved were concerned, such rescues were all in the day's work. As Walter Wood wrote in 1911, 'when a smacksman talks about a gale he means that something phenomenal took place. In the ordinary way bad weather means to him a breeze; if it's a real smashing snorter he'll let himself go a bit and call it a smart breeze or a hard blow, with a big lump of sea; but the weather has to be something of a hurricane before he'll call it a gale'. [8]

The fishermen's reaction was similar when war broke out in 1914 and the Germans began an onslaught on the British fishing boats, sinking smack after smack, usually by placing an explosive charge with a timing device in the fish hold or forepeak. In just one day, 9th June 1915, five smacks, the *Edward*, LT951, *Qui Vive*, LT702, *Britannia*, possibly R9, *Welfare*, LT555, and *Laurestina*, LT426, were blown up in that way, followed next day by the *Intrepid*, LT709. Worse still, on 30th July eight smacks, *Coriander*, LT153, *Fitzgerald*, LT197, *Achieve*, LT198, *Quest*, LT1080, *Prospector*, LT554, *Strive*, LT70, *Athena*, LT1036, and *Venture*, LT1093, were all sunk in an area 25 to 35 miles from Lowestoft.

In the face of such a fierce campaign the fishermen carried on just the same, working on the fishing grounds and bringing their catches to market as though everything were normal. 'Dozens of trawlers had been sunk by mines, submarines, or raiding surface craft, and yet. . .at the end of 1915 we met many groups working on their accustomed fishing grounds, without any escort, 70 to 80 miles off the coast, as if no war was raging, and things were quite normal,' said Lieutenant George Muhlhauser, a Royal Naval Reserve officer serving at that time with the minesweeping force.[9]

When the 3rd Destroyer Flotilla from Harwich went into action against four German destroyers off the Dutch coast in October 1914, sinking all four of them, Noah Ayers' steam trawler *United*, LT396, moved in to help pick up survivors; she brought two of the rescued German seamen back to Lowestoft. And when the German submarine U.9 torpedoed the three armoured cruisers *Aboukir*, *Hogue* and *Cressy* close to the Dutch coast that September two

Skipper George Jacobs of the Lowestoft smack *J.G.C.* who with Tom Phillips of the *Coriander* rescued 156 survivors from three torpedoed cruisers in 1915. Also shown is a commemorative certificate presented to Skipper Jacobs by the Norfolk and Suffolk District of the Independent Order of Rechabites.

Lowestoft smacks, the *J.G.C.* and the *Coriander*, ignored any danger from the submarine and sailed in to help in the rescue work, picking up 156 men from the water.

The skippers of the two smacks, Tom Phillips and George Jacobs, were awarded the Board of Trade Medal for Saving Life at Sea, more commonly known as the Sea Gallantry Medal, for their work that day. And a most remarkable tribute to the bravery and excellent seamanship displayed by the fishermen was made by Commander Bertram Nicholson of HMS *Cressy* in a letter to Tom Phillips, returning the trousers and jersey that Skipper Phillips had lent him; he declared 'you may be sure that, when you see the White Ensign first dipped to your vessel before you dip your flag, that is the ship in which I am afloat'.[10] Coming from a career naval officer, that was indeed a great tribute.

Lost without trace

However skilled the men and however seaworthy their boats, there were times when they could not withstand the violence of the North Sea weather. Working in relatively shallow seas along the edge of the banks, the smacksmen faced conditions that in bad weather could all too easily overwhelm a smack. In 1883 two disasters hit the Essex village of Brightlingsea, three of the fifteen oyster-dredging cutters that had been working on the 'Skilling' grounds off the Dutch coast failing to return after a very severe storm in March and two more smacks being overwhelmed on the Terschelling banks in December.[11]

What it was like to experience a storm such as that in which the *Recruit*, *Conquest* and *Mascotte* were lost without trace was described by the skipper of the *Express*, a 26-ton cutter that had been built at Brightlingsea in 1855.[12] He told how she had been struck by a heavy sea that carried away the mainsheet, broke the boom and washed the helmsman overboard. The rest of the crew tumbled out in time to see their friend being washed away; with the smack crippled by the damage she had received it was impossible to do anything to save him. The broken boom was thrashing about and threatening at any moment to hole the smack; it took the crew three exhausting hours to clear the boom, get the mainsail below and set a jib abaft the mast to bring the smack under control.

Their ordeal was by no means over. A few hours later another violent sea struck the vessel, carrying everything before it except the mast. The helmsman had taken the precaution of lashing himself at the tiller and was safe, but the smack was forced on to her beam ends, the cabin stove was thrown into one of the bunks and 11,000 oysters, together with the dredges, warps and other gear, were shot into the leeside of the hold right under the deck. With all that weight thrown to one side the smack could not right herself.

'To us who were below deck it fared to be some time before the deck could be reached,' Skipper George Butcher said. 'The side of the cabin answered for the floor, so that we could not reach the hatch.'

When they did escape from the cabin they hurriedly cast two oyster dredges overboard to bring the smack head to sea, then managed to clear up and trim the vessel. And when the weather improved a little they sailed her home under jury rig.

A fleet of East Anglian luggers fishing for mackerel in the same area off the Dutch coast had been caught by a succession of severe gales in May 1860; very nearly 200 men died. As far as Lowestoft was concerned, fifty-two men were lost, leaving thirty-two widows and forty-seven orphans. A relief fund was quickly raised and brought in more than £9,000, a vast amount of money in those times when a man's wages were counted in shillings and pence rather than in pounds. Each of the eighty-eight widows received five shillings (25p) a week and the 166 children each got a half-crown (12½p).

However, two months after the disaster it was decided to cut the allowances to two shillings and sixpence (12½p) a week for widows and a shilling (5p) a week for each child, with an additional sixpence (2½p) for the eldest member of a family. This reduction in benefit aroused some surprised comment, but it was pointed out that the pittances to be doled out would absorb £1,000 a year, and as the interest on the money invested would produce no more than £300 a year it was obvious that the money would run out relatively quickly.

Few of those who were lost in the 1860 gales had been as provident as Charles Calver, a young man from the inland village of Westhall who was washed overboard from the lugger *Leader*; he had insured his life for £50, so ensuring that his dependents were not left penniless.

The 1860 fund was still paying out when another gale overwhelmed the Lowestoft smack *Spider* with her entire crew in December 1863.[13] A month later, when all hope of her return had been given up, an 'appeal to the benevolent' was made on behalf of the widows and orphans of the lost men. And so it went on, disaster after disaster being followed by appeals to save those left behind from utter destitution.

Then in 1877 there occurred one of those January gales that caused particularly heavy losses, both of fishing craft and of life. The smacks *Dove*, *Enterprise*, *Flying Foam*, *Kingfisher*, *Langford*, *Protector* and *William and Sarah* failed to return from the North Sea fishing grounds, and a search by the coastguard gunboat *Seamew* and the paddle frigate *Valorous* failed to reveal any trace of the seven Lowestoft vessels.

An entry in the Lowestoft Vestry Book records that the churchwardens were requested to call a public meeting 'to take into consideration the best means of providing for the fourteen widows and twenty-eight children left destitute by the loss of life from seven fishing smacks in the recent gale'. At that meeting, held in the Public Hall at Lowestoft on 6th March, it was agreed that a subscription be raised not only 'to aid the necessities of the fourteen widows and twenty-eight children and four aged persons left destitute' by that particular disaster but also 'to form a nucleus for a permanent Society for Fishermen lost or permanently or temporarily disabled while engaged in Fishing, provided they subscribe thereto'.

Thus was born the Lowestoft Fishermen's Widows' and Orphans' Fund, which has ever since played a most useful part in relieving distress among the families of the town's fishermen. While it might be supposed that the coming of the Welfare State in the mid-twentieth century rendered such charitable organisations superfluous, the Lowestoft Fishermen's Widows' and Orphans' Fund, now known as the Lowestoft Fishermen's and Mariners' Benevolent Association, continues to play a valuable role even now that the British fishing industry is withering almost to the point of extinction.

Salvagers and lifesavers   **16**

With a constant procession of ships making use of the channels that intersect the offlying sandbanks, the Suffolk coast could prove dangerous in bad weather. Year by year the Board of Trade issued a wreck chart of the British Isles showing how many ships had been lost through stranding, collision or springing a leak in the preceding year; while that rock-bound coast of Cornwall where wreckers were reputed to tempt vessels ashore with false lights had just a smattering of wreck symbols, the map bore whole rows of dots representing wrecks by the score off the East Anglian coast.

In his book on the lifeboat service, published in 1874, Richard Lewis, then secretary of the Royal National Lifeboat Institution, pointed out that almost half the wrecks on the whole coasts of Great Britain including Ireland occurred on the east coast. Working his way up[1] the east coast from the Firth of Forth southwards, he remarked on the number of disasters in the vicinity of the Tyne, Wear and Tees and their busy ports, and then noted that 'all along the Eastern Counties, from Yarmouth to Dunwich and Misner Haven, the wrecks lie thick together. They are pretty frequent as we pass down to Harwich . . .'.[2]

That said, it is not at all surprising either that groups of skilled boatmen sprang up at places such as Lowestoft, Southwold and Aldeburgh to carry out salvage work and generally to provide services to passing shipping or that Suffolk has a very special place in the history of lifesaving and lifeboats. Not only were two of the earliest lifeboats stationed on the Suffolk coast but the world's first sailing lifeboat was built by a Lowestoft boatbuilder and put into service in the town.

For as long as men have gone to sea there have been wrecks on the beaches and on the offlying sands in the Lowestoft area; mention has been made in an earlier chapter of the legal difficulties that arose in 1353 after a number of ships had been driven ashore south of Lowestoft, and Daniel Defoe in *A Tour Through the Whole Island of Great Britain* (1723) told of a storm in 1692 that resulted in the loss of more than 200 ships and cost the lives of more than a thousand men.

An eyewitness account by Robert Reeve, a Lowestoft merchant and lawyer, of the great storm of 18th December 1770 gives one a stark idea of the conditions against which seamen struggled when the elements combined against them. He told how the wind, which had been blowing from the south-west, backed abruptly to the north-west and for two hours 'raged with a fury that was hardly ever equalled'.[3]

Opposite: One of the beach companies' yawls, rigged with only two masts instead of the three of the earlier craft, seen ready for service on Southwold beach about 1890.

Anchors and cables proved too feeble a security for the ships, which instantly parting from them, and running on board each other, produced a confusion neither to be described nor conceived. At daylight a scene of the most tragic distress was exhibited; those who first beheld it assert that no less than eighteen ships were on the sand before this place [Lowestoft] at one and the same time, and many others were seen to sink; of those on the sand, one half were entirely demolished, with their crews, before nine o'clock; the rest were preserved a few hours longer; but this dreadful pause served only to aggravate the destruction of the unhappy men who belonged to them, who betook themselves to the masts and rigging; these continuing breaking, eight or ten were not unfrequently seen to perish at a time, without the possibility of being assisted.

Fifteen only, about two in the afternoon, were taken off one of the wrecks, and about as many more were saved by taking to their boats, or getting on board other ships when they boarded each other. It is impossible to collect with certainty how many lives, or how many ships were lost in this terrible hurricane. Twenty-five at least, perhaps thirty ships, and two hundred men, do not seem to be an exaggerated account. This, indeed, is too small a calculation, if credit is to be given to one of the seamen, who declares he saw six vessels sink not far without the Stanford,[4] among which was a large ship bound for Lisbon, with sixty or seventy passengers on board. One or two of the ships which are left belong to Yarmouth, and one to Plymouth, but the generality are colliers, and belong to Sunderland, Shields, and other places in the north.

The concern this destructive scene occasioned to the spectators of it was increased by the following circumstance: when the masts of one of the ships, on which were eight or nine men, fell, two of them were some time afterwards seen struggling among the wreck, and at length, after unremitted efforts, got upon the hull. In the afternoon, a pilot-boat ventured from the shore, but it was found unpracticable to administer any relief to the unfortunate sufferers, whom they were compelled to leave in their forlorn state; an approaching dark, cold, stormy night, heightening the horrors of their situation.

The next day, to the astonishment of every body, one of the men was observed to be alive, and about noon the boat again attempted to save him, and approached so near as to ask the poor fellow several questions; but the hull, on which he was, being surrounded with wreck, and the sea running high, it was impossible to rescue him from the impending danger.

'The ensuing night put a period to his misfortunes and his life,' Mr Reeve's account ends.

The pilot boat whose crew endeavoured to reach the men on the wreck would have been one of the local beach yawls – pronounced *yoll* – fine, weatherly open boats of 40-50ft long that were used for putting pilots aboard ships in the offing and for salvage and rescue work not only at Lowestoft but all along the east Norfolk and Suffolk coast. Double-ended, clinker-built craft that could be launched from the beach, they had three masts on which were set large lugsails that gave them a good turn of speed.

As an appendix to his account of the 1770 storm Gillingwater recommended to his readers 'the possibility of constructing a vessel, or some other machine, upon such principles as shall not be liable to overset, but should be capable of approaching any vessel in distress, during the most violent storms, and when surrounded with the most tumultuous waves'.

His plea went unheeded at the time. It was not until 1800 that a subscription was raised in Lowestoft for the purchase of a lifeboat designed and built by Henry Greathead, of North Shields. He had constructed his first lifeboat for use at the mouth of the River Tyne in 1789; intended for work within a fairly short distance of the shore, it was purely a pulling boat with no means of propulsion other than oars.

The subscription for the lifeboat, which arrived at Lowestoft in February 1801, was promoted by Robert Sparrow, of Worlingham Hall near Beccles and Sparrow's Nest at Lowestoft, and the Revd Francis Bowness, the incumbent of Gunton, a parish just to the north of Lowestoft.[5] At almost the same time the Revd Dr Richard Frank, of Alderton, and Mr P.B. Broke, of Nacton, father of Sir Philip Broke of the *Shannon*,[6] raised a subscription for a similar lifeboat to be stationed in Hollesley Bay near the mouth of the Deben, some forty miles south of Lowestoft. The Lowestoft boat was the sixth lifeboat built by Greathead, and the Hollesley Bay boat the seventh.

While the lifeboat stationed at Bawdsey succeeded in rescuing eight people from the brig *Pallas* after she had gone ashore and sunk on 13th February 1804,[7] the Lowestoft boat was so disliked and distrusted by the beachmen that they refused to use her even when offered generous rewards for doing so. Deeply disappointed at what he saw as the intransigence of the Lowestoft men, Robert Sparrow transferred the boat to Gorleston, where she could be launched into the harbour and rowed out to the rescue instead of having to be launched off the beach. Unhappily the North Country boat found no greater favour there, and when the gunbrig HMS *Snipe* was wrecked in Gorleston South Ham with heavy loss of life in 1807 the lifeboat remained unheeded in her shed. The loss of seventy people in the wreck prompted the artilleryman Captain George Manby to develop his line-throwing mortar, but he seems to have been unaware of the presence of a lifesaving craft within easy reach.

Wrecks were indeed all too frequent on the Suffolk coast, and the fate of the *Peace*, one of a fleet of transports that encountered a very severe storm off the Dutch coast when on its way to the River Weser to land British troops in Oldenburg as part of a plan to counter Napoleon's expansion in Europe, was by no means exceptional. The fleet was scattered by the storm; some of them found refuge in Harwich harbour, but the *Peace* was driven ashore at Kessingland on 18th November 1805. After spending an uncomfortable night exposed to the elements on the ship's deck the officers and 138 men of the 28th Foot[8] – later to become the Gloucestershire Regiment – were brought ashore on Kessingland beach by local fishermen. It was not a remarkable rescue, just a routine evacuation; the only casualty was a serjeant of the 28th who had apparently collapsed the previous night and had been left for dead, with the waves washing over him and men treading on his body as they busied themselves about the ship.

A North Country lifeboat designed and built by Henry Greathead, of South Shields, similar to those put on station at Lowestoft and Bawdsey in 1801.

Serjeant James Bubb's body was landed and dumped on the sand when the troops came ashore, and it lay there untended as they were formed up and marched off towards Lowestoft. Nobody cared about the man whom the officers had considered to be drunk, and who was now thought to be dead, except four farmworkers who fetched a cart to take the body up to the village. By chance a surgeon from Beccles, Mr William Henchman Crowfoot, had been visiting one of his patients in Kessingland, and it happened that as he walked down the road past the then semi-ruinous St Edmund's Church he saw coming towards him a cart loaded with the belongings of the officers. Mr Crowfoot spoke to the red-coated serjeant of the 28th in charge of the cart, who told him that a cart that was following him up the road contained the body of another serjeant of the regiment who had collapsed on deck the previous night.

The surgeon stopped the second cart and took a look at the body. The first thing he realised was that there was no smell of drink; the officers' supposition that the man was drunk was unfounded. Taking a closer look, he found the tiniest spark of life; the serjeant had collapsed from exposure and exhaustion, but there remained a faint chance that he could be restored to life. The surgeon told the four farm labourers to get him to an inn as speedily as they could, and as soon as they got there he set to work, aided by the four men.

After 'three or four hours unremitted perseverance ... I had the inexpressible satisfaction of finding I had succeeded in rescuing a fellow-creature from premature death and in preserving to his country a robust young soldier,' Mr Crowfoot later told the treasurer of the Royal Humane Society.[9] Not only did that society award him its silver medal but the saving of Serjeant Bubb led directly to the formation, appropriately enough at a meeting held at the King's Head in Kessingland, of the Suffolk Humane Society to promote 'whatever means may most effectually awaken the exertions of humanity in cases of shipwreck'.

Throughout its existence the society concerned itself with rewarding those who saved others from drowning, but far more significantly it took over the operation of the lifeboat that was at the time of its foundation being built at

Lowestoft – the world's first sailing lifeboat.[10]

By the early 1800s Lowestoft had acquired a reputation as a pleasant place for well-to-do business people and tradesmen to spend a few weeks relaxing with their families beside the sea. One of those who came in 1807 was a coachbuilder from London, Lionel Lukin, who had made a name for himself not only as a successful builder of fashionable transport but as the inventor of what he called an unimmergible boat. A native of Dunmow in Essex, he is said to have carried out some of his early experiments on the Doctor's Pond there and had designed a lifeboat on the lines of a traditional Norwegian fishing boat, a joll.[11]

Hearing of Lukin's presence in the town, Robert Sparrow approached him and sought his advice. Lukin discussed with the beachmen and pilots their objections to the Greathead boat and was shown one of their favourite yawls; if such a boat were built and rendered unsinkable, he was told, the men would gladly use it for lifesaving. The upshot was that some of the beachmen wrote to Sparrow telling him that they would willingly use a lifeboat designed on the lines of their yawls 'provided we are convinced, by proper experiments, that such a boat is manageable here, and that she will not sink if filled with water, in addition to her proper burthen – this being a degree of safety which we confess our yawls do not possess'.[12]

After asking the advice of Captain Gilfred Reed, an Elder Brother of Trinity House who had had charge of the earlier lifeboat, Robert Sparrow decided to order a new boat from a local boatbuilder, Batchelor Barcham. Lukin offered to prolong his stay in Lowestoft to oversee the building of the boat, which was equipped with a number of sealed casks lashed inside the boat and under the thwarts to provide buoyancy should the boat be swamped. Other barrels in the bottom of the boat could be filled with water 'when necessary to encrease her ballast'. The new boat also had the protruding cork 'padding' that was to be a feature of all future Norfolk and Suffolk type lifeboats built for stations in those counties and in Essex; in most of those later craft the buoyancy barrels were replaced by canvas-covered wooden air cases made to fit the internal shape of the hull.

Although she was provided with fourteen oars for use in calm weather or when manoeuvring close to a wreck, the boat's main means of propulsion was her three lugsails; she was the first sailing lifeboat to be built. Named *Frances Ann* after the daughter of Lord Rous, the president of the then-newly-formed Suffolk Humane Society, the new lifeboat was launched for the first time on a most unpleasant November day when incessant heavy rain discouraged would-be spectators from coming down to the beach to watch the trials. During those trials the plugs (more than one according to the newspaper report) were removed and the boat was allowed to fill with water until she was floating on the air casks. Though full of water, she sailed well and proved very stable, even when the sixteen people who had gone out in her all gathered on the lee side; some of them even climbed on to the lee gunwale without affecting her trim.[13]

That was no pleasure trip. A strong south-easterly wind created a heavy sea on the offlying sands, but all the same she was taken right across the Corton Sand without shipping any water. It is interesting to read how well she sailed even when full of water; later boats of the Norfolk and Suffolk type were ordinarily sailed in that state so that any water coming aboard found its way out through the enlarged plugholes.

It would seem that the cost of building of the *Frances Ann*, some £350, came partly from funds remaining from the 1800 subscription and partly from Sparrow's own pocket, but it was the Suffolk Humane Society that was destined to operate her for the coming forty years and also to run the lifeboat service at both Lowestoft and Pakefield for more than sixty years.

An opportunity to test the *Frances Ann* in service was not long in coming. She was called out on 24th February 1808 when two colliers grounded on the sands to the north of Lowestoft; wind and tide being against the boats from Lowestoft, the Gorleston boats were first on the scene, but the Gorleston men did not attempt to board the stranded ships until the lifeboat was close by. Both vessels were eventually refloated by the Gorleston boatmen. At the annual meeting of the Suffolk Humane Society that year medals were presented to Mr Garrard, of Walberswick, and to two Lowestoft pilots, James Stebbens and James Buxton, for having 'at great hazard to themselves' saved the lives of others, but no details of the rescues were given.

A tremendous gale in December the following year drove many vessels ashore between Lowestoft and Yarmouth and strewed the beaches with wreckage. The Sunderland collier *Catherine* was driven on to the Holm Sand off Lowestoft, but it seems that there was a delay in getting the lifeboat afloat; 'from the position of the ship and the violence of the sea, it was impossible for some time to ascertain whether any persons were on the wreck,' says a newspaper report of the incident. 'At length one man was discovered, and the Life Boat launched as soon as possible. . .'.[14]

By the time the boat reached the wreck only one man, the carpenter, was left hanging in the rigging, the others having been washed away and drowned. In getting him into the lifeboat he was somehow crushed, breaking some of his ribs, but he was taken safely ashore and eventually recovered from his injuries.

The *Frances Ann* had made her first rescue and had shown her worth, but when another severe gale struck the coast in November 1810 and a vessel struck on the sands off the town she was not launched. 'The life boat was hauled down, but the sailors, so great was the danger to be apprehended, were unwilling to make any effort to approach the wreck, although twenty-five guineas were offered to them by some gentlemen who were spectators of this distressing scene.'[15] It seems that the best of the local sailors were at Corton saving the crew of a beached ship with Manby's life-saving mortar, but clearly there remained a prejudice against the lifeboat among some of the seafaring community.

However fine a boat the *Frances Ann* undoubtedly was, she was no use at all without a crew; and a crew is little use without the right leadership. That essential element was supplied by a naval lieutenant who settled in Lowestoft after his marriage in 1814 to his cousin, a daughter of the rector of Margate. A member of a Sudbury family, Samuel Thomas Carter had joined the Royal Navy as a first-class volunteer in 1800 and been confirmed in the rank of lieutenant in 1808; his seafaring career was not undistinguished and certainly not uneventful, but it came to an end so far as the Navy was concerned when he was placed on half pay in 1813.

Lieutenant Samuel Fielding Harmer, who while serving with the Coastguard acted as Lieutenant Samuel Thomas Carter's second-in-command in the *Frances Ann*. He was given command of a steam gunboat in 1840 and died in China in 1843.

He was in command of the *Frances Ann* when she was launched on a Sunday morning, 22nd October 1820, to the aid of ships caught in a heavy gale from the SSW that was whipping the sea into foam and sending a most tremendous surf to break on the shore. One vessel that attempted to gain the shelter of Lowestoft Roads struck the Beacon Ridge as she came through the Stanford Channel, and a second soon followed her; both ships broke up within minutes, and the crews were lost before any aid could reach them from the shore. Then the Woodbridge sloop *Sarah & Caroline*[16] grounded on the Newcome Sand and the crew of five climbed into the rigging as she sank beneath them.

Once the lifeboat was afloat – and it must have been a difficult task to launch her through the tremendous surf – she was towed by a large gang of men on the beach a considerable way to the southward to bring her into a position from which it was hoped she could reach the sloop. When the tow was let go the ebb tide carried the lifeboat to leeward of the wreck, and it was only when the tide began to flow that it proved possible to reach the vessel. The crew were taken off in the nick of time; one man was so exhausted that he was just about to fall from the rigging as he was grabbed and hauled into the lifeboat. The lifeboatmen then turned their attention to the brig *George*, of London, which was in a sinking state; a further seven men were taken into the

A painting in the Lowestoft Maritime Museum of the *Frances Ann* setting off to a wreck. Like the yawls of the early nineteenth century, on which she was based, the lifeboat left her mainmast ashore in heavy weather.

A homeward bound brig hove to off Lowestoft and signalling for a pilot, from a print published in the town in 1840. The Stanford lightvessel can be seen under the brig's bowsprit, and at left is a beach company's yawl, possibly bringing out the pilot. At the right is a herring lugger.

lifeboat, which landed all twelve rescued men on the beach about six o'clock that evening 'without the smallest accident whatever'.[17]

A leading part in manning the lifeboat was taken by the pilots, licensed but not employed by Trinity House and engaged in navigating vessels in coastal waters and into the Thames; they were the elite of the seafaring community. Prominent among them was Henry Beverley Disney, who gained his licence first in 1810 at the age of twenty-three and did not retire until 1871, when Trinity House granted him a pension of £28 a year. He was among those who gave evidence in favour of the Norwich and Lowestoft Navigation Bill in 1826; some of the townspeople sent a private carriage to Pakefield to bring him home when he returned from London by coach.[18]

Disney was in the crew of the *Frances Ann* when in January 1815 she rescued three men from the billyboy sloop *Jeanie* of Hull, watched by hundreds of people standing on top of the cliff.[19] The billyboy had sprung a leak when bound for London with a cargo of potatoes. He was also in the crew when the lifeboat carried out the rescue described above.

In 1841 he was awarded a gold medal by the South Holland Royal Humane Association for a rescue carried out on the Dutch coast,[20] and then the following January he had a narrow escape when washed overboard from the *Frances Ann* during a particularly difficult rescue from a ship on the Newcome Sand; he managed to hang on to a safety line and was hauled back into the boat by other members of the crew.[21]

While the pilots seem to have been the backbone of the lifeboat crew there were beachmen who willingly served in the boat, yet the beachmen's attitude to the *Frances Ann* was decidedly ambiguous. At Lowestoft, as well as elsewhere, those who gained their livelihood by assisting ships in trouble preferred to use their own yawls whenever they could, since the gentlemen who sat on the committee of the Humane Society and similar organisations stipulated that the lifeboat should never under any circumstances be used for salvage work; it was solely for the saving of life.

There were those among the members of the beach companies who saw the lifeboat as being unfair competition, and this led to serious trouble when the 108-ton brig *Westmoreland* of Stockton struck a point of the Newcome Sand as she endeavoured to pass through the Stanford Channel on 7th December 1821. The *Frances Ann* was one of five boats launched from Lowestoft beach when the *Westmoreland* hoisted a signal of distress.[22] The yawl *Seaman's Assistance*, belonging to Denny's Company, was the first to reach the casualty and ran alongside, putting two men, John Stebbings and a young man named William Butcher, aboard the brig.

What happened next is by no means clear. Conflicting accounts appeared in consecutive issues of the local newspapers, the second, based on sworn statements by the beachmen concerned, rebutting the earlier one.[23] However, a seaman from the *Westmoreland* was later to tell the Admiralty Court in London that he asked Stebbings to help him throw a warp to the lifeboat, but instead of helping him the beachman leaned over the bow and cut the line by which Lieutenant Harmer had made the boat fast. 'Damn yer eyes, let go and take that thing ashore, you've no business here!' Stebbings shouted to the men in the *Frances Ann*.

Figureheads and other relics of wrecked ships decorate the Old Company's shed at Lowestoft, photographed in 1939. The shed was destroyed during the Second World War.

'The villains have cut the lifeboat away!' the seaman said he told Captain Rydcr. Hearing the horror in the man's voice, Stebbings told the captain 'They'd no business here! The ship is ours – we've got the job. We're your safeguards and protectors – why, you're as safe as if you were ashore. . .'

Fine words, but when the brig floated on the rising tide and was found to be taking water the beachmen returned to their yawl, taking with them only a woman passenger and an apprentice, and sailed off. Seeing the *Seaman's Assistance* leaving the helpless vessel Lieutenant Carter assumed that the crew of the brig were safe in the yawl. As the doomed *Westmoreland* drifted on to the flats at Pakefield the *Frances Ann* and the yawl made for Lowestoft beach. It was only when the *Seaman's Assistance* was beached about a quarter of an hour after the lifeboat that it was realised that there were still men on board the wreck.

Darkness had fallen by the time Lieutenant Carter had returned to the wreck in the lifeboat, and try as he might he could not make contact with those on the brig. It was only when the beachmen took a skiff to Pakefield behind a team of horses and launched her close to the wreck that two survivors were rescued, thanks to the bravery of Lieutenant Harmer, who insisted on going out in the beachmen's skiff.

Had Captain Ryder ordered the signal of distress to be lowered? Had he threatened his crew with a gun when they sought to leave the ship, as the beachmen alleged? The captain could not answer such questions; he had died when struck by the tiller as the ship hit the sand. Nevertheless, much of the story came out when John Stebbings, William Butcher junior, T. Ellis, W. Butcher senior and John Denny, the owner of the company, were tried at the Admiralty Court on an indictment that they did conspire to prevent assistance being given to the *Westmoreland* and that in the pursuance of such conspiracy they did cut away a rope fastening the lifeboat to the said brig, by which four lives were lost.[24]

During the hearing of the case Henry May, a Trinity pilot who had been in the crew of the lifeboat, told the court that there was an impression on the coast that in cases of ships in distress a doctrine of 'first come, first served' was

A woodcut illustration of a sailing lifeboat designed by Captain George Manby and built at Yarmouth on very much the same lines as the *Frances Ann*.

held with respect to salvage. He was interrupted by the president of the court, Lord Stowell, who declared that 'if any such impression exists, nothing can be more erroneous; it is without the slightest foundation of fact'.

He went on to say that 'it is most absurd to suppose that, because a boat gets alongside a vessel in distress, the crew have a right to take possession of her, supersede the authority of the captain, and say who shall or shall not afterwards come on board'.

After much evidence had been heard and the lawyers had conferred, the High Court of Admiralty acquitted the beachmen of conspiracy; young Butcher, who was said to have been the one who cut the lifeboat adrift, not Stebbings, was bound over to be of good behaviour.

In spite of Lord Stowell's authoritative statement of the law, the Lowestoft beachmen stubbornly held to the principle of 'first come, first served'. What did he, sitting up there in his legal robes and wig, know about getting a stranded vessel off the sands? On the Newcome and the Holme, it was their word that was the law.

There was a tragic sequel to the case: the *Seaman's Assistance* was lost off the Suffolk coast in January 1823; William Butcher and his son, both of them pilots, and six beachmen died.

Beachmen at Lowestoft in a well-known photograph by a young Harry Tansley. He was apprenticed at the time to local photographer Thomas Boughton.

For the preservation of life   17

Where the Suffolk Humane Society had shown the way, others sought to follow – not always successfully. In the same gale in October 1820 in which the *Frances Ann* succeeded in rescuing the crews of the Woodbridge sloop *Sarah & Caroline* and the collier brig *George*, a Whitby vessel, the *Ann*, was wrecked near the entrance to Harwich harbour; a detachment of the 6th Royal Regiment[1] from Landguard Fort was helped by men of the Revenue service to rescue seven of the crew, who were given hospitality in the fort.[2] Then on 28th October a schooner was wrecked on the Cork Sand five miles or so off Landguard Point with the loss of nine men.[3]

Commenting on the loss of ship and life, the editor of the *Colchester Gazette* lamented that the establishment of lifeboats on the Essex coast had been neglected, and at the beginning of December the mayor of Harwich, Anthony Cox, convened a meeting that resulted in the formation of the Essex Life Boat Association. Within a commendably short time a boat on the lines of the *Frances Ann* was ordered from George Graham, who was at that time operating the Navy Yard at Harwich, but the building of a second boat to have been stationed at Brightlingsea was 'unavoidably deferred until the benevolent object of the Association receives a more general support from the friends of humanity'.[4]

At the same time a subscription was raised at Ipswich for the building of a rather different lifeboat designed by Captain Richard Hall Gower, a leading role in promoting this project being taken by Rear-Admiral Benjamin Page, a redoubtable old naval veteran living in retirement in his native Ipswich.[5] Unlike the Harwich lifeboat, this was a light boat on the lines of a whaler 'that ten or twelve men can quickly launch, and six, or even four, easily manage'. She was 29ft 6in long, with a 6ft beam, and had two short masts on which were set spritsails.

Built by Jabez Bayley at his St Peter's Yard under the superintendence of Captain Gower, she was launched on 4th April 1821; the launching was watched by a 'multitude of persons collected in the shipyard, on the several quays, on board the shipping, in boats, and on the banks of the river'. Indeed, the number of spectators was only exceeded by the crowds watching the launching of the Indiaman *Orwell* from Bayley's Halifax Yard in 1817, so it was said.[6]

After the launching Benjamin Hamblin, master of the Suffolk and Norfolk Shipping Company's hoy *Stevens*, took charge of the boat and six young seamen rowed her down the river and back to show her off to the assembled 'multitude'.

Opposite: One of the crew stands ready with a line as the Southwold No. 2 lifeboat *Rescue* comes ashore. She served at Southwold from 1897 to 1920.

The Orford lifeboat approaching a wreck on the Ness, seen in a print published in 1838.

And when the Harwich lifeboat *Braybrooke* was ceremonially launched the following September 'seven unemployed men were indiscriminately taken off the beach' at Harwich and rowed over to Landguard to form a crew for the *Ipswich Life Boat*. 'The whole was done at a moment's notice, without the least preparation' and the lifeboat was rowed over to Harwich 'in less than an hour'.[7]

Most unfortunately that was typical of the arrangements made for the Landguard lifeboat. In the event of the boat being called out it was assumed that suitable men could be found in Harwich, be ferried over the stormy waters of the harbour, get the boat ready and set off to the rescue, without the least preparation; there was no regular crew, nobody in command on the spot, and little real organisation.

The *Braybrooke* at Harwich performed her first service in May the following year, assisting a London fishing boat off the West Rocks in the harbour approaches,[8] and then in January 1823 she went to the assistance of HM cutter *Surly* after she had gone ashore; the Commissioners of the Navy awarded her crew £10 for 'their meritorious exertions'.[9] So far as is known the Landguard boat did not perform her first service until 19th February 1824, when she was taken out by a coxswain and six men of the Coast Blockade, forerunner of the Coastguard, to the Sunderland collier brig *Malvina*, which had grounded on the Platters, a shoal just to the east of Landguard Point; the collier was assisted off the shoal and into harbour.[10]

In spite of her success with the *Malvina* the Landguard lifeboat seems to have been a rather unsatisfactory craft, and when the Suffolk Association for Saving the Lives of Shipwrecked Seamen, only the second such county organisation to be formed, came into existence later in 1824 one of its first decisions was to have the boat rebuilt by her builder, increasing her beam to 8ft 6in.[11] Nevertheless, in 1825 it was reported that the Landguard station was 'of no use whatever' and the boat stationed there was 'totally inefficient'. She was withdrawn, sent back to the yard in which she had been built and converted into a yacht, surely the first lifeboat to be so converted; she was put up for sale at the Great White Horse Tavern, Ipswich, on 31st March 1827.[12]

While agreeing to abandon the Landguard station the Suffolk Shipwreck Association, as it was often called, decided to build a lifeboat for Orford and to place lifesaving mortars at Corton, Sizewell Gap and between Landguard Fort and Woodbridge.[13] Later it was decided to build a lifeboat for Sizewell Gap, both the new boats to be built by a firm of boatbuilders in the town of Newbury in Berkshire; they were brought from London by vessels trading between Orford and the Thames.[14]

Some time in the 1830s the Orford boat was transferred to Woodbridge Haven to replace the ageing North Country boat placed in Hollesley Bay as long ago as 1801, but that station was closed in 1852; at about the same time the Sizewell boat was transferred to Aldeburgh, where there were beachmen and fishermen in sufficient numbers to form a crew more easily than at Sizewell. The town has continued as a lifeboat station ever since. Little is known of the work of these two boats, but on 19th November 1838 the Woodbridge Haven boat saved four men from the Newcastle sloop *Friendship* and in 1841 the Sizewell boat rescued the exhausted crew of the sloop *Catherina* of Goole and subsequently, with the help of a boat from Thorpe, took the potato-laden vessel into Yarmouth.

In 1839 there were moves to station a lifeboat at Pakefield, then a village some distance to the south of Lowestoft rather than a suburb of that town, and the Suffolk Humane Society agreed to provide a boat on condition that 'the boat and its crews and the management thereof must be under the sole and absolute controul, direction and management of this Society'.[15] A 45ft boat built by William Teasdel at Yarmouth entered service the following year, and at about the same time Teasdel built a similar but smaller boat named the *Solebay* for a newly-formed Southwold Life Boat Society.

It was clearly the presence of beachmen and fishermen at Aldeburgh who could man the lifeboat that influenced the Suffolk Shipwreck Association in moving the Sizewell boat to the town. The ineffectiveness of the Landguard lifeboat had underlined the stupidity of stationing a boat where there were no seamen to provide a crew, and at Bawdsey it is apparent that insufficient thought had been given to the manning of the boat; when it was launched to the London-registered brig *Pallas* on 13th February 1804 it was at first unable to reach the vessel, the crew being partly landsmen, and it succeeded only at the second attempt when a crew entirely of seamen had been mustered – by then the unfortunate crew of the brig had spent six hours in the rigging.

The beachmen were professional boatmen and salvagers, entirely dependent on their seamanship, their knowledge of local waters and their other undoubted nautical skills to earn a living for themselves and their families. Occasionally hailed as heroes when they performed a notable rescue of a shipwrecked crew, they were branded as 'longshore sharks' and worse when they demanded payment for their services in refloating a stranded ship or assisting a leaky vessel into port. The landed gentry and successful businessmen who gave a few guineas to finance the lifeboats and ran organisations such as the humane society and the shipwreck association insisted that under no circumstances should any of their lifeboats be used for salvage work; when the Pakefield men, after rescuing the crew from a ship in distress, went out again in the lifeboat to bring the casualty into port they were castigated by the committee of the Suffolk Humane Society and told that such use of the lifeboat was strictly forbidden.[16]

The result was that when a call came to a wrecked ship on the sands the beachmen used their own yawls, and time after time it was only when they found it impossible to reach the casualty in a yawl that they returned ashore for the lifeboat or signalled to their colleagues ashore to bring the lifeboat. All too often the delay cost men's lives. It is not difficult to understand the ambivalence of the Suffolk beachmen's attitude to the introduction of lifeboats.

To perform their work the beachmen formed themselves into companies, each with a number of yawls, gigs and other boats and with a shed which served both as a meeting place for the men and as a store for their boats' gear. Some of the companies had a lookout close to their shed; at Aldeburgh, where there were two companies, the combined sheds and lookouts built in the mid-nineteenth century still exist, one of them having been extended to serve as the RNLI inshore lifeboat shed in fairly recent years.[17]

Gorleston, which was a part of Suffolk until being 'transferred to the county of Norfolk for administrative purposes' in the twentieth century, had three companies of boatmen – they operated mainly from the harbour and were termed boatmen rather than beachmen – whose members saw the advantage of augmenting their yawls with lifeboats of their own, all of the Norfolk and Suffolk type. The Ranger Company had the *Rescuer* built in 1855 by James Beeching, who had four years earlier been awarded the Duke of Northumberland's premium for a self-righting boat, referred to deprecatingly by beachmen as a 'roly-poly'.

Possession of a lifeboat enabled the boatmen to put to sea in foul weather in which others wished they were safely in harbour, but which promised them the chance of remunerative employment. In the new year of 1857 Henry Leggatt and Charles Salmon with eighteen other members of the Ranger Company were at sea in the *Rescuer*, assisting the barque *Elizabeth* into Lowestoft on 5th January in a heavy easterly gale. Next day the weather was no better, with frequent snowstorms, so they put out from Lowestoft 'for the purpose of rendering assistance to any vessel that might require it'.[18]

Off Hopton, between Lowestoft and Gorleston, they found the 257-ton brig *Magnet*, with a cargo of 420 tons of coal for London, lying with two anchors down in a most dangerous position a mere two cables (1,200ft) off the beach. They bore down on her and, seeing the brig's crew signalling to them for help, ran the lifeboat under the starboard quarter; a rope was thrown to them from the brig, and twelve of the boatmen boarded her, to find the master with the leadline in his hand. He told them there was only four and a half fathoms (27ft) and he didn't like the position he was in; his vessel was drawing 14½ft.

Without more ado he asked the boatmen to get his vessel to safety. They tried to get the anchors, but this proved too dangerous in the prevailing conditions, so they set the main stays'l, foretopmast stays'l, two double-reefed tops'ls and fore course and slipped both chain cables. By keeping her under as much canvas as she would bear they worked her off the shore while they set to work to pump her out. With the boatmen and the crew working together the *Magnet* was extricated from her perilous position and eventually taken into Lowestoft harbour. For that service the Rangers were awarded £215 10s. 4d., hardly a prince's ransom.

Even when employing such boats as the *Rescuer* the boatman faced risks that could never be discounted. In January 1866 the *Rescuer* overturned as she left the harbour in response to signals from a vessel out at sea, and twelve men died; even worse, twenty-five people drowned less than two years later when the same boat was in collision with a fishing lugger as she came in with men picked up from the full-rigged ship *George Kendall*, aground on the Cross Sand.

At Lowestoft there were three beach companies, the Old Company, in its early years known as Denny's, the New and the North Roads Company; the Old

The Aldeburgh lifeboat *Alfred & Patience Gottwald* seen at her station on the beach in 1976. When a call came the turntable platform on which the boat rested would be tipped forward and she would slide down the shingle beach into the water, a somewhat unusual method of launching.

Company was at different times the owner of five yawls named *Happy New Year*, the last of them designed for them by yacht designer G.L. Watson. Southwold also had three companies named after the part of the shore where they had their watch-houses cut into the cliff and kept their boats, the New York Cliff, Long Island Cliff and Kilcock Cliff companies. At Aldeburgh there were two, the more northerly company known as the 'downtowners' and the other as the 'uptowners'.

Of the companies situated in villages that at Pakefield was the largest, at one time having a membership of seventy. To the north of Lowestoft the village of Corton had a company that was never so large or so vigorous as that at Pakefield, and to the south Kessingland had a company that had a yawl, the *Sophia*, built by John Chambers as late as 1912; she was launched on only a very few occasions, and lay on the beach until broken up in 1933.

All the early lifesaving societies suffered severely from a shortage of funds; the Southwold society was so poor when it built the *Solebay* that it could not afford to reward the crews in any way until in 1844 a member of its committee offered to pay £5 to the crew 'upon their bringing in safety the first man they shall have actually saved by their exertions'.[19] And when in 1850 the Suffolk Humane Society had to have a new boat, the *Victoria*, built by Samuel Sparham to replace the pioneering *Frances Ann* they economised by giving the new lifeboat her predecessor's masts and sails, in spite of the fact that the new one was a larger boat.[20] Financial matters came to a head in the 1850s, when the Suffolk Association for Saving the Lives of Shipwrecked Seamen handed over the stations under its control to the Royal National Lifeboat Institution and the Southwold Life Boat Society became the Southwold branch of the RNLI. In 1855 the Suffolk Humane Society resolved to unite with the RNLI, although in that case the society retained the running of the Lowestoft and Pakefield stations until 1873.[21]

The first service of the new Lowestoft boat appears to have been on 6th January 1853, when she was towed out by the paddle tug *Imperial*[22] to the aid of the Ipswich brig *Marys*, which had gone on the Holm Sand and been forced over that bank and on to the Newcome. The *Victoria* and the Pakefield lifeboat together saved six men and a boy from the brig.[23] Though the newspaper reported that the crew had found fault with the new boat and particularly with the spars and sails inherited from the *Frances Ann*, complaining that 'if a sea should catch the sails, the masts would break like a carrot', the minutes of the Humane Society contain no mention of this.

Members of the beach companies did fine work in assisting ships in trouble, of that there is no doubt, but they attracted criticism at times not only for driving a hard bargain but for their profligate habits. The Old Company of Lowestoft received no less than £170 for their services in assisting the Yarmouth schooner *Abeona* off the Holm Sand one winter day in 1850, sufficient to dole twenty-seven shillings for each man of the company. It provoked the comment that 'it is a sad pity these sons of the ocean are not more provident; many of them who recently applied for parish relief and whose families were wanting bread were seen, after they had taken their money, in a state of intoxication'.[24]

On the occasion of the *Victoria's* first service the tugmen and the lifeboatmen collaborated successfully, but some three years earlier the beachmen's resentment had boiled over when the tugs belonging to the railway and harbour company at Lowestoft had begun to compete with them in salvage work.[25] The tugmasters paid no heed to the beachmen's premise that the first boat on the scene was given the job but instead sought to undercut the beachmen's charges whenever they could.

A salvage case in which a company of Lowestoft beachmen was claiming for assistance given to the schooner *Glory* of Hamburg came before the Admiralty Court on 15th May 1850; the schooner had run on to the Corton Sand about three in the morning, but it was not at all clear what had happened next. 'With the exception of the facts that the vessel got upon the sand; that the salvors came to her assistance and offered their services, which were at first refused, but afterwards accepted, and employed in carrying out an anchor and lightening the vessel, which on the following morning was towed off by a steam tug and taken into Lowestoft harbour – all the points were in dispute,' a local newspaper reported.[26]

That, of course, was nothing out of the ordinary; salvage cases before the magistrates were normally contentious, the salvors' case being that the weather was stormy in the extreme, the ship was in great danger and the work was carried out at great risk, while the owner's legal representative invariably argued that the sea was calm, the ship was in no danger and the services rendered were really of little or no value. This case, however, was before the Admiralty Court in London, and it would seem that the evidence revealed something more than just an ordinary difference of opinion.

'The Learned Judge, after adverting to the contrary statements contained in the evidence, said that in his opinion the salvors had behaved with great impropriety when the steam tug first came up, and still more so on her second approach.' One does not have to use much imagination to fill in between the lines.

'Had there been no misconduct he would have allotted them £300, but there [sic} misconduct had been so gross that he would now give them £100 only, and instead of their whole costs he would allow them only two-thirds.'

The feeling that the tugs were taking the food out of the mouths of the beachmen's families festered on, and violence erupted on 18th October 1850 when the brig *Luna* of Aberdeen, bound from Archangel for London with a cargo of linseed, grounded on the Newcome. Beachmen of the Young

Company went off in both
a yawl and a gig, and two
or three of the men went
on board the stranded
brig, but they were told
by the master, Captain
David Pretty, that he
did not require their
services. However, when
the tug *Lowestoft*[27] came
up Captain Pretty went on
board the tug and made

an agreement with the tugmaster for £50, which he seems to have thought
would be much less than the beachmen would demand; he might well have
been right.

To begin with two of the beachmen, perhaps leading members of the company
involved, went ashore with a letter demanding that Captain W.S. Andrews, the
harbourmaster, should withdraw the tug and leave the salvage work to the beachmen.
Captain Andrews was ill in bed, but on his behalf the deputy harbourmaster, James
Balls, rejected the beachmen's demand out of hand. This so incensed the beachmen
that they filled a gig with large stones from the beach and took them out to provide
their fellow beachmen with ammunition for an attack on the tug. Other beachmen
launched their boats and went to the support of the Young Company, taking with
them a good supply of beach cobbles.

'Immediately afterwards, an attack of the most violent kind was made by
the crews of the several boats upon the master and crew of the steam vessel,'
it was afterwards reported.[28] 'Laying their boats athwart the head and stern
of the steamer, they commenced pelting the crew with the stones they had
brought off, many being more than a pound weight, rendering it impossible
for anyone to keep the deck for a single moment without endangering their
lives; so thickly were the stones thrown that they struck against each other
and broke in pieces in the air, and upwards of a bushel of stones were picked
up on the deck of the steamer after the affray was over. About 5pm the master
of the steam-tug was felled by a large stone. . .'.

The tugmaster, John Cooper, had been creeping along the deck to reach
the wheel when one of the stones hit him and apparently knocked him out.
He had to be taken ashore by boat for medical treatment, and eventually the
Lowestoft was withdrawn and another tug, the *Pursuit*, was sent out to tow the
Luna off the sand.

The following Monday two of the beachmen appeared at the Lowestoft
magistrates' court accused of assaulting the tugmaster. One of them, William
Rose, was fined £4 but the other, John Saunders, was acquitted of trying to
stab Cooper with a boathook, 'for want of evidence'.

One of the magistrates, Charles Steward, told the beachmen that they must
adjust to the changing times; whereas once they had had no rivals they were
now faced with the competition of the harbour company steam tugs, and they
must accept that and not break the law in opposing the new situation. Steward
was on the Suffolk Humane Society committee at that time.

That, however, was not the end of the matter. At a later court on 4th

Photographs of lifeboatmen at sea in the days of sail are very rare; this picture of the crew of the Southwold No. 1 lifeboat *Alfred Corry* was taken by Ernest Read Cooper, who sometimes went to sea in the boat with a camera tucked down the leg of his oilskins.

November William Norman and John Saunders appeared on a charge of 'having on 18 October unlawfully molested and impeded John Cooper, James Barnes Swan, Charles Bemment and James Balls, who were then and there lawfully employed in saving a certain ship, then and there in distress, to wit, upon the high seas. . .'.[29] The complainant, it transpired, was Captain Andrews, the harbourmaster. Both men pleaded not guilty, but they were convicted and fined £10 each, or in default of payment sentenced to two months' imprisonment with hard labour. Thirteen other men who admitted the offence were bound over to keep the peace for six months.

Not surprisingly some of the national newspapers were highly critical of the beachmen, who were described variously as 'plunderers' and 'wreckers', though the *Norfolk Chronicle* was sympathetic, pointing out that 'for some months in the year, these men have nothing to depend on but what is earned by these yawls, which are kept up at a heavy expense.

'We have known many of them kept off the parish in the winter season, solely from this source. This is another reason why they cling with such tenacity to their self-constituted rights and for their looking with so jealous an eye on the interference of the steamers in an employment to which they think themselves alone entitled.'[30]

Robert Hook, a member of the Old Company, was appointed coxswain of the *Victoria* in 1853. Then a man of twenty-five, he was to command the Lowestoft lifeboats through thirty turbulent years, carrying out not a few meritorious rescues and winning the RNLI Silver Medal twice; he was also to witness the painful decline of the beach companies. His first outing as coxswain came on 25th April 1853 when the *Victoria* was called out to the Ipswich brig *Mary Young*, which had touched on the Newcome Sand at low water and had unshipped her rudder; the lifeboat took off the brig's crew of ten.

Today the coxswain is the master of the lifeboat and is in sole command when the boat puts to sea; in the 1850s Bob Hook was not in such a position, for there was a superintendent of the lifeboat, Lieutenant Richard Joachim, who was at the time chief officer of the Coastguard at Lowestoft and was for some

years an active member of the Suffolk Humane Society committee. He seems
to have taken precedence over Hook and assumed command of the *Victoria*
on 5th January 1857 when she was launched to the aid of the brig *Tennant*.
The timber-laden vessel had struck the northern part of the Newcome Sand
while on her passage from Danzig to London; her crew of eight was landed by
the lifeboat.

A further attempt was made by the beachmen to re-establish their
monopoly in 1859 when they drew up a petition that they proposed to send
to the Board of Trade, but it would seem the document was never submitted.
It was the action of the paddle tug *Powerful*, built at Poplar two years earlier,
in plucking the barque *Lisbon* off the Newcome when the Pakefield beachmen
considered themselves 'in treaty for the job' that provoked the drawing up of
the petition.

One of the points they made was that there were at Lowestoft and
Pakefield 330 beachmen with fourteen yawls and ten gigs valued at £2,100 and
costing £400 a year to maintain; even if they were guilty of some pardonable
exaggeration that is still an indication of the economic importance of the beach
companies. One of the magistrates who had shown considerable sympathy for
the beachmen told them after reading their petition 'you must make up your
minds to make the best of it and act together, tug and beachmen'.[31]

That was exactly what the Pakefield lifeboatmen did in November that year
when they were called to the aid of the two-year-old iron steamer *Enchantress*,
which had smashed her rudder in crossing Brille bar on her way out of the
Maas. The lifeboat acted as steerage while the *Powerful* and another tug towed
the disabled steamer into harbour. The resulting salvage claim was settled for
£750, half of which went to the lifeboat crew and the beach company. That
was a very satisfactory result for them, but when the Suffolk Humane Society
decided that in accordance with the then-current RNLI rules two shares
should be paid for the maintenance of the lifeboat one of the Pakefield crew
shocked his hearers by 'most discourteously and disgracefully' bursting out
with the remark 'Then we shall never go off in the boat again!'

Much the same intransigence surfaced a little more than twenty years later
when the local committee, considering a service on 7th March 1882 by the
lifeboat *Samuel Plimsoll* to a smack from which the Pakefield lifeboat, *The Two
Sisters, Mary and Hannah*, had just taken the crew, decided to recommend
the payment only of a launching fee to the Lowestoft crew rather than the full
amount for a service. The men indignantly refused the reduced payment and
declined to serve any longer in the lifeboat.

So it was that on 28th October that year when there was urgent need for
the lifeboat to save the crews of several ships wrecked both north and south of
the harbour the doors of the lifeboat shed remained locked and no effort was
made to launch the boat. The beachmen were in fact very busy assisting those
vessels that ran for the harbour, taking their lines and helping those that were
thrown against the piers as they sought safety within, but when a vociferous
demand was made for the lifeboat to be brought into action it was, as one
beachman put it, a case of 'let them that robs the crew save their lives'.[32]

The beachmen certainly found themselves the villains of the day, but the
subsequent RNLI inquiry by Captain Henry Chetwynd and Commander St
Vincent Nepean, both of them future Chief Inspectors of Lifeboats, did not

Robert Hook, who became
coxswain of the Lowestoft
lifeboat at the age
of twenty-five.

A chart of the coast between
Lowestoft and Southwold,
the area in which the
Lowestoft and Pakefield
lifeboats operated. The chart
was originally surveyed by
Captain William Hewett in
the surveying sloop *Fairy*;
Captain Hewett perished in
the *Fairy* in a severe gale in
1840, but he is remembered
in the name of the Hewett
Channel off Gorleston.

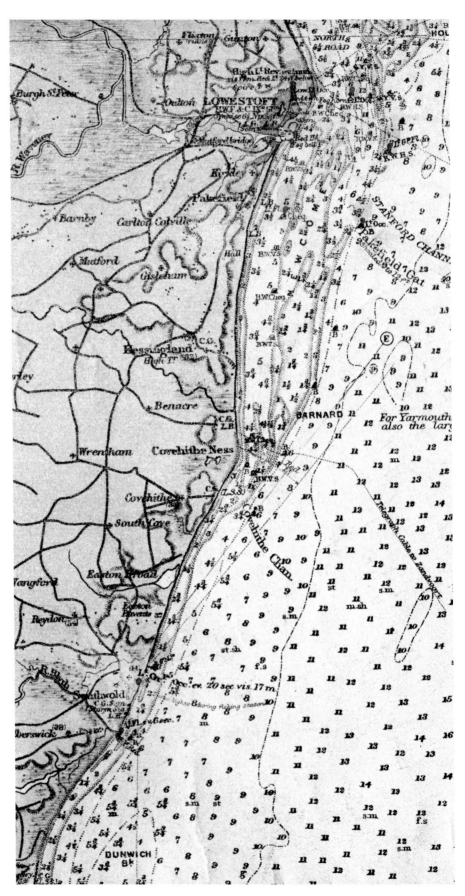

The Pakefield lifeboat *The Two Sisters, Mary and Hannah*, built at Lowestoft by Samuel Sparham in 1872, served in local waters until 1910.

heap all the blame on them. They found that the local secretary had erred through a misconception of the duties and and responsibilities of his office, the lifeboat superintendent who had actual charge of the boat had unpardonably and unaccountably neglected his duties, and that Coxswain Hook deserved the severest possible censure for gross and wilful neglect of his duties.

The beachmen were, however, given a chance to redeem their good name when on a wild and stormy 14th November the same year the Norwegian barque *Berthon* was seen running towards the Corton lightvessel displaying a signal for a pilot. Knowing that the flood tide was likely to set her on the sands, the beachmen manned the *Samuel Plimsoll* and left the harbour towed by the paddle tug *Despatch*,[33] which was recalled from sea by the harbourmaster, Captain Robert Massingham, who later received the thanks of the RNLI for his co-operation.

Sure enough the *Berthon* went on the sands and was being swept by the waves as the lifeboat approached. Six of the crew were dragged into the boat, leaving the captain and a young boy still on the disintegrating ship. A line was thrown to the captain, but he lacked the strength to tie it around the boy and, as one of the lifeboatmen said later, 'the poor little fellow fell amongst the wreck'. Another line was thrown to the captain, and he was successfully hauled into the boat, but the boy remained; eventually a well-aimed line fell right across him, he wound it around his wrist and was also dragged into the lifeboat.

All this was watched by townspeople from the back windows of the houses in the High Street and by crowds on the beach. As the lifeboat passed between the piers with the eight rescued sailors the curses of a fortnight earlier were replaced by cheers; 'the saving of that crew was worth more than a hundred pound,' Hook told the Rector of Lowestoft, 'for it seemed as if an Almighty power had sent it in our time of trouble'.

An anonymous Lowestoft beachman expressed the feelings of his fraternity rather neatly in a letter to one of the local newspapers: 'We are allowed to go into danger for the good of others, and it may be to sacrifice our own lives … then we are brave fellows; but if we go out to vessels to prevent them getting into dangerous positions and obtain some remuneration for our services, then we are branded with the title of "money grubbers" or "longshore pirates".'

The herring fishery   18

When Robert Gylbank the elder of Lowestoft made his will in 1545 he left to his son Thomas 'my fish house and salthouse beneath the cliff, with the billet and salt that is there'. Also mentioned in that will were three of his ferry boats in which fish was carried ashore from the larger fishing craft, 'with the appurtenances that belong to them, as proppes, hores [props and oars] and such other things'.

In his will Gylbank also left to his son 'my boat called the *Anthonie* with all her tackle that belongeth to her, as anchors, cables, warples, nets both herring and mackerel, with warroppes and boys, barrels and all manner of things.' One has no difficulty in recognising the drift nets, the warps to which the nets were made fast, and the buoys or floats that were fastened to the top of the nets to keep them hanging vertically just below the surface.

Clearly enough fishing was of considerable importance on the Suffolk coast in the sixteenth century, as indeed it had been in earlier centuries. The significance of the herring fishery was reflected in the long-drawn-out dispute between Lowestoft and its neighbour to the north, Great Yarmouth, whose corporation claimed jurisdiction over the landing of fish and goods in Kirkley Roads and at Lowestoft. It was a claim that was strenuously contested by the Lowestoftmen, who steadfastly refused to submit to domination by the townsmen of Yarmouth.

There is little doubt that the original settlement was an inland one around St Margaret's Church, now Lowestoft's parish church but originally that of the village of Akethorpe. Exactly when the first fishermen and traders occupied the strip of land at the top of the cliff and the Denes that lay at the cliff's foot is uncertain, but the move had certainly been made by the end of the fifteenth century. In 1539 John Powle, mariner, left in his will 'my tenement in Lowestoft and all the appurtenances above the cliff and beneath. . .'. It would seem that John Powle had his home somewhere in the area of the present-day High Street, and also had property including 'my salt and my boat with other things that is mine at the day of this present will-making' on the Denes at the foot of the cliff.

The wills made by the townsmen between 1444 and 1550, translated and transcribed by Peter Northeast, show plainly that Lowestoft was at that period as prosperous a community as any in Suffolk, with merchants as well as fishermen having their habitation in the coastal settlement. A goodly proportion of that prosperity was undoubtedly due to the activities of the fishing fraternity.

Opposite: 'Uvver she go in the name o' the Lord.' Shooting the nets on the motor drifter *Harold Cartwright* during the Home Fishing of 1953; she returned from this trip with a catch of some thirty crans.

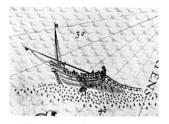

The earliest known picture of a herring buss, found on Lukas Waghenaer's chart of the North Sea, produced in 1583.

We have no idea what kind of a craft Robert Gylbank's boat the *Anthonie* might have been, but it was certainly small enough to be hauled up on to the shore, since there was no harbour at Lowestoft in those times. Not until late in the sixteenth century do we have any reliable information on the craft employed in herring fishing, referred to in documents as 'great boats' or busses. It is interesting that the term 'great boats' remained in use into the twentieth century at Sheringham, where it was used by the elderly fishermen who in the 1950s told me about the larger decked boats owned in the town that used to go crab fishing off the Yorkshire coast and also took part in the autumn herring fishing in the southern North Sea.

Two busses hauling their drift nets or flews as they were known at that time appear on Lukas Waghenaer's chart of the North Sea produced in 1583. That is the earliest known depiction of this type of craft, and a most intriguing picture it is. Both the boats have their masts lowered on to a gallows near the stern, just as the much later luggers did, and the steam drifters that succeeded them. A third vessel shown on the chart appears to be a three-masted buss under sail; she carries a single square sail on the fore and main masts, and no canvas on the mizzen.

From such scanty evidence a model was made for the Science Museum in South Kensington, representing a three-master with square sails on all three masts and a square topsail on the main. It has been suggested that the English busses were copied from the Dutch herring boats that fished in the North Sea in large fleets in the sixteenth century, but in fact there were significant differences between the Dutch craft and the English. It seems likely that the latter had a different ancestry from the Dutch, belonging to the same family as the Humber keels and billyboys which shared much the same bluff hull form. Development was slow, and the busses built for the Free British Fishery established at Southwold in 1750 bore a distinct resemblance to their forebears of some two centuries earlier. They had adopted a two-masted rig with headsails set on a long bowsprit, but in hull form they had not changed a great deal.

A most significant change came when the square sails of the old busses developed into lugsails, fore-and-aft sails that undoubtedly improved the sailing qualities of fishing craft. By about 1830 lugsails had entirely replaced the old square sails in fishing vessels, and the hull form had also been modified considerably.

Long before those changes had come about the herring fishery had assumed great economic importance at Lowestoft, bringing prosperity to at least a proportion of the town's seafaring community. A few not only became rich but climbed the social ladder, leaving the sea to participate in the processing and marketing of fish and in time becoming both wealthy and influential. Some seventeenth-century merchants both engaged in the processing of the catch and owned shares in the boats, no doubt relying on the fact that in a poor season when catches were sparse they could recoup their losses incurred as boatowners by selling the fish they processed at premium prices.

Given luck and good business sense some fishermen were able to gain access to the merchant class. In the course of the seventeenth century the Pacy family rose in just three generations to became the wealthiest merchants in Lowestoft. Towards the end of the century Samuel Pacy and his wife Elizabeth

A three-masted herring buss under sail, from Lukas Waghenaer's chart of the North Sea, 1583.

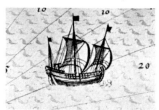

lived in a fine timber-framed house on the seaward side of the High Street that had been the family home for three generations, and they enjoyed a very comfortable lifestyle, with paintings and mirrors on the walls, leather-seated chairs and Spanish tables in the parlour, and heating in three of the four bedrooms.[1]

BEACH, LOWESTOFT.

To Fish Merchants, Smack Owners, and Others.

TO BE SOLD BY PRIVATE CONTRACT,

A NET CHAMBER,

WITH WAREHOUSES AND STABLE,

WELL situated near the Bath House, Whapload Road, Lowestoft, within a short distance of the Fish Market, Railway Station, and Harbour, and occupied by Mr. William Rose. Possession may be had at Christmas next.

For Selling Price and further particulars apply to Mr. W. T. BALLS, Auctioneer and Estate Agent, Lowestoft.

Auction and Estate Agency Offices, 12, London Road.

An advertisement from the *Norwich Mercury* of 1871 for a net chamber and other property on the Beach at Lowestoft.

On his death in 1680 Samuel was worth the very considerable sum of £2,849. The provision he made for his three sons enabled the eldest to set himself up as a gentleman and for his brothers to carry on fishing and fish-curing, the trades that had brought their father much of his wealth.[2]

Under her husband's will Elizabeth Pacy gained part-ownership of the trading vessel *Black Lyon*, of which Samuel Munds was master. Munds was another of those who managed to climb the social ladder, though not in such a spectacular fashion as the Pacy family; by the time he died in 1710 he was the owner of the fishing vessel *Mayflower* and had diverse interests in farming and brewing as well as fishing and fish-curing. At the time of his death his worldly goods were worth the not-inconsiderable total of £258 8s. 3d.

Samuel Munds lived in a house on the east side of the High Street at its northernmost end. Until the early nineteenth century there was no residential development on the Denes, the only buildings below the cliff being those connected with the fishing industry, including the smokehouses in which herring, and to a lesser extent other fish such as sprats, were turned into succulent smoked fish. In the early days the product of these buildings was mainly red herring for export to countries bordering the Mediterranean, smoked so hard that the fish could be pressed down into the barrels by screw presses to ensure that the barrels were well packed. Even so delay due to storms, adverse winds or other adversities could result in the contents of the barrels deteriorating seriously before reaching Leghorn (now Livorno), Venice, Civita Vecchia or some other destination, with sometimes devastating loss to the merchant consigning them.

The separation of the fish processing from the residential part of the town was considered by the Lowestoft people to be a great advantage, not only because the reek of fishy smoke was kept largely out of the town but because it was thought that the separation of the smokehouses from other buildings resulted in a better quality product. Whether any difference in quality was evident when expansion of the industry led to the building of smokehouses within the town has never been revealed.

Whether or not the building of the smokehouses in relative isolation really did result in a better product, that isolation was certainly advantageous when

A sixteenth-century herring buss hauling its nets, which are supported in the water by a series of wooden 'bowls' on the headrope, from Lukas Waghenaer's chart of the North Sea. Amidships one of the crew is using a 'thief-net' to catch fish dropping from the nets as they are hauled.

Herring luggers on Lowestoft beach in a nineteenth-century print. The Low Light is barely visible at extreme left.

towards the end of the eighteenth century Lowestoft began to develop as a seaside resort to which affluent businessmen and members of the gentry and aristocracy from Norwich and to some extent also from London moved their families for the summer. In 1797 the 'company' included the Duke of Gloucester and Prince William of Gloucester and their suite.

'The slope of the hill, upon which the town is built, and which was formerly one continued declivity of barren sand, is now converted, by modern improvements, into beautiful hanging gardens, by a gradual descent, from the dwelling-houses above to the bottom of the hill, and extending nearly from one end of the town to the other,' wrote the anonymous author of *The Lowestoft Guide*, published in Yarmouth in 1812.[3] 'At the bottom of these gardens the fish-houses are erected, for the purpose of curing the herrings which are caught on this coast; and are so numerous that, had they been built more compactly, they would have been sufficient to form a small town of themselves.

'Lowestoft derives many conveniences from the fish-houses being

Smokehouses and other fishing premises can be seen in this print of Lowestoft High Light; a number of three-masted herring luggers can also be seen close inshore.

thus detached from all other buildings, not the least of which are the easy conveyance of the herrings from the boats, and the avoiding those offensive smells which arise from the draining and smoking of them.

'The superior quality of the Lowestoft herrings, both in respect of color and flavor [sic], is evident, and is to be attributed solely to the arrangement of the fish-houses, which secures to them the benefit of a free, unobstructed current of air.'

A good contemporary description of what went on in those fish-houses is to be found in a court baron minute of December 1584.[4] As part of an agreement for the sale of the Swan Inn messuage in High Street to John Archer, the merchant George Phifeld was to supply the purchaser with twenty lasts (200 barrels) of red herrings; they were to be 'full red herrings, good, able and marchant, of one night's taking, to be roared in vats with sufficient salt before they be two nights old, dried with ashen billets of the best usual manner and order of making of herrings for Leghorn beyond the sea, with a bright and clear colour, and without gorge to be packed in such good and dry cask as usually is transported to Leghorn aforesaid.'

That is to say, they were to be of the finest quality as exported to the Italian port of Leghorn, were to be *full*, containing milt or roe, to have been caught in one night and landed the next day, and salted in vats rather than in heaps on the floor before being hung in the smokehouse over a fire of billets of ash. And finally they were to be packed carefully *without gorge*, not crammed into the barrels too tightly; perhaps that screw press was not to be used.

A three-masted lugger lying beached puts her gear ashore with the help of beachmen, seen in a print after a drawing by E. Duncan, 1854.

A beetster at work repairing herring nets in one of the Lowestoft beeting chambers about 1960.

A ransacker setting up a drift net in one of the netstores in Whapload Road, Lowestoft.

It might well be that the herrings to be supplied by George Phifeld were only relatively lightly cured, being for home consumption. When in 1790 Edmund Gillingwater described the curing process as then carried out it was longer and harder: 'As soon as the herrings are brought on shore, they are carried to the fish-houses, where they are salted, and laid on the floors in heaps, about two feet deep; after they have continued in this situation about fifty hours, the salt is washed from them by putting them into baskets and plunging them into water; from thence they are carried to an adjoining fish-house, where, after being pierced through the gills by small wooden spits about four feet long, they are handed to the men in the upper part of the house, who place them at proper distances as high as the top of the roof, where they are cured or made red.[5]

'The upper part of the house being thus filled with herrings, many small wood fires are kindled underneath, upon the floor, whose number is in proportion to the size of the room, and the smoke that ascends from these fires is what dries or cures the herrings. After the fish have hung in this manner about seven days, the fires are extinguished, that the oil and fat may drip from them, and in about two days after the fires are re-kindled, and after two more such drippings, the fires are kept continually burning until the herrings are perfectly cured, which requires a longer or shorter time according as they are designed either for a foreign or home consumption. After the herrings have hung a proper time, they are taken down (which they call striking), and are packed in barrels containing 800 or 1,000 herrings each, and then shipped off for market, which formerly was chiefly confined to foreign ports, especially those belonging to Roman catholic countries. . .'.

Gillingwater records that in 1755 no fewer than 70,000 barrels of fish were cured in Lowestoft and Yarmouth, of which only 18,000 barrels were for home consumption, chiefly in London. Some 39,000 barrels were consigned to southern Europe and the Mediterranean, with 13,000 going to Leghorn, 7,500 to Naples, 5,700 to Venice, 5,500 to Genoa and 4,500 to Ancona; smaller numbers went to Trieste, Civita Vecchia, Cadiz and Bordeaux. Holland took 13,000.[6]

Alongside the smokehouses and particularly along the landward side of Whapload Road were the long netstores in which the drift nets and other fishing gear were stored when not in use and in which the beetsters repaired the worn and torn nets when they were brought ashore at the end of a trip. The beetsters were skilled women employed in the beeting chambers on the upper floor of the netstores to make good the damage caused by dogfish, which snapped at the herring caught in the netting and in doing so cut through the meshes, and by rough seas. Using a sharp knife they cut out the broken meshes and deftly filled in the gaps with beeting cotton wound on their beeting needles, small shuttles made of wood or bone, or in more recent days of plastic or even metal.

The word beet is derived from the Old English word *boetan* meaning to make good, a word that had passed out of ordinary use before the year 1500 but survived in the fishing industry and in forestry, where it described the replanting of an area of damaged woodland. Other terms used in

Drift nets being 'barked' in the tan copper outside one of the netstores in Whapload Road, Lowestoft.

Hanging herring nets which have just been tanned on the drying rails on Lowestoft Denes.

the netstores were equally archaic; the beetsters searched for sprunks, a word with Dutch connotations meaning broken meshes, crow's feet, where two adjacent meshes were broken, and holes which were larger areas of damage.

When the beetsters had finished their work the nets were set up by the ransacker, who was often an older fisherman who had given up going to sea and had taken up a less arduous occupation ashore. The title of ransacker reflected the fact that in days when much of the repair work was done not in the beeting chambers but as outwork in the workers' homes he ransacked or searched the nets to assess the amount of work required to be done. Working on the lower floor, he would connect the head of the net by the ossels or norsels to the cork rope, a double line bearing corks that kept the net upright in the water. Possibly the word norsel originated from 'an ossel' which if carelessly pronounced would become 'a norsel'.

The complete nets were then taken outside and put into the tan copper and boiled up in a solution of cutch[7], a preservative agent imported mainly from Russia. Sometimes referred to as 'barking', since oak bark had once been used before cutch became available, this treatment helped to preserve the nets from being rotted by the seawater. After being boiled for a sufficient time the nets were hoisted out and allowed to drain, then hung on wooden rails on the Denes to dry.

Until the nineteenth century herring nets were made by hand of hemp twine produced by the many twine-spinners; an 1844 directory lists no fewer then seventeen rope and twine-spinners in Lowestoft. These rough nets, as they were called, had the warp, the main rope, set above the net because there was sufficient weight in the hemp to make the nets hang down in the water, but when James Paterson invented a machine loom that wove nets from cotton the warp was moved to the bottom of the net so that its weight should cause the lighter cotton net to hang correctly. A net factory was introduced at Musselburgh near Edinburgh in 1820 and by the end of the century the cotton Scotch nets had entirely replaced the old rough nets.[8] There were by then a number of firms in Lowestoft making nets by machinery.

On the Beach

With the town's population growing in the course of the nineteenth century and the fishing industry flourishing following the end of the Napoleonic Wars the smokehouses and netstores on the Beach, that area between the cliff and the sea, came to lose their isolation as a new community of beachmen and fishermen grew up below the cliff. That community on the Beach – the term Beach Village came into use only in the second half of the twentieth century – survived the flooding of 1953 but was soon thereafter to give way to an industrial estate.

A few of the once-isolated smokehouses and netstores were still to be found along the Whapload Road and on the Beach as late as the 1950s, at least one dating back to Elizabethan times, but almost all have given way to modern commercial buildings. In many cases the smokehouses were the oldest part of a complex of buildings that had grown up around them and of which they formed an essential part. The flint curtain wall of the property frequently survived, with the brick wall

Workers salting fish on Lowestoft fish market.

of a much newer packing shed built on top of it and the owner's residence inserted into a corner of the enclosure as the Beach community built up.[9]

Lowestoft was not the only place to take part in the herring fishery, of course. The large village of Kessingland, just five miles to the south, was in the early years of the twentieth century reputed to be the

The Walberswick-owned herring lugger *Esther*, LT505, using her steam capstan to warp herself out of Southwold harbour. On the Walberswick side of the river is the *Uranus*, LT104, also owned in that village.

most prosperous village in Suffolk as a result of its involvement in the fishing industry. Several of the leading drifter owners were residents of Kessingland, and men from the village crewed their boats, which worked out of Lowestoft harbour; the nets were brought from Lowestoft to be repaired in netstores in the village. Kessingland beetsters employed practices quite different from those of the Lowestoft beetsters; whereas in Lowestoft the nets under repair were suspended by a piece of twine from iron hooks attached to a socket on the wall, at Kessingland a wooden peg took the place of the hook.

The harbour at Southwold was home to a number of boats taking part in the herring fishery, and as that fishery reached its peak in the early years of the twentieth century Southwold Corporation sought to absorb the overflow

The first boat to moor at the new Southwold quay wall on 13th June 1907, the Lowestoft-owned *Amelia*, built at Rye in Sussex in 1879.

A catch of herring being landed on the new Southwold harbour quay. There is already an ominous sign of the paving subsiding. Note the lugger's mitchboard lantern amidships.

of steam drifters and Scots fifies and zulus from the increasingly overcrowded docks at Lowestoft. A good deal of money was spent on improving the harbour, reconstructing the quay at Blackshore and erecting a sale ring on the new quay. The outbreak of war in 1914 curtailed the fishing, and when peace returned four years later there was little need for the additional facilities provided on the Blyth.

In the mid-eighteenth century Southwold was chosen as the base for the Free British Fishery, an ill-fated and relatively short lived attempt to rival the highly successful Dutch fishing effort. Established in 1750 following the passing of an Act of Parliament that promised a bounty of thirty shillings annually to each decked vessel of 20 to 80 tons built and based in home ports for the herring fishery,[10] the Free British Fishery Society set up warehouses,

Herring luggers in Southwold harbour about 1890. Their bowsprits are run in, and on the outboard boat the mitchboard on to which the mainmast is lowered when lying to the nets is prominent. In the distance a billyboy, possibly the *Woodland Lass*, lies at Blackshore.

nethouses and other premises and proceeded to have fifty busses built in British yards. Like other attempts at state intervention by means of bounties, the scheme failed and the society's remaining assets were sold up in 1772. It was said in the town that the only person ultimately to benefit from the scheme was John May, the proprietor of the Southwold salt works, which had been expanded to cope with the demand from the society's fleet.

Towards the end of the century there was a further attempt to boost the herring and mackerel fishery by means of bounties.[11] In 1811 the Overseers of Lowestoft reported that the fishery was thriving, 'great numbers of Persons having been induced to employ their capitals in the concern, encouraged by the Bounties given by Government. These Bounties were granted at a time when the Fisheries were in a very declining state and they had every good effect which could be expected from so salutary a measure.'

Nevertheless, the Overseers sounded a note of caution, saying that 'the Bounties have now ceased, and a total stop being put to exportation, and the home markets being found incapable of consuming the quantity of herrings taken, there is too much reason to fear that the Fisheries will again decline. . .'.

With the final defeat of Napoleon at Waterloo in 1815 the Mediterranean trade was restored and by the middle of the century the spread of railways was providing the fishermen with inland markets that had hitherto been out of reach. Samuel Morton Peto, railway contractor and entrepreneur, promised the fishermen of Lowestoft in the 1840s that he would provide them with the means of getting their fish fresh to the industrial conurbations of the Midlands the same day that it was landed in the new harbour, and the link he made to the Norfolk Railway at Reedham achieved just that. In the course of the nineteenth century new docks carved out of the sandy waste north of the outer harbour provided accommodation for a vastly expanded fishing fleet.

The coming of the Scots

For almost a hundred years the autumn herring season attracted Scottish fishermen and their boats and also both men and women workers who processed the fish brought ashore by Scots and East Anglian fishermen. The first to be lured to the East Anglian fishing was James Murray of Cellardyke, who first came south in 1858,[12] and he was followed six years later by two sailing drifters from Anstruther (Anster to those who hailed from the East Neuk of Fife). Their success was sufficient to persuade others to follow them in succeeding years, and the Fife men were joined first by fishermen from Leith on the other side of the Firth of Forth and then by men from the Moray Firth.[13]

The annual influx of migrant fishermen presented considerable problems at a period when there were more than fifty beer houses alone in Lowestoft and Kirkley, to say nothing of the inns and taverns with more extensive licences. The local detachment of the East Suffolk police, consisting of deputy chief constable Major Peter Allez, an inspector, two sergeants and eleven constables, found their hands full endeavouring to keep order, especially during the autumn fishing season. In 1871 Major Allez told the Improvement Commissioners, forerunners of the town council, that with the arrival of sixty-five Scots boats and the imminent arrival of others there were likely to

A team of Scots workers
topping up barrels with
brine on the pickling plots
at Lowestoft during the
autumn herring season in
the early twentieth century.

be four or five thousand fishermen in the town of a night when the boats did
not put to sea; there were just four policemen, with the inspector and himself,
to do the 'night work'.

In the early days the catches made by the Scots boats were sold to local
buyers at Lowestoft and Yarmouth, helping to swell both the supply to domestic
markets in the English south-east and that to merchants smoking red herring
for export to the Mediterranean. Whereas Lowestoft had concentrated
largely on the smoking of herring – red herring in the parlance of the trade
– the Scots curers produced what were known as white herring, gutted and
pickled in brine. In the 1870s some Scottish curers began sending agents to
the East Anglian ports to purchase herrings that were sent north by railway
for processing in Scotland. It was but a short step to some Scottish curers
following the increasing numbers of boats and fishermen and beginning to

Scotswomen working at the
farlanes at Lowestoft during
the autumn fishing of 1902.
They select the size of fish
as they gut them and
throw them into the
appropriate basket.

Packing herring into barrels in carefully arranged layers, each successive layer having the fish laid at right angles to the last layer.

process herrings in East Anglia, bringing their own workers and establishing the tradition of an annual autumn migration of both male workers and fishergirls that survived to the end of the North Sea herring fishing in the 1950s and 60s.

Year by year fishermen from the Scottish east coast came south in their fifies and zulus, and by 1900 the number of Scots boats taking part in the East Anglian fishing had reached 634. Between 1905 and the outbreak of war in 1914 more than a thousand Scots boats participated in the autumn fishing, considerably outnumbering the local fleet, and the migrant labour force reached a peak of between six and seven thousand, recruited from both the east and west coasts of Scotland, from the western isles and from Shetland.

The task of the Scots women was to gut the herrings and pack them with layers of coarse salt into barrels that would be filled with brine. This work was

Scots fishergirls working at the farlanes overshadowed by the great piles of herring barrels built up by the coopers in preparation for the Home Fishing.

Oilskin skirts and boots
were the essential working
dress for those engaged at
the farlanes.

performed largely in the open air on the 'pickling plots' between Whapload Road and the sea. Equipped with razor-sharp gipping knives, the girls stood at the farlins or farlanes, large wooden troughs into which the fish were tipped as they were carted from the Waveney Dock where they had been landed and sold. Pre-1914 the farlins were deep boxes, but after the war a long, sloping type was introduced which speeded up the work as the girls did not have to reach down so far to grasp a fish. Taking the fish one at a time, they deftly inserted the knife and extracted the gut, at the same time selecting the fish according to size and condition and throwing it into one of the five or six tubs that were arranged behind them. There were various grades known as smalls, matties, matfulls, fulls and large fulls, and with experience the selection became almost instinctive.

Matties were herring not less than nine inches long from which the long gut had been removed; matfulls were full of milt or roe and not less than 9¼ inches in length, while fulls were herring not less than 10¼ inches and large fulls not less than 11¼ inches. The word *mattie* appears to be derived from the Dutch *maatje*, a word used for herrings that contained neither milt nor roe but had a good fat content; a popular delicacy, they used to be sold from stalls and barrows on the streets of Amsterdam and other Dutch towns.[14]

The girls worked in crews of three, two gutters and one packer who was effectively the senior member of the team. The crew would live together in lodgings in the town, sometimes two crews occupying a room together; apart from bunks there would be no furniture in the room, and the girls would use their kists, wooden chests in which they packed all their clothes and other belongings, as seats. The rooms they occupied would be cleared of the normal furniture before their arrival, since the smell of herring would quickly attach itself to the upholstery.

When the tubs were full of herring they would be carried across to the packer, who placed the fish carefully into a barrel in layers. The bottom layer of herring were laid dark back uppermost, subsequent layers being packed alternately back uppermost and back down, a scoop of salt being thrown over each succeeding layer. When the barrel was almost full the last row would be laid with the silver belly uppermost so that there would always be a gleam of silver when the head of the barrel was knocked off, whichever end was opened.[15]

Before starting work each girl would bind her fingers with strips of white cloth or linen – 'cloots'- which not only enabled her to grasp the slippery fish but to some extent protected her fingers from sores caused by the salt being rubbed into the skin and creating ulcerations. In spite of what has sometimes been said, their purpose was not to avoid them cutting themselves with their gutting knives; the 'cloots' afforded little protection from sharp knives, and the Church of Scotland nurse who manned a first-aid post on the pickling plots too often had to deal with such injuries.

A vivacious young Scots girl carries two baskets of herring to the packers during the 1902 autumn fishing at Lowestoft.

When the migration was at its height special trains were run both from the Scottish east coast, originating on the Great North of Scotland and North British railways and travelling by the East Coast route, and from the west coast, originating on the Highland and Caledonian railways and using the West Coast route, to bring the workers to East Anglia. The first of these special trains were organised by Alfred Bloxham, the stationmaster of Yarmouth Beach, eastern terminus of the Midland & Great Northern Joint Railway, at the beginning of the twentieth century. Trains using the M & GNR incorporated coaches for workers heading for Lowestoft which were detached at Yarmouth Beach and run on to Lowestoft Central over the Norfolk & Suffolk Joint line. The Great Eastern Railway and later the London & North Eastern also ran daily fish trains from Lowestoft during the autumn season to distribute the herring catches.

Arrangements both for travel and for accommodation at Lowestoft were made by the curers, who would send their representatives around the fishing towns and villages in the early part of the year recruiting workers for the autumn fishing. On accepting engagement the workers were given a sum of money known as 'arles' – a shilling in the early days but a rather more substantial payment later. Acceptance of that payment, which was not considered an advance on the season's earnings, signified a binding unwritten contract on the part of both curer and employee.

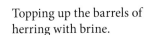

Topping up the barrels of herring with brine.

Whereas the Lowestoft boats that had landed a catch on Saturday would put to sea on Sunday morning the Scots boats always laid in on the Sabbath. Religion has been important to the Scots coastal dwellers at least since Thomas Rosie of Orkney founded the Edinburgh-based Scottish Coast Mission in 1852, followed by the Glasgow-based West Coast Mission in 1855 and the Aberdeen-based North-East Coast Mission in 1858, a year before the great revival movement swept in from America, spreading across Scotland like a prairie fire. The leader of the revival so far as the east coast of Scotland was concerned was James Turner, a Peterhead cooper and herring curer, who is said to have been the means of converting more than eight thousand people along the coast.[16]

The crew of a lugger counting out herring at Lowestoft in the first decade of the twentieth century. That laborious method of tallying the catch became extinct with the passing of the Cran Measure Act in 1908.

Peter Anson gives a vivid example of the preaching of an earlier revival preacher who was minister of Linktown in the kingdom of Fife from 1750 to 1803: observing 'lang Tam Gallowa',' a well-known mariner of the time, with some boatmen on their way to Pettycur harbour, he broke off his sermon and addressed them with his characteristic energy.

'Boatmen, aho!. . . The boats, aho . . . to Leith, aho, you cry . . . we cry, Sal-va-ti-on, aho; you sail aneath Skipper Gallowa', there . . . we sail aneath Christ . . . we hae Christ for oor skipper, the Holy Spirit for oor Pilot, an' God himsel' at the helm. Your boat, let me tell ye, is but a bit fir deal frae Norawa'; the keel o' oor boat was laid in Bethlehem, built in Judea, rigg'd in Jerusalem, launch'd on Mount Calvary, we hae the Cross o' Christ for a helm, a cedar o' Lebanon for a mast an' the Redemption o' mankind for a freight. . .'.[17]

It was during the East Anglian autumn fishing of 1921 that there occurred another extraordinary religious revival among the Scottish fishermen and their womenfolk in which a cooper from Wick, Jock Troup, played a leading part. He preached at open-air meetings in Yarmouth, to which he had come with other Scots workers for the season. Similar meetings were held in Lowestoft. It was a time of remarkable religious fervour: in the engine room of a steam drifter on the way out to the Smiths Knoll fishing grounds Robby Ritchie flung his packet of cigarettes into the boiler furnace in earnest of his sudden decision to turn to God, and ashore three lassies from the Isle of Lewis were so overcome that they refused to go to work at the farlins until Jock Troup had satisfied them of God's forgiveness for their sins.[18] That event had a deep and lasting influence on the Scots fisherfolk.

The 'joskins'

As the Lowestoft fishing fleet grew in the course of the nineteenth century farmworkers from a number of inland villages as well as from the coast were drawn by the chance of good earnings during the Home Fishing, which fitted conveniently into a slack period in the farming calendar. At first these 'landsmen' went as capstan hands, their main task being to tramp round the manual capstan winding in the warp as the nets were hauled, an occupation that required brawn rather than skill. Having got the harvest on the farms, many young men took the opportunity of work in the luggers, always hoping that the boat would have a good fishing and they would return home with pockets full of sovereigns. With the crews paid on the share system there was always a chance they might.

When the introduction of steam capstans rendered the 'joskins' redundant as capstan hands many farmworkers continued to go to sea each autumn as crew members on the drifters. The tradition was particularly strong in the village of Westhall, north of Halesworth and a twelve-mile walk from Lowestoft; the parish church contains a memorial to men from the village lost at sea rather similar to the larger one in St Margaret's at Lowestoft.

Official crew agreements now in the Lowestoft branch of the Suffolk Record Office reveal that in 1876 out of a sample of 272 men making up the crews of Lowestoft boats only thirty came from Lowestoft itself and another thirty from Pakefield; thirty-four came from Kessingland, nineteen from Carlton Colville, eleven from Blythburgh, eight from Westleton, eight from Southwold and seven from Walberswick, while others came from Blundeston, Burgh Castle, Gisleham, Henstead, Hopton and Hulver, Lound, Mutford and Rushmere and from a number of other villages in the area.

One boat, the *Halcyon*, was owned in the inland village of Barnby – always pronounced Barnaby by its natives – and had a crew recruited exclusively

Close up of a nineteenth-century model of a lugger with three joskins walking around the capstan and other members of the crew hauling the nets over the rail and shaking out the fish; one man has a dydle with which to catch the herring that fall from the rough net as it is brought aboard.

from Barnby and adjoining Mutford. One of those from Mutford was a sixteen-year-old 'landsman' who was making his first voyage as 'boy'; he had probably been employed on the land for three or four years before deciding to try his luck at the fishing.

Typical of those who left the land for a life at sea at a tender age was George Youell, the son of a horseman working on a farm at Toft Monks, on the Norfolk side of the River Waveney some three miles north of Beccles. Born in 1868, he shipped as cook in the lugger *Eclipse* at the age of thirteen bound for North Shields and the east coast of Scotland. 'For this, my first voyage, I was outfitted almost entirely with articles of clothing which my older brothers gave me,' he wrote many years later. 'They were woollen and had shrunk to somewhere near my size.[19]

'My berth was that of cook. We spent three or four days getting the boat ready for the voyage, bending sails, taking on the fishing gear, salt, and other supplies. During these few days we lived entirely on bread and cheese, which fact did not develop any problems for the new cook.

'It was anticipated that herring would be the major item in our diet, and they were. The men ate enormous quantities of them, as many as fifteen each for breakfast. From the list of groceries described' – salt beef, some kind of lard substitute kept in a three-gallon pail, pieces of suet, flour, sugar, tea, treacle, baking powder, sea biscuits, margarine, vinegar, pepper, salt and raisins for plum puddings on Sundays – 'and the addition of the herring, a thirteen-year-old boy with no previous experience and working under the handicap of cooking on a small craft which was seldom on an even keel was expected to provide appetizing and nourishing meals. With the exception of the bread used when we were outfitting, bread on the *Eclipse* was limited to sea biscuits which anyway, when soaked in hot tea, were quite acceptable. As we had no spoons, the men would retrieve the biscuits from their pots of tea by using their unwashed fingers.'

Those sea biscuits were sometimes known in Lowestoft as Cooper's rusks, since one of the main providers of this hard tack was the firm of W.B. Cooper, whose bakery was in Mariner's Street. In 1871 Lewis B. Cooper introduced to his bakery machines worked by steam power for the production of ships' biscuits. A report in the *Suffolk Mercury* states that 'The flour and the requisite liquor are put into an iron drum, inside of which are also iron arms termed "kneaders". The drum is revolved by steam power . . . the dough is placed on another machine, and worked through two rollers into the requisite thickness, and a set

An advertisement for W.B. Cooper, 'baker, grocer and chandler to the fishing trade' from the 1912 *Fisherman's Nautical Almanack*. William Beckett Cooper was the successor to Lewis B. Cooper who introduced steam power for the production of ships' biscuits.

128   Advertisement—Lowestoft.

THE NOTED PROVISION STORES.

W.B. COOPER,

OPPOSITE

THE HERRING AND

TRAWL DOCKS.

BAKER, GROCER,

— AND —

CHANDLER,

To the **FISHING TRADE.**

Quality and Excellence Unsurpassed.

Prompt and Careful attention to Every Order.

Note the Address—

FISH DOCK STORES,

LOWESTOFT.

Tel. 83.

of moulds fall on to it cutting the biscuits clean out and marking them as required by the maker.'

Life began in real earnest when the *Eclipse* arrived on the fishing grounds, George Youell goes on. 'The nets would be laid out before dark, and hauling them in usually commenced very early in the morning, often as early as two or three o'clock. This interrupted my sleep. . . Preparing the meals was but a small part of my many duties. To make tea I had only to add to the quantity of leaves that were already in the two-gallon kettle, the amount of tea prescribed as the daily ration. To secure impartial distribution the sugar was added at the same time. It was then brought to the boiling point, when it was ready to serve.

'My biggest job was in connection with hauling in the nets. As the nets were in a continuous string more than a mile in length, the boat hauled to the nets. . .Heaving the heavy boat to the nets was a most laborious task, which was made much more so in proportion to the strength of the wind blowing at the time. It was often a steady grind of six or eight hours. I held back on the rope and coiled it in a small square hold in even layers, much the same way that cable is stowed in a cable-laying ship. This had to be done carefully or the rope would foul when running out. If I allowed the rope to slip – or surge – on the capstan, curses and imprecations would ensue. While I was quite a large boy for my age, still I was not strong enough to perform some of my duties properly. My incompetence brought much verbal abuse on me, the men blaming me for keeping a more competent boy out of a berth.'

Incompetent he might have been at that time, but the boy from Toft Monks remained in the crew, learning all the while, as the *Eclipse* followed the herring up the North Sea, working out of Scarborough and then Grimsby and eventually returning to Lowestoft. At the beginning of October the boat sailed from there, the skipper taking her a long way to the north-eastward in search of the herring shoals, which had not at that stage reached the Smiths Knoll grounds. The nets had just been shot when it was noticed that the barometer was falling rapidly, a sure sign of imminent bad weather. The crew set to work to haul the nets, which proved difficult in the worsening conditions, and it was daylight before they were all in.

'Our skipper was anxious to be getting to the westward; the glass had dropped to the lowest point any of the crew had ever seen. There was something terribly ominous about the situation. The men did not swear. That in itself was significant, for never previously had it seemed possible for them to talk without the use of some profanity. None of them ate any of the herring which I had fried for breakfast, a task of great difficulty owing to the tossing of the boat. The mainsail was barely set before it had to be lowered for the third reef, quickly followed by a fourth, which was the last . . . the boat had been tacked to the NE while the last reef was taken, the storm jib set, the mizzen and foresail close reefed. This was the minimum of sail to which she could be reduced with the hope of making any headway whatever . . .'.

'I stood in the companionway and watched the mighty waves. It was one of the grandest sights I have ever witnessed, at least at a time when I had any sense of appreciation. I could see only a short distance from the boat because of her low freeboard and the spray which filled the air. The sea was streaked with foam, and when a wave rolled up to form a crest the wind tore off the crest

'She was kept off the wind…'
A drawing by L. Jeffery of
the predicament in which
the *Eclipse* and her crew
found themselves.

and scattered it in the form of spray . . . While during the day it had seemed that it would be impossible for the wind to blow any harder, still as darkness closed around the *Eclipse* the wind increased in fury to one continuous and deafening roar.'

George Youell and the *Eclipse* survived what was remembered for many a year as the October Gale of 1881, but many boats and many fishermen did not. The lugger *Young Agnes*, owned by C. Pye of Corton, returned to Lowestoft some days after the gale had abated with the news that five men had been washed off the deck by a heavy sea and three of them had been drowned; by a miracle the other two were actually washed back again. The boat also sustained a serious loss of gear. On board the *Gratitude*, owned by G.H. Doughty, one of the crew was severely injured when he was thrown to the deck and washed overboard; other members of the crew used a boathook to pull him back on board, but when the boat reached Lowestoft he had to be taken to hospital with a compound fracture of the thigh and other injuries. A Dutch fishing boat was thrown on to the beach at Trimingham with five men and two boys dead in the cabin; it was thought it had been capsized while at anchor.

The changing 'lugger'

Although the fishermen continued to refer to the boats in which they fished for herring and mackerel as luggers, during the course of the nineteenth century the dipping lugsails that had to be lowered and shifted to the other side of the mast each time the boat went about were replaced by loose-footed gaff sails that were much easier to handle. The Scotsmen, on the other hand, retained the lugsail in their scaffies, fifies and zulus right up to the time motors replaced sail.

Alongside the change in rig the Lowestoft boatbuilders evolved a new hull form, eventually changing from the old clinker build with overlapping planks to carvel, with the planking fastened to a previously erected wooden skeleton; in the clinker tradition the planks were fastened to each other before the timbers were inserted.

Until about 1880 the herring luggers were quite different from the boats employed in trawling and would be laid up when not fishing for herring or

The Elliott and Garrood capstan of the *Lydia Eva*, a preserved steam drifter, still to be seen at Lowestoft and Yarmouth.

The crew of the Lowestoft steam drifter *Good Friend*, built at Lowestoft in 1908 and owned by J. Beamish of Kirkley. She later passed to Peterhead ownership. The large lamps on the front of the wheelhouse are fuelled by acetylene gas.

mackerel. In the summer of 1883 Henry Reynolds, who had a yard on the south side of Lake Lothing, built two large sailing drifters, the *Ocean Queen*, LT617, and *Rosebud*, LT594, which were intended to be used for trawling as well as for drifting. A list of Lowestoft fishing vessels published in 1896[20] includes four boats that were said to be for both drifting and trawling, but oddly enough the *Ocean Queen* was described in that list as a trawler and the *Rosebud* as a drifter.[21]

Already by 1912, when this advertisement appeared, Elliott & Garrood had sold more than 3,200 of their revolutionary steam capstans. No longer was it necessary for the capstan hands to trudge around a manual capstan to haul in the nets.

The dandy *Neptune* leaving Lowestoft harbour towards the end of the nineteenth century. Owned in Walberswick, she had been built in 1885 as the *Uranus*, LT401, which number can just be made out on the sail beneath the new registration LT66 given her when her name was changed..

The converter smacks, as they were sometimes called, were rigged with a lofty mainmast with topmast carrying a large mainsail with gaff and boom that gave them the power to tow the beam trawl. In preparation for the Home Fishing the mainmast and its gear would be hoisted out and a pole mast and loose-footed mainsail substituted. Some of the pierhead artists who produced paintings of fishing craft for their owners and crews made ship-portraits in pairs, one picture showing a boat in its lofty summer rig and the other showing the same vessel hauling its nets on the Smiths Knoll grounds in the autumn.

Despite the fact that the Lowestoft boatyards built many drifters for Yarmouth owners, those boats owned in Lowestoft differed from Yarmouth drifters in a number of respects. Lowestoft 'luggers' had lofty mizzen masts raked well for'ard, while the Yarmouth fishermen preferred a shorter mizzen set upright. The rake of the Lowstermen's mast allowed the mizzen boom to be steeved up higher without spoiling the flat set of the large sail, avoiding the necessity for the helmsman to duck every time the boat went about.[22]

An improvement that considerably mitigated the manual labour of hauling the drift nets was the introduction of steam capstans operated by an engine with a vertical boiler fitted below deck. A particularly compact and useful steam capstan was invented by William Elliott, a partner in the engineering firm of Elliott & Garrood which was in the 1880s mainly concerned with the manufacture of agricultural machinery at the Ingate Iron Works in Beccles. Instead of putting the capstan engine below deck, he designed a very small twin-cylinder horizontal engine which he placed on top of the capstan, bringing the steam pipe up through a hollow steel post which served as the capstan spindle. The first such capstan was fitted in 1885 in the Lowestoft drifter *Beaconsfield*, built at Lowestoft four years earlier and owned by Robert Capps, who lived in Arnold Street. Ten years later the Beccles firm claimed in an advertisement that some 900 vessels were fitted with their patent capstan, and by then all but four of the 190 drifters on the Lowestoft register were fitted with some form of steam capstan. In another advertisement in O.T. Olsen's *Fishermen's Nautical Almanack* for 1912 the company announced that more than 5,300 of their capstans were then in use. By 1896 Elliott & Garrood had branches at Lowestoft, Yarmouth and Brixham, and later also at Newlyn, Buckie and Fraserburgh.

It seems to have been Scots fishermen who were the first to experiment with steam engines as a means of propulsion for their drifters.[23] The first steam drifter built in Lowestoft was the *Consolation*, LT718, launched in 1897 from the yard of Chambers & Colby at the west end of the North Quay which later became John Chambers' No. 1 yard. Built to the order of George 'Mouse' Catchpole of Kessingland Beach, she was fitted with a 40hp compound engine by Elliott & Garrood that was possibly the Beccles firm's first marine engine.

Further wooden steam drifters followed the *Consolation* from the Chambers & Colby and other Lowestoft yards, some of the early steamers being equipped with relatively low-powered compound engines from Elliott & Garrood that bore the soubriquet of *Elliott Pots* – the vertical boiler in which the steam was raised had a domed top which stood above deck level.

With the Home Fishing gaining importance and prosperity, Lowestoft boatowners rapidly replaced their sailing drifters by steamers and by 1912 there were no fewer than 294 steam drifters in the Lowestoft fleet, roughly a third of all the fishing vessels owned in the port. Many of the Scots fishermen also turned to steam, and some of the steamers entering the fleets at Buckie, Banff, Fraserburgh and Kirkcaldy were built in yards at Lowestoft and Oulton Broad. The wooden steam drifter *Peep o' Day* was built at Lowestoft in 1898

One of the last generation of diesel-engined drifter-trawlers, the *Harold Cartwright*, built in 1950 by Richards Ironworks at Lowestoft, passes an angler fishing from the north extension as she leaves Lowestoft harbour in the early 1960s. Sold to Capetown in 1966, she was lost in August the following year south of Cape Agulhas, the most southerly point of Africa.

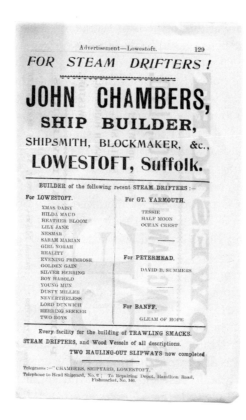

Advertisement—Lowestoft.   129

FOR STEAM DRIFTERS !

JOHN CHAMBERS,

SHIP BUILDER,

SHIPSMITH, BLOCKMAKER, &c.,

LOWESTOFT, Suffolk.

BUILDER of the following recent STEAM DRIFTERS :—

For LOWESTOFT.	For GT. YARMOUTH.
XMAS DAISY	TESSIE
HILDA MAUD	HALF MOON
HEATHER BLOOM	OCEAN CREST
LILY JANE	
NESMAR	
SARAH MARIAN	
GIRL NORAH	
REALITY	
EVENING PRIMROSE	For PETERHEAD.
GOLDEN GAIN	
SILVER HERRING	DAVID B. SUMMERS
BOY HAROLD	
YOUNG MUN	
DUSTY MILLER	
NEVERTHELESS	
LORD DUNWICH	For BANFF.
HERRING SEEKER	
TWO BOYS	GLEAM OF HOPE

Every facility for the building of TRAWLING SMACKS.
STEAM DRIFTERS, and Wood Vessels of all descriptions.
TWO HAULING-OUT SLIPWAYS now completed

Telegrams :—" CHAMBERS, SHIPYARD, LOWESTOFT."
Telephone to Head Shipyard, No. 2 ; To Repairing Depot, Hamilton Road,
Fishmarket, No. 146.

for David Stewart, of Wick, but by 1912 she had returned to her birthplace as LT187 and was owned by C.A. Gouldby of Kessingland and others.

Reading through the list of those steam drifters that were fishing out of Lowestoft in 1912 brings into mind a picture of boats laden down with fish racing for the harbour entrance and crowding the Waveney Dock, moored side by side with their heads to the quay, quarter-cran baskets being swung ashore as the coal wherry transfers fuel into the bunkers of drifter after drifter. The names arouse their own memories: *Girl Ena, Herring Fisher, Vesper Star, Bon Espoir, Children's Hope, Rose of Sharon, Tryphena, Supernal, All's Well* and *Peacemaker*. Then there was the *Pecheur*, a French word for a fisherman but rendered *Pe-chewer* in the local idiom.

The list of owners contains many well-remembered local family names: Allerton, Beamish, Breach, Capps, Catchpole, Colby, Durrant, Gouldby, Jenner, Mitchell, Offord, Pye and Reynolds, Strowger, Turrell and Utting, all of them names familiar in the fishing trade for several generations.

The year 1913 saw the East Anglian herring fishing reach its peak, the fleet of some 770 boats working out of Lowestoft – 359 local and 420 Scottish drifters – landing nearly 535,000 crans.[24] 'How wonderful it all was among all those boats, all the fishermen, the market workers, the Scots girls, the fish workers, the horses, the carters, the terrific hustle and bustle, all the many people working

day and night,' wrote Ted Frost, who experienced the 1913 Home Fishing as a boy in his early teens – a market ranger, he calls himself. 'It was a marvellous period for any boy with a love of ships and the sea to be living in Lowestoft … shipwrights and fitters were working on board many of

Some East Anglian steam drifters performed an annual circumnavigation of the British Isles in search of herring, working their way down the east coast in the summer and returning to home waters in time for the Home Fishing. A number of Lowestoft boats are seen here in Scarborough; at left is the *Dick Whittington*, LT61, and at right the steel drifter *Norfolk County*, LT103, built at Selby in Yorkshire in 1908.

the vessels repairing damage, possibly sustained through collision, in order to get them to sea again as quickly as possible. Time was indeed money as the shoals of herring slowly but surely worked their way south past Lowestoft and Yarmouth.'[25]

The outbreak of war with Germany in August 1914 brought herring fishing in the North Sea to a stop for more than four years, and the drifters were hired as patrol boats, minesweepers and netlayers to maintain anti-submarine nets in the Dover Straits and elsewhere. No fewer than 504 steam drifters from Lowestoft and Yarmouth served with the Royal Navy, and fifty-four of them were lost, along with many of the fishermen who manned them.[26]

When fishing resumed after the war strenuous efforts were made to replace the boats destroyed by enemy surface craft, U-boats and mines, but contrary to expectations catches proved by no means as plentiful as in earlier years. In the period between the two world wars some steam drifters made an annual circumnavigation of the British Isles in search of fish, leaving Lowestoft in

East Anglian drifters ranged widely in search of fish, and the Lowestoft men were well known in Milford Haven. Indeed some east coast men settled in the Welsh port.

Bill Soloman, who took the *Lord Wenlock* all round Britain in search of herring in 1939. During the Second World War he commanded a large naval trawler.

Built at Selby in 1925, the *Shepherd Lad* was originally owned by Alexander Tait and others of Fraserburgh and bore the registration FR123. She later passed to Lowestoft ownership and is seen here leaving Lowestoft in the 1950s.

April or May and steaming down Channel and into the Irish Sea. They would fish for a time out of Milford Haven and then perhaps work out of Dunmore East in Waterford Harbour, southern Ireland, and Buncrana in Lough Swilly, Donegal. From Ireland they went on to Stornoway on the Isle of Lewis and then to Lerwick in the Shetlands, from where they followed the herring shoals up the east coast, arriving at Lowestoft in time to fit out for the Home Fishing.

Bill Soloman, one of those who set up the Lowestoft maritime museum at Sparrows Nest, made that voyage in 1939 as skipper of the *Lord Wenlock*, LT1143; he claimed to have been the last skipper to take a steam drifter around the British Isles in search of herring. Lowestoft boats continued to use Milford Haven and the Irish ports in the 1950s, but they no longer made the round-Britain voyage.

One of the last steam drifters built in a Lowestoft yard was the *Lord Suffolk*, launched for Lowestoft Steam Herring Drifters Ltd by John Chambers Ltd in 1929; of 115 gross registered tons and 92ft in length, she had a triple expansion engine by William Burrell of the Victoria engineering works in Southtown, as did her sister ship *Lord St Vincent*. Both vessels served with the Royal Navy during the Second World War along with other drifters from the same company; the *Lord Suffolk* returned to fishing when peace came but the *Lord St Vincent* fell victim to a mine in the Thames Estuary in 1941. Altogether 107 drifters were lost on war service, a number of them from the Lowestoft fleet.

New drifters built in the 1950s were all motor vessels, and some of the steam drifter-trawlers that survived the war were converted to diesel, one of them being the *Thrifty* that had been built at Leiderdorp in Holland in 1916. Like the *Comrades*, built at Selby in 1928, and the *Kindred Star*, launched by Chambers in 1930, the *Thrifty* was fitted with a diesel engine specially designed for fishing vessels by a Lowestoft firm, AK Diesels Ltd.

The fishery struggled on through the 1950s, but with catches declining both the number of local drifters and the number of Scots boats coming south for the East Anglian autumn fishing were much reduced. The Scots 'girls' – almost all of very mature years since the youngsters were no longer being recruited into their ranks – continued to come to Lowestoft, but they no longer had a special train to themselves; and when landings were poor they spent much of their time drinking tea in the Bethel on Battery Green.

In 1963 the Lowestoft fleet numbered twenty-one boats, with ten Scots boats taking part in the autumn fishing from the Suffolk port. In succeeding years the number of boats declined further until in 1968 the last Lowestoft herring drifter, the Fraserburgh-built *Wisemans*, gave up the search for herring before the end of November after landing only half a cran as the result of three nights' fishing.

And then it was all history; the herring fishery was no more.

The Lowestoft steam drifter *Fisher Girl* putting to sea on a dull day in the 1950s. Built of wood at Lowestoft in 1914, she served with the navy in both world wars andd was sunk by air attack in Falmouth harbour in 1941, but was raised and survived to be one of the last steam drifters working out of Lowestoft.

Lowestoft was for a long period the east coast base of the Royal Navy's fishery protection squadron, whose vessels not infrequently escorted into harbour continental trawlers caught fishing within British territorial waters or using illegal nets.

Above: The torpedo gunboats HMS *Leda* and HMS *Halcyon* dressed overall for Lowestoft Regatta just before the First World War. The *Halcyon* remained at Lowestoft throughout the war and did some excellent work, ramming and sinking a U-boat in 1917.

Left: The fishery protection gunboat HMS *Halcyon* berthed in Lowestoft inner harbour about 1912. Her lofty foremast carries early wireless aerials.

Above: The third class
cruiser HMS *Barham* of
1889 in Lowestoft inner
harbour about 1904.

Right Particularly well
known at Lowestoft
in the years before the
First World War was the
fishery protection vessel
HMS *Hearty*, here seen
in the smart black and
white paintwork and buff
funnels of earlier years. Her
concert party, the Hearty
Snowflakes, were popular in
the town.

Shipwrights and shipyards   19

At a time when small shipyards all around the coast were turning out little ships that sailed worldwide as well as fishing boats that played a very significant part in feeding the growing population of England, the shipwrights were among the elite of the workforce. Not only did they know how to handle the adze to shape and mould timber but they also acquired a great deal of empirical knowledge of ship design, drafting and stability.[1]

Shipwrights from various Suffolk ports, including Ipswich, Dunwich, Southwold and Lowestoft, were impressed in 1512 for the building of Henry VIII's massive warship *Henri Grace a Dieu*, popularly known as the *Great Harry*, at his dockyard at Woolwich. Twenty-five went from Ipswich, fifteen from Southwold, and ten from Dunwich. Altogether 252 men were conscripted from as far afield as Cornwall and Yorkshire; Ipswich was one of just four places that mustered twenty or more men each.[2]

The Petts who made such a name for themselves as royal shipwrights in the sixteenth and seventeenth centuries were a Harwich family and might have come originally from Aldeburgh. The surname is said to have its origin in the appellation 'atte Pitt', he who lives at or beside the claypit, sandpit or stonepit; the change from Pitt to Pett might well be an indication of a Suffolk origin, bearing in mind the Suffolk tendency to change the vowel. The Petts and their relations the Chapmans moved from Harwich to Chatham and Rotherhithe, the latter being the official centre of the shipwrights' craft.

Although at the beginning of the seventeenth century Ipswich shipbuilders were constructing so many ships for the merchants of London that the town was gaining a reputation as 'the shipyard of London', the Thames was the main centre of shipbuilding in England. There were four royal dockyards and at least 160 private shipyards beside the rivers Thames and Medway, and in the course of three centuries the royal yards built more than a thousand ships; perhaps four times this number were turned out by the private yards.[3]

Most famous of those private yards was undoubtedly the celebrated Blackwall yard, which launched more than 550 vessels between 1613 and 1901 and at one period was sub-let to members of the Johnson family, who had come from Aldeburgh. Henry Johnson was a cousin of Phineas Pett, to whom he was apprenticed in 1639.

Born in 1570, Phineas Pett is reputed to have come of a line of shipwrights stretching back for some two hundred years. There was a William Pette of Dunwich who in his will of 1497 left to his brother John 'my new boat and all my working tools', though there is no evidence that he was an ancestor

Opposite: The barquentine *Thomas* on the slip at Lowestoft. Built at Barnstaple in 1837, she was owned at the time of the photograph by John Stewart, of Carlton Colville.

of Phineas, whose father Peter was a Harwich shipwright. It is possible that brother John was the same John Pette who in 1499 was paid for caulking the *Regent*, probably at Portsmouth – the mobility of shipwrights in that period is illustrated clearly enough by the impressing of all those Suffolk men for the building of the *Great Harry* at Woolwich.

When King James I gave a charter to 'the Master, Wardens and Commonalty of the Art or Mystery of Shipwrights of England' in 1605 he named Phineas Pett as one of the twelve Assistants, along with Thomas Cole of Woodbridge, Robert Wilkinson of Ipswich and Thomas Pryme of Yarmouth and eight others. It is indeed significant that representatives of the three East Anglian ports were prominent in the new organization that had been set up, as a result of agitation by the shipwrights themselves, in an attempt to improve the standard of ship design and construction.

The links between the Petts and Thomas Cole of Woodbridge are difficult to unravel, but in 1633 Phineas and his son Peter set off from Chatham in the pinnace *Henrietta* for a visit to Woodbridge to arrange the marriage of Peter to Catherine Cole, Thomas's eldest daughter. The wedding duly took place that September in St Mary's Church at Woodbridge 'after the sermon'.[4]

A Peter Pett built the 4th rates *Advice* and *Reserve* at Woodbridge in 1650, but this was not the same Peter Pett who married Catherine and was Commissioner at Chatham from 1647 to 1668, when he was made the scapegoat for the disastrous failure to prevent the Dutch attack on the Medway the previous year. He was pilloried for having concentrated on saving the models, but those dockyard models were the designs of the next generation of English warships and it was of prime importance that they should not fall into Dutch hands. There were so many Petts with the given names of Peter and Phineas in various generations and different branches of the family that one becomes hopelessly confused when trying to sort out which one did what; indeed it has been said that the Navy Board of the time not infrequently confused one with another.

Records of shipbuilding in the early days are hard to find; the accounts of the building of a galley and barge at Ipswich in 1294, quoted in chapter two, are a rare survival. It is apparent from the tenor of those documents that shipbuilding was already well established on the Orwell by the thirteenth century, and it is fairly evident also that the trade was carried on elsewhere around the coast at that time. Dunwich also was required to assist King Edward's galley-building drive, and is thought to have had a galley-house in which such a craft might be protected from the elements.[5]

The requirement for a shipyard in the days of oak and hemp were simple enough; an area of gravel providing a firm foundation for the stocks on which the ship was constructed, a gentle declivity to facilitate launching and deep water close to the shore, that was all. The only other requirements were supplies of good timber and a sufficiency of skilled labour, both of which might be brought in from outside the immediate area. Ships might even be built on the open beach, as they certainly were at Lowestoft.

For the most part the only buildings on the old shipyards would be weatherboarded and pantiled sheds providing storage for the shipwrights' tools; on the walls would he hung augers, some of them ten feet and more in length, used to make holes for the fastenings which would include oaken treenails (pronounced trennels or trunnels) produced with the aid of a tool called a mute. One of the larger sheds might be a two-storey affair, the upper floor being the mould loft. This would have a well-laid uninterrupted floor on which the moulds of the vessel to be built could be laid down at full size; a yard building large vessels would require a loft of considerable extent.

Outside would be the sawpit in which the two sawyers, one top, one bottom, would cut up the tree trunks into strakes and also cut to shape the curved and twisted branches or 'wrongs' selected for frames, knees and other structural members. The top sawyer would guide the saw, his colleague in the pit pulling the saw on its downward, cutting stroke. The sawyers were specialists well able not only to produce all the various pieces of timber needed to build a ship but also to go out to the woods to select and fell trees from which to fashion that timber.[6]

When sawn the wood was stacked flick above flick, with sticks in between each to allow air to circulate and help the wood to season. The use of 'green' unseasoned wood was generally frowned upon, although in the case of the East Indiaman *Orwell* built by Jabez Bayley at Ipswich in 1816-17 the Suffolk oak of which she was built was considered at the time to be very green; it was, however, found to be only partially decayed when she was broken up more than twenty years later.[7]

Early ships like the 1294 Ipswich galley, and fishing craft until the nineteenth century, were clinker built, a term that derived from the fact that the overlapping planks were fastened to one another with iron or copper nails clenched on the inside over 'roves', slightly conical washers over which the end of the nails were riveted. In this form of building the shape of the ship was determined by the shaping and fitting of the strakes, the internal timbers being inserted only when the outer skin was complete.

By contrast, in carvel building, a technique which might have been introduced to northern Europe from the Mediterranean, the frame of the vessel consisting of heavy timbers was set up on the keel and completed before planking up was commenced, the planks being fastened to the timbers. By the seventeenth century this method was used for the building of all large vessels.

Stacks of seasoning timber and heaps of 'wrongs' awaiting selection for cutting out as knees and floors would take up a corner of the yard, and in another corner would be a steam chest in which strakes could be steamed to give them the necessary flexibility to take up the correct form when being fastened in place. This could be a long wooden box or an iron or steel box or cylinder, often fed by a vertical boiler close by, fired by waste wood.

Some yards did not possess a steam chest but employed a more primitive method of rendering the strakes supple. Bundles of burning reeds were held close enough to the boards to warm them but not so close as to scorch them.

For hauling vessels out of the water for repair a horse would be hitched to a simple but heavy windlass or capstan, a tackle giving the power required to haul the ship up temporary ways laid under keel and bilge. A similar method was used as late as the 1920s to set up steam drifters for launching at John Chambers' yard at Oulton Broad, as can be seen in a drawing by Ted Frost, a shipwright who served his apprenticeship on that yard.

A number of east coast yards were equipped with a patent slip or 'marine railway' invented by Scottish shipbuilder Thomas Morton in 1818. It consisted

A wooden steam drifter ready for launching from John Chambers yard in 1917, a drawing by Ted Frost, who was an apprentice on the yard at the time of the launching.

A large vessel, possibly an East Indiaman intended for the service of the Honourable East India Company, under construction just a few years after Jabez Bayley built similar vessels at the Halifax shipyard in Ipswich; an etching by E.W. Cooke.

of a wheeled carriage which would be lowered down rails into the water and on to which a vessel could be manoeuvred; when the ship was in position the carriage would be hauled up the rails, bringing the craft clear of the water so that repairs could be carried out.

One of the earliest patent slips was installed at the Harwich Navy Yard in 1825, well shown in a print in Dale's *Season at Harwich*. Two Post Office packets, the *Earl of Leicester* and the *Prince of Orange*, were the first vessels to be hauled out on the Navy Yard slip, the operation of which was thus described by a local newspaper of the time: 'The vessels were fixed upon a frame, to which were attached four rows of small iron wheels, placed laterally upon an inclined plane; the only moving power was a capstan with a few men, who ran it round with great facility.'

When the Dutch ship *Friesland* ran aground on the Longsand in 1859 while on her way to Batavier in the Netherlands East Indies (renamed Jakarta by Indonesian nationalists) with troops for the Dutch garrison there and was brought into Harwich by the tug *Amazon* for repair it was the soldiers who manned the capstan to bring their ship on to the yard. She was the largest ship to be hauled up the Harwich slip, and extra purchases had to be employed to get her up.[8]

Two such slips were installed at Lowestoft, one on what is now the Excelsior Yard, base of the Excelsior Trust which operates the Lowestoft sailing smack *Excelsior*; the other at Laundry Lane was much used for the refitting of steam drifters in preparation for the Home Fishing. Several such slips were installed in Ipswich shipyards, the first, in place by 1830, being that in William Bayley's St Clement's Yard which is still in use.

The Harwich Navy Yard also had a treadwheel crane which is thought to date back to the establishment of the yard in the mid-seventeenth century. The treadwheel is housed in a timber structure that was originally largely open at the sides, though since the removal of the crane from the yard to Harwich

Green about 1930 the sides have been boarded. Surprisingly, no brake of any kind was fitted to the treadwheel; more than one accident occurred as a result of the load taking charge and rotating the drum at high speed. On one occasion a youngster was badly injured when his older colleague stepped out of the wheel to see if the load had been hoisted high enough; the boy's weight proved insufficient to hold the load of timber that was being lifted.

That was probably the only such crane to be installed on any shipyard in the area. The remarkable thing is, perhaps, that it is the sole survivor in the country of such cranes installed at this and other royal dockyards. It should be regarded as a national monument.

Although established as a naval dockyard in 1657 when the Commonwealth was in conflict with our Dutch neighbours, and known throughout its existence as the Navy Yard, the Harwich shipyard was for much of its life occupied by private shipbuilders. Even before the laying out of the yard on land leased from the Corporation at the tip of the peninsula, Harwich had been employed during the first Dutch War of 1652-54 as a stores base. Those who have dipped into Sam Pepys's incomparable diary will know of the everlasting lack of money and the problems of getting supplies to the fleet, and will have sympathy for Major Nehemiah Bourne, who was put in charge at Harwich.

A former London merchant and a serving naval officer of some distinction, Bourne proved an able administrator and carried out excellent work at Harwich in the face of considerable difficulties. In 1653 he hinted at the problems he faced when he wrote that five warships were ready to sail from Harwich but were held up by the non-arrival of a ship with stores from the depot at Deptford. 'Hitherto I have quieted the seamen with promises of payment and have encouraged them to go on with the buisness [sic] of fitting their shippes,' he wrote, 'but now they begin to be a little Impatient, Crying out they want Cloathes and they shall be forst away to sea and what will their money do them good, not having time to lay it out'.[9]

The fact that Major Bourne – he was always referred to by his army rank – was indeed doing a good job at Harwich was confirmed by General Monk,

The Dutch ship *Friesland* hauled out on the Harwich Navy Yard for repairs after running aground on the Longsand in 1859

The jib of the Harwich dockyard crane, believed to date from the mid-seventeenth century, when the crane was still in its original position at the tip of the Harwich peninsula. It now stands on Harwich Green, the sole survivor of the treadwheel dockyard cranes that were once a feature of naval establishments.

in command of the fleet, in a letter to the Navy Commissioners of 20th July 1653: 'It is strange that 20 ships should be so long fitting out from Chatham, Woolwich and Deptford,' he told the Navy Board, 'when there have been 22 or more fitted out from Harwich in half the time by Major Bourne'.[10]

Quite a lot of what we know of the early days of the Harwich Navy Yard is to be learnt from the pages of that diary kept by Samuel Pepys, the man who laid the foundations of the country's naval administration. The genius of Samuel Pepys lay in his realisation that he needed to know all about other people's jobs as well as he knew his own. For instance, only by understanding the intricacies of timber measurement could he detect when suppliers were cheating the King; cheating the customer was a popular way of making a fortune in the seventeenth century. He was made aware of 'the whole mystery of off-square, wherein the King is abused in the timber that he buys,'[11] by his friend Anthony Deane, who was appointed Master Shipwright at Harwich in 1664 on Pepys's recommendation.

A Harwich man, Deane served his apprenticeship with Christopher Pett, Master Shipwright at Woolwich Dockyard, where he became Assistant Master Shipwright to Pett. He was in his mid-twenties when he first became known to Pepys, and like many at that age had more than his share of self-confidence: 'I find Deane a pretty able man, and able to do the King service,' Pepys noted. 'He would fain seem a modest man, and yet will commend his own work and skill and vie with other persons, especially the Petts. But I let him alone, to hear all he will say.'[12]

Pepys did indeed learn a good deal from him, and the two became firm friends, though when Deane quarrelled with the storekeeper and the Navy Commissioner at Harwich Pepys did find cause to caution him as to his behaviour. Pepys was a good judge of character, and Deane went on to become perhaps the most significant naval architect of the seventeenth century and the first to apply scientific principles of ship design to the construction of warships.

The Navy Commissioner with whom Deane had differences was Captain John Taylor, who had earlier demonstrated his abilities at Chatham under the Commonwealth. The storekeeper, Silas Taylor, was not, in spite of having the same surname, in any way related to the commissioner; he owed the appointment in Harwich to other influential friends and was a man of many parts, antiquary, composer and playwright. Pepys did not think highly of him, to judge of the remarks he noted down after hearing an anthem he had composed: '. . .a dull old-fashioned thing of 6 or 7 parts that nobody could understand; and the Duke of York, when he came out, told me that he was a better store-keeper than anthem-maker, and that was bad enough too.'[13]

The first ship that Deane built in the Harwich Navy Yard, the 66-gun 3rd rate *Rupert*, was launched in January 1666. She won considerable praise for her design and construction. On 19th May that year Pepys took Deane home to dinner and they discussed the new ship, 'which succeeds so well, as he hath got great honour by it, and I some by recommending him – the King, Duke and everybody saying it is the best ship that was ever built', Pepys noted in his diary. 'And then he fell to explain to me his manner of casting the draught of water which a ship will draw beforehand – which is a secret the King and all admire in him; and he is the first that hath come to any certainty beforehand of foretelling the draught of water of a ship before she be launched. I must confess I am much pleased in his success in this business. . .'.[14]

As ever, there were old hands who decried any development of that kind. William Castle, the shipbuilder son-in-law of Surveyor of the Navy Sir William Batten, took one look at the draught of the ship that Deane had sent to his friend and asked Pepys 'whether he that laid it down had ever built a ship or no'.

Whatever the opinion of lesser craftsmen, the warships that Deane built at Harwich won high praise in those quarters that really mattered. When Charles II and the Duke of York paid their visit to Landguard Fort in October 1668 and also had a look at the Navy Yard, guided around by Silas Taylor, they praised the *Rupert* and the *Resolution*, which they knew had been built there by Deane.

Although the yard was extended and a second building slip laid down when in 1677 war with France seemed likely and four new warships, the *Restoration*, *Bredah*, *Sandwich* and *Albemarle*, were built there by Master Shipwright Isaac Betts, lack of money and a preference for the dockyard at Sheerness at the mouth of the Medway resulted in the Navy Yard being run down. Deane had been transferred to Portsmouth and Captain Taylor was probably not sorry when his term at Harwich came to an end; letters in the National Archive tell rather eloquently of the difficulties with which he was faced while in charge of the yard.

Nonetheless, the Navy Yard continued as a private shipyard, and in about 1742 an Ipswich shipbuilder, the younger John Barnard, leased the yard. He had already built for the Navy on his St Clement's yard in Ipswich the 6th rate *Biddeford*, one of five 20-gun ships ordered from private shipbuilders in 1739 as war with Spain loomed. He had also built the 4th rate 50-gun *Hampshire* in 1741 at John's Ness, just below where the Orwell Bridge now carries the Ipswich by-pass road over the river. Both vessels were towed down to Harwich for fitting out and rigging at the Navy Yard, as was the bomb vessel *Granado* which he built at his Ipswich yard in 1742.

The Harwich Navy Yard in the early eighteenth century when it was turning out warships for the Royal Navy. On the right is a hulk sunk to provide a breakwater.

The reason for his going downriver to John's Ness for the building of the *Hampshire* was that this vessel was too large and drew too much water to be launched from any of the yards in the town. From the yard at John's Ness she could be launched into the length of Back Again Reach, where the channel of the Orwell turned sharply across the river from one shore to the other. Back Again Reach was later to be eradicated by one of the improvements made by the Ipswich River Commissioners.

A painting by the elder John Cleveley in the National Maritime Museum at Greenwich shows all three vessels, the *Hampshire* on the ways at John's Ness, the *Biddeford* on the way down to Harwich for fitting out, and the *Granado* at anchor.[15] A certain amount of artistic licence is involved, since all three vessels could not have been in the one place at the same time. It seems very likely that this picture was commissioned by John Barnard as a record of his Navy Board contracts.

It was normal for the Navy Board to appoint an overseer to supervise the construction of ships contracted out to private yards, and in the case of Barnard's early warship contracts this was a shipwright from one of the royal dockyards named Thomas Slade. It was presumably during his superintendence of Barnard's contracts that he met Hannah Moore, an Ipswich woman whom he married at Nacton Church in 1747.[16] A man of outstanding ability, Slade became Master Shipwright at Deptford and was appointed by George Anson, First Lord of the Admiralty, one of the two joint Surveyors of the Navy in 1755; he was largely responsible for the introduction of the 74-gun ship and the classic frigate, and was the designer of HMS *Victory*, built at Chatham between 1759 and 1765.

When he died at Bath as Sir Thomas in 1771 he was brought to Ipswich to be buried in St Clement's churchyard alongside his wife, who had predeceased him nearly eight years earlier. The exact site of his grave is unknown, but a new memorial installed as part of a landscaping scheme commemorates a man who did so much not only to improve warship design but to revolutionise naval shipbuilding policy.

After Barnard had been given the contract for the *Hampshire* suggestions were made that John's Ness was an unsuitable site for the building of a vessel of such a size. The Surveyor of the Navy, Sir Jacob Ackworth, wrote to Slade demanding an explanation. John Barnard's reply to the allegations that had been made was firm and very much to the point. He wrote that, having been shown the letter by Slade, 'he was very much surprised that any new difficulty should be started about the place which by Mr Slade's own opinion was thought both a convenient and safe place to launch and carry down the *Hampshire* or a 70-gun ship if required'. To back up his and Slade's opinion he wrote 'I have since consulted most of the ablest Pilots and old experienced Masters who all agree to a man 'tis easy and safe to carry down a ship of that Draft of Water without difficulty or hazzard'.[17]

There seems to have been no further correspondence on that matter, but letters between Barnard and the Navy Board during the course of work on the *Hampshire* reveal the many problems facing a private shipbuilder engaged on such a contract. One of those difficulties concerned the issue of certificates of protection to men working on naval ships against the activities of the press gang, which was very active in seaports such as Ipswich. It might not be entirely

coincidental that in 1762 a petition was sent to the Lords Commissioners of the Admiralty asking 'to be relieved from the violence and oppression of the Press Gang commanded by Captain John Lloyd, then quartered at Orford,' and a number of members of the press gang appeared in court accused of assault, illegal impressment and other offences in Suffolk.

Another worry for John Barnard was the defence of the Harwich yard from possible attack. In 1744, when he had in hand a 60-gun ship and one of 50 guns as well as a sloop, he represented 'the dangerous situation of that place, being so much exposed to the enemy that it is in the power of every little privateer, or even a boat, to burn the ships there on the stocks'. As a result of what he said it was agreed that a hulk armed with twelve nine-pounders should be stationed there and that the shipyard workers as well as the hulk's crew should be given small arms.

The Barnards, like other Suffolk shipbuilding families before them, eventually moved to the Thames, and William Barnard was building warships and other vessels at Deptford in the last twenty years of the eighteenth century. While there the Barnards turned out a dozen East Indiamen as well as more than twice that number of warships. The many hundreds of East Indiamen produced in the course of the eighteenth and early nineteenth centuries to meet the requirements of the Honourable East India Company were almost all River-built; produced, that is, by the Thames yards. Among the exceptions were a small group built at Ipswich by the Bayleys, perhaps the most interesting of all the Ipswich shipbuilding families. Thanks to the researches of John Leather we know quite a lot about this family, which originated in Kent or Sussex and produced some great characters.[18]

John Bayley, born at Rotherhithe and apprenticed there as a shipwright and boatbuilder, moved to Burnham-on-Crouch and ultimately to Ipswich with a

The East Indiaman *Orwell* under construction at Jabez Bayley's Halifax Yard at Ipswich in 1817. Bayley lost heavily on the contract for her building as he had to dredge a channel out to Ostrich Creek for her launching on 17th August of that year.

Jabez Bayley in a
contemporary sketch.

relative, William Bayley, an instance of the usual migration to the Thames working in reverse. It was the youngest of John's sons, Jabez, who built the majority of the Indiamen launched into the Orwell. While his brother Philip, 'who was not overstocked with brains,' according to a nephew, 'remained a working man all his life with a working man's thoughts and habits', Jabez became a leading figure in local maritime circles.

His nephew George described him as 'one of those good natured impulsive men on whom one cannot rely with confidence'; significantly we also learn that he had a 'fondness for distinction and was susceptible to flattery'. Perhaps that helps to explain why he overreached himself with the building of the Indiaman *Orwell*, for the launching of which he had to dredge a channel across the mudflats from his Halifax yard to the deep water of Ostrich Creek. The profits from the building of the 1,335-ton ship went into the dredging of that channel.

Jabez had taken over four of the town's shipyards, and when he lost heavily on the building of the *Orwell* he found himself in deep trouble. In due course he crashed in the same way as so many others had done, and everything, even his copies of Steel's and Stalkartt's *Naval Architecture*, was sold for the benefit of his creditors. His property at that time included standing trees at places as far away as Colchester and Ixworth.

The nephew whose unflattering comments on Jabez and Philip make such interesting reading was George Bayley, who as a lad of eighteen was employed as an under-foreman on the building of the *Orwell* and as foreman on the even bigger Indiamen which followed in the 1820s, the David Scott and William Fairlie. He it was who distinguished himself by building in 1825 the first two steamers to be launched in Ipswich; he went on to greater things after a period of financial misfortune and in 1834 was appointed in effect if not in

A group of Leith smacks
seen in an etching by
E.W. Cooke. Some of these
craft were products of the
Ipswich shipyards.

title the first principal surveyor to Lloyd's Register. George was no unschooled shipwright unable to make use of theoretical knowledge; he had supplemented what he learnt during his work on the Indiamen and other vessels by reading and by seeking the advice of those who superintended the building of those vessels.

The Indiamen were big ships for their day, and were by no means typical of the vessels turned out by the Ipswich shipyards. Both at Ipswich and on the River Colne in Essex there were shipbuilders who were adept at designing and producing relatively small fast-sailing vessels such as the Leith smacks that ran regular services along the east coast from Scotland to London, fruit schooners and the 'buttermen' that brought dairy produce from the Channel Islands.[19] The fruit trades from the Azores and from the eastern Mediterranean demanded fast craft able to make a quick passage carrying a relatively small cargo, and there were those like the firm of Thomas Harvey & Son of Wivenhoe on the Colne and Halifax yard, Ipswich, who specialised in the design and building of such vessels.[20]

Apart from the shipbuilders themselves, one of the most interesting characters to be involved with the trade at Ipswich was a former officer in the Honourable East India Company's sea service, Richard Hall Gower, whose home was at Nova Scotia House on the west bank of the Orwell a short way below the town. One of those men whose minds were wont to think beyond the conventional, Gower wrote of himself as 'an officer accustomed to pass his mid-night watch on ship-board, during the quietude of steady weather in considering the imbecility of shipping and the wants of seamen on the ocean, with the intention of supplying their defects'.[21]

Having experienced for himself the defects, as he saw them, of the sailing vessels in commercial use towards the end of the eighteenth century, Gower

Thomas Harvey and Son's Halifax Shipyard at Ipswich in 1858, the birthplace of many fruit traders and other speedy vessels. Hugh Moffat has recorded that the figure to be seen on the second vessel from the left is Thomas Harvey junior, and the next vessel, with a mast stepped, is the fruit schooner *Nonpareil* of Ipswich, which had been built on this yard in 1848. The yard closed in 1864.

A portrait of Captain
Richard Hall Gower,
Honourable East India
Company officer and
designer of some most
interesting and
unusual vessels.

determined to put them right in the most practical way possible; he designed a vessel incorporating his own ideas and, having persuaded six of his East India Company friends and two others to subscribe towards the cost, had it built at Itchenor on Chichester Harbour in 1800. According to his own account that vessel, the *Transit*, 'was framed by house carpenters, but planked by shipwrights, and launched, as rigged and complete for sea, on the tenth day of May 1800'.[22]

The *Transit* was indeed a revolutionary vessel, both as regards hull form and rig. In some respects the hull form anticipated that of the later clipper ships, long and lean and with fine lines at bow and stern; the midship section showed inward-tapering sides and a deep V-shaped bottom with a deep keel. Her rig was as unconventional as her hull shape; she had four masts, the foremast being square rigged and the others carrying fore-and-aft gaff sails that were each divided into three sections for ease of handling. When she entered service she was very fast and left all contemporary vessels well astern, if Gower's own writings are to be believed.

Gower was not a man to understate his achievements, and there is little doubt that his actions sometimes proved counter-productive, gaining him no support. After her launching at Itchenor the *Transit* sailed under his command to Portsmouth, where 'the novelty of her structure gave great amusement to the Jack Tars on board the Channel Fleet, then at anchor on the Spit,' Gower wrote later. 'As the vessel wrought through the fleet, the sailors absolutely swarmed the rigging of the ships, seemingly highly gratified by the ready manoeuvring of the *Transit*'.[23]

A little later Gower sought to interest King George III in his project. Rebuffed when he tried to obtain an interview with the king, Gower decided to give His Majesty a display of the *Transit's* abilities as the king was rowed out to the royal yacht in Portsmouth Harbour; the *Transit* 'was sailed so close to the barge as to view the surprise of the party, and to catch the enquiring words of His Majesty respecting this novel vessel'.[24] Those enquiring words

The brigantine *Clementine*
on the ways at St Clement's
Yard, Ipswich, in 1885.
Registered in London
and intended for the
Newfoundland stockfish
trade, she was the last
round-bottomed sailing
craft to be built in the
Ipswich yards

were probably something like 'who the devil is that confounded fool. . .'

No doubt the royal party expressed similar sentiments rather more strongly a few minutes later. 'When the Royal Family were on board the *Royal Charlotte* yacht, and while she was getting under-way, the *Transit* sailed three times round her, quite close, the water being extremely smooth, which drew the particular attention of the King, Queen, and Princesses, who kept walking round the quarter-deck of the yacht, with their eyes fixed on the movements of the *Transit*' – probably nervously expecting a collision at any moment.

Perhaps predictably, Gower received a cold shoulder wherever he sought support. Eventually a Portuguese government cargo was fixed for Lisbon, and this country being at war with France it was necessary for the *Transit* to sail in convoy. When the signal was made for the ships of the convoy to weigh anchor and leave Torbay Gower chose the moment to send his boats ashore to fill the ship's water casks; it was a deliberate ploy to enable him to show off the *Transit's* sailing qualities.

The *Transit* beat out of Torbay against the south-easterly wind without difficulty and quite soon caught up with the convoy, but it was not the kind of antics to endear her commander to the commodore of the convoy, who issued Gower with a strong reprimand for disobedience to his signal. Naval officers intensely disliked convoy work, because merchant ships were never able to keep station as they were expected to do – and here was a ship whose commander deliberately flouted instructions.

 Some time after her return from Lisbon the *Transit* was purchased by Messrs St Barbe, Green & Bignall[25] and put into the Mediterranean trade, making two round passages to Constantinople (now known as Istanbul) and Smyrna (now Izmir) in the course of a year. After what appears to have been a successful career Lloyd's List of 18th December 1810 reported her loss by stranding on a reef when bound from Hayti for Smyrna.

In the end Gower's persistence paid off and in 1808 the Navy ordered a second *Transit* from Jabez Bayley as an 'advice cutter'. She was 130ft overall length with a beam of 22ft 6in. and her tonnage was 262, but in 1809 she was shortened, having 20ft cut out amidships, reducing her tonnage to 214.[26] Gower of course reckoned that the changes ruined her performance. She was sold out of the Navy in 1815.

Bayley also built a three-masted yacht, also named *Transit*, for the Hon. George Vernon of Orwell Park, Nacton, descendant of Admiral Vernon, 'Old Grog', who is credited with having introduced the dilution of the Navy's rum issue. It was reported that between three and four thousand people had watched the launching,[27] which no doubt gratified Thomas Simmons of the Ostrich Inn at Wherstead who had advertised a week earlier that his tea gardens, which had been 'lately fitted up with arbours and benches in a stile of superior elegance', would be a most suitable site from which to view the proceedings.[28]

Again Gower complained that modifications made to his design had marred her sailing qualities, passing on the comment that 'she had more rigs than months in a year'. Gower was also responsible for the design of a lifeboat stationed at Landguard Fort, as mentioned in chapter seventeen, and for a rather remarkable cargo vessel built by George Bayley in 1824 for the British Copper Company,[29] whose mill in Walthamstow closed in 1857.

Sail to steam, oak to steel　　20

The relatively small town of Woodbridge, lying at the head of the Deben, had a long history of shipbuilding and, in spite of the restrictions imposed by a narrow and relatively shallow river, saw the launching of several quite large warships in the seventeenth century, as mentioned earlier. Besides the 4th rates *Advice* and *Reserve* built by a Peter Pett in 1650 there were the *Preston*, built three years later by William Carey and renamed *Antelope* at the Restoration, and the *Maidstone*, launched the following year by Edmund Munday and later renamed *Mary Rose*. Munday, who was a churchwarden at St Mary's, was also responsible for the *Ludlow* in 1698. These ships all seem to have been taken downriver and towed to one of the dockyards for fitting out and rigging; it was by no means unknown for ships to be towed by sailing vessels.

There were two shipyards, the more northerly one at Lime Kiln Quay above the tidemill pond and the other at the Lord's Quay more or less where the railway station is now. One of these was for sale in 1751, the occupier, Edward Darley, having succumbed to that scourge of shipbuilders, bankruptcy.[1]

It was at the Lime Kiln Quay that William Dryden, who is said to have begun business in 1796, turned out a succession of trading and fishing vessels, including the sloop *Constant Trader* of 1803 which was rerigged as a brig in 1815 and lost off Lowestoft five years later. Another of his sloops, the 70-ton *Britannia*, launched in 1810, traded for a little over fifty years before being run ashore at Palling on the Norfolk coast after a collision; she was broken up where she lay.

Dryden suffered a fire in his yard in 1812 when his store was burnt out, greater damage being prevented 'by the assistance of inhabitants'. He sold out six years later to William Bayley, his last vessel being the sloop *Albion*, which was lost in 1846; Dryden died in 1819. Bayley later moved to Ipswich, and Dryden's son William Holland Dryden took over the yard in 1826, when he 'Returned thanks to the friends of his late Father, for the favours conferred upon him during the many years he conducted the above business' and respectfully solicited their patronage and support for himself. The younger Dryden built the 134-ton schooner *Elizabeth* in 1826 and another schooner, the 89-ton *Mary and Betsey*, the following year.

William Taylor took over the yard about 1830, apparently after the retirement of W.H. Dryden, who died in 1838 at the age of only thirty-four. Taylor launched the schooner *Grecian Daughter* for a Manningtree owner in 1837, and business at that time was said to be so good that the keel of another vessel for the same company was laid that same day. In 1839 he launched

Opposite: Herring luggers on the yard at Walberswick, where shipbuilding and boatbuilding were carried on somewhat spasmodically. The photograph was taken between 1867 and 1880 by Southwold photographer James Court or possibly by his wife Eliza, who was also very capable with a camera.

the 'Humber-keel sloop' *Monarch*, said to be the first billyboy to be built in Woodbridge.[2]

The year 1840 was one of considerable activity at the Lime Kiln Quay yard, but Taylor found time in February to celebrate the wedding of Queen Victoria and Prince Albert of Saxe-Coburg-Gotha, an event that was observed in Woodbridge 'in a manner that must entail everlasting disgrace upon us', according to the *Suffolk Chronicle*. 'Not a single public demonstration but the pealing of bells …'. William Taylor did, however, enjoy the newspaper's approbation for giving his men, their wives and families, upwards of ninety people all told, an excellent tea on his new mould loft, a building well adapted and fitted up for the occasion.

Later the same year Taylor launched the schooner *Bernard Barton*, named after the Woodbridge poet of that name. Edward Fitzgerald is said to have been told of the schooner's impending launch just as he was about to dine with Barton. With that odd sense of humour of his Old Fitz at once removed himself and his chair into a far corner of the room, saying that 'he could not profess to sit at the same table as one about to have a ship named after him'.

A section of Isaac Johnson's map of Woodbridge in 1828 showing at top right and bottom left the two shipyard sites.

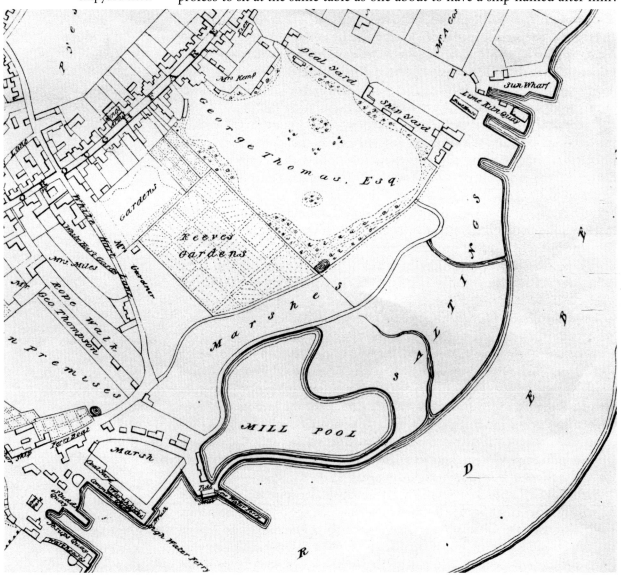

The billyboy ketch *Woodland Lass* at Blackshore Quay, Southwold about 1880. Although typical of a type of trading craft that originated in Yorkshire, she was built at Yarmouth in 1851 and registered at Lowestoft. At least one of these craft, the *Heart of Oak,* was built at Southwold in 1836

The poet himself amusingly commented that 'if my Bardship never gets me to the muster-roll of Parnassus, it will into the Shipping-List'.

She had a long life, for she did not meet her end until the fifty-ninth anniversary of her launching. She had by then passed into West Country ownership, being registered at Bridgwater and owned at Minehead; she was lost in the Bristol Channel when her pumps choked during a voyage from Chichester for Cardiff.

Taylor launched the big schooner *Leader* for a Harwich owner in 1841, the schooner *Princess Royal* and the billyboy sloop *Charlotte* in 1843 and another billyboy sloop, the *Laura,* the following year. The *Princess Royal,* one of the fleet of vessels owned by the Cobbold family of Ipswich, was lengthened in 1855 and her rig was changed to a brig.

Also operating in the 1830s was William Garrard, who although listed in the directories of the time as a boatbuilder built the schooner *Gleaner* in 1832 for a group of eight local people, three of them master mariners and one the wife of a master mariner. He was also the builder of several sloops, one of which, the 78-ton *Lark,* was owned by William Row, the Woodbridge postmaster.

It fell to William Taylor's son, also William, to launch the last Woodbridge-built schooner into the Deben, the 61-ton *Ellen,* in 1853; she was lost in Yarmouth Roads in 1875. Though the town has remained a popular yachting centre with a number of boatyards, that was the end of shipbuilding on the Deben.

At Slaughden Quay on the Alde several generations of the Hunt family were ship and boatbuilders, William Hunt being described as a shipbuilder in 1830. Most of the craft built on their yard were fishing boats, including three-masted luggers that changed their rig according to the season, adopting a powerful cutter rig when trawling and reverting to the lug rig when drifting for herrings or mackerel.

Edward and a younger William Hunt built the schooner *Jane* in 1840 for the Leiston ironfounders Richard Garrett and his sons Richard and John Dunnell Garrett, and were probably responsible for lengthening her in 1858.

Caulking tools used for caulking the seams of a wooden vessel: the caulker's mallet and a selection of caulking and making irons.

She was sold to Lowestoft in 1869, by which time John Dunnell Garrett was said to be 'of Magdeburg, Prussia', where he had set up his own ironworks.[3]

It might well be that when trade was slack the Hunts would build a smack or lugger 'on spec'. Edward Hunt owned the 47-ton smack *Mary Ann* from the time of her building in 1838 until 1863, when she was lengthened and sold to Samuel Barley of Aldeburgh. In 1849 he also acquired the 25-ton smack *Two Brothers*, built on the family yard in 1822, selling her to the Aldeburgh merchant Newson Garrett five years later.[4]

There was also a small yard operating at Snape, where Newson Garrett built a large maltings in mid-century. From that yard was launched in 1860 the 68-ton ketch barge *Percy* for Garrett's own fleet.

Ship and boatbuilding became a rather precarious business towards the end of the 1800s, and by about 1880 Allen Edward Hunt had seen the need to diversify. His entry in the 1879 *Post Office Directory* describes him as ship and boatbuilder, custom house agent, harbourmaster and coal merchant at the Quay.

At the same period there were two women boatbuilders in Southwold, both members of families that had a long involvement with the trade. Mrs Sarah Critten and John Critten, possibly her son, were listed in the 1879 directory as boatbuilders at East Green in the town and Mrs Elizabeth Ladd was listed on Gun Hill.[5] In both cases it would seem that these were home addresses, and it is thought that the ladies were probably managers of the family businesses rather than hands-on boatbuilders. Henry Ladd had built a number of fishing boats, including the *Andrew*, the first of the 'half-and-halfers', around the 1850s and James Critten was responsible for several beach yawls and gigs for the Southwold beach companies, among them the yawl *John Bull*.

Shipbuilding at Southwold and Walberswick seems to have been a rather fitful business. James Maggs records that William Williams built the ship *Suffolk* at Walberswick in 1804 but 'failed the same year and left the place', while Thomas Johnson launched the schooner *Norfolk* at Walberswick in 1826 for Halesworth coal merchant Hamond Ringwood after having moved

The interior of the Crittens' boatbuilding shop on Southwold beach about 1900. Several generations of the Critten family built fishing boats and beach yawls there.

A herring lugger on the beach at Lowestoft in the 1820s, after a painting by James Stark, whose name appears on the stern of the coble in the right foreground. Members of one of the town's beach companies, one of them with a telescope, are on watch for ships requiring their services.

from Lowestoft. At Blackshore on the Southwold side of the harbour the brig *Effort* was built in 1834, but she was lost on her first voyage; the *Vigilant* was launched there the same year and the billyboy schooner *Heart of Oak* in 1836.[6]

Thomas King, who with his brother John emigrated to America in 1838 in search of employment but returned the same year, began shipbuilding at Blackshore in 1843, launching the schooner *Sole Bay* the following year for G. Butcher of Wenhaston and others. He launched the *Ruby* in 1848 but then left the town for Yarmouth, and shipbuilding at Blackshore came to an end.

Long before the construction of the harbour ships were being built on the beach at Lowestoft. Early records of shipbuilding activity barely exist, but David Butcher records that a family of shipwrights, the Barnards, who might have been the forebears of the Ipswich shipbuilders of that name, were operating in the town in the second half of the sixteenth century and the first part of the seventeenth. They owned houses on the seaward side of the High Street with yards running right down to the Denes, where they would have set up the stocks on which their vessels were built.[7] William Barnard 'signed' his will in 1580 with a representation of an adze, a tool with which he would have been most familiar.[8] Another shipwright, Thomas Hawes, who was plying his trade in the middle of the seventeenth century, had a house and yard in the same location as the property occupied by the Barnards.

Rather more is known about the Johnsons, who were 'raising' ships on Lowestoft beach towards the end of the eighteenth century, thanks to the research of Les Moore, one of the founder-members of the Port of Lowestoft Research Society.[9] Thomas Johnson was a Yarmouth man who had served his apprenticeship with Drury and Crabtree in that town. In 1785 he obtained permission from the Lord of the Manor of Lowestoft to erect a shed on the

Two of the shipwright's basic tools, the adze and the maul.

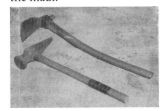

A wooden barge framed up
on John Chambers' No. 3
yard at Oulton Broad in the
1920s

beach – the 'waste of the manor' – 'abutting on the Whapload Way' and to
occupy a plot of ground there as a shipyard, for which he paid a rent of a
shilling a year. The agreement was ratified at a Court Baron or manor court
held on 23rd February 1786.

Thomas moved himself to Lowestoft, taking over a High Street property
formerly occupied by Breathard Tilmouth[10] and beginning work on his first
vessel, believed to have been the 140-ton brigantine *London*, a two-masted
craft square-rigged on the foremast. Two schooners, the *Samuel* and the
Johnson, followed in 1787, and he is thought to have built two three-masted
luggers, fishing craft, the next year.

Between 1787 and 1817 the Johnson yard is credited with twenty-one vessels,
mainly square-rigged ships, though it is possible that the total might have been
somewhat greater. The largest of them was the 260-ton *Young Henry*, which
Thomas built in 1801 for London owners. Besides launching ships for owners in
Yarmouth and Southwold he built vessels for much more distant ports including
Boston, Sunderland and Glasgow as well as for London. Some of these were
intended for the Baltic, Mediterranean and transatlantic trades. The 93-ton brig
Lowestoft, built in 1799 and said when put up for sale in 1802 to carry 650 or 660
quarters of corn at a draught of 9ft, almost certainly came from his yard.

Johnson's son, also named Thomas, joined him in the business in 1817 but
moved to Southwold after it ran into financial trouble in 1819, resulting in
bankruptcy for his father in 1820. It could be that they overreached themselves,
since it is said that they launched ten vessels in three years.

With the opening of Lowestoft harbour the Norwich and Lowestoft
Navigation Company laid out a shipyard which was leased to John Korff,

Planking up the dandy
Challenger at John
Chambers' yard at Oulton
Broad in 1920, a drawing by
Ted Frost. The *Challenger*
was one of the smacks built
shortly after the First World
War to replace boats lost
during the war years.

The same, or a similar, barge planked up and almost ready for launching.

who in 1831-32 built the 134-ton schooner *Lightning* for the Mediterranean fruit trade. Launched on 19th March 1832 in front of 'an immense number of persons of all classes congregated together to witness this grand and imposing sight', the *Lightning* was still in the Liverpool register in 1857. Korff also launched the schooner *City of Norwich* for the London, Norwich, Lowestoft and Beccles Shipping Company a few weeks later, but by the end of the year his name appeared in the list of bankruptcies and the 'spacious enclosed Ship-Yard and Staithe' that he had occupied was advertised for sale by auction at the Queen's Head Inn, that same hostelry at which the directors of the navigation had dined after opening the harbour some eighteen months earlier.

While boatbuilders like Batchelor Barcham, who built the world's first sailing lifeboat, the *Frances Ann*, in 1807, continued to work on the beach those craftsmen who produced larger vessels found it more convenient to carry on their operations on the shores of the harbour. Barcham is known to have continued building until 1843; among at least forty craft known to have come from his yard were the luggers *Britannia* of 1819 and *George Dillwyn* of 1828, both lost in the gale of 28th May 1860.[11]

Another who built small craft on the beach was William Thomas Ellis, who turned out the pilot cutter *Jenny Lind* and a number of lifeboats including the *Stock Exchange*, the Lowestoft No. 2 boat from 1890 to 1892 when she was transferred to Gorleston as the third *Mark Lane*, serving there until 1921

A dry dock in which vessels could be refitted and repaired was constructed on the north side of the inner harbour by the North of Europe Steam Navigation Company in 1853, and just to the west of that was a yard occupied for some years around the 1850s by what was referred to simply as the Shipbuilding Company, managed by Robert Westaway. From this yard was launched the 89-ton ketch *Kate & Emily* in 1851, followed the next year by the schooner *Emma & Mary*, both owned by Lucas Brothers, a firm of building contractors of international renown who had a large joinery works on the south side of the harbour as well as a London depot in Belvedere Road, Lambeth.

At the end of the North Quay D. & J. Fuller had a yard from 1874 to 1878, after which it was occupied by Page & Chambers, a firm that in due course became John Chambers Ltd, acquiring a reputation that long outlasted the company itself. In 1897 Chambers & Colby, as the firm was known at that time, built the *Consolation*, the first steam drifter to be launched in Lowestoft, and in the First World War Chambers became the parent firm for the Admiralty's standard wooden steam drifters, building sixteen of them as well as three steel standard drifters.

Overleaf: Hoisting the boiler into a newly launched steam drifter using the sheerlegs on the north side of the inner harbour, as depicted by Ted Frost. The triple expansion engine waits on the quayside to be lifted aboard when the boiler is in place.

A Lowestoft fisherman's certificate of discharge recording his service in the steam drifter *Lilith* during the Home Fishing of 1919.

S. 1.
FISHING.

ISSUED BY THE
BOARD OF TRADE.

Seaman.

Countersigned

CERTIFICATE OF DISCHARGE.
FOR THE FISHING TRADE.

NAME OF VESSEL.	PORT OF REGISTRY.	Letters & Number.
Lilith	*Lowestoft*	*LT 247*

OFFICIAL NUMBER.	NATURE OF FISHING EXPEDITION.
84267	*Drift Fishing*

NAME OF SEAMAN.	AGE.	CAPACITY.
Robert Pye	*18*	*Net Ropeman*

DATE OF JOINING.	DATE OF DISCHARGE.	PLACE OF DISCHARGE.
19th Oct. 1918	*8th Jany. 1919*	*Lowestoft*

CHARACTER FOR CONDUCT.

CHARACTER FOR ABILITY.

I Certify that the above particulars are correct, and that the above-named Seaman was discharged accordingly.

Dated this *10th* day of *Feby.* 19*23*

Signed *Mitchell Bros.* ~~Skipper~~ *Agent.*

NOTE.—One of these Certificates must be filled up and delivered to every Seaman when he is discharged from a trawler of 25 tons registered tonnage and upwards.

N.B.—Should this Certificate come into the possession of any person to whom it does not belong, it should be handed to the Superintendent of the nearest Mercantile Marine Office, or be transmitted to the Registrar-General of Seamen, Tower Hill, London, E.

(C8A8) (72680) Wt. 961/33 12500 4-16 W B & L

In its heyday Chambers had three yards, that at the end of the North Quay being their No. 1 yard; No. 2 at Horn Hill, on the south side of the harbour, was used for the repair and storage of small craft and No. 3 yard on the north side at Oulton Broad built steam coasters, tugs and barges in both wood and steel as well as a considerable number of fishing craft. They owned a 300-acre estate near Worlingham from which they obtained their timber.[12]

Chambers had a reputation second to none; there was a saying on the yard, 'Don't say you work for John Chambers, say you work *with* John Chambers'.[13] In 1930 the business was acquired and closed down by National Shipbuilders Securities Ltd, whose remit was to remove over-capacity from the British shipbuilding industry; the last vessel launched by Chambers, the steam drifter *Kindred Star*, was yard no. 584.

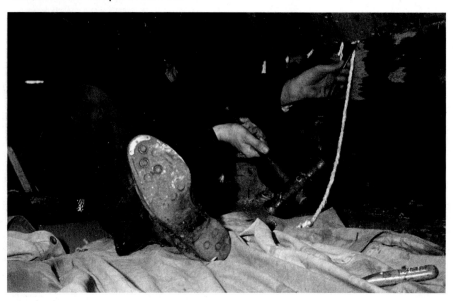

Caulking the keel of s Broads cruiser.

The new yard laid out by Brooke Marine on the south side of Lake Lothing in the 1950s pioneered new methods of ship construction, large sections of the vessel being prefabricated in the shops and then moved outside for erection on the building berth. The vessel seen here is a freezer trawler for Aberdeen owners.

The Oulton Broad yard had been laid out in 1900 by Henry Reynolds, who built a number of wooden sailing smacks and steam drifters after moving there from a yard on the south side of Lake Lothing where he had built the beach yawl *Happy New Year* – fourth yawl to bear that name – in 1894 and four RNLI lifeboats, including the Norfolk and Suffolk type boat *Rescue* for the Southwold No. 2 station in 1897.

Another yard on the south side of Lake Lothing was set up by John Colby in 1913. Colby Brothers, as the firm was known, turned to steel construction in 1917, launching its first steel drifter, the *Flash*, the following February. Post-war conditions forced Colby's to close their yard, the firm moving to the Beach as blacksmiths.

Longest lived of all the Lowestoft yards was that on the east of Kirkley Ham established by Sam Richards, who moved from Penzance to Lowestoft in 1876, completing his first vessel, the 52ft dandy *Nil Desperandum*, LT111, three years later. A watercolour painting of the *Nil Desperandum* under

The launching of the offshore safety and standby vessel *Seagair* from the Lowestoft yard of Richards Shipbuilders in December 1981. Built for BP Petroleum Development Ltd, she was intended for firefighting, pollution control and general safety at offshore installations but was later converted to a diving support vessel under the name *Toisa Sentinel*: she was later renamed DSV *Whale*.

The launching of the bulk carrier *Jack Wharton* from the Lowestoft shipyard of Richards Shipbuilders in 1977. Built for J. Wharton (Shipping) Ltd of Scunthorpe, she had a length of 297ft and was at the time the largest vessel built by Richards. The local tug *Ala* and the *Hector Read* from Yarmouth are seen taking charge of the ship as soon as she is afloat.

construction shows that the yard then had few if any facilities, there being not even a shed in which the workers might store their tools. Carvel built with brightly varnished topsides, the *Nil Desperandum* was a smart little craft, attracting further orders for the builder, who seems to have established himself well enough in his early years in the port. Yard no. 20 was the 35ft sailing yacht *Ormonde*, which Sam Richards built in 1885 for his own use.

She was not the only pleasure craft built on the yard. In 1887 the Lowestoft engineer J.W. Brooke placed an order with Richards for a 42ft river launch, the *Nellie*, which was fitted with a little triple expansion steam engine made by Brooke himself. In later years Brooke's firm became boatbuilders as well as engineers, beginning by fitting their petrol engines into some very early racing speedboats; ultimately Brooke Marine turned to shipbuilding and with Richards Shipbuilders Ltd were the last to build ships in Lowestoft.

Most of the craft that began their lives in the Horn Hill yard in the first decade of its existence were fishing vessels, either trawling smacks or sailing drifters. The introduction of steam drifters presented Sam Richards with a challenge: while the first steam drifter built in a Lowestoft yard had an engine made by Elliott & Garrood of Beccles, Richards made the bold decision to construct his own steam engines, and at the turn of the century a foundry was set up in which all the parts for the firm's engines could be manufactured. The first two steam drifters to be launched by Richards, the *Adventure*, LT80, and the *Test*, LT270, were laid down side by side, both being completed in 1899. They were quickly followed by many others, including several ordered by the Steam Herring Fleet Ltd of Aberdeen.

When war came in 1914 Lowestoft became the main minesweeping depot on the east coast, and large steam trawlers from the Humber ports and Aberdeen arrived in the port to be fitted out as minesweepers; Richards in common with other yards found themselves fully occupied with Admiralty work. In 1918-19 the Horn Hill yard launched eight wooden standard drifters, *Midnight Sun*, *Nadir*, *Nightfall*, *Nimbus*, *Hailstorm*, *Heatwave*, *Hurricane* and *Mistral*, for the Navy to help replace the many boats that were lost to enemy action.

German warships and U-boats instituted an onslaught on British fishing vessels that resulted in serious losses for Lowestoft boatowners, and in the immediate post-war years the yard constructed seven sailing smacks as replacements for some of those destroyed. The days of sail were coming to an end, however, and just at the time that the great depression was causing difficulties for firms like Richards one Lowestoft smackowner, W.H. Podd, gave an order for the fitting of Deutz diesel engines to four of his smacks, *Flag Jack*, LT1224, *Lucky Hit*, LT961, *Pathway*, LT397, and *Pilot Jack*, LT1212; other such conversions followed.

Just as Sam Richards had espoused the steam engine at the turn of the century, in the late 1920s his sons Sidney, Cyril and Lewis saw that the future lay with the diesel engine and showed the way with the building of the first motor drifter, the *Veracity*, giving her a 200bhp Deutz engine. The boat had a successful Home Fishing that year under the ownership of her builders, and proved extremely economical, but none of the local boatowners were interested. Eventually after a period laid up in the harbour the *Veracity* was sold to an adventurer who was planning an expedition to Cocos Island, in the Pacific, in search of a treasure said to have been hidden by pirates. The *Veracity* reached Cocos Island safely, but the treasure proved extraordinarily elusive, and the little drifter never returned home.

In 1931 W.H. Podd, impressed with the trawling smacks that had been motorised earlier, ordered the diesel-engined trawler *J.A.P.*, LT245, named after Mrs J.A. Podd. The following year W.F. Cockrell, head of the East Anglian Ice and Cold Storage Co., came to the aid of the struggling yard, resulting in the setting up of a new company, Richards Ironworks Ltd, with himself as chairman. Sidney Richards set to work to design a 75ft diesel-engined trawler, and Cockrell was so taken with this entirely new concept that he ordered twelve boats; the first of them, the *Ala*, LT347, was launched in 1933. The *Willa*, LT43, and *Eta*, LT , followed in 1935, the *Gula*, LT179, *Rotha*, LT208, and *Rewga*, LT234, in 1936 and 1937, and the *Celita*, LT236, in 1939. Then events brought the building of such craft to an end.

When war broke out in September 1939 Richards Ironworks was at the centre of efforts to deal with the magnetic mine, which the Germans employed to block the east coast shipping channels and waterways, laying them both from surface craft and by parachute from the air. To begin with the yard fitted out six wooden drifters, the *Formidable*, LT100, *Fisher Boy*, LT334, *Jacketa*, LT296, *Lord Cavan*, LT680, *Ray of Hope*, LT230, and *Silver Dawn*, LT194, to be employed by HMS *Vernon*, the Royal Navy mining and torpedo school, in a desperate attempt to recover one of the new mines. Working day and night, a hastily assembled team of shipwrights completed the task in just eight days and the six drifters, known throughout the Navy as 'Vernon's private navy', began their dangerous task; *Ray of Hope* was blown up by a mine that exploded as it was being hauled up.

One of the first countermeasures to the magnetic mine was a wooden skid carrying a large magnetic coil that could be towed behind a protected minesweeper. Richards made six of these towing skids in 1940 while plans were drawn up for a class of wooden motor minesweepers that it was hoped would themselves be immune to the mine's magnetic detonating device. Design staff at the Lowestoft yard were brought into the preparations, and the first vessel, *MMS 1*, was built on the yard in 1940; subsequently Richards Ironworks became 'parent yard' for the 105ft motor minesweeper, advising other yards throughout the country on the construction of these vessels. *MMS 1* was launched in August 1940, and by the end of 1941 Richards had

Early motor-boats racing off Lowestoft about 1910. Some of these craft were built on the Brooke yard on the north side of Lake Lothing.

completed nine boats; altogether seventeen 'Mickey Mouse' minesweepers, as they were dubbed by the Navy, were built by Richards as well as another three by East Anglian Constructors Ltd, a wartime subsidiary of Richards Ironworks, using what had earlier been Colby Brothers' yard. The two yards together also built twelve of the later 126ft motor minesweepers.

Richards' achievements in converting six drifters in eight days in 1939 and in later developing and building the first motor minesweepers so expeditiously brought a letter of appreciation from the then Controller of the Navy, Vice-Admiral William Wake-Walker, an officer who is remembered for his work in organising the fleet of small craft during the Dunkirk evacuation.

The two yards also turned out a number of 60ft motor fishing vessels, used by the Navy for a multitude of tasks, and then turned to the production of a 90ft version designed by George Herring, who during the course of a lifelong career with the company rose from apprentice to managing director. Altogether forty-two MFVs were completed by the two yards, another thirty-six being turned out by other yards in Oulton Broad and Lowestoft.

In the postwar years some much larger vessels were launched from the yard, ranging from tugs to molasses tankers and from coastal minesweepers for the Royal Navy to large motor trawlers for the Boston Deep Sea Fishing Co. and other local owners; between 1954 and 1962 Richards launched seventeen vessels for the Boston company.

The firm changed its name to Richards Shipbuilders Ltd when taken over by United Molasses in 1957. Twelve years later the Fellows yard at Yarmouth was acquired and shipbuilding continued at both yards, an order for twelve River class minesweepers being split equally between the two yards. While earlier coastal minesweepers, of which eight were built by Richards between 1954 and 1960, were of composite construction, with aluminium frames and double mahogany planking to give the lowest possible magnetic attraction, providing the greatest possible safety factor when sweeping, the River class had steel hulls.

The company remained buoyant, turning out twenty-six vessels, eight of them at the Yarmouth yard, between 1970 and 1975, but the British shipbuilding industry went into terminal decline in the 1980s and the company closed in 1994, six years after the demise of the town's other major shipyard, Brooke Marine. As the yard was cleared strict orders were given that all the company's half-models, used in the design of ships over more than a hundred years, were to be burnt.

Brooke Marine, a very significant company that had had links with Richards as long ago as 1888, suffered a somewhat lingering death. Nationalised in July 1977 and absorbed into British Shipbuilders, the Brooke yard was closed ten years later, its work being carried on until 1992 by a firm known as Brooke Yachts.

Originally known as J.W. Brooke, the firm was conceived in 1874 when John Walter Brooke opened a foundry in Lowestoft which he named Adrian Works, after the town of Adrian in Michigan where he had earlier spent some time. In its early years the foundry made steam engines and steam capstans for locally built fishing craft, but at the turn of the century switched to the production of internal combustion engines which were installed in boats built by Henry Reynolds and other Lowestoft boatbuilders.

Watched by two of the shipwrights who have built her, the General Steam Navigation Company cargo vessel *Plover* enters the waters of Kirkley Ham from the Lowestoft yard of Richards Shipbuilders Ltd in 1965. She was handed over to her owners exactly a year after the signing of the contract for her building.

The Oulton Broad yard of J.E. Fletcher, now the International Boatbuilding Training Centre, was one of the few boatyards chosen by the Royal National Lifeboat Institution for repairing and refitting its wooden lifeboats. Here the Cromer lifeboat *Ruby and Arthur Reed* is returned to the water following a refit during which her upperworks, formerly coloured grey, have been repainted in dayglow orange to render the boat more easily visible from the air.

This view of Lake Lothing about 1970 shows two eras of shipbuilding at Lowestoft. In the foreground is the derelict fitting-out quay of John Chambers No. 3 yard and in the background is the Brooke Marine shipyard, at the time of its laying out in about 1950 probably the most up-to-date shipyard in Britain.

In 1910, however, John Brooke acquired land on the north shore of Lake Lothing and in the following year began to build his own hulls there. Soon he was busy with Admiralty work, and during the war started a yard on the south side of the harbour to build steel steam drifters; this was given up when peace came, existing contracts for coasters and oil barges being taken over by the neighbouring Colby Brothers yard while Brookes concentrated on the production of motor yachts and powerboats.

Among the many boats turned out by Brookes was the *Bulldog*, which in 1925 set up a world speed record for 1½-litre boats of 38.175 knots; she was fitted with the first supercharged marine engine built in Britain.[14]

Between the wars the firm continued to build mainly motor yachts, though in 1929 and 1930 they turned out thirty-three high-speed launches for the Brazilian Customs service. With the outbreak of the Second World War the firm turned to the building of high-speed fighting craft for the Navy and seaplane tenders and refuellers for the Royal Air Force, and in 1940 was taken over by industrialist Harry Dowsett and renamed Brooke Marine. During the war years the yard turned out eleven motor torpedo boats and motor gunboats and sixteen Fairmile 112ft motor launches and was engaged also in repairing battle damage and in maintaining such craft.

In the 1950s a new shipyard, the biggest and most modern south of the Humber, was laid out on the south side of Lake Lothing to cope with a Russian contract for the building of twenty large trawlers, an order that occupied the yard for several years. Besides the building berths there were spacious erecting shops in which prefabricated sections were prepared; completed sections were moved outside to the slipways on multi-wheeled trolleys for assembly. Such a system of prefabrication had never before been employed in a British shipyard.

The new yard received its steel stock by way of the goods-only railway line that ran to Kirkley along the southern side of the harbour, until that line was closed down. The railways had killed off the coasting trade, but they in turn were emasculated by political doctrine that decreed that railways should carry only passengers between one conurbation and another and that all alternative routes, feeder branches and goods lines should be closed and torn up without delay.

The old yard on the north side of the harbour closed in 1955 as activity in the new yard was stepped up, and the bridge channel between the inner and outer harbours had to be widened to allow the larger ships being built to pass out to sea. In 1958 and 1959 Brooke Marine built two 2,740-gross-ton cargo ships, the mv *Bolton Abbey* and mv *Melrose Abbey*, for Associated Humber Lines and the 3,099-gross-ton refrigerated ship *Constable* for Lamport & Holt; in 1962 the *Constable* was transferred to the Blue Star Line and renamed *Santos Star*.

Very different in almost every way were the fast attack and patrol craft built for navies across the world. The four steel-hulled 24-knot patrol craft built by Brooke Marine for Pakistan in 1965 had an unfortunate history, for three of them were sunk in the war which resulted in Bangladesh gaining independence; one of the three was subsequently raised and put into service by the breakaway state, while the survivor remained in Pakistani service. Four similar craft were built for Nigeria in 1974 and 1977; the first pair returned to Lowestoft in 1981-2 to be re-engined and modified.

The naval forces of the Sultanate of Oman in the Persian Gulf very largely originated in Lowestoft, the Sultan's yacht *Al Said* being built in 1971 by

The first of the 50ft Thames class lifeboats built by Brooke Marine for the RNLI undergoing a self-righting test in 1973. Named *Rotary Service*, she was stationed first at Falmouth and then at Dover.

Brookes. The Lowestoft yard also supplied seven fast attack craft and a 2,000-ton landing ship capable of carrying tanks, guns and troops and small landing craft. One of the fast attack craft, *Al Bushra*, was lost overboard in hurricane force winds in the Bay of Biscay from the ship in which it was being returned home in December 1978 after a refit. The Sultan's yacht was converted into a training/patrol ship and renamed *Al Mabrukah* in 1983.

When in 1977 Australia decided to acquire a number of 137ft patrol craft the design was entrusted to Brooke Marine, who also built the lead craft, *Fremantle*, which was commissioned in 1980. The other fourteen were built in Queensland to the Brooke design.

Nearer home, the Lowestoft yard built four coastal/inshore survey vessels for the Royal Navy and two logistic landing craft for the Royal Corps of Transport. The survey vessels, *Bulldog*, *Beagle*, *Fox* and *Fawn*, were all commissioned in 1968 and the landing craft, *Ardennes* and *Arakan*, entered service in 1977 and 1978.

Possibly the most prestigious order of all was that received from the United States Navy for three big salvage and rescue ships capable not only of ocean towage and firefighting but of supporting diving operations to a depth of 850ft. Seldom does the US Navy look across the Atlantic for the building of its ships. Fitted with four Paxman diesels made in Colchester, driving two shafts, these vessels were fitted with a bow thruster to facilitate precise manoeuvring.[15] The first of these ships, the USS *Edenton*, entered service in 1971, with the USS *Beaufort* and the USS *Brunswick* being commissioned the following year. When paid off in 1996 the *Beaufort* and *Brunswick* were transferred to the South Korean navy; the *Edenton* was commissioned as the US Coastguard cutter *Alex Hayley* in 1999.

With the closing of Richards Shipbuilders and Brooke Marine the thousand-year story of shipbuilding in Suffolk came to an end. Vessels still come to Lowestoft to be dry-docked and refitted, and the Excelsior Yard provides facilities mainly for historic craft like the *Excelsior* herself, but it seems extremely unlikely that large ships will ever again be built in the county.

The port of Felixstowe　　21

The port of Felixstowe, now Britain's busiest container port, used by the world's largest merchant ships, was the creation of a somewhat eccentric Victorian landowner. George Tomline, who bought the Orwell Park estate[1] at Nacton in 1847 and in the following years acquired neighbouring farms and land until he had the second largest estate in Suffolk, saw the establishment of the dock as a way of improving the prospects of people living in the area; rather than offering charity, he preferred to provide employment and opportunity.

Often known as Colonel Tomline, he was not in fact a military man; his title derived from his being honorary colonel of a militia regiment in his native Lincolnshire.[2] In 1876 he opened a railway from Westerfield on the East Suffolk line to Felixstowe, terminating on a short pier built out into Harwich harbour, his intention being that a line of steamers should run from there to northern Europe. It seems likely that an extension of the line across Suffolk to link with the Midland Railway at Chesterford, near Cambridge, was envisaged; this could have given Felixstowe first-class connections with the industrial Midlands and have provided the Midland Railway with a much-desired access to the North Sea trade routes, but it failed to gain parliamentary approval in 1886.

That year of 1886 saw the opening after a somewhat protracted period of construction of a small dock excavated from the marshes on the north side of the harbour; like the railway, this was paid for by George Tomline. The first ship to use the new facility on 7th April 1886 was the steam collier *Crathie*, a little ship of ill repute which in 1895 was involved in a disastrous collision with the German liner *Elbe*, as described in chapter 15.

The proposed passenger service to northern Europe had failed to materialise, and the trade of the dock did not develop to the extent that had been hoped. On the other side of the harbour a steam packet service to the Continent had been started in 1851, initially employing the 300-ton paddle steamer *Arab* belonging to the North of Europe Steam Navigation Company at Lowestoft.[3] That experiment failed, but another attempt to run a service to Antwerp in conjunction with trains to and from London was made when the railway branch line to Harwich opened in 1854, using two new iron ships, the *Aquila* and the *Cygnus*, just delivered to the North of Europe company by the Renfrew yard of James Henderson & Sons and chartered to the Eastern Counties Railway.[4] This service, however, was discontinued at the end of the 1855 season, having made a considerable loss.

Nevertheless, on the formation of the Great Eastern Railway in 1863

Opposite: Looking towards the sea along the line of quays at the Port of Felixstowe, which can accommodate the world's largest container ships. The first container terminal, Landguard Terminal, completed in 1967, can be seen at the top of the picture.

Walton Creek meandering across the marshes where work on Felixstowe Dock was just beginning in 1881. The lower part of the creek was navigable, and a story that a Dutch smuggler was chased into it and burnt by its crew to avoid capture was confirmed in the 1960s when the wreck was discovered during extensions to the dock complex.

application was made to Parliament by the new company, an amalgamation of the Eastern Counties Railway and other lines in the East of England, for a Bill authorising the operation of steamships from Harwich to Antwerp, Rotterdam and Flushing. In spite of strenuous opposition the Bill passed both Houses of Parliament and received Royal Assent on 28th July 1863, significantly the same day that the Harwich Harbour Conservancy Board came into being.[5]

The building of Felixstowe Dock: casting of the concrete caissons, or 'monoliths' as they were termed at the time, goes ahead on the site of the south quay

Excavation taking place within one of the 'monoliths' to cause it to sink into the ground in the same way that a well was sunk. This was a very recently introduced technique in civil engineering when used at Felixstowe.

The Newcastle steamer *Millicent* aground at Felixstowe in November 1889. Three spritsail barges are alongside taking off some of her cargo of coal preparatory to an attempt to refloat her.

The continental service opened in the autumn of 1863 employing chartered cargo vessels that were fitted for the carriage of cattle, but with little or no accommodation for passengers. Even when two passenger paddle steamers, the *Avalon* and the *Zealous*, were built for the railway company by J. & W. Dudgeon at Cubitt Town on the Thames in 1864 the services offered to the 150 passengers left much to be desired, and travellers expressed their dissatisfaction. One reason for their disgruntlement was the distance they had to walk between the railway station at Harwich and the pier where they boarded the steamers.

As the number of travellers increased and the continental services were expanded a decision was taken to construct a new steamer terminal in the Stour some distance above Harwich and to divert the railway line to a new

The original railway station at Harwich, from which passengers had to walk to the pier from which the continental steamers sailed.

Work at the Port of Felixstowe goes on day and night in order to achieve a speedy turnaround for the great container ships, sophisticated computer systems being employed to organise the receipt and dispatch of hundreds of containers, laden and empty.

Loading wind generator components at Felixstowe in 2008.

station immediately adjacent to the quay. Work began on Ray Island, a marshy piece of land on the south bank of the river, in 1879 and was not completed until 1883, when the new quay was opened by the Great Eastern chairman, Mr Charles Parkes, after whom it was named Parkeston Quay. It had cost half a million pounds.[6]

At the same time that the upriver quay was being brought into being far-reaching developments were taking place on the other side of the North Sea that would eventually have a most beneficial effect on the GER services from Parkeston Quay. One was the opening of a new navigation channel to provide a better approach to the port of Rotterdam and another was the building of a railway to link that city with a new terminal at Hoek van Holland,[7] at the entrance of the Nieue Waterweg.

With its own extensive facilities, including a luxurious hotel, at Parkeston Quay the Great Eastern, which had taken over Tomline's Felixstowe railway,

was distinctly disinclined to support a rival port on the other side of the harbour. Time after time Edward Woodmancy, the Felixstowe Dock & Railway Company's manager, complained at the punitive charges imposed by the Great Eastern on coal being distributed locally by rail after having been unloaded in the dock or at the 'inability' of the railway's district goods manager at Ipswich to supply the number of trucks required to handle goods landed at the dock. 'For the provision of trucks we are entirely at the mercy of the GER, who take care that we play second fiddle when any of their other places are short,' he told the directors of the dock company in 1913.[8]

Coal and water

Harwich harbour remained a minor base for the Royal Navy, and Felixstowe benefited from this when in 1898 the early torpedo boat destroyers

While Felixstowe is regularly visited by the world's largest container vessels it also handles smaller short-sea vessels like this one operated by Seago Line, a Maersk subsidiary, seen passing the Harwich Haven Authority radar tower on Landguard Point.

The Maersk Line container ship MSC *Renee* leaving her berth at Felixstowe's Trinity Terminal. She was built in South Korea in 2012.

using the harbour began to visit the dock for bunker coal. The following year, coincidentally the year the training ship HMS *Ganges* took up moorings in the harbour, the Admiralty accepted the dock company's tender for the supply of Welsh coal; at the same time it was agreed that the dock company should supply water to warships in the harbour, which led to the company having a water tender, the *Bheestie*, built at South Shields in 1910.[9]

When the Royal Navy began experimenting with oil fuel – the destroyer HMS *Spiteful* was the first warship to be fitted to burn oil in 1904 – the dock company entered into an agreement with the Admiralty to supply bunker fuel and two 2,500-ton tanks were erected close to the dock. When war broke out with Germany in 1914 and Harwich Force under Commodore Reginald Tyrwhitt fought so aggressively and so successfully in the North Sea, sinking a German minelayer off the Suffolk coast only hours after the declaration of war, it was to Felixstowe that the ships came both for bunkering and for water.[10] Parkeston Quay became a base for submarines, which regularly went into Ipswich Dock for refitting.

Felixstowe was also the site of a Royal Naval Air Station, established in 1913, which not only operated patrols over the North Sea but played a significant part in the development of maritime flying. Under the guidance of the extremely talented John Porte a series of Felixstowe flying boats was developed, culminating in the Felixstowe Fury, a large triplane flying boat powered by five Rolls Royce Eagle VII engines. Between the wars the station was the home of the RAF Marine Aircraft Experimental Establishment, which moved to Helensburgh on the Clyde when war broke out afresh in 1939.

During the Second World War Felixstowe Dock was home to HMS

Parkeston Quay seen on a chart published about 1890. It would appear that in the beginning boat trains had to travel to Harwich and then reverse to the new upriver quay; later the Manningtree-Harwich line was diverted to run direct to the quay station.

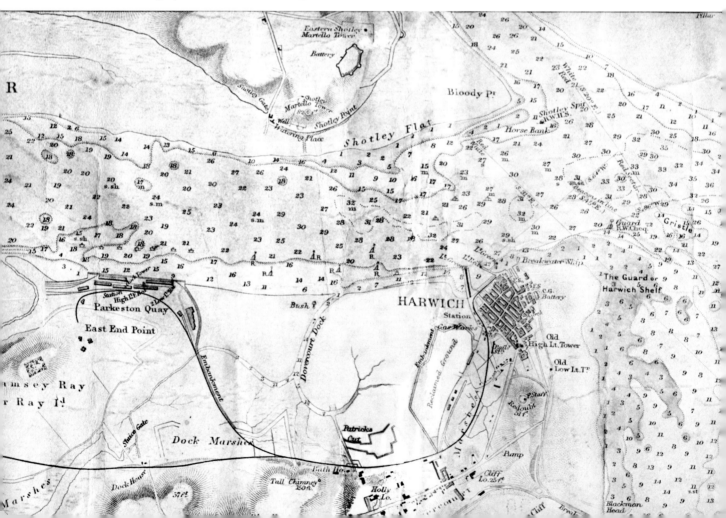

Beehive, a very active light coastal forces base from which motor torpedo boats and motor gunboats carried out offensive operations against enemy shipping. One of the officers sailing from *Beehive* was Lieutenant-Commander Ian Trelawney, who in later years was to play a very significant part in the spectacular growth of the port of Felixstowe.

Parkeston Quay again became a naval base under the name HMS *Badger* and Cliff Quay at Ipswich, named HMS *Bunting*, became a base for patrol trawlers while HMS *Ganges* at Shotley, by then purely a shore establishment, trained hostilities-only entrants to

A guidebook issued by the Great Eastern Railway for German tourists travelling by way of the Hook of Holland to Parkeston Quay route. On the cover is an illustration of London's Liverpool Street Station.

the Navy by the hundred. Woolverstone Hall on the Orwell was taken over as HMS *Woolverstone*, a landing craft base that played a considerable part in the preparations for the D-Day invasion of Europe in June 1944.

In the post-war years almost the only trade at Felixstowe Dock, apart from sailing barges delivering wheat to the big dockside flour mill, was that of two salvage companies salving the cargoes from the numerous wartime wrecks that cluttered the shipping channels all along the East Anglian coast. Those channels had in the early 1940s earned an unenviable reputation as 'E-boat Alley' owing to the activities of the German schnellboote, the wartime rivals of the light coastal forces of HMS *Beehive*; those fast, well-armed craft called by the German S-boote were known to the British as E-boats, standing for enemy boats.

It seemed likely that Felixstowe Dock would lapse into obscurity; there was a possibility that with the railway network contracting fast it might lose its vital rail connection. Then in 1951 an agricultural merchant from West Norfolk engaged in the barley export trade, H. Gordon Parker, purchased the port of Felixstowe for a mere £50,000. The bank refused to advance him the money for the purchase, considering that the investment was unwise; Gordon Parker did not forgive them for that.

Primarily the new chairman and owner of the Felixstowe Dock and Railway Company sought an outlet to the Continent for his grain, but his vision was much wider; he realised that the money required for improvements to the little dock could be raised by using the dock sheds for storage. The 1950s was the era of the ill-fated Groundnuts Scheme in East Africa, sponsored by the British government, and the relatively few monkey-nuts that resulted from that scheme were stored at Felixstowe Dock along with a variety of other

Container ships from all parts of the world unloading their cargoes at Felixstowe.

products. The oil tanks that once held bunker fuel for warships were cleaned out by the few dock company employees and refilled with vegetable oils.

The 1953 flood

Then came the terrible tidal surge of 31st January-1st February 1953 when the seas burst over the Felixstowe sea front and the tide, rising four or five feet above the eight-foot railway embankment in the vicinity of the dock, rushed into the lower-lying part of the town, drowning forty people in their homes. A great deal of damage was done to the dock and the storage sheds were flooded as a wall of water surged through, smashing everything that stood in its way.

The dock workers who made their way down to the dock along the railway embankment – the only available access remaining – on the morning after the disaster found a scene of utter desolation. Yet Gordon Parker was not a man to admit defeat. Picking his way along the damaged embankment, he discussed

Its bow door still open, a Townsend Thoresen roll-on roll-off ferry prepares to depart for the Continent in 1975.

The *Prinz Hamlet* leaves
Harwich for the German
port of Hamburg. For a
time there was a passenger
and ro-ro service from
Felixstowe, but it closed as
the Suffolk port expanded
and concentrated more and
more on the container trade.

the situation with company officials and planned an eventual comeback; then
he made his perilous way back along the railway sleepers in the darkness of a
February night, the discussions having continued long after dusk.

As the struggle was waged to restore the wrecked dock facilities and to
bring the little port into profit Parker recruited a remarkable assistant to
help him with the task. Ian Trelawney knew the dock well from his wartime
service with HMS *Beehive*, and his drive and energy contributed very largely
to the phenomenal development of the port in the second half of the twentieth
century. For some time the company found it hard to finance activities at
the dock; Trelawney was later to recall how one week he had to borrow the
money to pay the men, and on other occasions Gordon Parker contributed the
necessary cash from his own pocket.[11]

Unable to afford to purchase hardcore required for making up roads and
providing foundations for new buildings, the dock company contracted to
break up runways and perimeter tracks on disused wartime airfields in East
Anglia. Redundant buildings from those same aerodromes were acquired for

A brightly-lit Stena Line
ferry enters Harwich,
passing Landguard Fort
as it follows the deepwater
channel that at this point
runs close to the
Suffolk shore.

The big steam mill at Felixstowe Dock built by the Colchester milling firm of E. Marriage & Son in 1907 which received many cargoes of imported grain by sailing barge. In the first full year of operation Marriage's imported 56,629 quarters of wheat and exported 4,207 tons of flour and offal by sea.

re-erection as storage sheds and similar facilities; other buildings came from a former Ministry of Aircraft Production factory in North London.

As improvements were made to the facilities at Felixstowe Ian Trelawney cast around energetically for new business. While dockers in some of the major British ports resisted the introduction of new methods and stuck determinedly to outmoded practices, the expanding workforce at Felixstowe was prepared to accept mechanisation and to adopt new working practices which have since become universally employed. Felixstowe was the first port in England to use pallets and fork lift trucks, the first fork lift truck being introduced in 1956. Three or four men with a fork lift truck were able to handle the same amount of cargo that in London required a whole gang of stevedores. It was typical of the Felixstowe approach that the pallets were made in the port.

In 1975, when the Felixstowe Dock and Railway Company celebrated its centenary, the British Transport Docks Board made a £5,250,000 offer for the company which Gordon Parker had acquired for £50,000. Nationalisation seemed inevitable, but then in February 1976 European Ferries Group, which had been operating out of Felixstowe for some years in the guise of the Transport Ferry Service and Townsend Thoresen, made a counter-bid for the company. The defeat in the House of Lords in October 1976 of the Bill promoted by the Docks Board opened the way for European Ferries to acquire the company; an immediate investment of £670,000 for new equipment followed as Felixstowe was added to the group's other port interests at Harwich, Larne in Northern Ireland and Cairnryan in Scotland.

The Transport Ferry Service was a pioneer of roll-on, roll-off shipping, Lieutenant-Colonel Frank Bustard having inaugurated such a service when at the end of the Second World War he purchased some tank landing ships and put them into commercial operation carrying lorries between British ports and the Continent. The roll-on, roll-off technique had been employed earlier in the train ferries which began running from Harwich to Zeebrugge in 1924.

The Swedish passenger ferry *Tor Britannia* wears the Red Ensign as a courtesy flag while in Harwich.

The three original ferries had been built in 1917, two of them on the Tyne and the other at Govan on the Clyde, to operate between the military port of Richborough in Kent and Dunkirk. The service was resumed after the Second World War, but it lost money and closed in 1982.

Felixstowe was to the forefront in building facilities for that form of traffic, bringing the first ro-ro berth into use in 1965, with two bridges linking a large floating pontoon to the shore. Further ro-ro berths came into use in subsequent years, employing a hydraulically operated link span between ship and shore instead of having a floating pontoon.

A Tor Line brochure from 1975 advertising a short-lived service from Felixstowe.

Container revolution

Felixstowe was equally quick to espouse the container revolution. Small containers had been employed by the railway companies in the 1930s to introduce door-to-door transport of goods, but those were small things compared to the 20ft. containers introduced to world trade in the 1960s. A 32-ton Scotch derrick crane was erected beside the dock basin in 1966 to handle containers and unit loads to and from the United States by way of continental ports, but that was only the beginning. Work on the construction of the first container terminal, Landguard Terminal, began in November 1966, and when it was completed in June 1967 it was the first purpose-built container terminal to become operational in Britain. It had a single Paceco Vickers Portainer crane.

By 1980 Felixstowe was the largest container port in the country; in that year it handled 252,802 containers. The following year two new terminals, the Dooley and Walton terminals, came into operation, the Walton terminal being separately managed by the C.H. Tung Group. The Dooley Terminal took its name from the Napoleonic-era Dooley Fort, the remains of which disappeared under the new quay.[12]

TOR LINE

Fares and schedules

Felixstowe-Gothenburg
Immingham-Gothenburg
Immingham-Amsterdam

TOR LINE

16th March 1975 to
25th October 1975

TOR LINE

Developments came thick and fast as the once-moribund port grew in size and importance, and with them George Tomline's little old dock was filled in and disappeared beneath the concrete. Work began on a second railfreight terminal served by a new branch off the Ipswich-Felixstowe line in 1982, and two years later Felixstowe became the first UK seaport to introduce computerised Customs clearance. The initial phase of another new terminal, Trinity Terminal, came into operation in 1986, and subsequent phases opened in 1990, 1996 and 2004, expanding the quays as far as Fagbury Point in the lower part of the River Orwell.

In the early days of the container revolution Felixstowe had received its containers by way of Rotterdam in relatively small ships that loaded from the much larger ocean-going vessels there. When Felixstowe began receiving cargoes direct from much more distant places it became necessary to improve the approaches to the Suffolk port, and in 1985 the Harwich Haven Authority – the old Harwich Harbour Conservancy Board under a new title – dredged the four-mile navigation channel to a minimum 11 metres. Eight years later the channel was deepened to 12.5 metres over a length of 12 miles at a cost of £19 million, and then in 1998 another £27 million was spent increasing the depth to 14.5 metres, making it possible for the largest container ships to access the port.[13] Indeed, it is claimed that Felixstowe provides some of the deepest water close to the open sea of any European port.

To ensure that a least depth of 14.5m is maintained in the approach channel dredgers remove 3.5 million cubic metres of silt every year in a regular programme of maintenance dredging. The material is taken some twenty miles to the Inner Gabbard disposal site, where the hopper doors of

Container storage areas take up a good deal of land behind the quays, as seen in this aerial view in 2017. Commercial and industrial development attracted by the port occupies sites further inland.

The trailer suction hopper dredger *Willem van Oranje* engaged in maintenance dredging at Felixstowe in July 2015. The Harwich Haven Authority has a contract with two of the world's leading dredging contractors to carry out regular dredging to ensure that a sufficient depth is maintained in the approach channel for the largest container ships using the port.

the dredger are opened to release the mud into deep water; it does not fall immediately to the seabed but is dispersed over a wide area.

One of the large trailing suction dredgers employed in this work in recent years is the *Willem van Oranje*, built in Holland and named in 2010 by Queen Beatrix of the Netherlands after William the Silent, leader of the Dutch revolt against the Spanish Habsburgs in the sixteenth century. Owned by Royal Boskalis Westminster, one of the world's largest dredging contractors, the *Willem van Oranje* is an impressive vessel, 136m long with a gross tonnage of 13,917.

Financing such developments as the construction of new container terminals and the reclamation of land to gain space for them did not prove easy. In 1987 the port was acquired by the P & O Group, and in that year it became the first British container port to handle more than a million TEU – twenty-foot equivalent units, based on the early 20ft. containers – in a year. Then in 1991 two companies registered in Hong Kong, Hutchison Whampoa

In the early days of the port of Felixstowe a customs officer was rowed over from Harwich when necessary, but today there is a large staff of customs officials inhabiting the glass-walled modern Customs House close to the port complex.

The original office of
the Felixstowe Dock
and Railway Company
was one of a number of
Scandinavian sectional
buildings imported to the
town in the 1880s.

and Orient Overseas Holdings, jointly paid more than £100 million for the port, and three years later Hutchison Whampoa purchased Orient's 25 per cent holding to assume total control; in 1998 Hutchison also acquired Harwich International on the other side of the harbour.

While Ipswich at the head of the Orwell remains very much a working port, it is somewhat overshadowed by the downriver complex whose quays now stretch for more than two miles along the shore of Harwich harbour and into the river. The depth of 16 metres alongside the quays allows the world's biggest container ships to berth, some of them 400 metres in length and with a beam of 60 metres. Some 3,000 ships come in a year, and with some thirty shipping lines of many different nationalities regularly using the port Felixstowe handles around ninety services to and from four hundred ports around the world.

The two railfreight terminals handle no fewer than sixty-six trains a day. In 2016 a new curve was installed at the Ipswich junction to enable trains from

Belching smoke from one of
her twin funnels, one of the
original train ferries, *Train
Ferry No.2,* approaches
the end of her voyage from
Zeebrugge and will soon be
going astern into her berth
at the Harwich train
ferry terminal.

Felixstowe to travel on to Ely and the Midlands without having to reverse in the goods yard at Ipswich. And on the roads 4,500 trucks are handled each weekday, the average turnaround being only 32 minutes.

The statistics are as impressive as is the view of the dock complex from across the water in Shotley. One above all would delight George Tomline: in place of the handful of men who worked on the old dock, the complex now has some 2,500 employees drawn not just from Felixstowe itself but from a wide area around. His aim to provide employment and prosperity for the people of the Colneis region has been achieved, albeit more than a hundred years after his death.

It is difficult to conceive how the modern Port of Felixstowe seen on the left has grown from a tiny dock dug by hand by the little band of workers seen below.

References

1   Saxon Seamen

1   Charles Green, Sutton Hoo: *The Excavation of a Royal Ship-Burial*, Merlin Press, 1963, chapter 7.
2   *Ipswich Journal*, 24 November 1860; Hugh Moffat, 'Victorian Archaeology', East Coast Mariner, 19 (1971), p. 25.
3   It has been discovered that one of the fastenings kept by Charles Phillips after the 1939 excavation is non-magnetic; no iron survives, the nail and rove having become entirely oxidised.
4   Martin Carver, 'The Anglo-Saxon Cemetery at Sutton Hoo: An Interim Report' in Carver, ed., *The Age of Sutton Hoo*, Boydell Press, 1992, p. 360.
5   *Blazer*, a wooden paddle sloop, built at Chatham Dockyard in 1834, became a surveying vessel in 1843, broken up at Portsmouth, 1853.
6   Martin Carver, p. 346.
7   Robert Markham, *Sutton Hoo Through the Rear View Mirror*, Sutton Hoo Society, 2002, p. 25.
8   Washer-like fittings over which the inner end of the nail was clenched or riveted.

2   Galleys and Warfare

1   SROI, C1/8/1.
2   Ian Friel, *The Good Ship*, British Museum Press, 1995, p. 41.
3   Ibid., p. 41.
4   N.A.M. Rodger, *The Safeguard of the Sea*, HarperCollins, 1997, p. 122.
5   May McKisack, *The Fourteenth Century 1307-1399*, Oxford University Press, 1959, p. 128.
6   N.A.M. Rodger, p. 96.
7   Ibid., p.97.
8   McKisack, p. 129..
9   N.A.M. Rodger, p. 99.

3   Fishermen and traders

1   C.M. Fraser, *The Accounts of the Chamberlains of Newcastle Upon Tyne 1508-1511*, The Society of Antiquaries of Newcastle Upon Tyne, 1987. I am indebted to Peter Northeast for having called my attention to this invaluable work.
2   It is difficult to differentiate between 'empty' and 'in ballast'; possibly the two terms indicate the same thing.
3   Fraser, pp. xiii-xiv.
4   Ibid., pp. xv, 76

Opposite: The Swedish barque *Abraham Rydberg* is towed from Ipswich Dock to Cliff Quay to load ballast for the homeward voyage in 1934; she had brought a cargo of Australian wheat for Cranfields' mills. She made another visit to Ipswich with grain from the Spencer Gulf in 1939, and was the last square-rigged ship to bring a cargo to the Suffolk port. The era of sail had come to an end.

[5] Ibid., pp. xv, 84.

[6] SROI HD2448/1/1/6

[7] SROI HD2448/1/1/6

[8] David Butcher, *Rigged for River and Sea*, Hull, North Atlantic Fisheries History Association, 2008.

[9] SROI HD2448/1/1/

[10] SROI HD2448/1/1/291

[11] David Butcher, *Medieval Lowestoft*, Boydell, 2016, pp. 243, 248.

[12] John Morris, ed., *Domesday Book: Suffolk*, Phillimore, 1986.

[13] R. Malster, *The Norfolk and Suffolk Broads*, Phillimore, 2003, p. 65.

[14] H.C. Darby, *The Domesday History of Eastern England*, Cambridge University Press, 3rd. edn. 1971, p. 142.

[15] Jezz Meredith and Bill Jenman, *Life and Death at Barber's Point*, Aldeburgh and District Local History Society, 2016.

[16] F.M. Davis, *An Account of the Fishing Gear of England and Wales*, Her Majesty's Stationery Office, 4th edn., 1958.

[17] David Butcher, *The Half-hundred of Mutford*, Lowestoft Heritage Workshop Centre, 2013, pp. 95-6.

[18] Nicholas Amor, *Late Medieval Ipswich: Trade and Industry*, Boydell, 2011, pp. 114-138.

[19] David Butcher, *Medieval Lowestoft*, Boydell, 2016, pp. 242-5.

[20] Wolf-Dieter Hoheisel, 'The Hanseatic Cog', in Jenny Bennett, *Sailing into the Past. Learning from Replica Ships*, Seaforth Publishing, 2009, pp. 72-83.

4   The port of Orwell

[1] Keith Wade, 'The urbanisation of East Anglia: The Ipswich perspective', in *Flatlands and Wetlands: Current Themes in East Anglian Archaeology, EAA 50*, Scole Archaeological Committee for East Anglia, 1993.

[2] Anne Savage, *The Anglo-Saxon Chronicles*, Macmillan, 1982, p. 97.

[3] W.G. Arnott, *Orwell Estuary*, Norman Adlard, 1954, pp. 7-8.

[4] John Fairclough, *Boudica to Raedwald: East Anglia's relations with Rome*, Malthouse Press, 2010, pp. 154, 179-181, 186.

[5] Hundred Rolls, 3 Richard II, quoted in Carlyon Huhes, *The History of Harwich Harbour*, Harwich, 1939, p. 12.

[6] A parcel or bundle of goods.

[7] Historical Manuscripts Commission Ninth Report, 1883, p. 259.

[8] Nathaniel Bacon, *The Annalls of Ipswich*, edited by W.H. Richardson, Ipswich, 1884, p. 64.

[9] Calendar of Patent Rolls, 12 Edward III, pt. II, 16.

[10] Bacon, *op. cit.*, pp.80-1.

[11] [Richard Canning], *The Principal Charters Which have been Granted to the Corporation of Ipswich in Suffolk Translated*, Ipswich, 1754.

[12] A French chronicler accused Sir Thomas of having called on a devil named Nostrok to aid the English. In fact what he misheard was the order to the archers to loose their arrows, given in broadest Norfolk – 'Naow, Stroike!'

[13] E.F. Jacob, *The Fifteenth Century 1399–1485*, Oxford University Press, 1961, p. 493.

[14] Roger Virgo, 'The death of William de la Pole, Duke of Suffolk', in *East Anglian Society and the Political Community of Late Medieval England*, 1997, p. 248.

[15] Ibid., p. 249.

[16] Ibid., p. 251.

[17] Nicholas Amor, *Late Medieval Ipswich Trade and Industry*, Boydell Press, 2011.

[18] Ibid.

[19] HMC, p. 258.
[20] G.H. Martin, 'Shipments of wool from Ipswich to Calais, 1399-1402', in *The Journal of Transport History*, vol. II, 1956, pp. 177-81.
[21] Mark Bailey, *The Bailiffs' Minute Book of Dunwich, 1404-1430*, Suffolk Records Society vol. 34, 1992.
[22] Information from Peter Wain, 'The Medieval Port of Goseford', *Proceedings of the Suffolk Institute of Archaeology and History*, vol. 43 (2016), pp. 582-601

5   Merchants and adventurers

[1] Richard Hakluyt, *The Principal Navigations, Voyages, Traffiques & Discoveries of the English Nation*, Everyman's Library, J.M. Dent, 1913, vol. 3, pp. 38-50.
[2] Ibid., vol. 8, pp. 206-55.
[3] Ibid., vol. 6, p. 133.
[4] Port Desire has other East Anglian links: in 1670 John Narborough, the Norfolk-born admiral who conducted himself with such conspicuous valour at the Battle of Sole Bay that he was knighted by Charles II and promoted to rear-admiral, visited Port Desire and claimed the territory for England, but no effort was made later to assert the claim.
[5] Not Rio Dulce in Guatemala, today much visited by yachtsmen and tourists, but another 'Sweet River' on the coast of what is now Ecuador.
[6] *Lives and Voyages of Drake, Cavendish and Dampier*, Edinburgh, 1832, p. 194.
[7] *Oxford Dictionary of National Biography*, Oxford University Press, 2004-2016.
[8] John Webb, *Great Tooley of Ipswich*, Suffolk Records Society, 1962, pp. 4-5.
[9] G.R. Clarke, *The History of Ipswich*, 1830, p. 300.
[10] Webb, p.73.

6   To the New World

[1] Brian Dietz, 'The Royal Bounty and English Merchant Shipping in the Sixteenth and Seventeenth Centuries', *The Mariner's Mirror*, vol. 77, p. 18.
[2] M.L.R. Peterson, 'The Sea Venture', *The Mariner's Mirror*, vol. 74, pp. 37-48.
[3] It is said that the wreck of the *Sea Venture* provided the inspiration for William Shakespeare's play *The Tempest*.
[4] Winifred Cooper, *Harwich, The Mayflower and Christopher Jones*, Phillimore, 1970, p. 2.
[5] Ibid., p. 5.
[6] Nathaniell Bacon, *Annals of Ipswich*, pp. 523-4n.
[7] Charles Edward Banks, *The Planters of the Commonwealth*, 1930.

7   The Dutch wars

[1] Robert Malster, *A History of Ipswich*, Phillimore, 2000, p. 25.
[2] Robert Malster, *Maritime Norfolk*, part two, Poppyland Publishing, 2014, p. 6.
[3] A.G.E. Jones, 'The sick and wounded in Ipswich during the First Dutch War, 1651-1654', *The Suffolk Review*, vol. 1 no. 1 (1956), pp. 1-6.
[4] G.R. Clark, *The History of Ipswich*, 1830, p, 240.
[5] A.G.E. Jones, p. 6
[6] R.C. Latham & W. Matthews, eds., *The Diary of Samuel Pepys*, vol. 6, G. Bell & Sons, 1972, p. 113.
[7] A.G.E. Jones, 'The sick and wounded in Ipswich during the Second Dutch War', *The Suffolk Review*, vol. 1 no. 2 (1956), pp. 26-31.
[8] *The Diary of Samuel Pepys*, vol. 6, p. 76.
[9] Ibid., p. 78.
[10] Ibid., p. 76.
[11] Ibid., p. 116.

[12] Ibid., p. 121.
[13] Ibid., vol. 10. p.69
[14] Frank Hussey, *Suffolk Invasion*, Terence Dalton, 1983, p. 39.
[15] *The Diary of Samuel Pepys*, vol. 7, pp. 145-6.
[16] Hussey, p. 39.
[17] Ibid., p. 59.
[18] Ibid., p. 107.
[19] Ibid., p. 119.
[20] Sir George Clark, *The Later Stuarts 1660-1714*, 2nd edn, Oxford University Press, p. 76.
[21] Ibid., p. 77.
[22] William Laird Clowes, *The Royal Navy, A History from the Earliest Times to 1900*, Chatham Publishing, 1996, vol. 2, p. 299.
[24] Ibid., p. 302.
[25] Ibid., p. 304.
[26] Leonard T. Weaver, *The Harwich Story*, privately published, 1975, p. 58.

8   The Dunkirk menace

CPSD: Calendar of State Papers Domestic.
[1]   Frederik af Chapman, *Architectura Navalis Mercatoria*, facsimile edition, Adlard Coles, 1971, p. 88.
[2]   Godfrey Davies, *The Early Stuarts 1603-1660*, Oxford University Press, 2nd ed., 1959, p. 22.
[3]   CSPD 1625-6, p. 131.
[4]   Davies, p. 22.
[5]   CSPD 1625-6, p. 415.
[6]   CPSD 1625-6. p.239.
[7]   CPSD 1625-6, p. 251.
[8]   CPSD 1625-6, p. 265.
[9]   CPSD 1625-6, p.285.
[10] CSPD 1627-8, p. 84.
[11] Davies, p. 67.
[12] CPSD 1627-8, p.265.
[13] Davies, p. 43.
[14] CPSD 1625-6, p. 274.
[15] CPSD 1631-3. p. 450.
[16] CSPD 1625-6, p. 409.
[17] C.J. Palmer, *The Perlustration of Great Yarmouth*, 1875, vol. 3, p. 162.
[18] *Ipswich Journal*, 9 March 1745.
[19] *Ipswich Journal*, 11 July 1744.
[20] *Ipswich Journal*, 4 Aug 1744.
[21] *Ipswich Journal*, 28 April 1744.
[22] *Ipswich Journal*, 7 September 1745.
[23] *Ipswich Journal*, 3 January 1745.
[24] *Ipswich Journal*, 14 August 1762.
[25] *Ipswich Journal*, 17 November 1804.
[26] SROI G2/4/1.
[27] *Norwich Mercury*, 20 March 1880 supplement.

9   New harbours and old

[1]   *Norwich Mercury*, 3 April 1830.
[2]   *Norwich Mercury*, 11 June 1831.
[3]   Hugh Moffat, *Ships and Shipyards of Ipswich 1700-1970*, Malthouse Press, 2002,

pp. 95-96.

4   *Norwich Mercury*, 2 July 1831.

5   *Norwich Mercury*, 17 October 1835.

6   *Norwich Mercury*, 24 October 1835.

7   James Maggs, *Hand Book to the Port and Shipping of Southwold,* Halesworth, 1842, p. 6.

8   Ibid.

9   Edward Paget-Tomlinson, *The Illustrated History of Canal and River Navigations*, Sheffield Academic Press, 1993, pp. 330-1.

10   Bob Malster and Bob Jones, *A Victorian Vision, The building of Ipswich Wet Dock*, Ipswich Port Authority, 1992, p. 5.

11   1 Victoria, Cap. LXXIV.

12   SROI EL1/5/2.

13   SROI EL1/1/4/2.

14   *Ipswich Journal*, 22 January 1842.

15   See Chapter 21.

10   Colliers, billyboys and barges

1   Daniel Defoe, *Tour Through the Eastern Counties*, East Anglian Magazine, 1949, pp. 57-9.

2   *Ipswich Journal*, 29 January 1743.

3   Daniel Defoe, *Tour Through the Eastern Counties*.

4   R. Keys, *Dictionary of Tyne Sailing Ships*, 1998. Thanks to Adrian Osler for information on the Tyne connection.

5   Hinged boards on either side of the hull that could be lowered to counteract the flat-bottomed vessel's tendency to blow down to leeward.

6   P.R.V. Marsden, *A Roman Ship from Blackfriars*, London, Guildhall Museum, London, n.d., p. 35.

7   F.G.G. Carr, *Sailing Barges*, 3rd edn, Terence Dalton, 1989, p. 126.

8   *Suffolk Chronicle*, 4 December 1841 and 1 January 1842.

9   An ale with good keeping qualities especially brewed for export to India, where it was much appreciated by British troops and officials.

10   *Suffolk Chronicle*, 31 October 1840; Hugh Moffat, *Ships and Shipyards of Ipswich 1700-1970*, Malthouse Press, 2002, p. 123.

11   R. Malster and R. Jones, *A Victorian Vision, The building of Ipswich Wet Dock*, Ipswich Port Authority, 1992, pp. 26-7.

12   Taylor and Dale, *The History and Antiquities of Harwich and Dovercourt in the County of Essex*, 2nd edn.,1732.

13   Hervey Benham, *Down Tops'l, The story of the East Coast sailing barges*, George G. Harrap, 1951, p. 117.

14   Told to the author by Captain Polley about 1965.

15   Information given to the author by Alderman J.E. Cann in 1967.

16   *East Anglian Daily Times*, 24 December 1927.

17   see R. Malster, *North Sea War 1914-1919*, Poppyland, 2015.

18   F.G.G. Carr, *Sailing Barges*, 3rd edn,, pp. 122-3.

11   The coasting trade

1   Defoe, *A Tour Through the Whole Island of Great Britain*, ed. P.N. Furbank & W.R Owens, Yale University Press, 1991.

2   *Ipswich Journal*,

3   *Ipswich Express*, 2 February 1847.

4   William White, *History, Gazetteer and Directory of Suffolk*, 1855, p. 517.

5   SROI. HA28/50/23/1.13 (2).

[6]   SROI. HA28/50/23/1.13 (2), letter to Woodley of 3 March 1827.
[7]   A sailing barge has a flat bottom and employs leeboards; the vessels owned by the Mingays were all round-bottomed and depended on the keel to prevent leeway.
[8]   SROI. HA28/50/23/1.10 (4).
[9]   SROI. HA412/1/6/1.
[10] SROI. HA28/50/23/1.10 (10).
[11] Inquiries along the Tyne have failed to identify the quay.
[12] SROI. HA28/50/23/1.6 (4).
[13] H.E.G. Rope, 'George Rope of Blaxhall and Orford (1814-1912)', *Suffolk Review*, vol. 2 no. 2, 1959.

12   The life of a river

[1]   David Cleveland, *Manningtree and Mistley*, Malthouse Press, 2007, p. 34.
[2]   For the full story of the Ipswich whale fishery see Hugh Moffat, *Ships and Shipyards of Ipswich 1700-1970*, Malthouse Press, 2002, chapter two.
[3]   *Ipswich Journal*, 11 August 1787.
[4]   G.R. Clark, *The History and Description of the Town and Borough of Ipswich*, 1830, p. 406.
[5]   SROI FB132/G4/1.
[6]   William White, *History,Gazetteer and Directory of Suffolk*, 1844, p. 219.
[7]   Lennie Knowland, ed., *Samuel Dove's Debenham*, Debenham Vernacular Architectural Group, 1986, p. 13.
[8]   *Norwich Mercury*, 20 May 1837.
[9]   *Ipswich Journal*, 20 May 1837.
[10] *Ipswich Journal*, 7 May 1836.
[11] *Ipswich Journal*, 14 May 1836.
[12] *Ipswich Journal*, 21 May 1836.
[13] *Ipswich Journal*, 13 August 1836.
[14] Nathaniell Bacon, *The Annals of Ipswich*, edited by W.H. Richardson, Ipswich, 1884, p. 482.
[15] *Ipswich Journal*, 10 March 1753.
[16] The Wherry public house was actually in the neighbouring parish of Mistley, the boundary being just at the end of Manningtree High Street.
[17] G.R. Clarke, *The History & Description of the Town and Borough of Ipswich*, London, 1830, pp. 121-2.
[18] *Ipswich Journal*, 11 December 1841.
[19] Captain John Washington's report to the Admiralty, in Carlyon Hughes, *The History of Harwich Harbour*, Harwich, 1939, p. 36.
[20] Thomas Wright, *The History and Topography of the County of Essex*, London, 1836, p. 18,
[21] William White, *History, Gazetteer and Directory of Suffolk*, 1845, p. 250.
[22] William White, *History, Gazetteer and Directory of Suffolk*, 1855, p. 219.
[23] *Ipswich Journal*, 21 April 1838.
[24] The word *gaff* generally used for the spar at the head of a fore-and-aft mainsail was in East Anglia pronounced with a long a and a final t.
[25] Information from Hugh Moffat's notes.
[26] *Suffolk Chronicle*, 7 August 1840.
[27] *Ipswich Journal*, 17 September 1842.
[28] *Ipswich Journal*, 13 March 1841.
[29] *Ipswich Journal*, 8 May 1841.
[30] *Ipswich Journal*, 31 December 1842.
[31] *Ipswich Journal*, 27 May 1843.
[32] Carlyon Hughes, *The History of Harwich Harbour*, Harwich, 1939, p. 36.
[33] *Ipswich Journal*, 12 August 1843.

34 Suffolk Chronicle, 17 January 1846.
35 *Ipswich Journal*, 12 December 1846.
36 Leonard Weaver, *The Harwich Story*, Harwich, 1975, p. 126.
37 *The Post Office Directory of the Counties of Cambridge, Norfolk and Suffolk*, Kelly & Co., 1879, p. 821.
38 Richard W. Smith and Jill Freestone, *The Port of Ipswich, Its Shipping and Trades*, Malthouse Press, 2011, pp. 194-7.

13 The Sudbury navigation

1 C.G. Grimwood and S.A. Kay, *History of Sudbury, Suffolk* (1952), p. 103.
2 E.W. Paget-Tomlinson, *The Illustrated History of Canal and River Navigations* (1993), p. 350.
3 J. Boys and R. Russell, *The Canals of Eastern England* (1977), p. 79.
4 Ibid., p. 82.
5 IV Anne, cap. XV. An Act for making the river Stower navigable, from the town of Maningtree in the county of Essex, to the town of Sudbury in the county of Suffolk, 1705.
6 William White, directory of Suffolk, 1844; Post Office Directory of Suffolk, 1879.
7 W.A.B. Jones, *Hadleigh Through the Ages* (1977), p. 88.
8 Jenny Robinson, *Boxford, A Miscellany* (1998), p. 25.

14 Life and death at sea

1 H. Holman, *A Handy Book for Shipowners and Masters*, 5th edn., London, 1900, p. 16.
2 *Suffolk Chronicle*, 22 May 1830.
3 *Suffolk Chronicle*, 5 June 1830.
4 Ashton Booth, 'Shipwrecks on the coast of Norfolk and Suffolk in the early 19th century', *The Norfolk Sailor* no. 5, 1962.
5 *Ipswich Journal*, 16 and 23 March, 20 April and 19 October 1844.
6 *Ipswich Journal* and *Suffolk Chronicle*, 29 February 1840.
7 *Ipswich Journal*, 14 November 1840,
8 [Richard Canning] An Account of the Gifts and Legacies that have been given and bequeathed to Charitable Purposes in the Town of Ipswich, Ipswich, 1747, p. 180.
9 Ibid., pp. 180-1.
10 *Ipswich Journal*, 4 July 1829.
11 *Suffolk Chronicle*, 1 February 1840.
12 *Suffolk Chronicle*, 8 February 1840.
13 *Suffolk Chronicle*, 15 February 1840.
14 SROI HA65/1/22.
15 SROI HA65/1/7.
16 SROI HA65/1/25.

15 The smacksmen

1 *Essex Standard*, 21 January 1842.
2 *Essex Standard*, 18 November 1842.
3 Hervey Benham, *The Salvagers*, Essex County Newspapers, 1980, p. 18.
4 *Essex Standard*, 3 and 24 January 1851.
5 *Essex Standard*, 7 November and 12 December 1851.
6 *Suffolk Mercury*, 1 February 1895.
7 H. Holman, *A Handy Book for Shipowners and Masters*, 5th edn., London, 1900, pp. 15, 147-8.
8 Walter Wood, *North Sea Fishers and Fighters*, London, 1911, p. 222.

9   G.H.P Muhlhauser, *Small Craft*, The Bodley Head, 1920, p. 51.
10   Robert Malster, *North Sea War 1914-1919*, Poppyland Publishing, 2015, p. 17.
11   *Essex Standard*, 17 March 1883 and 5 January 1884.
12   *Essex Standard*, 17 March 1883; Robert Malster, *Wreck and Rescue on the Essex Coast*, D. Bradford Barton, Truro, 1968, pp. 24-6.
13   *Norwich Mercury*, 26 December 1863.

16   Salvagers and lifesavers

1   Up the east coast – in the direction of the flood tide, which runs from north to south.
2   Richard Lewis, *History of the Life-Boat and its Work*, London, 1874, pp. 42-3.
3   Edmund Gillingwater, *An Historical Account of The Ancient Town of Lowestoft*, London, 1790, pp. 65-7.
4   The Stanford Channel running from NNW to SSE between the Holm and Newcome sands off Lowestoft.
5   *Ipswich Journal*, 4 October 1800.
6   Captain Broke, in command of HMS *Shannon*, boarded and took the Ameerican warship *Chesapeake* during the war of 1812.
7   *Ipswich Journal*, 18 February 1804.
8   The 28th Regiment of Foot was at that time the North Gloucestershire Regiment, known in army slang as 'The Old Braggs'. Serjeant Bubb might well have been serving at the time of the Battle of Alexandria, fought in Egypt in 1801, when the regiment won the distinction of being allowed to wear a badge at the back of the shako as well as in the normal position at the front as a result of their cool behaviour when attacked in the rear by French cavalry; without hesitation the commanding officer gave the command '28th, front rank stand fast, rear rank about face,' and the attack was repulsed.
9   Letter of 7 December 1805, reproduced in the minute book of the Suffolk Humane Society.
10   For a detailed account of the Suffolk Humane Society see R. Malster, *The Minute Books of the Suffolk Humane Society*, Suffolk Records Society, 2013.
11   The same word and same pronunciation that was used in Suffolk for the beach company's sailing boats.
12   *Ipswich Journal*, 24 October 1807.
13   *Ipswich Journal*, 28 November 1807.
14   *Norwich Mercury*, 23 December 1809.
15   *Ipswich Journal*, 20 January 1810.
16   Built at Ipswich in 1802.
17   *Suffolk Chronicle*, 28 October 1820.
18   *Lowestoft Journal*, 25 January 1890.
19   *Ipswich Journal*, 21 January 1815.
20   *Norwich Mercury*, 15 January 1842.
21   *Norwich Mercury*, 29 January 1842.
22   *Suffolk Chronicle*, 15 December 1821.
23   *Suffolk Chronicle*, 22 December 1821.
24   *Colchester Gazette*, 26 January 1822; *Ipswich Journal*, 26 January 1822.
25   *Colchester Gazette*, 25 January 1823.

17   For the preservation of life

1   This is possibly the regiment that later became the Royal Warwickshire Regiment, though that was not officially granted the Royal title until 1832.
2   *Suffolk Chronicle*, 28 October 1820.
3   *Colchester Gazette*, 18 November 1820.

4   *Colchester Gazette*, 17 February 1821.

5   Benjamin Page retired as a captain and achieved flag rank only in retirement.
    There is a portrait of him in Ipswich Town Hall, but it is an unflattering one of
    him as a very old man; his uniform no longer fits him, and hangs loosely on his
    shrinking frame. Admiral Page paid a small pension to a local watercress seller on
    condition that he did not cry his wares in Tower Street, where the admiral had his
    home.

6   *Suffolk Chronicle*, 7 April 1821.

7   *Ipswich Journal*, 15 September 1821.

8   *Colchester Gazette*, 1 June 1822.

9   *Colchester Gazette*, 1 February 1823.

10 *Ipswich Journal*, 28 February 1824.

11 *Ipswich Journal*, 13 November 1824 and 18 December 1824.

12 *Ipswich Journal*, 22 April 1826, and *Suffolk Chronicle*, 24 March 1827.

13 *Ipswich Journal*, 8 January 1825.

14 The cargo book of George Mingay's sloop *Idas*, now in the Suffolk Record Office
    at Ipswich, shows that she brought what must have been the lifeboat for Sizewell
    Gap from London in January 1827.

15 *The Minute Books of the Suffolk Humane Society*, R. Malster, ed., Suffolk Records
    Society, 2013, p. 30.

16 Ibid., p. 58.

17 For a detailed account of the growth of the beach companies see David Higgins,
    The Beachmen, Terence Dalton, 1987.

18 *Norwich Mercury*, 24 January 1857.

19 Ernest R. Cooper, *The Southwold Lifeboats from 1840 to 1912*, The Southwold
    Press, 1912, p. 8.

20 *Norwich Mercury*, 15 January 1853; *The Minute Books of the Suffolk Humane
    Society*, p. 53.

21 *The Minute Books of the Suffolk Humane Society*, p. 71.

22 Predecessor of the paddle tug *Imperial* built at Blackwall in 1879 for the Great
    Eastern Railway Company.

23 *Norwich Mercury*, 15 January 1853.

24 *Norwich Mercury*, 9 February 1850 .

25 Lowestoft harbour and the tugs were owned by the Eastern Counties Railway, and
    later its successor the Great Eastern, since railway interests had predominated
    following the purchase of the harbour by the railway entrepreneur Samuel
    Morton Peto in 1842.

26 *Norwich Mercury*, 18 May 1850.

27 A paddle tug built of iron at Blackwall in 1846 and not to be confused with the
    later screw tug *Lowestoft* of 1898. The first *Lowestoft* later went to Australia and
    was registered at Melbourne; she was still in the Mercantile Navy List at the very
    end of the century.

28 *Norwich Mercury*, 26 October 1850.

29 *Norwich Mercury*, 9 November 1850.

30 *Norfolk Chronicle*, 20 October 1850.

31 *Norwich Mercury*, 19 March 1859.

32 For a full account of the events of 'Black Saturday' see Robert Malster, *Saved from
    the Sea*, Terence Dalton, 1974, pp. 103-110.

33 Built of iron on the Thames in 1875 and owned by the Great Eastern Railway
    Company.

18   The herring fishery

1   David Butcher, *Lowestoft 1550-1750, Development and Change in a Suffolk Coastal
    Town*, Boydell, 2008, pp. 125-7.

[2] Ibid., p. 154.
[3] *The Lowestoft Guide: containing a Descriptive Account of Lowestoft and its Environs*, by a Lady, W. Alexander, Yarmouth, 1812.
[4] SROL. 194/A10/4, p. 104; Butcher, p. 181.
[5] Gillingwater, *History of Lowestoft*, pp. 95-6.
[6] Ibid., p. 97.
[7] A hard material prepared from the resin of the *Acacia catechu* tree.
[8] David Butcher, *The Driftermen*, Tops'l Books, 1979, p. 21.
[9] Author's own observation of buildings on the Beach prior to their demolition in the 1970s.
[10] 23 Geo. II, cap. 24, An Act for the Encouragement of the British White Fishery.
[11] 26 Geo. III, An Act for the More Effectual Encouragement of the British Fisheries, see Gillingwater, *History of Lowestoft*, p. 441.
[12] Peter Smith, *The Lammas Drave and the Winter Herring*.
[13] James R. Coull, *The Sea Fisheries of Scotland, A Historical Geography*, Edinburgh, John Donald, 1986, p. 213.
[14] Hodgson, *The Herring and its Fishery* (1957), p. 19.
[15] Susan Telford, *In a World A Wir Ane, A Shetland Herring Girl's Story*, Shetland Times Ltd., 1998, p.5.
[16] Peter Anson, *Fishermen and Fishing Ways*, George G. Harrap, 1931, p. 89.
[17] Henry Farnie, *The Coast of Fife* quoted in Peter Anson, *Fishing Boats and Fisher Folk on the East Coast of Scotland*, J.M. Dent, 1930, reprint 1971, p. 47.
[18] Jackie Ritchie, *Floods upon the dry ground: God working among fisherfolk*, Peterhead, 1983.
[19] George Youell, *Lower Class*, Seattle, Washington, 1938, pp. 112ff.
[20] *The East Norfolk Annual 1896*, The East Norfolk Printing Company, Yarmouth, 1896.
[21] *Norwich Mercury*, 11 August 1883.
[22] Edgar March, *Sailing Drifters*, Percival Marshall, 1952, p. 65.
[23] See Robert Malster, *Maritime Norfolk part two*, Poppyland, 2013, pp. 110-11.
[24] David Butcher, *The Driftermen*, p. 14.
[25] Ted Frost, *From Tree to Sea*, Terence Dalton, 1985, p. vii.
[26] See Robert Malster, *North Sea War 1914-1919*, Poppyland Publishing, 2015.
[27] Bill Soloman, 'Steam drifters', *The Norfolk Sailor* no. 12, 1966, pp. 7-12.

19   Shipwrights and shipyards

[1] Examples of failure to employ such knowledge include the *Mary Rose* and the *Vasa*.
[2] Ian Friel, *The Good Ship*, British Museum Press, 1995, p. 41.
[3] Philip Banbury, *Shipbuilders of the Thames and Medway*, David & Charles, 1971.
[4] W.G. Perrin, ed., *The Autobiography of Phineas Pett*, Navy Records Society, 1918, pp. 151-3.
[5] N.A.M. Rodger, *The Safeguard of the Sea*, Harper-Collins, 1997, p. 69.
[6] Ted Frost, *From Tree to Sea*, Terence Dalton, 1985, pp. 2-10.
[7] Hugh Moffat, *Ships and Shipyards of Ipswich 1700-1970*, Malthouse Press, 2002, p. 113.
[8] *Ipswich Journal*, 23 July 1859.
[9] CPSD Inter., xli, p. 51.
[10] CPSD Inter., xxxvi, p. 59.
[11] R.C. Latham & W. Matthews, eds., *The Diary of Samuel Pepys*, vol. 3, p. 169.
[12] Ibid., vol. 3, p. 170.
[13] Ibid.,
[14] Ibid., vol 7, p. 127.
[15] Hugh Moffat, *Ships and Shipyards of Ipswich 1700-1970*, p. 84.

16   Ibid., p. 87.

17   John E. Barnard, *Building Britain's Wooden Walls, The Barnard Dynasty c. 1697-1851*, Anthony Nelson, 1997, p. 15.

18   John Leather, 'The Shipbuilding Bayleys', *Mariner's Mirror*, vol. 51, pp. 131ff.

19   The latter gave a name to Buttermans Bay below Pin Mill in the Orwell.

20   Hugh Moffat, *Ships and Shipyards of Ipswich*, pp. 127-30.

21   R.H. Gower, *Original observations regarding the inability of ships to perform their duty with promptitude and safety, with suggestions for their improvement, as practised on board the Transit, an experimental vessel, invented, built, and commanded by the author*, Ipswich, 1833.

22   Ibid.,

23   Ibid., p. 19.

24   Ibid, p. 21.

25   Ibid., p. 34.

26   David Lyon, *The Sailing Navy List*, Conway Maritime Press, 1993, p. 163.

27   *Suffolk Chronicle*, 11 September 1819.

28   *Suffolk Chronicle*, 4 September 1819.

29   *Ipswich Journal*, 4 September 1824.

20   Sail to steam, oak to steel

1   *Ipswich Journal*, 19 October 1751.

2   *Ipswich Express*, 19 November 1839.

3   Ipswich shipping register, transcription by Hugh Moffat, Ipswich Transport Museum IPSTM:2014A.657.

4   Ibid.

5   E.R. Kelly, *Post Office Directory of Cambridge, Norfolk and Suffolk*, 1879, pp. 978-9.

6   Alan Bottomley, Ed., *The Southwold Diary of James Maggs 1818-1876*, Suffolk Records Society, vols. 1 and 2, 1983-4, passim.

8   David Butcher, *Lowestoft 1550-1750, Development and Change in a Suffolk Coastal Town*, Boydell Press, 1008, pp. 27-8.

9   Ibid., p. 281.

10   *Lowestoft Journal*, 20 February 1970.

11   Later members of this family, including two named Breathard Tilmouth, were in the 1830s sailmakers in Lowestoft.

12   See chapter 15.

13   Jack Mitchley, 'Built Lowestoft', *The Norfolk Sailor no. 8*, 1964, p. 15.

14   Ted Frost, 'John Chambers', *The Norfolk Sailor no. 12*, 1966, p. 13.

15   Jack Mitchley, p. 16.

16   *Jane's Fighting Ships 1988-89*, Jane's Publishing, 1988, p. 762.

21   The port of Felixstowe

1   Orwell Park had earlier been the home of Admiral Vernon, known as 'Old Grog' from the grogram cloak he wore. He is remembered as the man who introduced grog, a rum-and-water mix, to the Royal Navy in a move to reduce drunkenness – the watered rum would not keep and could not be stored up for a later binge.

2   The statement that he was a Royal Engineers officer and that he served in the Crimean War, which has appeared in print, is no more than a sample of the extraordinary folklore that grew up around him. To his contemporaries George Tomline was an enigma; and thanks largely to the almost impenetrable smokescreen of myth and legend surrounding him, he remains an enigma to this day. For an account of his family and early life see Robert Malster, 'Colonel George Tomline of Orwell Park', *Suffolk Review* new series 41, autumn 2003,

pp. 23-34.

[3]   *Suffolk Chronicle*, 6 September 1851.

[4]   *Illustrated London News*, 19 August 1854, 30 September 1854 and 28 April 1855.

[5]   For the history of the Harwich Harbour Conservancy Board see Graham Stewart, *Time & Tide. The History of the Harwich Haven Authority 1863-2013*, Wild ReSearch, 2013.

[6]   For a full account of the railway steamers see Stephen Brown, *Harwich Ferries, Parkeston Quay under Railway Ownership*, Ferry Publications, 2014.

[7]   Hook of Holland, literally translated as the corner of Holland.

[8]   Robert Malster, *Felixstowe, 100 Years a Working Port*, Port of Felixstowe, 1986, p. 17.

[9]   Bheestie was the word used in Anglo-Indian households for the domestic servant responsible for supplying the family with water, which he carried in a mussuck or goatskin on his back.

[10] See Robert Malster, *North Sea War 1914-1919*, Poppyland, 2016.

[11] *Felixstowe, 100 Years a Working Port*, p. 66.

[12] The name Dooley was derived from Dulali Tat, the site of a military lunatic asylum in nineteenth-century British India. Officially known as Walton Battery, this small fortification incorporating a martello tower was in so secluded a position that it was assumed by their comrades that those stationed there would rapidly become insane, if they were not already mad when they arrived.

[13] Graham Stewart, *Time & Tide. The History of the Harwich Haven Authority 1863-2013*, p. 108.

Bibliography

Amor, Nicholas, *Late Medieval Ipswich, Trade and Industry*, Boydell Press, 2011.

Bacon, R., *The Dover Patrol*, vol. 2, Doran, 1919.

Benham, Hervey, *Once Upon a Tide*, George G. Harrap, 1955, 1971.

Benham, Hervey, *The Codbangers*, Essex County Newspapers, 1979.

Benham, Hervey, *The Salvagers*, Essex County Newspapers, 1980.

Benham, Hervey, *The Smugglers' Century*, Essex Record Office, 1986.

Benham, Hervey, and Finch, Roger, *The Big Barges*, Harrap, 1983.

Bennett, Jenny, ed., *Sailing into the Past: Learning from Replica Ships*, Seaforth Publishing, 2009.

Boys, J., and Russell, R., *The Canals of Eastern England*, David and Charles, 1977.

Brown, Stephen, *Harwich Ferries, Parkeston Quay under Railway Ownership*, Ferry Publications, 2014.

Butcher, David, *The Driftermen*, Tops'l Books, 1979.

Butcher, David, *The Trawlermen*, Tops'l Books, 1980.

Butcher, David, *Living from the Sea*, Tops'l Books, 1982.

Butcher, David, *The Cliffhanger, Landscape and Fishing As Elements in the History of Lowestoft*, EARO, 1983..

Butcher, David, *Following the Fishing*, Tops'l Books, 1987.

Butcher, David, *The Ocean's Gift, Fishing in Lowestoft during the Pre-Industrial Era, 1550-1750*, Centre of East Anglian Studies, 1995.

Butcher, David, 'The Herring Fisheries in the Early Modern Period: Lowestoft as Microcosm', in Starkey, Reid and Ashcroft, *England's Sea Fisheries*, Chatham Publishing, 2000.

Butcher, David, *Rigged for River and Sea*, Hull, North Atlantic Fisheries History Association, 2008.

Butcher, David, *Lowestoft 1550-1750*, Boydell Press, 2008.

Butcher, David, *Fishing Talk, The Language of a Lost Industry*, Poppyland Publishing, 2014.

Butcher, David, *Medieval Lowestoft*, Boydell Press, 2016.

Cable, James, *A Lifeboatman's Days*, Leiston Abbey Press [1921].

Carlyon Hughes, B., *The History of Harwich Harbour*, Harwich Harbour Conservancy Board, 1939.

Carr, F.G.G., *Sailing Barges*, 1st edn., Hodder & Stoughton, 1931; 2nd edn., Peter Davies, 1951; 3rd edn., Terence Dalton, 1989.

Carus-Wilson, E.M., *Medieval Merchant Venturers*, Methuen, 1967.

Cooper, E.R., *Seventy Years' Work of the Southwold Lifeboats*, The Southwold Press, 1912.

Cooper, E.R., *A Suffolk Coast Garland*, Heath Cranton, 1928,

Cooper, E.R., *Mardles from Suffolk, Tales of the South Folk*, Heath Cranton, 1932.

Cooper, E.R., *Storm Warriors of the Suffolk Coast*, Heath Cranton, 1937.

Cooper, E.R., *Storm Warriors of the Suffolk Coast*, new edition with additional material by Robert Malster, Poppyland Publishing, 2013.

Cone, Philip J., *100 Years of Parkeston Quay and its Ships*, Harwich Printing Co., nd.

Corin, J., *Fishermen's Conflict*, Tops'l Books, 1988.

Cowsill, Miles, Haalmeijer, Frank, and Hendy, John, *Hawich-Hoek van Holland, 100 Years of Service*, Ferry Publications, 1993.

Darby, H.C., *The Domesday History of Eastern England*, Cambridge University Press, 3rd. edn. 1971.

Davis, F.M., *An Account of the Fishing Gear of England and Wales*, Her Majesty's Stationery Office, 4th edn., 1958.

De Caux, J.W., *The Herring and the Herring Fishery*, Hamilton, Adams, 1881.

Finch, Roger, *Sailing Craft of the British Isles*, Collins, 1976.

Finch, Roger, and Benham, Hervey, *Sailing Craft of East Anglia*, Terence Dalton, 1987.

Fraser, C.M., *The Accounts of the Chamberlains of Newcastle Upon Tyne 1508-1511*, Society of Antiquaries of Newcastle Upon Tyne, 1987.

Foynes, Julian, *East Anglia against the Tricolor*, Poppyland Publishing, 2016

Friel, Ian, *The Good Ship: Ships, Shipbuilding and Technology in Britain 1200-1520*, British Museum Press, 1995.

Frost, Ted, *From Tree to Sea, The building of a wooden steam drifter*, Terence Dalton, 1985.

Goodey, Charles, *The First Hundred Years: The Story of Richards Shipbuilders*, Boydell Press, 1976.

Greenhill, Basil with Morrison, John, *The Archaeology of Boats and Ships*, Conway Maritime Press, 1976, 1995.

Grimwood, C.G. and Kay, S.A., *History of Sudbury, Suffolk*, 1952.

Hakluyt, R., *The Principal Voyages, Traffiques and Discoveries of the English Nation*, 8 vols., J.M. Dent.

Higgins, David, *The Beachmen*, Terence Dalton, 1987.

Hodgson, W.C., *The Herring and Its Fishery*, Routledge & Kegan Paul, 1957.

Horlock, A.H., *Mistleyman's Log*, Fisher Nautical Press, 1977.

Hussey, Frank, *The Royal Harwich*, Boydell Press, 1972.

Hussey, Frank, *Old Fitz: Edward Fitzgerald and East Coast Sailing*, Boydell Press, 1974.

Hussey, Frank, *Suffolk Invasion: The Dutch Attack on Landguard Fort, 1667*, Terence Dalton, 1983.

Hutchinson, Gillian, *Medieval Ships and Shipping*, Leicester University Press, 1994.

Jay, H.H., *Fishy Tales*, Lowestoft Heritage Workshop Centre, nd.

Jenkins, Ford, *Port War: Lowestoft 1939-45*, W.S. Cowell, 1946.

Jenkins, J.T., *The Herring and the Herring Fisheries*, P.S. King, 1927.

Jones, W.A.B., *Hadleigh Through the Ages*, 1977.

Kent, Peter, *Fortifications of East Anglia*, Terence Dalton, 1988.

Latham, R.C., and Matthews, W., eds., *The Diary of Samuel Pepys*, G. Bell and Sons,

Malster, Robert, *Wreck and Rescue on the Essex Coast*, Bradford Barton, 1968.

Malster, Robert, *Wherries and Waterways*, Terence Dalton, 1971, 1986.

BIBLIOGRAPHY

Malster, Robert, *Saved from the Sea*, Terence Dalton, 1974, 1980.

Malster, Robert, *Ipswich, Town on the Orwell*, Terence Dalton, 1978, 1986.

Malster, Robert, *Lowestoft, East Coast Port*, Terence Dalton, 1982,

Malster, Robert, *Felixstowe, 100 Years a Working Port*, Felixstowe Dock and Railway Company, 1986.

Malster, Robert, *A History of Ipswich*, Phillimore, 2000.

Malster, Robert, *Maritime Norfolk part one*, Poppyland Publishing, 2012.

Malster, Robert, *Maritime Norfolk part two*, Poppyland Publishing, 2013.

Malster, Robert, *North Sea War 1914-1919*, Poppyland Publishing, 2015.

March, Edgar, *Sailing Trawlers*, Percival Marshall, 1953.

March, Edgar, *Sailing Drifters*, Percival Marshall, 1952.

March, Edgar, *Inshore Craft of Britain in the Days of Sail and Oar*, 2 vols., David and Charles, 1970.

Mitchley, Jack, *The Story of Lowestoft Lifeboats, 1801-1876*, Port of Lowestoft Research Society, 1973, 1974, 2001.

Mitchley, Jack, Jones, Stuart and Keith, William, *The Story of Lowestoft Lifeboats, 1877-1924*, PLRS, 1996.

Moffat, Hugh, *Ships and Shipyards of Ipswich 1700–1970,* Malthouse Press, 2002.

Morris, John, ed., *Domesday Book: Suffolk*, Phillimore, 1986.

Norden, John, *Orford Ness; A Selection of Maps mainly by John Norden*, W. Heffer and Sons, 1966.

Paget-Tomlinson, E.W., *The Illustrated History of Canal and River Navigations*, Sheffield Academic Press, 1993.

Richards, Lewis, *Eighty Years of Shipbuilding and Designing*, Richards Ironworks Ltd, 1956.

Robinson, Jenny, *Boxford, A Miscellany*, 1998.

Robinson, Robb, *Trawling, The Rise and Fall of the British Trawl Industry*, University of Exeter Press, 1996.

Rodger, N.A.M., *The Safeguard of the Sea*, HarperCollins, 1997.

Rodger, N.A.M., *The Command of the Ocean*, Allen Lane, 2004.

Rose, Jack, and Parkin, Dean, *The Grit, The Story of Lowestoft's Beach Village*, Rushmere Publishing, 1997.

Simper, Robert, *Over Snape Bridge*, 1967.

Simper, Robert, *East Coast Sail*, David and Charles, 1972.

Simper, Robert, *British Sail*, David and Charles, 1977.

Simper, Robert, *The Deben River, An Enchanted Waterway*, Creekside Publishing, 1992.

Simper, Robert, *The River Orwell and the River Stour*, Creekside Publishing, 1993.

Simper, Robert, *Rivers Alde, Ore and Blyth*, Creekside Publishing, 1994.

Simper, Robert, *Beach Boats of Britain*, Boydell Press, 1984.

Smith, Richard, and Freestone, Jill, *The Port of Ipswich, Its Shipping and Trades*, Malthouse Press, 2011.

Stacy-Watson, C., *The Silvery Hosts of the North Sea*, Home Words Publishing Office, 1883.

Stewart, Graham, *Time & Tide, The History of the Harwich Haven Authority*, Wild ReSearch, 2013.

Trinder, Ivan, *The Harwich Packets 1635-1834*, privately published, 1998.

Weaver, Leonard, *The Harwich Story*, privately published, 1975.

Weaver, Leonard, *Harwich-Holland, The story of the service and the boats since 1661*, The Lindel Organisation, 1975.

Weaver, Leonard, *Harwich, gateway to the continent*, Terence Dalton, 1990.

Weaver, Leonard, *Harwich Papers*, The Harwich Society, 1994.

Webb, J., *Great Tooley of Ipswich*, Suffolk Records Society, 1962.

White, Malcolm R., *Down the Harbour 1955-1995*, Malcolm White, 1998.

White, Malcolm R., *A Century of Fishing*, Malcolm White, 1999.

White, Malcolm R., *Fishing with Diversity, A portrait of the Colne Group of Lowestoft*, Malcolm White, 2000.

White, Malcolm R., *Crownies of Lowestoft, The steam trawler fleet of Consolidated Fisheries*, Malcolm White, 2000.

White, Malcolm R., *Drifting, Trawling and Shipping, A portrait of Small & Co (Lowestoft) Ltd*, Malcolm White, 2001.

White, Malcolm R., *The Boston Putford Story*, Malcolm White, 2003.

White, Malcolm R., *Herrings, Drifters and the Prunier Trophy*, Malcolm White, 2006.

White, Malcolm R., *Dockside Delights, dock, harbour and seaside scenes by Ernest Graystone*, Malcolm White, 2011.

White, Malcolm R., *Lowestoft Fishing Vessels Remembered*, Malcolm White, 2013.

General index

Index of named vessels